DEEP DEMOCRACY

Community, Diversity, and Transformation

Judith M. Green

Rowman & Littlefield Publishers, Inc.
Lanham • Boulder • New York • Oxford

ROWMAN & LITTLEFIELD PUBLISHERS, INC.

Published in the United States of America
by Rowman & Littlefield Publishers, Inc.
4720 Boston Way, Lanham, Maryland 20706

12 Hid's Copse Road
Cumnor Hill, Oxford OX2 9JJ, England

British Cataloging in Publication Information Available

Library of Congress Cataloging-in-Publication Data

Green, Judith M.
    Deep democracy : community, diversity, and transformation / Judith
M. Green.
        p.   cm.
    Includes bibliographical references.
    ISBN 0–8476–9270–1 (cloth : alk. paper). — ISBN 0–8476–9271–X
(paper : alk. paper)
    1. Democracy.   2. Community life.
    JC423.G735   1999   98–55977
    321.8—dc21   CIP

Printed in the United States of America
♾™ The paper used in this publication meets the minimum requirements of American National Standard for Information Sciences—Permanence of Paper for Printed Library Materials, ANSI/NISO Z39.48–1992.

Contents

Acknowledgments

For the experience-based wisdom about deep democracy that this book offers to its readers, its author is indebted to many people for memories and hopes they have shared, as well as support and guidance they have offered. My parents, Leo Green and Helen Louise O'Keefe Green, shared with my older brother, James, my younger sister, Shannon, and me, their middle child, many rich cross-generational memories of the Irish and American struggle for religious liberty and social justice; of friendly cross-difference encounters in mid-nineteenth century Minnesota with our first neighbors, the Dakotas; of a rural life made up of beauty, poverty, and cooperative making-do; and of the union movement's contribution to the realization of their hopes for our education, economic sufficiency, and practical freedom to develop our gifts. In conversations at the dinner table and through the examples of their lives, they taught us unforgettable lessons about listening carefully, speaking up diplomatically, supporting one another, and always acting as if deeply democratic values matter. I am likewise indebted to my great-hearted spouse, David Woods, who is my partner in transformative activity, in ongoing education, and in our shared life adventure. Together we are blessed with a large network of extended families whose diverse memories, loving interest, and hopes for the future feed our place-connected roots, and thus, energize our work. I am greatly indebted to my excellent teachers in the Minnesota public schools, to my undergraduate mentor at Michigan State University, Edmund F. Byrne, and to graduate professors and friends at the University of Minnesota who supported the emergence of my own philosophical voice and vision, especially Rolf Sartorius, Naomi Scheman, John Dolan, John Wallace, Marcia Eaton, Jasper Hopkins, H. Eugene Mason, Carl Brandt, Harlan Smith, and Sara Evans, as well as members of the Wittgenstein Group, the Political Economy Group, and the Women's Center. I learned a great deal from gifted colleagues and loyal friends during my Florida years at Eckerd College, especially Carolyn Johnston, Jewel Spears Brooker, Dudley DeGroot, William McKee, Keith Irwin, J. Stanley Chesnut, Dallas Albritton, Bruce Foltz, Linda Lucas, Gregory Padgett, Suzan Harrison, and Blanche Radford Curry. I am very grateful to colleagues at Seattle University and fellow members of the Northwest Reading Group in American Philosophy who supported my early work on this book as well as my development of courses in African American Philosophy and Native American Philosophies, especially

Kenneth W. Stikkers, Erin McKenna, Scott Pratt, Jamie Ross, J. Patrick Burke, Rosaleen Trainor, Michael Holloman, and Joseph McGowan, who also led me to the Shades of Praise Gospel Choir. I owe a great debt to members of the Fordham University community who taught me to be at home in New York City as I finished this book, especially John Conley, James Marsh, Judith Jones, Mark Naison, Mark Chapman, Margaret Walker, Brian Davies, Christopher Gowans, Merold Westphal, Dominic Balestra, Raymond Grontkowski, Robert O'Brien, Astrid O'Brien, Joseph Koterski, Maria Terzulli, Donald Moore, E. Doyle McCarthy, Robert Carrubba, Mark Van Hollebeke, Anne Pomeroy, Judith Bradford, Kory Sorrell, and Danielle Poe. I owe more than I can express to the founding members of the Society for the Advancement of American Philosophy, especially John McDermott, John Lachs, Beth Singer, and Ralph Sleeper, as well as to other members whose generous support and critical insights have helped me greatly, especially Charlene Haddock Seigfried, Vincent Colapietro, Peter Hare, Frank Oppenheim, Thomas Alexander, Larry Hickman, and Leonard Harris, who read and commented on earlier drafts of this book. I thank the members of the Society for Women in Philosophy, especially Margaret Simons and Linda Lopez McAlister, for their empowering support for diverse women's voices, including my own. I thank my fellow members of the Society for the Study of Africana Philosophy for their welcoming cross-difference solidarity in liberatory democratic theorizing. I deeply appreciate the support of Maureen MacGrogan, my wide-ranging editor at Rowman & Littlefield who believed in this book, of Howard McGary, whose encouraging review led to its publication, and of Dorothy Rogers, who created the index and read the final page proofs with attentive care. I gladly acknowledge my debts to those past and present generations of philosophers, activists, and democracy-minded citizens in various parts of the world upon whose visionary legacy of struggle I draw in these pages, and to which I hope to contribute. Finally, I acknowledge with confidence the future contributions to the deepening of democracy that will be made by the rising generations, a precious few of whose members I am privileged to call my students.

Introduction

We live in a paradoxical, global, millennial era that is a descendent of the problem situation the great American pragmatist philosopher, John Dewey, described in the years between the two world wars that shook and shaped the twentieth century. However, it is an offspring its parents and grandparents might have had a very difficult time recognizing and understanding. New technologies were once expected to end poverty while allowing enough leisure for all the world's people to devote to re-creation of our mental and physical energies, reflection on the meaning of our times and our lives, and reconstruction of our civic institutions and our civilities in ways that would make them liberatory and inclusive beyond all past separations and oppressions. This phantom leisure, however, has largely been lost to a stepped-up pace of doing more, being more, or at least seeming to do and to be more than any of us really can. As Dewey prophetically suggested, the economic realm moral philosophers long treated as beneath their notice has taken its revenge. Many, perhaps most, of the beneficiaries of our forebears' struggle to educate us, their children, so that we could have better jobs, longer lives, and the leisure to enjoy them find ourselves overcommitted, stressed out, and unable to care enough about rebuilding our communities to attend one more meeting.

Meanwhile, the great American divides of race, class, and gender that Dewey and other progressives confidently believed were being eliminated as the idea of democracy gained momentum have instead angrily revived like monsters sighting new prey during a time of famine—prey being herded toward them by proudly conservative political and religious ideologues, using as their means of antidemocratic historical reversal the very mass communications technologies that Dewey hoped could be used to raise up a self-conscious "Public" capable of transforming what he called "the Great Society" into a "Great Community." The practical meaning of this backlash has been millions of homeless men, women, and children; an increase in domestic violence; and a growing gap between the "haves" and the "have-nots" that seems to be creating a permanent urban underclass, such that a young black man in America has one chance in three of being scarred for life by prison, probation, and "priors," and is more likely to die from homicide than from any other cause. On the other side of the tracks, "controlled-access communities" have sprung up for the wealthy who prefer to send out for security and civic leadership as they would for dry cleaning or a pizza. Under the guise of affirming perennial "family values," voices of political and religious authority call for sending women back to the kitchen and to tending the cradle while simultaneously driving into the low-wage workforce those women who bear children and seek to raise them without benefit of a legitimacy-conferring, breadwinning husband, no matter what the circumstances. An epidemic, acquired immune deficiency syndrome (AIDS), is killing millions worldwide because its victims are said to "deserve to die," or at least to be unworthy of the dedication of scarce resources to finding a cure that will let them live.

America's painfully initiated, periodically progressing cross-racial conversation has become strident and hurtful once again. Other conversations have also become screaming matches: between environmentalists and timber workers and ranchers; between advocates for illegal immigrants fleeing conditions of poverty and war and those who argue that these people are polluting or diluting American culture, or at least ruining the American economy for American workers; between an aging population and their children who worry about whether their basic needs will continue to be met with dignity and a majority of U.S. voters who elected and reelected a Congressional majority dedicated to cutting back on government spending for Medicare and making Social Security contributions voluntary, because the richest nation on earth "can no longer afford them" and they "undercut the motivation of free enterprise." Warp-speed technological development and a libertarian consumer mentality combine with global warming, influential demands to "deregulate" the environment, and refusal to preserve ancient forests and wild lands because legal requirements to do so might violate individual liberty. Meanwhile, America's traditional conservators of Mother Earth, the Native Americans, struggle with alcoholism, substance abuse, teen suicide, and widespread despair while simultaneously struggling in the courts for legal authority to operate high-stakes gambling casinos that offer the possibility of desperately needed economic empowerment, while ironically violating virtually every tribe's ethical traditions.

In recent years, an odd international alliance of conservative and liberal political theorists has advocated *a purely "formal," institutional conception of democracy* for very different reasons: as an expression of filial piety to America's Founding Fathers, or as the most extensive conception of democracy compatible with individualistically conceived liberty, or in the belief that no shared conception of the goods or goals of social life can be justified. Such a limited, formal conception of democracy contrasts with *a deeper conception of democracy* that expresses the experience-based possibility of more equal, respectful, and mutually beneficial ways of community life and "habits of the heart"—those characteristic, feeling-based, culturally shaped and located frameworks of value within which we perceive the world and formulate our active responses to it.[1] It is an overarching paradox of our global millennial era that more than half the world's nations have become or are in the process of becoming formal democracies, yet recent developments within the United States of America, a nation widely regarded as democracy's world-historic model, suggest that *a purely formal democracy is existentially unsustaining and culturally unsustainable, as well as ideologically hollow and operationally subvertible.*

In societies like America that are formally but not deeply democratic and that are increasingly dominated by a powerful and pervasive transnational capitalist economic sector, the existentially unsustaining and culturally unsustainable character of such a limited instantiation of democracy has recently become visible in the forms of two interactive social pathologies: existential nihilism and ontological rootlessness. In an insightful, millennium-conscious collection of essays, *Race Matters* (1994), Cornel West diagnosed a widespread lived experience of *existential nihilism* growing out of America's failures to sufficiently deepen our realization of democracy during the years since Martin Luther King, Jr., identified racism, poverty, and militarism as its chief threats. West focuses on poor, urban, predominantly African American communities in which educational opportunities are inadequate, unemployment is widespread, and many people depend on an "informal," drug-based and violence-regulated economy for income and identity; where many of the traditionally sustaining institutions of civil society have broken down; where youth suicide is on the increase; and where a widespread lack of the sense of agency that might have made greater goals possible fuels a fairly common, short-term focus on sources of pleasure and status that have been given their significance by the commodity-focused hype of the profit-motivated mass media. This nihilistic "disease of the soul" West diagnoses is a more concentrated, highly virulent form of a dangerous malaise that has been spreading across differing geopolitical and cultural locations within American society, even among the relatively privileged. It manifests itself in a generalized insecurity, a shared loss of the sense of agency that once allowed diverse people to believe that they could participate in shaping the public terms of social life, a shared lack of meaningfulness in daily activities, and a widespread loss of permanence in life commitments that leads many people to focus on pleasure-seeking and pain-killing, rather than risk a more complex kind of pursuit of happiness.

West's democracy-deepening prescription for curing this widespread existential nihilism is also applicable to another contemporary American pathology: *ontological rootlessness,* a loss of lived connection with particular places, and with what the classical American pragmatist philosopher Josiah Royce called "communities of memory and hope." Voluntary or involuntary relocation for education and jobs is one of the most common reasons for severing the connections to particular, localized, face-to-face communities that give people a sense of place and involvement in processes and purposes that have a longer history, a more stable direction, and a broader meaning than their own narrowly individual lives. A second social development that has undercut the capacity of local communities to provide such a life-sustaining sense of place and purpose is usurpation of their functions, capacities, and connections by expert-directed governance at local and higher levels, by economic institutions and forces that allow powerful business firms to radically reshape local conditions through action at a distance, and by nationally centralized, profit-motivated, mass-communications media that we increasingly depend on for our ontological sense of the real, our epistemic sense of the true, our ethical sense of the worthy, our aesthetic sense of the fitting and the beautiful, our political sense of the possible, and our economic sense of the necessary.

These social developments have revealed the *ideological hollowness* and *operational subvertibility* of formal democratic institutions and mechanisms that lack a more deeply democratic social grounding. Issue-eluding, "sound-bite" political campaign advertising and the sale of influence to pay for it have subverted the operations of democratic governance in recent years. Simultaneously, in the absence of effective, critically multicultural education about the purposes and processes of democratic community life, ideologues of control, fear, and blaming who rationalize in terms of an unrestricted right of the majority to rule and a need to preserve shallowly conceived "democratic values" from economic and political attack have misdirected attention away from our real problems while problematizing and politicizing historically grounded democratic equity entitlements, as well as democratically imperative humane and environmental values. Such ideological displacements and institutional subversions cannot be prevented or even effectively criticized in a society that lacks a diversity-respecting, dynamic social unity. Such *democratic social unity* grows out of a widespread sense of citizen agency and a broadly shared commitment to support those daily, local, face-to-face communities that ground our broader, multiple memberships in geographically dispersed communities of memory and hope. It is fostered by a publicly supported, realistic and idealistic model of critical multicultural education that replaces historical patterns of dominance, oppression-based resentment, xenophobic demonizing, and fear of the new with knowledge-based understanding and democratic skills for cross-difference respect and practical cooperation.

These manifest vulnerabilities of *formal* democracy do not imply, however, that some alternative, *nondemocratic* form of social organization is preferable. The forms of social life within which modern peoples have developed their identities, their sensibilities, and their understandings of how to get things done depend upon cooperative relationships within which each person expects to exercise judgment rather than to bow to arbitrary authority, and within which each person expects to meet human existential needs and to find opportunities for a particular, self-defined variety of human flourishing. However, the democratic ideal has achieved only a shallow and incomplete realization thus far, and many of the ideas advocated in its name actually work against it, given the emergent realities of our times. Thus, the standard political institutions of "formal" democracy have become empty, anachronistic, even counterproductive in the absence of vital relationships of community life and the overpowering presence of technology-enhanced concentrations of economic, cultural, and military power. It is true that learning to "do democracy" takes time, as societies attempting to accomplish the transition from totalitarian modes of political economy to even minimally democratic ones soon learn. Yet experienced "formal" democracies like Britain, France, Canada, and the United States also are vulnerable to antidemocratic sentiments and are in need of a deeper democracy in their institutions and their shared social lives.

Deeply understood, democracy is more than an increasingly widespread type of "formal" institutional framework for which America provides the model, a preferable alternative to the various totalitarianisms that have ravaged and distorted social life around the world during the twentieth century. At its core, as

Dewey understood, democracy is *a realistic, historically grounded ideal, a desired and desirable future possibility that is yet to be.* So understood, the democratic ideal indicates a direction for further evolution of the full range of formally democratic institutions, as well as for growth of democratic habits of the heart and of the processes of inquiry and education that support them. In those areas of community life and to the extent that this deeper social and cultural background is lacking, formally democratic institutions tend to generate the kinds of crises we are now experiencing because their inner logic is conceptually incomplete.

"The cure for the ailments of democracy is *more democracy,*" Dewey frequently asserted, or as we might say in the language of our own times, a *deeper democracy.* Many environmental philosophers have argued that we need a *deep ecology* to articulate the meaning and imperative of effective caring for the shared, fragile ecosystem in which we humans find our natural home. Likewise, we need a clear, contemporary articulation of *deep democracy* to interpret the origins and the imperative, historically unfolding transformative implications of the democratic ideal. Deeply understood, the democratic ideal is a normative guide for the development of diversity-respecting unity in habits of the heart that are shaped and corrected by reflective inquiry. Such ideal-guided democratic deepening in habits of the heart is a necessary concomitant to democratic institutional evolution within our increasingly globalized, highly vulnerable, shared social life.

The purpose of this book is to frame the kind of philosophy of deep democracy that can guide individual and social transformation as we address our urgent contemporary problems and opportunities. Dewey's own appreciative yet critical reconstruction of the Western philosophical tradition is the best starting point for this project because he was, as his student John Herman Randall, Jr., called him, the greatest "traditionalist" of his era.[2] Dewey insisted that instead of treating the philosophical achievements of earlier generations as hallowed museum pieces, they must be treated as active responses to their own historical problem situations that may still carry living implications for future generations, and thus, they must be critically reconstructed using experience-based intelligence to meet the needs of our own times. To contemporary readers, many of Dewey's books and essays are still alive with insightful implications for our own quest for meaning and the good life within our problematic present. Yet they occasionally seem slightly "off" or incomplete for our era, when Western and non-Western philosophies and bodies of experience meet in the daily congress of interactive diversity. This is, Dewey warned us, to be expected—philosophy must be continually reconstructed in order to fulfill its ongoing cultural role of articulating and mediating the conflicts of successive historical eras in the development of civilizations. Thus, insofar as we understand and value Dewey's contribution, we must critically reconstruct it in order to frame the kind of philosophy that can most effectively guide and reflect democratic transformation in our own times.

Our current problems of community life are deep and serious, and many of the world's citizens have had limited experience of democracy's successes. Therefore, we need to draw upon philosophical imagination to clarify and to extend the prophetic intimations of the democratic community's ideal possibilities that are revealed to us in those hope-based transformative activities that even partially satisfy the democratic impulse that motivates them. As we come to realize the existential and practical implications of the democratic ideal, we become aware of the need for a deeper social realization of democracy than the world has yet seen. "The end of democracy is a radical end," Dewey wrote in 1937, "for it is an end that has not been adequately realized in any country at any time."[3] Dewey rightly suggests that, instead of being a *justificatory ideal* for existing institutions, democracy is a *transformative ideal* that leads us to work for their further evolution.

Such a philosophy of deep democracy must play both critical and reconstructive roles in today's intellectual and social climate. It must critically engage with liberalism, communitarianism, postmodernism, critical theory, feminism, and cultural pluralism, learning from each, yet challenging any intellectual obstacles they may create through misguided aspects of their methodologies and ideal visions. At the same time, a philosophy of deep democracy must help to reenergize civic institutions and extrapolitical networks into effective public voices calling for more deeply democratic social reconstruction by reinvigorating the public role of philosophy and its influence within engaged transformative praxis. It must help to rehabilitate bases for trust that can overcome historically well-warranted suspicions by outlining effective processes of participatory democratic inquiry and by displaying the merits of a dynamic, individual-transforming, community-rebuilding ethic of democratic mutual commitment.

Each chapter of this book plays both critical and reconstructive roles in framing a philosophy of deep democracy. The first chapter, "The Diverse Community or the Unoppressive City: Which Ideal for a Transformative Politics of Difference?" focuses on an important intellectual obstacle to the project of deepening democracy: the postmodernist critique of the ideal of community. As represented by the brilliant and influential work of Iris Marion Young, the postmodernist critique claims that the concept of community (and, thus, its related ideal conception of democracy) is necessarily tied to a totalizing metaphysics with unavoidably diversity-repressive political consequences. Therefore, Young argues, it might better be replaced with a less metaphysically committed, difference-respecting ideal of "the unoppressive city" as the goal of liberatory struggle. The purpose of this chapter is to show that Young's rejection of the ideal of community rests on a series of mistakes and misinterpretations that derive from viewing common language and community life through a distorting and ideologically suspicious postmodernist philosophical lens. Such a postmodernist perspective leads to reductionistic conclusions with counterproductive, antiliberatory consequences in practice, especially in contrast with the liberatory potential of reconstructing our experience-based, common language–embedded ideal of the democratic community to reflect our increasing awareness that it must be necessarily and positively inclusive of diversity. Nonetheless, Young's counterideal of the unoppressive city can play a valuable role as an interim goal for theorizing and praxis in relation to the broader, action-guiding ideal of the diverse democratic community.

If we take this twin-faceted ideal of the diverse democratic community seriously, what roles should philosophy play in articulating and realizing it, and what philosophical methodologies will be most effective in fulfilling these transformative roles? Chapter Two, "Transformative Communication toward Democratic Communities: Pragmatism or Critical Theory?" argues that philosophy has a fourfold purpose within the larger democratic transformative project: (1) to show the need for more deeply democratic social and intellectual transformation, and to critically remove intellectual obstacles to deepening democracy; (2) to contribute to studies of actual social transformation processes and of particular contemporary situations that have democratic change potential; (3) to create effective, democratic tools of inquiry and communication for existing communities to use in their democratic transformation processes; and (4) to reflectively interpret and synthesize experiences in actual transformation processes in order to deepen our understanding of the ideals of democratic community life. Focusing appreciatively yet critically on John Dewey's pragmatism and Jürgen Habermas's critical theory, this chapter argues that these apparently competing philosophical methodologies are largely complementary, mutually corrective, yet conjointly inadequate for fulfilling these four roles within the ongoing collaborative project of deepening democracy. However, if they are brought into critical conversation with compatible streams of feminism and cultural pluralism, a collaborative philosophical methodology emerges: *a radical critical pragmatism* that can theorize a caring, cultivated pluralism that arcs toward the universally humane while celebrating diversity, creating models and methods for deepening democracy through open, reciprocal communication within liberatory praxis.

The third chapter, "The Deeply Democratic Community: Reconstructing Dewey's Transformative Ideal," collaboratively revises Dewey's still-resonant contextualized insights about the democratic ideal and its practical implications in light of critical pragmatist insights from subsequent experience. So reconstructed, Dewey's discussions of how to democratically deepen community life and to raise up an institution-transforming democratic public offer helpful leadings on five crucial, interconnected questions within contemporary democratic transformative praxis: (1) How can we shape educational experiences to support the democratic growth of individuals, cultures, and societies? (2) How can we build up transformative cross-difference coalitions and diverse democratic communities amidst the differences that presently divide us? (3) How can we develop effective processes of intelligent communication within democratic social inquiry, choice, and action? (4) How can we reflectively revise our goals, objectives, and strategies as we learn from transformative experience? (5) How can we effectively coordinate and sustain our transformative efforts over the extended period of time it will take to institutionalize the progressive changes that will make deep democracy real in our experience? Of course, even when it is reconstructed to factor in diversity, Dewey's theoretical standpoint, grounded as it is within transformative praxis in the first half of the twentieth century, offers incomplete direction to and expression of contemporary experience. It must be supplemented by the insights of culturally differing and later philosopher–activists.

Chapter Four, "Cosmopolitan Unity Amidst Valued Diversity: Alain Locke's Transformative Vision of Deep Democracy," harvests the culturally pluralistic insights of a now too-little-known African American critical pragmatist whose work offers invaluable transformative guidance for our global millennial times. Believing that William James's pragmatist pluralism must be expanded to acknowledge cultural differences, Alain LeRoy Locke proposed a transformative understanding of the democratic ideal as expressing "cosmopolitan unity in diversity," and he developed a feeling-focused value theory that includes methodological principles for a critical-empirical social science of values he called "anthropology in the broadest sense."[4] Locke argued that such a new, cross-disciplinary approach to values research would discover an empirical basis for identifying functionally equivalent "common humane values" while demonstrating that many differing cultural values are democratically tolerable.[5] This knowledge could then be used to foster peace-making coalition-building between historically antagonistic peoples, deepened and sustained by a critically multicultural approach to education that would teach students "to convert parochial thinking into global thinking."[6]

Nonetheless, the urgent project of transforming democratically deficient habits of the heart as well as flawed institutional structures on interconnected local, national, and international levels requires more broadly participatory and more deeply motivated democratic transformation processes than Dewey's and Locke's insights can guide. Chapter Five, "Prophetic Pragmatism: King, West, and the Beloved Community," aims to show that a deeper, prophetic model of democratic transformation can have great imaginative and motivational power in future years, as did the model that guided the world-historic transformative leadership of Martin Luther King, Jr. In his final book, *Where Do We Go from Here: Chaos or Community?* (1967), King offers an insightful analysis of the successes and failures of the American Civil Rights Movement of the 1950s and 1960s, coupled with a prophetic vision of "the World House," as the basis for his prescription of goals and strategies for future democracy-inspired transformative activism. Implicit within King's analysis and prophetic prescription is a theoretical framework for guiding transformative praxis that complements yet deepens those of Dewey and Locke. Drawing on Royce's concept of "the Beloved Community," King's final theoretical approach enriches the motivational appeal of the ideal of deep democracy while contributing more fully developed insights about urgent problems in transformative praxis. Building on the lived examples and the theoretical inheritance of both Dewey and King, Cornel West has proposed some initial elements of a deeply democratic approach to contemporary transformative praxis that he calls "prophetic pragmatism." When West's theorizing is critically dislocated from a misguided allegiance to Richard Rorty's ironic postmodernism, and relocated within the classical pragmatist stream that gave rise to King's final prophetic transformative framework, the resulting model of prophetic pragmatism, though still incomplete, offers helpful guidance for democratic transformative praxis while clarifying areas in which additional work is needed.

One of the most important of these areas is political economy. Chapter Six, "Transforming World Capitalisms through Radical Pragmatism: Economy, Law, and Democracy," argues that our three-fold global crisis in culture, ecology, and political economy reveals deep flaws in the now-dominant neocapitalist theoretical model as well as the institutional practices it guides and justifies. The family of differing global capitalisms has become a voracious Leviathan, increasing the economic welfare of the few by the immiseration of the many. Instead of democratizing interlinked societies, this family of world capitalisms is deeply damaging all cultures' lifeworlds as well as the integrity, stability, and beauty of Earth's ecosystems. Effectively resolving our three-fold global crisis requires changes in current "formally democratic" institutional structures of economy, law, and democracy, as well as in the neocapitalist economic model that presently guides them. Both the successes and the failures of recent local and international crisis-intervention experiences show that the only transformative approach that can help existing institutions to work well enough, soon enough, and sustainably enough is a *radical pragmatism* that is experimental, culturally pluralistic, location-specific, and deeply democratic. At the same time, such a radical pragmatism will guide us in developing more deeply democratic theoretical models and more existentially and locationally sensitive economic measures that will help us to assess our needs and our progress relative to our interlinked goals of pluralistic human flourishing and care for the Earth.

Finally, Chapter Seven argues that our focal challenge during these times of three-fold global crisis must be "Deepening Democracy: Rebuilding the Public Square"—the set of infrastructures, institutions, and social relations that interlink our destinies—in ways that transform its presently adverse outcomes while democratically deepening our hearts and minds. We must create the context for each human person to experience "the good life" that satisfies our shared existential needs in individually specific, culturally connective ways within an institutional framework and related cooperative practices that are socially and ecologically sustainable. Fortunately, diverse philosopher–activists' experiences in transformative praxis, including my own, suggest how we can do this: through collaborative participation of local citizens and other stakeholders in planning for their community's future, with consulting assistance from "public philosophers" who have particular relevant skills and who draw on a broader transformative framework in helping participants to tailor and to communicate their own locally appropriate transformative solutions to others. In addition to effectively addressing local problems, creating locally desirable futures, and educating participants' hearts and minds in the ways of deep democracy, such a collaborative participatory approach allows citizens to contribute widely dispersed knowledge and differing embodiments of values to a fund of deeply democratic experience on which others' transformative efforts can draw. Although *cross-difference coalitions* may be the initially best attainable character of such locally focused transformative collaborations, my experience suggests that, in order to be successful over time, and as they become progressively more successful, the developmental dynamic of cross-difference coalitions arcs toward becoming *deeply democratic communities* in which participants experience *cosmopolitan unity amidst valued diversity,* expressed in the mutual personal support and caring that allows the shared memories and hopes of *beloved communities* to emerge, to stabilize long-term commitments, and to give meaning to shared struggle.

Deep democracy so understood—as a realistically imaginative philosophical expansion of the implications of the democratic ideal into habits of the heart and a shared way of life—is profoundly preferable to a merely formal, institutional conception of democracy because it is preferable "all the way down."[7] Deep democracy can guide the development of characters with socially conscious responsible agency, as well as the emergence of a more sensitive awareness of each individual's gifts and needs, and a fuller realization of our most valuable human potentials. It can guide the formation of equal and unoppressive social relations of various kinds that can supportively contextualize each person's lived experience, including families, neighborhoods, communities, working collegialities, friendships, political and economic relationships, semi-autonomous cultures, and a whole multicultural social web. In comparison to a merely formal, institutional democracy, deep democracy is ontologically and epistemologically more realistic, as well as ethically, aesthetically, politically, and economically preferable, because it would prepare people to understand and to act effectively within the relational processes that are actually emerging within our shared social and natural environment. Deep democracy would equip people to expect, to understand, and to value diversity and change while preserving and projecting both democratically humane cultural values and interactively sustainable environmental values in a dynamic, responsive way. Existentially, deep democracy would reconnect people in satisfying ways, thus healing our currently dangerous pathologies of existential nihilism and ontological rootlessness. It would direct and support collaborative local communities in reconstructing civic institutions, processes, and expectations. Deep democracy is both the goal and the process that can facilitate the emergence of "publics" that can exert effective transformative influence within our democratically deficient world societies.

In writing this book and in beginning to imagine the book that will follow, my aim is to write "public philosophy" that can frame the transformative dimensions of a comprehensive philosophy of deep democracy. I hope to assist scholars working on related projects in a wide range of disciplines: political science, sociology, psychology, law, business, economics, urban and regional planning, ecology, literature and the other arts, history, religion, and education, as well as philosophy. I hope to welcome many students into the conversation. I also hope to encourage and to reflect what I have learned from listening to teachers, preachers, business leaders, urban and regional planners, government officials, economists, citizen–activists, and other philosophers who seek to discover the deeper meanings of the democratic ideal and its transformative implications for solving the critical problems of our times.

We need not wait for "another Martin Luther King" to lead us. "We lie in the lap of an immense intelligence," as Dewey said, quoting Emerson. Grassroots collaborative processes of tapping that great intelligence to realize the ideal of deep democracy worldwide have already begun. The needs and challenges are enormous. The potential for life-illuminating meaning for participants in the democratic struggle, as well as for gradual and eventually great differences in the quality of humanity's lived experience, are real and exhilarating.

Notes

1. See Alexis de Tocqueville's *Democracy in America* (1835 and 1840), p. 287. His valuable analytic concept "habits of the heart" was revived by Robert Bellah and his collaborators in an influential study of late-twentieth-century American society, *Habits of the Heart: Individualism and Commitment in American Life* (1985). Unfortunately, this study is flawed by a false universalism that fails to consider the diversity of such value-laden, action-cueing perceptual frameworks in American society today, as Vincent Harding and others have pointed out.

2. See John Herman Randall, Jr.'s "Dewey's Interpretation of the History of Philosophy," in *The Philosophy of John Dewey* (1939), volume 1 in *The Library of Living Philosopher* eds. Paul Arthur Schilpp and Lewis Edwin Hahn.

3. See John Dewey, "Democracy Is Radical," *Common Sense* 6 (January 1937), in *John Dewey: The Later Works*, volume 11. All citations of Dewey's works in this book refer to the now-standard critical editions edited by Jo Ann Boydston and published by Southern Illinois University Press. However, because I believe it is more respectful and more meaningful to readers to note Dewey's original titles and dates of publication, I do so.

4. For examples of Locke's use of the concept of "cosmopolitan unity in diversity," see "Pluralism and Intellectual Democracy" in Harris (1989:53 and 61). For "anthropology in the broadest sense," see, for example, "Cultural Relativism and Ideological Peace" in Harris (1989:72).

5. See, for example, Locke's "Pluralism and Intellectual Democracy" in Harris (1989:56).

6. See Locke's "The Need for a New Organon in Education" in Harris (1989:268).

7. I discuss this claim that deep democracy is preferable "all the way down" more fully in "Educational Multiculturalism, Cultural Pluralism, and Deep Democracy," in *Theorizing Multiculturalism: A Guide to the Current Debate,* ed. Cynthia Willett (1998).

Chapter 1

The Diverse Community or the Unoppressive City: Which Ideal for a Transformative Politics of Difference?

> *The cure for the ailments of democracy is more democracy*
>
> —JOHN DEWEY, *The Public and Its Problems* (1927)

The coherence and desirability of the ideal of community have been forcefully attacked by Iris Marion Young, among others, as inextricably entangled within what Jacques Derrida calls "the metaphysics of presence," Theodor Adorno calls "the logic of identity," and Julia Kristeva calls "the repression of heterogeneity."[1] In a highly influential essay, "The Ideal of Community and the Politics of Difference" (1990), Young argues that communitarian theory, in all of its widely varying expressions, is metaphysically flawed by traditional Western dualistic logical and ontological oppositions, fixed essential kinds with associated less-valued deviations, and a static, unitary conception of the self. Moreover, Young argues, communitarian theory is bound to a false and restrictive view of language as closed and common. Finally, she argues, the ideal of community itself is inescapably implicated in social and political practices that exclude and punish differences relative to a heterogeneous norm that serves the psychic security and will-to-power of the dominant few. Therefore, Young concludes, the ideal of community should be jettisoned by participants in the development of a transformative politics of difference in favor of her counter-ideal of "the unoppressive city," which does not attempt to specify shared values other than the rejection of oppression in all forms, relying instead on mediating social institutions to reduce face-to-face contact among those who differ in order to prevent enforced uniformity. Partly due to Young's influence, many other feminists, postmodernists, and theorists of liberatory transformative change have rejected the ideal of community in all of its possible formulations. Surely, they are right to do so if these central claims of Young's brilliant and complex analysis are correct. However, whereas Young's criticisms might be insightful if they were focused on the liberal individualist ideal and its various theoretical expressions, they are mistakenly applied to the ideal of community and at least some of its egalitarian theoretical expressions, including those of Michael Sandel, John Dewey, Josiah Royce, and Alain Locke. Contrary to Young's conclusion and to the beliefs of those who have been influenced by it, when the ideal of community is understood as valuing diversity within unity, it can guide a highly desirable and more feasible path for a transformative politics of difference. Within a politics of difference guided by the ideal of the diverse community, a version of Young's counter-ideal of the unoppressive city, separated from its postmodernist underpinnings, can play a valuable intermediate role.

In her intellectually dazzling essay, "The Ideal of Community and the Politics of Difference," Young's critique runs along the following lines.[2] Both Western theorizing and everyday language exhibit a misguided urge to characterize things in terms of overarching wholes and subordinate parts as a way of representing and thus grasping reality. This way of thinking leads inevitably to hierarchical oppositions between the pure and the impure examples of things of a kind, given that the common nature of the kind is expressed by giving privileged attention to certain characteristics that are widely shared among favored examples and by marginalizing other characteristics in which things of the kind differ. At the same time, the bearers of the marginalized characteristics are treated as lesser because impure examples of the kind, even though the differences are treated as less important than the commonalities in order for the kind itself to be conceptually constituted. The kind-constituting human self is treated as a *fixed unity* that originates the language and thought that fully map reality, thereby capturing it for control.[3] Thus, according to this picture, the meaning of language and thought is never out of the self's referential grasp. Because selves also form an essentially similar kind, in their role as subjects they can fully grasp each other as objects of thought and expression.

However, this traditional Western picture is unrealizable and undesirable, Young argues, because the very process of attempting to represent reality in this way inevitably leaves out, downplays, or attempts to repress real differences among "the irreducible particularity of entities" (304). This attempt to represent reality in terms of the fixed, common characteristics of members of natural kinds denies the importance of the context of particular relationships to other entities as part of a thing's being. Thus, this quest for unity and totality also, as Adorno suggests, denies things their materiality and, as Derrida suggests, denies the relations of locations in place and time among signs that are important to the way language works and that always leave meanings incomplete and multiple. Moreover, as Kristeva suggests, this quest falsifies the real character of the self, which is not a unified, finished thing, but a thing in process.[4]

Young's crucial but mistaken premise is that the ideal of community is inextricably tied into this hopeless quest for unity and totality. Community, she claims, is frequently posed as the polar opposite of the inferior ideal of individualism, understood as the modern problem to be overcome. Moreover, she claims, the ideal of community "exhibits a totalizing impulse" and "denies difference" in privileging face-to-face relations unmediated by time and distance, and in contrasting the problematic present with a utopian alternative future without specifying a transformational process that links them (305).[5] If these were the real and necessary characteristics of communitarian thought, Young would be insightful in urging intellectuals who seek to advance the cause of social transformation of multiple oppressions to discard the ideal of community in favor of a less-flawed picture, perhaps her ideal of "the unoppressive city."

However, Young seriously misrepresents the communitarian model she discusses at greatest length, Sandel's as expressed in his *Liberalism and the Limits of Justice,* because she interprets what he has written through a suspicious lens that seems illuminating only to one who has already been captured by the playful language-games of the postmodernist critique. For example, in critically explicating Sandel's communitarian conception of the self, Young misleadingly shifts the burden of his language in a passage that she quotes in the process of restating his claim and attempting to show that it is totalizing and repressive of difference.

> And insofar as our constitutive self-understandings comprehend a wider subject than the individual alone, whether a family or a tribe or a city or class or nation or people, to this extent they define a community in the constitutive sense. And what marks such a community is not merely a spirit of benevolence, or the prevalence of communitarian values, or even certain "shared final ends" alone, but a common vocabulary of discourse and a background of implicit practices and understandings within which the opacity of the person is reduced, if never finally dissolved. Insofar as [John Rawls's liberal conception of] justice depends for its preeminence on the separateness and boundedness of persons in the cognitive sense, its priority would diminish as that opacity faded and those community values deepened. (Young, 306; Sandel, 172–173)

Young claims that this passage is an example of communitarianism's hopeless captivity to the same old Western quest for unity and totality, in that it depends on a simple opposition between a communitarian ideal of social "fusion" and a liberal individualist ideal of separation. "As Sandel puts it," she says, "the opacity of persons *tends to dissolve* as ends, vocabulary, and practices become *identical*" (307). However, this is not what Sandel said; he said "the opacity of persons is reduced if never finally dissolved" rather than "tends to dissolve," and he referred to a "common vocabulary," rather that an "identical" one. These are important differences, and the substitutions of the second phrases for the first ones are seriously misleading. In the passage in question, Sandel proposes a countermodel of the self that contrasts with Rawls's liberal model, which he criticizes as lacking the real self's relational character, and thereby obscuring the importance of other important social entities, such as families, tribes, cities, classes, nations, and peoples. Such relational entities, Sandel argues, are necessary to particular constitutive self-understandings among relational selves who are interconnected by a common language and a shared form of life that can give them some understanding of each other.[6] Sandel's point is that justice understood in the liberal individualist way as a boundary keeper is less primary in its importance to such cooperative relational selves than it is to individualist selves who are concerned about privacy and freedom from each other's interference. If Rawls's conception of the self is bounded by a high brick privacy wall, Sandel's is bounded by a low picket fence, easy to talk over and to let air currents and small creatures move through, allowing partial insights into each others' lives and inviting some social osmosis, but reminding us that self and other are not one. The either/or polarity between the individuated self and the social self is Young's, and perhaps Rawls's, but not Sandel's.

Expressing a contrast is not necessarily expressing a polarity. Our common or ordinary language holds subtly different, multiple possibilities of expressing contrasting relationships of things and ideas, in addition to polarities. Many ordinary people recognize this; so do some philosophers. Young is one of these in the subtle expression of her own vision later in her essay, but her view is distorted when she looks through the skeptical postmodernist lens and sees all other philosophers' language as part of the same traditional, dangerous Western quest for unity and totality.

Young is wrong in two ways in her further claim that this passage in Sandel's expression of the ideal of community reveals that, for communitarians, "community" is part of an opposition with "the separated self," each defined in terms of the other and existing in logical codependency. First, she has paired the wrong partners: communitarianism as a theoretical picture, not community as a concept, contrasts with liberal individualism as a theoretical picture. In the first picture, the community has a primary ontological status as part of a multiplicity of equally primary relational entities, including the self. In the second picture, only the atomic individual has primary ontological status, and the community is understood as an epiphenomenon that springs from many selves' conjoint willing. The contrast between these two pictures is more subtle than a simple polarity, in that each contains the elements of the other, but in a transformed ontological role. Second, Young has her oppositions wrong in regarding them as fundamentally logical. They are fundamentally historical and political, changing in their contents as "container concepts" in different eras as intellectuals have attempted to transform the use of the common political language to express a picture of a shared form of life that they hoped their transformative use of language-games would help to bring into being.[7] Historical opponents have frequently oversimplified each other's picture in order to fit it into a logical schema that would then allow them to apply a favored critical apparatus in order to undercut its perceived intellectual power. Sometimes historical partisans, including competing liberal individualists such as Rawls and Nozick, have even expressed their own picture in abstractly logical terms in an attempt to restrict the wide coattails and multiple connotations of our ordinary political language and, thus, to redirect toward their view our historically grounded intuitions, which are prompted by and implicated within our shared ordinary language.[8] However, the oppositions are fundamentally historical and always political, and the attempt to express and contain them as logical ones always, as Young herself would say, leaves something out and represses differences.

For most radicals, Young quite rightly suggests, the dichotomous opposition between individual and community that she claims to find in Sandel's work tends to break down. "Unlike reactionary appeals to community which consistently assert the subordination of individual aims and values to the collective," she suggests, "most radical theorists assert that community itself consists in the respect for and fulfillment of individual aims and capacities" (307). The radical reinterpretation of the dichotomy, Young says, is as a dialectic in which individualism and community are each conditions for the other. Again, Young makes a subtle mistake here. The ontological relationship she should be restating is between individual and community, whereas the historical relationship is between individualism and communitarianism, as well as other ideological models, including various forms of statism.

Interestingly enough, however, this "radical" understanding of the relationship between individual and community parallels Dewey's pragmatist analysis in *The Public and Its Problems* (1927). It is also characteristic of egalitarian communitarian analyses and those of contemporary pragmatists working in Dewey's classical stream. Thus, instead of presenting a critique of left-communitarian social ontology, Young has simply described it and implicitly characterized it as radical, though she is correct to sense a repressive, ahistorical, and reactionary tendency in communitarianisms of the right, including works by Alasdair MacIntyre (1984) and Allan Bloom (1987).

Young mistakenly claims, however, that left-communitarians' radical reinterpretation of the individual-collective dichotomy as a dialectic is also totalizing, repressive of difference, tied to a false conception of the self, and hopelessly utopian (307–309). Carol Gould's *Rethinking Democracy* (1988) is Young's example of theoretical totalizing that represses difference in its universal generalizations and its expectation that subjects can and should become fully transparent to each other. It also, Young claims, unrealistically puts closure to history in its teleological finality. However, Young simply miscategorizes Gould's work, which is a retrieval of Marx's social ontology, including a Marxian understanding of dialectic, and thus should not be regarded as an example of communitarian theory, although Gould herself regards it as an example of *democratic* theory, a label that left-communitarians also would claim.

Young argues that the complex of problems she has identified, especially "the difference problem" in intersubjectivity, is widely shared among a widely varying assortment of self-identified and Young-identified left-communitarians, among whom she includes Seyla Benhabib, Isaac Balbus, Roberto Unger, Dorothy Allison, Carol Gould, and once again, Michael Sandel. Young argues that all of these widely differing theorists share a composite formulation of the ideal of community: "Persons will cease to be opaque, other, not understood, and instead become fused, mutually sympathetic, understanding one another as they understand themselves" (309). In a sweeping critique that embraces all of these theories, Young draws on Hegel, Sartre, and Kristeva in arguing that a fully shared subjectivity of "complete mutual understanding and reciprocity" is impossible, both because subjects transcend one another's grasp and because, contrary to the Cartesian conception of the self as unified and originative, selves are heterogeneous subjects in process who cannot even grasp their own meanings, needs, and desires.

As pointed out previously, Young is in error in identifying all of these theorists as communitarians. Moreover, neither Sandel nor any other self-identified communitarian theorist, including Alasdair MacIntyre on the conservative end of the spectrum, actually advocates her caricature of their differing ideal models of self and community. None of them calls for a complete loss of mystery and the end of all opacity in social relations through the creation of a "fused self"—who would call for this outside of science fiction? Instead, Sandel and other egalitarian communitarians call for a lessening of misunderstanding and the discovery of important points of tangency amidst better-acknowledged differences among selves who can and do change in the flow and rapids of historical processes.

Nor do communitarians call for community members to "identify" with one another in the mathematical sense of perceiving or believing in one another's interchangeable sameness that Young claims is the real historical meaning of community identity in the United States. In Young's view, such an interchangeable sameness is described and intensified by contrast with the disvalued differences of others in America's indigenous processes of racism and xenophobia. Young's claim is not that appeal to an ideal of community is directly racist and xenophobic, but rather that in the real American historical context, these are its inevitable public implications. Although this crude sense of identity may be uncritically employed by some people, the wiser members of all of our various ethnic communities realize that mathematical sameness is very different from the sense of a shared, heterogeneous heritage and a shared, complex contemporary predicament that allows us to feel partial echoes of sympathy and a sense of tangency at certain points of experience. This is what many communitarian theorists and transformative change agents, including Martin Luther King, Jr., Malcolm X (El-Hajj Malik El-Shabazz), and James H. Cone, seek to evoke when they refer to a "community identity."[9] Wise people among African Americans do not think "we are all alike," nor do wise people among my own Irish Americans. When such self-identified, historically formed communities are under pressure, many of their members may feel that it is unwise to disclose some of their internal group differences to members of opponent groups. Yet the less ideologically limited members of such groups have always been able to see many of their own and their opponents' group differences beyond the political veils and smoke screens. Some have chosen to use these insights to promote adversarial advantage, whereas others have chosen to use them to work for peace and mutual benefit. Thus, there is no logically necessary or historically probable implication of racism and xenophobia, or in general, repression of differences, in an appeal to an ideal of community, especially when it is envisioned as *a diverse community* that includes multiple, partially overlapping, shared social identities that are also some of the constitutive elements of personal identities, understood in the classical pragmatist stream of Peirce, James, Royce, Mead, and Dewey as changeable and always in process.[10]

Nor does the process of building such "shared identities" ideally or actually require that our most important social relations be totally unmediated, as Young claims. She rightly points out that many communitarian theorists place great emphasis on face-to-face relations as part of the process of building valued, shared identities, understood as both a precondition for and an outcome of participatory democratic processes. Such face-to-face relations are emphasized by communitarians, Young claims, because they are immediate, meaning unmediated in any sense. However, this is impossible, she argues, because all social relations are mediated by language, gesture, and the presence of others who interject their own meanings into the midst of communication processes.

Here, Young makes a peculiar mistake about the connection between selves and language. If, as Wittgenstein argues (and Peirce, Royce, Dewey, and Mead suggest), there can be no private languages, but rather, linguistic meanings are socially learned, tied to social practices within shared forms of life and, thus, an active instrument in the social constitution of selves, social relations cannot rightly be understood as *mediated* by language, gesture, and the presence of others. Rather, social relations are *constituted* by language-games, which include not only words but also their inseparable social practices that weave together a social whole.[11] To suggest that language mediates social relations is to suggest, with liberal individualists, that selves are essentially separate and originative, in contrast with Kristeva's favorably cited analysis of dynamic, relational selves and Young's own earlier claims.

Moreover, although Sandel does not explain what he means by a "common" language, if we understand this concept in a Wittgensteinian or Peircean way, there is no reason to regard it as unitary, fully homogeneous, and "identical," or fixed, final, and "without location in place and time," as Young, in her evocation of Derrida's analysis, suggests the concept of a common language must be. Rather, following Wittgenstein's lead in his analysis of language-games as displaying "family resemblances," we might better understand differing people's uses of the concepts of a common language as displaying variety within interlinked, dynamic patterns without sharing some essential core meaning or set of necessary and sufficient conditions for their definition.[12] Because new "family members" can be added at any time to the set of versions of a concept linked by "family resemblances," there is nothing final or fixed about such language-games. Nor is a common language structured by such always-developing families of concept variants totalizing, because different groups within a language-sharing society may invent and employ distinctive patterns of concept usage that differ from those of other groups with whom their usages nonetheless share family resemblances. Moreover, a common language understood in this way contains within itself resources for transforming its socially shared form of life, especially given Wittgenstein's insight that some concept-focused language-games play a particularly powerful role within a form of life. He calls these language-games the "hinges" upon which other language-games turn.[13] Among these "hinge" concepts we might include justice, democracy, liberty, equality, individual, and community within our own shared American form of life, as well as their conceptual equivalents within many other modern forms of life. These concepts are understood in widely differing yet interlinked ways, and at least some of them play the role of container concepts that organize particular interpretations of other important concepts into patterns of thought and action.

Building on her mistakes about selves and language, Young argues that realizing a form of life organized through face-to-face relations unmediated by other agents and institutions would require that our society be balkanized into small, self-sufficient communities. This, she rightly points out, would be neither feasible nor desirable. However, the ideal of the diverse community does not require dismantling cities in order to build face-to-face communities. Rather, it requires their *transformation*, a necessity that Young acknowledges implicitly even when she correctly points out that "[many] people enjoy [some aspects of] cities"—although perhaps not solely or even primarily for the reason she gives, that they are places where "strangers are thrown together" (316). Surely she does not intend to suggest by posing her counterideal of "the unoppressive city" that suburbs, villages, and rural forms of life be abolished, or that all or any real cities in their present, untransformed conditions are model locations of the good life for all who enjoy the privacy of anonymity and just know how to see the beauty of differences.

Egalitarian communitarians call for changes within all of these differing yet interlinked geopolitical forms. Cities, for example, can develop neighborhoods and neighborhood organizations within them in which the face-to-face relationships amidst diversity that Michael Sandel, John Dewey, Alain Locke, and others have prized can become a part of citizens' lived experience, although not the whole of it. Even by 1927, when he published *The Public and Its Problems,* Dewey had become aware of a widely shared sense of rootlessness and impermanence in human relations combined with a sense of impotence in the face of enormous bureaucratic economic and political institutions over which people felt they had no control. Dewey's solution to the first part of this problem, the reestablishment of face-to-face democratic communities suited to new times and new technologies, was a precondition and ongoing part of his solution to the second part of the problem: the reemergence of a well-informed, energetic "Public" linked by effective use of modern mass communication and able to transform outdated "democratic" institutions into ones that could return democratic power to the people. Ongoing participation in and shared control of the institutions that shape the conditions of their lives was a necessary element of the democratic transformation Dewey envisioned. Thus, in Dewey's again-influential pragmatist example of a democratic transformative politics that bears close affinities to left-communitarian thought and has helped to influence its development, the face-to-face community is an important part of the picture, but not the whole or even the only important part.[14]

Young's most insightful and important charge is that communitarian theorists do not explain adequately how separate face-to-face communities would relate to each other, which is inevitable and desirable in the real world. Young is surely correct that an account of how communities are to be feasibly and desirably related to one another is a necessary feature of a complete and adequate communitarian model. She is right to fault Sandel's work and that of many other contemporary communitarian theorists for a tendency to slip back and forth too casually between descriptive and normative theory without taking responsibility to clearly characterize feasible and desirable transformative processes. This is a problem these communitarians share with many liberal individualists like Rawls and Nozick. Even if one adopts a communitarian account of constitutive self-understandings, of common language, and of shared group identity, one still has the problem of explaining how such communities can, do, or might interact with each other, as well as how the quality of such cross-community interactions in the real world can be improved relative to something like Dewey's democratic ideal.

However, this theoretical fault is different from the fatal flaw of questing after undifferentiated unity and totality, and it is a fault that our diverse communitarian philosophical heritage offers rich resources for overcoming, especially in the treasure trove of classical American pragmatism and cultural pluralism explored in the following chapters of this book. In addition to their transformative leadings, Royce's and Dewey's works show the misdirection of Young's Derridean critical claim that theorists of the community are inescapably wedded to a metaphysics of presence. Royce's *The Problem of Christianity* explores the human necessity and significance of two forms of absence, memory and hope, for the development and sustenance of communities; this work and others by Royce deeply influenced the development of Martin Luther King, Jr.'s conception of "the Beloved Community" as a yet-to-be embodied unity amidst diversity. Similarly, Dewey's way of explaining the functioning of ideals like community and democracy in *The Public and Its Problems* depends upon a gap between the actual and the possible, the experienced and the not-yet-experienced for which we strive, and his Jamesian emphasis on an ontological openness to change displays his sensibility to the lived inseparability of absence from presence. Dewey's work is a rich source of inspiration and provocation for many contemporary philosophers of the democratic community.

Likewise, the writings of Royce's and Dewey's younger contemporary, Alain Locke, whose critical pragmatist philosophy of cultural pluralism is an outgrowth in part of his early appreciation of James's pragmatist critique of absolute values and of Royce's conception of "loyalty to loyalty," is enjoying a renaissance of posthumous influence, in large part because of his transformative insights about the path to achieving democratic unity amidst diversity through respectful cooperation among culturally differing individuals and groups. Such classical pragmatist and cultural pluralist insights can be enormously helpful as we attempt to create a transformative politics of difference to serve us well in a new century. For example, in "Pluralism and Intellectual Democracy" (1942), Locke argued that there is no ground for objective justification of human values outside of human experience, which differs in important respects relative to geopolitical location, patterns of historical power relations, and other factors, and that various cultures' value systems represent differing functional adaptations to their differing lived circumstances. Nonetheless, Locke argued, a cooperative interdisciplinary "anthropology in the broadest sense" could discover basic humane values that express commonalities amidst these different systematic expressions of differing human experiences. These basic humane values can then become the common ground for democratic mutuality amidst diversity, and also for rejecting antidemocratic absolutisms and fundamentalisms as both intellectually unjustifiable and practically intolerable. In successive stages, cross-difference conversa-

tions on the common ground of basic humane values can lead to tolerant understanding of the historical roots of each others' differing perspectives, to deeper respect, to reciprocal exchanges, to some areas of agreement and experience-
founded trust, and eventually, to collaborative projects for mutual benefit. The
dual role of intellectuals in promoting such a democratic peace at all levels,
after clearing their own heads of narrow absolutisms in favor of "realistic world
mindedness," includes both critical removal of its intellectual impediments and
preparing future generations to contribute to the ongoing peace-building process
by teaching them the skills and perspectives of a historically located "critical relativism," in replacement for the combination of anti-evaluative relativisms and
ahistorical absolutisms that now shape their educational experiences. If we hope
to build a democratic politics of difference for the twenty-first century that will
effectively bring an end to historically ongoing group-based oppressions, we
need to retrieve these insights from Locke, as well as complementary ones from
other cultural pluralists, pragmatists, critical theorists, feminists, and various
philosophers of the diverse democratic community because, as Young so rightly
points out, we have no choice but to deal with each other across differences in our
practically entangled lives.

At the end of her essay, Young acknowledges that all of the inspiring claims
she makes for her ideal of the unoppressive city have also been made by some of
the proponents of the ideal of community, and she suggests that it may be just "a
matter of stipulation" into which ideal one packages a transformative politics that
reflects and operates through "the play of difference" (320). Young opts for the
ideal of the unoppressive city because she objects to what some theorists have
packaged into the ideal of community. Why not let the conservatives have that
language, she seems to suggest, and instead generate a new way of talking about
what we want and how to achieve it that does not require wrestling with them
over the meaning of terms and, by creating a sharper contrast, aids us in articulating a countervision among ourselves? It is ironic how difficult it is even for a
proponent of a postmodern politics of difference to escape the old dualizing tendencies that let us validate our intellectual likeness in valued contradistinction
from "them," those "demon others" that cause trouble for us and prevent us from
realizing our cherished visions. Not only has Young fallen into this same old trap,
but she has also yielded to her opponents the very field to which she calls radical
intellectuals to shift our game.

That field is transformative real-world politics, in America and in some other
parts of the world, in which the language of community has tremendous historical power as well as a current infusion of energy for revitalizing the quest for a
free and equal play of difference, including generating the material preconditions
for its progressive realization. Like other ideal container concepts such as liberty,
equality, and human dignity, "community" has a positive valence and motivating
power within our common languages and shared forms of life, even though there
is deep disagreement about just what it means. In recent years, this language of
community has become prominent in real-world American politics, partly be-

cause of the influence of communitarian intellectuals, but largely because this thread of thought and feeling that goes back to Thomas Jefferson and the roots of our shared, diverse intellectual heritage has seemed to express for many nonintellectuals what is missing now and what we want in our future life as an always-diverse people.[15] Amitai Etzioni's *The Spirit of Community: Rights, Responsibilities, and the Communitarian Agenda* (1993) was a bestseller for months, spawning a communitarian social movement, other books, and at least one scholarly journal. Likewise, experiments in local democratic participation under the ideal banner of community are springing up all over the country. *Governing*, a professional journal received and read by a large portion of the mid- and high-level civil servants in local and state governments, included "A User's Guide to Communitarianism" as a featured article that discussed some of the positive lessons in "bringing an ethic of personal responsibility back to American community life" that these local experiments in democratic participation offer.[16] As Chapters Six and Seven discuss in greater detail, experiments that aim to increase citizen participation in city planning under the banner of community are changing the ways cities decide the future of their mediating institutions, and also are bringing citizens from widely differing perspectives into mutually desired conversation with each other in order to build a shared vision and to jointly influence the conditions of their lives.

Although Young disparages a naive participatory democratic impulse among fellow American feminists as leading to intragroup dissension and wider political ineffectiveness (301), this very impulse is one of our deepest links to the political sensibilities of the larger citizenry we hope to influence. Perhaps the true energy sapper in recent American feminism has been a lack of real and extensive democratic participation amidst differences, both in feminist intragroup relations and in our relations as feminists to the political processes and forums of national and local life. The question is, how can we transform these limitations, both in feminist characters and praxis, and in the moral and political tendencies and institutions of the larger society? Young's suggestion that the language we use to evoke our transformative ideal may be just "a matter of stipulation" reveals an implicitly elitist belief that differences about ideals are matters for intellectuals to resolve. This suggestion ignores the importance of the ideal of community for many diverse people in our larger society. At the same time, Young's rejection of the ideal of community impedes the struggle of transformative democratic theorists and left-communitarian intellectuals to redefine the meaning of the ideal of community on the academic turf as well as in the political life of our larger societies.

If, as Young believes, intellectuals can offer anything helpful to a transformative politics of difference in the larger society, her suggestion that we trade in the history-laden popular language of community in favor of a new concept that repackages much of the same contents for the convenience of intellectuals is not wise. Our convenience should serve ordinary citizens' convenience in mere matters of stipulation so that we can connect meaningfully with the discourse of public life and play a useful, appropriately humble role in its deepening, its diversifying, and its enhanced transformative effectiveness. For those of us who advocate a transformative politics of difference to yield the language of community to conservatives is to give up the promise and the responsibility of our role as public intellectuals.

Therefore, Iris Marion Young's brilliant and influential critique of communitarianism and the ideal of community misses the mark, both theoretically and as a guide to transformative praxis. Nonetheless, her proposed counterideal of the unoppressive city can and must play an important intermediate role as an end-in-view within a transformative politics of difference guided by the ideal of community. Its invaluable role is to focus reconstructive attention on the transformation of our real cities into places where the free and equal play of difference within a mutually fulfilling democratic community life can be experienced. However, the way to achieve Young's unoppressive city is not through a merely negative politics of attempting to end present patterns of domination and interference, because there is no way urban people really can just leave each other alone. Rather, we must replace our presently oppressive social and political patterns and the institutions that sustain them with better ones that reflect our common and our differing needs, as well as the patterns of family resemblances amidst diversity among our positive ideals and our converging and diverging historical experiences. This can be achieved only through conjoint, cross-difference, participatory democratic processes that reflect dispersed knowledge, that provide opportunities to understand differing experiences, and that can bring into being the basis and the will for mutually beneficial cooperation. Such processes can be initiated, encouraged, and brought to fruition only if we start with the assumption that at least these limited first steps for developing a diverse, deeply democratic community are possible.

Notes

1. See Derrida's *Of Grammatology* (1976), Adorno's *Negative Dialectics* (1973), and Kristeva's, *Polylogue* (1977), all quoted by Young, "The Ideal of Community and the Politics of Difference" (1990), 302–304.

2. Unless otherwise noted, all parenthetical page citations in this essay are to Iris Marion Young's "The Ideal of Community and the Politics of Difference," *Feminism/Postmodernism* (1990), ed. Linda J. Nicholson. This chapter is an outgrowth of an essay with the same title that I published in *The Journal of Social Philosophy* 26:1 (Spring 1995).

3. John Rawls's self of the "original position" in *A Theory of Justice* (1971) exemplifies the conception Young treats as uniformly characteristic of Western philosophy, but contrasts markedly with pragmatist conceptions of the self in William James's *Principles of Psychology* (1890) and George Herbert Mead's "The Social Self" (1913).

4. These insightful criticisms of a major stream of Western philosophy from Descartes through Kant do not apply to the equally critical American pragmatist stream from Charles Sanders Peirce through John Dewey to the present.

5. Young may wish to evade the National Association of Scholars's conservative adversarial use of the concept of community, but Dewey's nonutopian use of the concept in *Democracy and Education* (1916) and *The Public and Its Problems* (1927) is very compatible with and useful in achieving the goals of inclusiveness, respect for differences, and free spaces in which to flourish advocated by Young.

6. "Shared form of life" is one of Ludwig Wittgenstein's analytic concepts in *Philosophical Investigations,* Third Edition (1958) remark 19ff, which he develops further in *On Certainty* (1969), preceding and following remark 358.

7. "Container concept" is John Schaar's term from "Equality of Opportunity, and Beyond," *Nomos IX: Equality* (1967), eds. J. Roland Pennock and John W. Chapman. "Language-games" is another of Wittgenstein's analytic concepts from *Philosophical Investigations* (1958), remark 7ff.

8. See John Rawls, *op. cit.*, and Robert Nozick, *Anarchy, State, and Utopia* (1974).

9. See Martin Luther King, Jr.'s *Where Do We Go from Here: Chaos or Community?* (1967), George Breitman's collection of some of Malcom (X) Shabazz's last speeches and letters, *By Any Means Necessary* (1970), and James H. Cone's *Martin & Malcolm & America: A Dream or a Nightmare* (1991).

10. See *The Essential Peirce: Selected Philosophical Writings*, 2 Vols. (1992 and 1998), eds. Nathan Houser and Christian Kloesel; and Vincent M. Colapietro's *Peirce's Approach to the Self: A Semiotic Perspective on Human Subjectivity* (1989); as well as *The Writings of William James*, ed. John J. McDermott (1977); *The Basic Writings of Josiah Royce*, ed. John J. McDermott (1969); George Herbert Mead's *Mind, Self, and Society,* ed., Charles W. Morris (1934); and *The Collected Works of John Dewey*, 37 Vols. (1969–1990), ed. Jo Ann Boydston.

11. Wittgenstein develops his "private language argument" in *Philosophical Investigations* (1958), remark 241ff.

12. Wittgenstein develops the concept of "family resemblances" within his analysis of the ordinary language concept of "games" in *Philosophical Investigations* (1958); see especially remarks 65–67 and following.

13. See Wittgenstein's *On Certainty* (1969), especially remark 341 and following.

14. Some recent works by American pragmatists that show Dewey's continuing influence include Cornel West's *The American Evasion of Philosophy: A Genealogy of Pragmatism* (1989); *Philosophy and the Reconstruction of Culture: Pragmatic Essays after Dewey* (1993), a collection of essays by various contemporary pragmatists edited by John J. Stuhr; Charlene Haddock Seigfried's *Pragmatism and Feminism: Reweaving the Social Fabric* (1996); *Reading Dewey: Interpretations for a Postmodern Generation* (1998), a collection of essays by various contemporary pragmatists edited by Larry A. Hickman; and Michael Eldridge's *Transforming Experience: John Dewey's Cultural Instrumentalism* (1998).

15. See Garry Wills's *Inventing America: Jefferson's Declaration of Independence* (1978).

16. See Rob Gurwitt, "A User's Guide to Communitarianism," *Governing: The Magazine of States and Localities* 6:11 (August 1993).

Chapter 2

Transformative Communication toward Democratic Communities: Pragmatism or Critical Theory?

The philosophers have only interpreted the world, in various ways; the point is to change it.

—KARL MARX, "Theses on Feuerbach" (1845)

Philosophy as a critical organ *becomes in effect a messenger, a liaison officer, making reciprocally intelligible voices speaking provincial tongues, and thereby enlarging as well as rectifying the meanings with which they are charged.*

—JOHN DEWEY, *Experience and Nature* (1925)

As soon as the theory of language is no longer semantically oriented towards the understanding of sentences but is pragmatically oriented *toward the utterances with which speakers come to an understanding with each other about something, it will be able to take relation-to-self and sentence form into account on the same level. In order to reach an understanding about something, participants must not only understand the meaning of the sentences employed in their utterances, they must also be able to relate to each other in the role of speakers and hearers—in the presence of bystanders from their (or from a) linguistic community.*

—JÜRGEN HABERMAS, "Metaphysics after Kant" (1988)

Introduction

How is just and effective democratic transformation of diverse predemocratic, anti-democratic, posttotalitarian, and only "formally" democratic societies to be accomplished in our globalized era? A practical philosophy of democratic transformation is greatly needed to guide and to learn from interlinked local struggles to improve the quality of life in our democratically deficient and rapidly changing world. Pragmatism in John Dewey's stream of influence and critical theory in Jürgen Habermas's stream are differing philosophical schools that share the project of developing such a practical philosophy of democratic transformation in community life. Although they agree in regarding transformative communication as the key, they are often portrayed as mutually exclusive contemporary rivals. For example, perhaps thinking of the work of post-Deweyan "neopragmatist" Richard Rorty, Steven Seidman claims that "in response to the relativist implications of hermeneutics, *pragmatism,* and poststructuralism, Habermas abandons the view of theory as a general interpretive framework since this suggests a historical–hermeneutic and therefore relativist standpoint. He wants to defend the proposition that there can be a purely objective theoretical standpoint."[1] Yet Deweyan pragmatism and Habermasian critical theory share common historical sources of influence, they agree on the central concepts to be clarified, and they share a common contemporary predicament to transform. This should be sufficient common ground for renewing an engagement that aims to increase the value of their contributions to world-changing democratic struggle. Although differences may remain, each can be helpfully clarified, corrected, and redirected in light of reconstructive criticisms of the other, helping each to make more valuable contributions to this shared transformative project.

This can be shown by critically interrelating Dewey's and Habermas's ideas about community, communication, the democratic ideal, and the need for a new kind of social science to guide real-world democratic transformation processes. Such a reconstructively critical conversation also reveals shared shortcomings of both philosophical approaches, which can be overcome by learning from feminists and cultural pluralists, especially Jane Addams, Alain Locke, and their contemporary inheritors, about the importance of *cultivated pluralism* within liberatory transformative praxis amidst deep, power-structured, culturally linked differences in participants' perspectives and life situations.[2] Some of the insights from these other, diversity-appreciating philosophical voices we need to draw on in developing a practical philosophy of democratic transformation focus on how to identify and build support for more deeply democratic values, how to bridge cultural and social–locational gaps in negotiating a collaborative basis for community building, and how to educate new generations through democratic communicative processes that deeply transform current undemocratic relations of dominance and exclusion.

Taking these insights from feminism and cultural pluralism seriously will stimulate the kind of "recovery of philosophy" from self-absorption Dewey called for in 1917, thereby changing the course of both pragmatism and critical theory. It will recall those pragmatists who have become preoccupied with the "problems of philosophers" to the "problems of men" while deepening pragmatism's democratic character beyond even Dewey's prophetic horizon.[3] It will recall those critical theorists who have become caught up in diverse projects of merely criticizing or, worse yet, justifying existing social, political, and economic institutions, to their original project of universal human liberation, which demands their active participation in concrete problems of institutional and attitudinal transformation.[4] Although pragmatism and critical theory may retain their characteristic "flavors" and emphases even after a critical–reconstructive engagement with feminism and cultural pluralism, a shared offspring will come into being: *a radical critical pragmatism* that can theorize a caring, cultivated pluralism that arcs toward the universally humane while celebrating diversity, creating models and methods for deepening democracy through open, reciprocal communication within liberatory praxis.[5]

Preliminary Critical–Reconstructive Negotiations: Pragmatism and Critical Theory

When Dewey published *The Public and Its Problems* in 1927, he was troubled about the same lacks and losses that presently concern Habermas and many of the rest of us who advocate a deeper realization of democracy in our world today: a lack of meaningful social connections with people we encounter in our daily lives, a loss of trust in the institutions of government and industry to operate on values and work toward goals we believe in, a lack in many of our lives of the material prerequisites to meet basic human needs as well as to undergird human flourishing, and a loss of a sense of power and direction to overcome the growing problems that overshadow our hopefulness about the future.[6] Unlike Habermas, Dewey wholeheartedly celebrated the growth of modern science and provisionally celebrated the technologies to which it has given rise, drawing on his own analysis of the method of cooperative, hypothesis-driven, experimental inquiry that he believed had made these developments possible as his model for transformative social inquiry.[7] With Dewey, Habermas affirms the importance of many of modernity's achievements, including the emergence of "formally" democratic government institutions, broader distribution of the material means of life, more widespread education, and a more generally shared sense of human equality. Both suggest that these modern developments indicate a democratic tendency in history, although Dewey did not believe that democracy in a fuller sense is historically inevitable, or that all of the developments associated with modernity have been positive. Rather, Dewey believed that an important dimension of a fuller human experience—the experience of community—has been unraveled and must be reknit in new forms to fit our new times if we are to overcome the lacks and losses that concern us.

Like his friend and pragmatist colleague George Herbert Mead, an acknowledged influence in the development of Habermas's ideas, Dewey viewed the widely posited dichotomy of individual versus community (or group, or society, or the collective) as a mistake. Thus, Habermas's depiction of "Dewey's model" as focusing on "an isolated actor's instrumental dealings with things and events" is a fundamental misreading that keeps him and those who draw on him from appropriating the rich critical–reconstructive resources Dewey offers for further developing Habermas's own contribution.[8] Our societies have no separate existence apart from the groups and the individuals who make them up, Dewey argued in

The Public and Its Problems and many other places. Yet there are no residual individuals who are not shaped in their development by their experiences of group membership within larger social processes. Dichotomous thinking of the kind that pits the individual against society or the community tends to emerge, Dewey suggested, during times of rapid social change, when new group relationships are forming and old patterns of intergroup relationship undergo new stresses. The real problem of such times, his and ours, he suggests, is how to intelligently reconstruct our patterns of social relationships so that mutual benefit can be advanced simultaneously with "more equable *liberation* of the powers of all individual members of all groupings" (Dewey 1927:355, emphasis mine). Solving this problem, Dewey argues, requires and amounts to democratically rebuilding our face-to-face communities as well as transforming the modern Great Society toward the Great Community: "Since every individual is a member of many groups, this specification [i.e., liberation both as individuals and as group members] cannot be fulfilled except when different groups interact flexibly and fully in connection with other groups" (Dewey 1927:328).

Reflecting the influence of the "absolute pragmatist" Josiah Royce that he, like Habermas, fails to sufficiently acknowledge, Dewey applied the concept of "community" to at least two differing levels of social organization of individuals, reflecting ordinary language as well as the aspirations of many people today in societies that have been reshaped by the forces of modernity.[9] At its most important, originative, and humanly sustaining level, Dewey's "community" refers to consciously interconnected patterns of face-to-face relationships in daily life that give us a sense of social identity and shared purpose, that motivate people to look out for each other and to work together toward goals of mutual betterment—a fast-fleeing American reality in Dewey's day and an extraordinarily rare one in our own times of walled suburban "lifestyle enclaves" and urban apartments with multiple locks on their doors. At its expanded, more complex level, Dewey's use of the concept of "community" in his ideal vision of "the Great Community" suggests a quality of life of a whole society in which the lacks and losses presently associated with the gains of modernity have been overcome through the emergence of a wider, consciously collaborative "public" that has the knowledge and the power to democratically transform the larger social patterns that frame the life conditions of individuals, families, groups, and face-to-face communities. Community life in both its face-to-face and its social–ideal senses is necessary for a fully human life, Dewey and Habermas agree. However, Dewey insightfully points out, neither kind of community experience can reasonably be regarded as an inevitable dimension or presumptive basis of associated life, as Habermas seems to suggest in his analysis of reason's operation in history and within linguistic communication. Rather, Dewey argues, beyond our "physical" interconnections created by shared patterns of actions and consequences, the development of communities requires the kind of conscious individual awareness that creates an active desire to cooperatively shape these patterns of interconnection in mutually beneficial ways. Community is an achieved quality of social interaction, not its rational antecedent.

Drawing on additional unacknowledged insights of the originary pragmatist Charles Sanders Peirce, whose influence Habermas does acknowledge, Dewey persuasively suggests that communities are constituted through the use of linguistic signs or symbols that allow people to preserve features of events as meanings that can be communicated and thus shared.[10] Echoing Royce's admittedly Peircean analysis of communication, Dewey argues that shared signs and symbols make possible certain convergent qualities and activities of mind: recollection (like Royce's memory) and foresight (like Royce's hope), as well as calculation, planning, and "a new kind of action" growing out of wants and needs that have been converted by common meanings into shared desires and purposes that make possible a "community of interest and endeavor" (Dewey 1927: 330–331). Creating Dewey's active "community of interest and endeavor" (like Royce's sustaining "community of memory and hope") through such symbolic chemistry is an ongoing, progressive, problem-solving process that spans generations.[11] Through educative communication that brings each new member into a community's particular traditions and flow of life, Dewey argues, one learns to be human, which means that one develops "an effective sense of being an individually distinctive member of a community; one who understands and appreciates its beliefs, desires and methods, and who contributes to a further [never-finished] conversion of organic powers into human resources and values" (Dewey 1927: 332). Habermas, following Mead as well as the protopragmatist leadings of the later Ludwig Wittgenstein, would agree.[12] Through communication and the cooperative action it makes possible, human individuals and communities are thus mutually constructive and continuously reconstructive, not only responding to incompletely resolved problems of the past but also taking account of new historical developments in the project of attempting to consciously guide transformation toward a fuller interactive realization of their ideal potentials.

In critically reconstructing Marx's analysis of the historical transformation process, a critique that Habermas has both partially corrected and insightfully detailed, Dewey persuasively argues that in addition to Marx's economic "engine of history"—technological changes working on a social base of productive relations—there is a second, moral–communicative engine within history that has counterpower to redirect Marx's economic engine. History's moral–communicative engine fuels and is fueled by the experience of community life, Dewey argues, which develops and changes slowly, rather than in revolutionary bursts. This explains, he suggests, "the essential continuity of history," within which both personal outlooks and transformative tools are "precipitates of the past" (Dewey 1927:336). Nonetheless, Dewey argues, consciously directed transformation toward a more fully human—and thus, necessarily a more democratic—stage of history can and does occur when the moral–communicative engine is effectively brought to bear on past-formed habits and customs. In arguing for his own closely related critique and counterview, Habermas insightfully reconstructs the Marxian concept of "crisis potential" as a way of expressing the possibility of social quantum leaps Dewey seems to overlook in this analysis. Profound social changes clearly do occur at times, signaling new historical eras—as we can see with hindsight about the twentieth century, in which a series of such profound social changes rocked humanity repeatedly, with increasing frequency. However, Dewey may be right in suggesting that the origins of such changes, as well as the dynamic continuities that hold our social worlds together, must be sought within historical processes that have been slowly aggregative.[13]

Habermas's analysis of how this moral–communicative engine works in history adds two very helpful, interrelated analytical concepts to the conversation: *lifeworld* (which refers to Dewey's sphere of community life) and *system* (which refers to Dewey's institutional apparatus of government and macroeconomy, though they disagree about where to locate science and technology).[14] Habermas's analytical concepts help to clarify the counterdynamics to which Dewey alluded, and also to bring out differences in operating principles between these two dimensions of society that are useful in diagnosing current problems that grow out of their relationship. If we interrelate their theories using these concepts, Dewey would agree with Habermas's implicitly normative claim that the lifeworld *should* regulate the system that exists to serve it, that the relationship has been reversed as capitalism has advanced, and that restoring the lifeworld to its appropriate dominance while reaping the benefits of positive developments within the system requires moral–communicative action guided by the democratic ideal.

Unfortunately, Habermas's general analysis is largely uncritical of traditional, power-structured social relations within and between the diverse lifeworlds he seeks to reelevate to dominance, which gives his critical analysis and his transformative prescription a peculiarly conservative character. Dewey, in contrast, recognized that problems of injustice within traditional social structures, especially as these become dysfunctional in progressively changing circumstances, motivate people to struggle together to change them, guided by a shared, historically evolving democratic ideal. His various articulations of the practical meaning of the democratic ideal require overcoming past exclusions on the basis of gender, race, and class. However, in *The Public and Its Problems,* the work from his prolific later years that is most focally concerned with conscious citizen collaboration in seeking democratic social transformation, Dewey's attention was less focused on America's "old problems" of still-unrectified oppressions based on gender, race, and class than on the new problem of how to reconstruct and start up the counterengine of moral communication within community life in order to gain transformative influence over an increasingly powerful capitalist political economy. Dewey's failure to interconnect the "old problems" with this new one—and with issues of power-structured cultural differences within and between societies—limits the adequacy of his social critique and the comprehensiveness of his articulation of the democratic ideal, as well as the efficacy of his transformative prescription. Nonetheless, as Chapter Three discusses in more detail, if these aspects of Dewey's analysis are reconstructed in ways that reflect critical yet compatible insights from feminists and cultural pluralists, it offers invaluable leadings for overcoming several key problems within contemporary democratic transformative praxis.

Although Dewey highly valued the development of modern technologies as potential tools for the democratic enrichment of all citizens' lives, he argued that problems in the relationship between the two parts of modern capitalist societies—Habermas's lifeworld and system—have arisen because an economic and political elite controls the new industrial and communications technologies. This controlling elite uses these powerful technologies for their own benefit, limiting democracy to "formal" institutional mechanisms perverted in their operation by the substitution of ideology for information, thereby diminishing others' practical experience of shared democratic influence and of valuable interconnection in their daily lives. Nonetheless, Dewey argued, it is possible to transform this power-distorted situation, because the shared democratic moral and political concepts that originally shaped our now-receding experience of community life, as well as the macro-level economic and political institutions to support it, still have power with us as signs and symbols that we can reinterpret to reconnect and redirect us in new times and circumstances. Our transformative challenge is to communicate such recontextualized meanings—and practical implications—of our traditional democratic moral and political concepts effectively, which is to say artfully, in his view.

Dewey offered only a few preliminary suggestions on how to effectively communicate such a transformatively inspiring reconception of the democratic ideal. He was as critical as the great critical theorist Herbert Marcuse concerning the ways in which elite-controlled mass-communications media distort information and pacify through entertainment, although Dewey was unable to foresee the stultifying, limiting, and enchaining powers of the vast bureaucracies that have become the norm, both in government and in the economic system that now creates the mass media's first imperatives.[15] Nonetheless, Dewey believed that the new mass-communications technologies could and must be brought into play in order to raise up an activist Public, inspired by the reconstructed signs and symbols of democracy artfully communicated, and informed through the agency of a reconceived social science about results of its critical inquiries. The question Dewey left unanswered in 1927 for democratic theorists of the future is *how* to actually rebuild the kind of face-to-face communities that so many people in modern societies now long for while transforming elite-controlled, ideology-purveying governmental, economic, and mass-communications institutions into tools for progressively realizing democracy. Clearly, Dewey did not think that such transformations in institutional purpose and content would be likely to emerge from some "conversion" to community-spirited motivations on the part of their profit-driven owners and managers, even if consumers used their power in the marketplace to express their democracy-serving preferences. By the 1930s, Dewey was calling for nationalization of the mass-communications media, although this did not happen in his lifetime and seems unlikely anytime soon. In any case, it is unclear that an elite-controlled government would convey different information than elite-controlled, for-profit mass media corporations.[16] The subsequent development in America of nonprofit mass media like National Public Radio and television's Public Broadcasting System has helped to bring out additional information and to bring in different voices, but these sources are insecurely funded and attended to by only a relatively small portion of the public. More recently, some theorists have expressed great hopes for the future of mass participation in the global computer Internet. Although it offers the advantages of easy, relatively uncontrolled access to interactive participation, thus far participating in the Internet has carried with it no responsibility for the *quality* of information, the other key element in the kind of effective democratic communication Dewey argued can revive and give a new shape to community life.

More than fifty years after Dewey wrote *The Public and Its Problems,* Habermas wrote in his complex and widely influential two-volume work, *The Theory of Communicative Action,* that within the "colonized" lifeworld of modern late capitalist societies, community is a memory, a language-borne intuition, and a universal human need, but the actual experience of community life is distorted by the formidable imperatives of the economic and administrative system. In contrast with Dewey's assignment of blame to an economic and political elite, and also in contrast with his own earlier focus on elite-controlled ideology, Habermas argues there that the system's clout derives in great part from past *choices* made by citizens whose goal was to limit the adverse impact of economic crises through greater government regulation and intervention in the market, a strategy that diminished *localized direct democracy* for the sake of building a more powerful *administered democracy.*[17] A concomitant result of these choices, Habermas argues, is the loss of the kind of social connection and personal voice that develops within a community that has some meaningful degree of shared autonomy. A further result, he suggests, is damage to the lifeworld culture that transmits and continuously redefines the values, such as freedom, justice, and equality, on which the late capitalist economic and administrative system's rationale depends. However, Habermas does not explain within this analysis why citizens of modern societies would make such costly choices. Although he is surely right to insist that citizen "choices" must be relevant somehow to these developments within formally democratic societies, if he is to offer an analysis with greater depth and transformative potential than the kind of merely justificatory liberal account of existing "formally" democratic institutions Dewey insightfully critiqued, Habermas must rejoin Dewey in looking for the *social forces* that shape such citizen "choices" so as to counteract their influence. This includes appropriately taking into account the importance of real-world disparities in the power various people have to gather information, to communicate with others, and to influence the outcomes of "formally" democratic institutional processes. If elite-controlled, democracy-limiting ideology is not the best explanation of why citizens of "formally" democratic societies contribute to their own disempowerment, then a better one must be found.[18] The challenge, as Dewey recognized, is to reconstruct processes of interactive citizen communication in ways that deepen the democratic quality of community life while transforming the macro-level social institutions that should exist to serve it.

For Habermas, as for Dewey, the ideal of democracy plays a central role in theorizing about community and communication. However, *methodological differences* about the derivation and operation of the democratic ideal lead to important *differences in their transformative prescriptions*, both of which require fuller development and justification. Habermas's implicitly democratic conception of the requirements of "communicative rationality" in "the ideal speech situation" continues to be the key to his entire social theory at its present stage of development.[19] In earlier works whose methodological and metaphysical standpoint reflects the minimally reconstructed influences of Kant and Hegel, Habermas claimed that the transcendent norms of communicative rationality—those which would characterize an ideal speech situation—are derived from the presumptive bases on which any rational person would enter into communication with another person. In an ideal speech situation, he argued, all participants would share as equals in the process of discovering generalizable, universal values that express self-identified, critically reflective needs, their own and those of others. Furthermore, such an "ideal speech situation" would require consensus among participants, and would treat this goal as the underlying rational presupposition of communication. This rational ideal, Habermas argued, operates both as an underlying expectation within almost all forms of actual lifeworld communications and as a criterion for evaluating their normative effectiveness. Although Habermas did not explicitly name the rational ideal that structures his ideal speech situation, its contents echo those of Dewey's twin-faceted ideal of the democratic community.

Although his theorizing takes what he calls a "pragmatic turn" in *The Theory of Communicative Action,* metaphysically and methodologically reconstructing his earlier idealist standpoint to some extent by drawing on Peirce and Mead, Habermas reasserts his earlier claims about the universal normative implications of the ideal speech situation—"I still view as correct my intention to reconstruct the general symmetry conditions that every competent speaker must presuppose are sufficiently satisfied insofar as he intends to enter into argumentation at all"—while acknowledging that his earlier explanation of this project "may be unsatisfactory in its details" (Habermas 1984:25). The only significant change in the scope of applicability he claims here for the "ideal speech situation" is that he confines to "theoretical, practical, and explicative discourse" the relevance of this "(often counterfactual) presupposition that the conditions of an ideal speech situation are satisfied to a sufficient degree of approximation . . . if only the argumentation could be conducted openly enough and continued long enough" (Habermas 1984:42). Because theoretical, practical, and explicative discourse are three of Habermas's five forms of "argumentation"—the most common forms and the only ones he subsequently refers to as "discourse"—this scope-limiting passage makes little difference in his position, leaving only aesthetic criticism and therapeutic critique as communicative contexts within which he believes the "ideal speech situation" lacks application.

This pragmatist-influenced reconstruction of his neo-Kantian "ideal speech situation" is the starting point for Habermas's subsequent work on "discourse ethics," as well as the point of theoretical commonality he recognizes between his own work and the contemporary liberal philosophy of John Rawls, whom he has urged to use it as a guide in rethinking his own ideal theoretical concept, "the original position."[20] In a 1995 exchange of papers, Habermas acknowledges important commonalities and shared intentions between his ideal-guided philosophical project and Rawls's as a starting point for his criticisms: "Because I admire this project, share its intentions, and regard its essential results as correct, the dissent I express here will remain within the bounds of a familial dispute."[21] Habermas's criticisms focus on Rawls's use of the original position as a way to reconceptualize the requirements of the public use of reason in terms of structural constraints on the social contract situation so as to maintain neutrality among parties while avoiding metaphysical and epistemic issues. Habermas argues that this strategy cannot work, in part because metaphysical and epistemic issues cannot and should not be avoided. As an alternative approach to the public use of reason as Rawls conceptualizes it, Habermas recommends Mead's "ideal role taking," which he incorporates within his own discourse ethics.

> Discourse ethics rests on the intuition that the application of the principle of universalization, properly understood, calls for a joint process of "ideal role taking." It interprets this idea of G. H. Mead in terms of *a pragmatic theory of argumentation.* Under the *pragmatic presuppositions* of an inclusive and noncoercive rational discourse among free and equal participants, everyone is required to *take the perspective of everyone else,* and thus project herself into the understandings of self and world of all others; *from this interlocking of perspectives there emerges an ideally extended we-perspective* from which all can test in common whether they wish to make a controversial norm the basis of their shared practice; and this should include *mutual criticism of the appropriateness of the languages in terms of which situations and needs are interpreted. In the course of successively undertaken abstractions, the core of generalizable interests can then emerge step by step.* (Habermas 1995:117–118, emphases mine)

This discussion of the requirements of democratic "ideal role taking" clearly echoes Habermas's earlier discussions of the "ideal speech situation" while reflecting his thoughtful efforts to respond to criticisms about the need to pluralize and contextualize his use of the ideal.[22]

In such recent works, Habermas's only explanation of why this implicitly democratic ideal of communicative rationality is not generally operative in actual late capitalist societies is that the economic and administrative system that depends on the lifeworld and that exists to serve it tends to colonize it. Thus, functional communication regulated by money and power replaces the consensus-seeking dialogue of communicative rationality. This analysis seems helpful as far as it goes, and Habermas's account of the rational assumptions that *should* underlie communication is attractive. Yet it fails to yield and to justify either a *particular set of actually shared universal values* or a *practical process of discovering or creating them* that could unite diverse peoples who are presently divided by cultural and social–locational differences into an effective coalition with the power to liberate their lifeworld from the present system's colonization.

What Habermas has not yet fully acknowledged is that the context of "modernity" that locates his theoretical project is itself a development within particular cultures that does not affect all of their members—or all cultures—in the same ways. His claims about the background assumptions that should and partially do underlie interpersonal communication are theoretically contextualized relative to what Wittgenstein called a "form of life," specifically, a *modern* form of life, which seems to be shared cross-culturally by at least the successful members of the dominant cultures of many of the "developed" nations, but not in identical ways. Instead of being a uniform set of social characteristics that cross cultural boundaries, modernity seems to display a pattern of what Wittgenstein called "family resemblances" among various "forms of life" that differ at least subtly in their specific social forces, institutions, processes, and shared habits, as well as the shared values that support and are shaped by them. Although Wittgenstein seems to have thought that all of those who share a form of life share it in the same way, this is not obvious—we must, as he exhorted us on many other subjects, "Look and see."[23] For example, whether American society is itself a single form of life or part of a larger one, its multicultural composition, in addition to its important power-structured differences in gender, race, and class, suggest that the "grammatical structures" of American people's lives may differ significantly relative to these and other group-based locations. A close study of African American philosophy since 1845, when Frederick Douglass published the first of his three slave narratives, suggests that many of America's shared ideal concepts like "freedom," "equality," and "democracy" have been taken very differently by many African Americans engaged in liberatory struggle than by America's controlling elite and most of its broad middle class. As to whether all of the variously located members of the world's globally interlinked forms of life should agree on the ideal presuppositions of communication, and on the kinds of social institutions and processes that are most likely to support the actualization of those presuppositions within daily life, if Habermas is not to fall back on an idealist appeal to transcendent reason, he must take his "pragmatic turn" even farther. He must ground his universal value claims in empirical evidence of an anthropological character that takes seriously the possibility of deep differences in the communicative presuppositions of differing forms of life, and also in praxis-based procedural proposals for reaching cross-difference agreement in actual conditions that could be implemented and tested by experience.

Successfully accomplishing Habermas's Meadean project of "tak[ing] the perspective of everyone else" in ways that "project herself into the understandings of self and world of all others" cannot be done without leaving one's armchair, no matter how much good will informs one's efforts, even if one has done one's homework by reading the careful scholarship of historians, sociologists, and anthropologists, as well as autobiographies, essays, and novels written by "other" voices. It requires *actual conversations,* collaboratively aiming for mutual understanding about self and world, with others who are differently located than oneself within a shared culture, as well as with others whose lifeworld is framed within different cultures—even if the background conditions of such conversations cannot be freed from our contemporary world's actual distortions in substantive equality that are created by power-structured hierarchies of interactive opportunity, benefit, and harm. *If* it is possible for an "ideally extended we-perspective" that authentically represents an "interlocking of perspectives" to emerge from such conversations in spite of such background conditions, this *could* serve as a unifying factor within cooperative action that aims to transform these conditions, which in turn *could* foster a broader sense of community amidst valued differences within a desirably pluralized global lifeworld.

Within such a collaborative process growing out of mutual understanding and progressively achieved trust, it may eventually be possible for "all [to] test in common whether they wish to make a controversial norm the basis of their shared practice." However, the relevant "testing" is not an individualistic, purely intellectual process that only requires a theorist to carefully consider cognitive inputs at varying levels of abstraction within her or his own frame of reference, like Rawls's "wide reflective equilibrium."[24] Rather, it is an *experiential* project that requires power-marginalized participants to put themselves and those who depend on them at further risk, after already attaining a stage of personal awareness and self-transformation that has involved risking their achieved self-understanding and the stability of their sociocultural location. Only if differences within and between forms of life have been appreciated, and more powerful participants have achieved an openness to deep transformation in the presuppositions of their own lifeworld, including their character tendencies and their achieved pattern of living as well as their ideas, values, and customary uses of signs and symbols, does "mutual criticism of the appropriateness of the languages in terms of which situations and needs are interpreted" make sense as a trust-funded activity in which cross-difference participants who have enough experience and understanding of the world to make the enterprise worthwhile *should* invest their time and risk their hope. Far more is involved in appropriately responding to locationally based criticism of one's "language" than just learning to use gender-inclusive word choices that occasionally substitute a generalized "she" for a humanly generic "he." Indeed, transformation of the language-games that organize deep levels of one's form of life may be required. Otherwise, such negotiations are likely to amount to little more than a pacifying gesture on the part of a controlling cultural elite that provides them with further information for broadening and deepening their control. However, if such cross-difference negotiations to build a common ground for understanding and a cooperative *modus vivendi* are authentic and productive, and if they continue over a long enough period of time, they should make possible a "course of successively undertaken abstractions," to the extent that these are needed and helpful to the overall transformative project or some of its aspects.

Nonetheless, it is not clear that some "core of generalizable interests" on which to base cross-difference cooperation and shared general norms can "emerge step by step" from some action-preceding process of abstraction that yields shared norms as a basis for further cooperation. Rather, in our actual, hierarchically power-structured world of differing visions and located experiences, it seems that the *opposite* generative relationship more typically holds: that semigeneral or at least convergent needs and interests make possible the first stages of cross-difference negotiation for sufficient mutual understanding and trust to make possible a first stage of cooperation in addressing them, and that more generalizable interests *may* emerge from this process *if* it is successful, and dependently, *may* lead to progressively fuller agreement on shared norms, practically understood.

Such a developmental process, though it shares certain programmatic features with Habermas's neo-Kantian reconstruction of the "ideal speech situation" in light of his appropriation of Mead's "ideal we-perspective," turns Habermas's ordering and dependency relations among the stages on their heads. Instead of "objective" scholarly delineation of common values, it calls for risk-filled practical engagement from which something new and better *may* evolve within a world in which we already have reason to think there are significant, power-structured differences in the deep grammars of culturally framed forms of life. What such a theoretical transformation would involve for Habermas and his stream of critical theory is not just further, pragmatism-flavored modifications at the margins of a neo-Kantian metaphysics and methodology. Rather, it requires completing "the pragmatic turn" with Peirce, Mead, and Dewey, incorporating Kant's best insights within a radically reconstructed metaphysical, methodological, and practical framework.

Habermas's "Struggles for Recognition in the Democratic Constitutional State" (1994), which was written during the same period as his 1995 critical–collaborative exchange with Rawls, shows that he has not yet completed the "pragmatic turn" that the difference-embracing practical implications of his own advocacy of Mead's "ideal we-perspective" require, but rather still clings to a neo-Kantian, abstract individualist conception of democracy and of the idealization process that can more fully actualize it. Habermas acknowledges that differences in the particular patterns of historical experience that have shaped modern, "formally" democratic French and German societies have led in recent years to their very different national interpretations of the practical meanings of democratic responsibility and international human rights in response to the challenge of deciding how many and which Third World immigrants to accept.[25] Emigrating members of predemocratic societies that have not experienced modernization from within but largely as a pressure from without, like members of societies that are emerging from a totalitarian but in some sense "modern" past like Poland's and Russia's, may interpret these concepts in still different ways, so that the kinds of cultural assumptions that underlie actual communication processes within such societies may differ significantly from those that operate within France, Germany, and other members of the family of modern, "formally" democratic societies. We must "Look and see." Although Habermas's analysis does not directly address members of these various culturally differing societies that are *not* long-term formal democracies, they are nonetheless implicated in his way of addressing those of us who *are,* because of his way of interpreting the contents and standing of the United Nations Declaration of Human Rights and subsequent international declarations, and also because of the practical realities of every society's increasingly globalized situation.

In arguing that any reasonable group-related demand for fair treatment and cultural recognition can be accommodated within the kind of individualistic legal, political, and ontological framework that is typical of modern, formally democratic societies, Habermas employs a historically based procedural analysis that focuses on their constitutional basis and their "common political culture." The practicality of his argument turns on the claim that those of us who are members of such societies should be "loyal" to their constitutional frameworks, making only those claims on others that can be accommodated within them, and understanding ourselves at least in our civic identities in the individualistic terms of their "common political cultures," rather than in the often collective terms of the various traditional cultural identities they frame and are obliged to protect.

> The political integration of citizens ensures *loyalty to the common political culture*. The latter is rooted in an interpretation of constitutional principles from the perspective of *the nation's historical experience*. To this extent that interpretation cannot be ethically neutral. Perhaps one would do better to speak of *a common horizon of interpretation* within which current issues give rise to public debates about the citizens' political self-understanding. The "historians' debate" in 1986–1987 in Germany is a good example of this. But the debates are always about the best interpretation of the same constitutional rights and principles. These form the fixed point of reference for any *constitutional patriotism* that situates the system of rights within the historical context of a legal community. They must be enduringly linked with the *motivations and convictions of the citizens*, for without such a motivational anchoring they could not become *the driving force* behind the *dynamically conceived project* of producing an association of individuals who are free and equal. (Habermas 1994:134, emphases mine)

Habermas's analysis of the kind of mutual moral commitment that should be involved in the social contract that constitutional frameworks of modern, formally democratic societies *claim* to represent is attractively deep, involving not just passive acceptance or fear of the coercive powers of the state, but the kind of loyalty that can shape one's framing of one's own needs, desires, and basic beliefs. Furthermore, it is realistic insofar as it regards the achievement of an "association of individuals who are free and equal" as a *goal* that shapes a "dynamically conceived project," rather than as an immediate condition of its framers that somehow could be substantially inherited by all future citizens in virtue of constitutional "guarantees" alone. Yet Habermas's implied claim that loyalty to *actual* formally democratic constitutional frameworks is *warranted* rests on two unrealistic assumptions: that "the nation's historical experience" is shared in the same way by all of its variously located constituent groups and individuals, in spite of their actual power-structured hierarchical differences; and that a "common horizon of experience" is created by a shared constitutional framework alone, instead of requiring ongoing negotiation for understanding and operative norms. The all-too-common response that such an inclusively representative, negotiated understanding was achieved once and for all future times and future citizens by the founders of modern formal democracies, and that this is adequately expressed in their constitutions, is precluded by Habermas's own reading of the diverse sociocultural groups whose members have what he regards as unacknowledged but legitimate claims to citizenship, and thus to constitutional expression in contemporary Germany.

Ultimately, Habermas's analysis rests on an appeal to natural law, rather than to any evidence that such formally democratic constitutional frameworks reflect negotiated historical achievement of shared interpretive horizons, or that they serve their societies better than would constitutional frameworks and interpretations informed by some alternative conception of democracy.

> Modern constitutions owe their existence to a conception found in *modern natural law according* to which citizens come together voluntarily to form a legal community of free and equal consociates. The constitution puts into effect *precisely those rights* that those individuals *must* grant one another if they want to order their life together *legitimately* by means of positive law. This conception presupposes the notion of individual [*subjektive*] rights and individual legal persons as the bearers of rights. While modern law establishes a basis for state-sanctioned relations of intersubjective recognition, the rights derived from them protect the vulnerable integrity of *legal subjects who are in every case individuals.* In the final analysis it is a question of protecting these individual legal persons, even if the integrity of the individual—in law no less than in morality—depends on relations of mutual recognition remaining intact. (Habermas 1994:107)

Habermas assumes without argument here that actual, formally democratic constitutions pick out and protect the *right* rights, and in the right order of priority when rights conflict. Moreover, he *assumes* rather than giving reasons and evidence for the claim that mutual democratic recognition, as structured in positive law by the decisions of legislators, organizes interactions between metaphysically, morally, and functionally separate individuals who *have* cultural and other group attachments, rather than between cultures and other groups *composed of* individual members, an alternative conception of individuals that might imply that cultures and certain other groups should be treated as having a kind of ontological and legal standing.

Against Charles Taylor and Michael Walzer, communitarian critics within other modern "forms of life" (Canada and the United States respectively) that share family resemblances as formal democracies with his own Germany, Habermas argues that formally "democratic" societies can *appropriately recognize* cultural and group attachments of individuals without reconceptualizing their constitutional structures. However, when Habermas starts from the artificial, individualistic assumptions of classical social contract theory and implicitly treats their actualization as a historical *fait accompli,* "The decisive move in the conjuring trick has been made," as Wittgenstein said in another connection.[26] Yet Habermas himself argues against rigid attachment to unchanging cultural traditions that can limit individual growth and overall social development; *if* it makes sense for him to refer to "common political cultures" at the level of national life, the same warning should apply to these as well, promoting openness to transformation rather than rigidity as the practical meaning of loyalty to one's nation.

> Cultural heritages and the forms of life articulated in them normally reproduce themselves by convincing those whose personality structures they shape, that is, by motivating them to appropriate productively and continue the traditions. The constitutional state can make this hermeneutic achieve-

ment of the cultural reproduction of lifeworlds possible, but it cannot guarantee it. For to guarantee survival would necessarily rob the members of the very freedom to say yes or no that is necessary if they are to appropriate and preserve their cultural heritage. *When a culture has become reflexive, the only traditions and forms of life that can sustain themselves are those that bind their members while at the same time subjecting themselves to critical examination and leaving later generations the option of learning from other traditions or converting and setting out for other shores.* (Habermas 1994:130, emphasis mine)

If, as Habermas has argued, the system deeply damages the lifeworld in modern, formally democratic societies, perhaps their constitutional structures and the assumptions that underlie them need to be reevaluated, as Taylor, Walzer, and Dewey argue. Especially if the "pragmatic turn" is not to be just a new way of making old idealist claims, supporters of universal democratic principles must offer a better argument than an appeal to the irresistible forces of modernization, bolstered by the individualist natural law theory favored by elite political reformers, in response to contempory internal and external critics. Such critics are *rightly concerned* about the various adverse impacts of modernization, and they are *not* persuaded that elite-controlled formal democracies can optimally promote human flourishing.

Habermas and Dewey rightly share an appreciation of the importance of an inherited tradition or fund of experience within an inclusive and dynamically self-transforming community life. Both insightfully emphasize the role of communication in creating a community's sustaining moral web and in bringing in new members. However, neither Habermas nor Dewey adequately understands and criticizes important, deeply undemocratic aspects of many real-world cultural traditions, including the "linguistic" patterns and the ongoing processes of educative communication that tend to sustain earlier patterns of traditional oppressions within modern formal democracies. In the closing pages of *The Theory of Communicative Action,* Habermas suggests that the great struggle of contemporary democratic social movements has been to beat back the colonizing impacts of the political and economic system within the culture-creating and person-sustaining lifeworld: "The issue is not primarily one of compensations that the welfare state can provide, but of defending and restoring endangered ways of life" (Habermas 1987:392). What Habermas fails to adequately appreciate here is that the *targets* of those democratic struggles by feminists as well as racially and culturally excluded groups he praises have included not only *oppressive usurpations of power by the economic and political system,* but also *an oppressive traditional lifeworld.* Habermas is insightful in his comment that these liberation struggles involve "questions having to do with the grammar of forms of life" (Habermas 1987:392), and not just equality within the existing, colonized lifeworld. However, like Dewey, he fails to address significant social–locational differences about the meanings of shared traditional signs and symbols including the democratic ideal, as well as cross-cultural differences in interpretation of experience within intersecting, globalized, language-sharing "forms of life" that interact within our power-structured, multicultural world today. These differences must be bridged through negotiation, collaborative reconstruction, and a more deeply democratic multiculturalism in education if transformative communication is to (re)create democratic community life on the face-to-face level, as well as on the national, international, and postnational levels that Dewey's ideal of the "Great Community" now requires.

Starting from the other end of the relationship between the real and the ideal, Dewey argues that, though the obstacles are formidable, a *deeper democracy* than we presently enjoy is *possible,* not because we can conceive of an abstract ideal like Habermas's requirements of communicative rationality in "the ideal speech situation" and can then contrast it with our experience of actual discourse, but rather because *the ideal of democracy is an extension to the limits of their implications of certain desirable social conditions we have already experienced,* insofar as we have experienced community life. The dimensions of that experience that we hope to develop more fully give particular contents to our broadly shared ideal of community life, which Dewey says is the same as our ideal of democracy—an ideal "in the only intelligible sense of an ideal: namely, the tendency and movement of some thing which exists carried to its final limit, viewed as completed, perfected" (Dewey 1927:328). Like ideal communities that completely fulfill their formative and guiding impulse, Dewey argues, *democracy in this fully ideal sense does not and cannot exist,* because other influences have affected and will continue to affect the development of associated life in the real world. Nonetheless, Dewey argues, "wherever there is conjoint activity whose consequences are appreciated as good by all singular persons who take part in it, and where the realization of the good is such as to effect an energetic desire and effort to sustain it in being just because it is a good shared by all, there is so far a community. *The clear consciousness of a communal life, in all its implications, constitutes the ideal of democracy"* (Dewey 1927:328).

Although Habermas's abstract analysis of the ideal of democracy in terms of the relations that *would* obtain in an ideal speech situation might appear to be totally incompatible with Dewey's analysis, it can be helpfully reconstructed from a different, Deweyan kind of "objective theoretical standpoint" to which Habermas also seems drawn. That is, the democratic ideal can be understood as *a demonstrable, directional tendency within history* that reflects widely shared, experience-grounded human needs and desires that, insofar as these embody a deep, reflective sense of the preciousness and precariousness of each person's life, combined with growing awareness of the ever-increasing mutuality of our life situations, take on an at least apparently universal aspect. The second strand of Habermas's recent work suggests that he might be attracted to this fully pragmatic regrounding of the objective theoretical standpoint he has been attempting to locate and to justify: that is, his effort to trace historical processes of democratic development to show that universal processes of social "rationalization" growing out of human needs and experience are actually at work in the world. Even if Habermas's "objectivity" claim were pragmatically regrounded in this way, however, what might *seem* to be a universal democratic ideal operating within history would call for *empirical confirmation and a pluralistic practical specification* in order to motivate concerted efforts to achieve its fuller realization in real-world conditions today.

Dewey's universal claims about the democratic ideal similarly require cross-cultural empirical confirmation and a more pluralistic practical specification. As chapter three shows, his various expressions of the experience-based democratic ideal that he believed was operating within actual processes of social evolution all project the progressive overcoming of past patterns of exclusion from equal participation in directing all aspects of a shared social life. However, Dewey never fully grasped the scope of the unsettlings of presently dominant cultural assumptions that active, equal inclusion of the now marginalized would require and imply for transformative social inquiry, institutional reconstruction, and deeply democratic education. Although Dewey's critics are right to charge him with failing to take adequate account of what I have called the "old problems"—power-structured relational differences like gender, race, culture, and class that make it very difficult to create communities that promote an equitable mutuality of benefit—he did not make the mistake that some have attributed to him of regarding communities as homogeneous social blocks, a shortcoming that is more true of Habermas's broad statements about the lifeworld. Rather, Dewey analyzes communities as dynamic, historically situated, heterogeneous constructions that reflect and grow out of the multiple group memberships of the persons whose lives they interconnect. This is why, in Dewey's view, the theoretical and practical solution to the problem of how to democratically transform existing, democratically deficient social conditions, including the weakening and loss of ties of community, cannot be a uniform "cookbook" answer, but rather must reflect the unique characters of the particular situations in question.

Such particular answers, Dewey argued, require a new kind of practically focused, critical–empirical social knowledge, formulated and communicated by a new approach to social science. Dewey offered preliminary outlines and helpful leadings to guide the development of such a reconceptualized, critical–empirical social science, including his living example, which modeled engaged, life-long experimental activism within real-world problem situations.[27] Habermas has added important descriptive and analytic details to Dewey's outline of the requirements for a critical–empirical social science, including the study of crisis potential. However, Habermas's efforts to shake off the influence of originary critical theorists Horkheimer's and Adorno's detached conception of "objectivity" have thus far been largely unsuccessful.[28] Furthermore, his involvement in transformative praxis since the 1960s has been very limited, and his theorizing seems at times almost perversely impartial, expressing only an occasional normative assessment almost reluctantly and without a normative philosophical argument that draws, as Dewey openly does, on the democratic values he clearly believes to be humanely defensible as well as operative within the actual historical processes he describes.

Unfortunately, both Dewey and Habermas treat the new critical–empirical social science they call for as almost entirely the work of academic specialists, granting at most some unclear role in its practical application to other participants in transformative struggles. Dewey's suggestion in *The Public and Its Problems* that his new transformative social science would be the work of experts, to be communicated through the mass media by other experts to influence the general citizenry in those daily conversations that create public opinion, both undemocratically and counterproductively limits the participatory scope of its epistemological processes. Fortunately, as the discussion later in this chapter shows, these problems in Dewey's analysis can be reconstructed to guide an active, inclusive transformative praxis.

Habermas's conception of a critical–empirical social science similarly requires a more deeply democratic reconstruction. In the final chapter of *The Theory of Communicative Action,* Habermas describes the role of his critical social science as follows: "Critical social theory does not relate to established lines of research as a competitor; starting from its concept of the rise of modern societies, it attempts to explain the specific limitations and the relative rights of those approaches" (Habermas 1987:375). Such a critical social theory does not challenge the historically exclusive processes and shared assumptions of our present social sciences, but only contextualizes and interprets their results. In defining the project of critical social theory so understood, Habermas claims an "affirmative role for philosophy" that seems to involve pointing those "radically differentiated moments of reason" that express themselves in the social countermovements he praises "toward a unity—not a unity that could be had at the level of worldviews, but one that might be established *this side* of expert cultures, in a nonreified communicative everyday practice" (Habermas 1987:398, emphasis in original). Like Dewey, Habermas recommends transforming the daily communicative practices of ordinary citizens by incorporating critically winnowed insights from social scientific research, calling for no return influence. However, in what sense such an "objective" critical theory of society can also be "affirmative" is unclear.

Jane Braaten has described Habermas's theory as "consciously activist," but this seems to mean only that an engaged stance motivates the production of critical–empirical analyses.[29] In her explanation of Habermas's transformative purposes, Braaten gives his work a more Deweyan activist cast than the work itself seems to support, perhaps because this is the way Habermas's work *must* be interpreted if it is to count as a normative–transformative theory, rather than a merely detached, objectivist kind of descriptive theory. However, even if Braaten's interpretation is taken as an insightful suggestion concerning how Habermas's work might fit into a larger, more complete philosophy and praxis of democratic transformation, it is only in this secondary, contextualized sense that it can reasonably be regarded as "activist," and there seems little or no evidence in his actual texts that it is consciously so.

From the perspective of the requirements of a comprehensive philosophy of democratic transformation, a fundamental gap in Habermas's work as developed thus far is the lack of a metatheoretical bridge between his theory of communicative rationality and a transformative democratic praxis to which it might be understood as helpfully contributing. Critical–empirical analyses alone will not achieve just and effective democratic transformations; at most, they can locate sites with relative crisis potential for transformation. The theoretical element that would engage critical–empirical analysis with democratic transformative activism is missing.

Toward a Comprehensive Philosophy of Democratic Transformation

A fully adequate philosophy of democratic transformation must address these problems on metaphysical, epistemological, and methodological levels, as well as in practical application, in order to reflect the difficult lessons of our contemporary experience while contributing effectively to the democratic transformation of real-world problem situations. This is not to suggest that the work of any one philosopher must or even could address every aspect of a comprehensive philosophy of democratic transformation. Rather, it is to say that a philosopher contributes an incomplete or only a partial philosophy of democratic transformation if his or her work leaves out any of its elements, and that the meaning and quality of various contributions should be assessed in light of this larger whole. Such a comprehensive—though never complete—philosophy of democratic transformation would include a background metaphysics and epistemology, an interactive philosophical methodology, a democratic participatory model of critical–transformative social science, an extensive range of critical studies of actual historical and contemporary transformative social experiments and of current social situations holding crisis potential, as well as diverse organizational and evaluational tools for guiding democratic transformation processes. All of these elements must reflect the engaged activism of collaborating interpreters, reconstructive thinkers, reflective evaluators, and retrospective synthesizers of the philosophical implications of democratic praxis.

Given the daunting scope of such a comprehensive philosophy of democratic transformation, it is not surprising that few if any philosophers address all of its aspects. Moreover, such work is *necessarily collaborative and multiperspectival,* in the theorizing process as well as in transformational praxis. Historically, however, there has been a tendency among Western philosophers to value work on the methodological and social scientific modeling aspects of such a complete philosophy of political transformation as of more serious or significant philosophical character than work focusing on critical–historical and contemporary studies, or on transformative means and processes. However, the transformative philosophical project as a whole is incomplete without these latter elements, which represent crucial tests of the adequacy of the former ones, given that the purpose of such a philosophy is not just to interpret the world, but to change it.

The gaps in Dewey's and Habermas's contributions to a comprehensive philosophy of democratic transformation become visible when we seek out their answers to the question with which we began this chapter, "How is just and effective democratic transformation of diverse predemocratic, antidemocratic, posttotalitarian, and only 'formally' democratic societies to be accomplished in our globalized era?" Instead of being a nonphilosophical or postphilosophical question, as Charles Sherover and others have claimed, this is *the key philosophical question* of justifiable means and methods that immediately focuses theorizing when social life is understood as dynamic and democratically deficient, rather than as governed by some approximation of ideal formal principles.[10] As Angela Davis insightfully argued in her 1969 *Lectures on Liberation,* philosophy as our shared Socratic inheritance must understand itself as midwifery to change, both in the individual and in society, and such changes are specific and practical matters.

Drawing on his own activist experience as well as his traditionally American hopes, Dewey's answer to our question in *The Public and Its Problems* is, "The cure for the ailments of democracy is more democracy" (Dewey 1927:327). He suggests there that the transformative means we need now combine better information with more effective communication. However, *how* we are to go about developing these transformative means within global capitalist, "formally" democratic societies, as well as how those activists are to proceed who do not have democratic cultural traditions on which they can draw, is beyond the scope of Dewey's insights, there and elsewhere, though he does offer promising leadings in many of his later works that are more fully developed in Chapter Three.

Habermas's answer, which may not be so different if it is pragmatically regrounded, is that democracy requires further communicative rationalization within our increasingly globalized lifeworlds, i.e., a fuller development of their possibilities to realize the characteristics of the "ideal speech situation." To achieve this goal, Habermas calls for critical–empirical analyses of particular communicative distortions within late capitalist societies that reveal their areas of crisis potential, which are also areas of transformative possibility. Thus, Habermas's current prescription is a more detailed voice of agreement with Dewey's call for a new critical–empirical social science, though Dewey rightly warned that focusing on crises alone does not employ a wide enough lens for the kind of critical inquiry an emerging democratic public will need. However, even assuming that Habermas's critical–empirical analyses are effective in accomplishing their task of revealing a society's areas of transformative potential, *how is democratic transformation to be effectively accomplished,* which is also to ask in Habermas's terms, how is the transformation to be *justly* accomplished? Like Dewey, Habermas seems to have no answer to this question.

Perhaps this is not a failure in either Dewey's or Habermas's theory as developed thus far, because neither claims to have offered a comprehensive theory. However, there are at least two reasons why answering this question is a requirement of the kind of comprehensive theory that both Dewey and Habermas should affirm and regard as the larger theoretical context of their work. First, as Dewey and Habermas agree, *realizing* democracy is a deep human need and a requirement for the good life; it is the purpose for developing Dewey's and Habermas's theories to this point. Secondly, given this purpose, the potential of their theoretical work to guide effective democratic transformation should be a key philosophical test of the insightfulness of their background metaphysics and epistemologies, of their methodologies, and of the kinds of critical–empirical analyses they propose.

Experiences of the twentieth century have amply illustrated that situations with crisis potential—including those in which crises actually occur—do not automatically change through *democratic* transformative means or toward *more democratic* forms of community life. Consider Stalin's transformative approach to feeding the people of the former USSR, Hitler's transformative approach to increasing Germany's social stability, South Africa's postcolonial transformation into an apartheid system, and Bosnia–Herzegovina's transformative experience of rape, mass execution, forced family relocation, and other techniques of so-called "ethnic cleansing" to resolve ancient ethnic hostilities following the breakup of communist Yugoslavia. In contrast, consider some seemingly miraculous events of recent years that keep alive hope for the fuller realization of democracy, such as the Philippines' nonviolent people's revolution, the destruction of the Berlin Wall, the Czech "Velvet Revolution," the popular protest-based rise of Boris Yeltsin to leadership in a post-Soviet Russia, and the transfer of power to Nelson Mandela's black-majority government through largely peaceful elections in South Africa. Like these other "miracles" in some ways, and unlike them in others, the South African "miracle" occurred as the result of a long, difficult, suffering-filled and often violent struggle, during which those who led and participated in efforts to achieve democratic transformation had to wrestle with difficult philosophical questions about justifiable means and processes—*effective, democratic, and locationally appropriate means and processes* that would reflect the highest and best values within multiple cultures' traditions, while helping those cultures to change in appropriate and necessary ways. These activists still struggle to work out a model of transformation in South Africa's economic and administrative system that will reflect, respect, and support this process of mutual, multicultural lifeworld adjustment.

These are areas of great need for further development within a comprehensive philosophy of democratic transformation, ones in which sincere and determined democratic change activists now wrestle largely alone and unaided. Philosophers can and should assist them by developing those aspects of a complete philosophy of democratic transformation that go beyond reconstructively articulating a Deweyan democratic ideal and developing Habermasian critical–empirical analyses of sites of crisis potential. Philosophers who have the requisite gifts and skills should also participate in democratic social transformation as scholar–activists. In addition to making practical contributions, they will learn valuable philosophical lessons about the adequacy of developed theory to guide actual praxis and about new, praxis-born theoretical needs. Philosophers should also contribute to cross-disciplinary, collaborative, critical–empirical analyses of actual social transformation processes in order to discover tools and techniques for steering current and future social transformation processes toward democratic goals using justifiable transformative means, including effective democratic communication. Surely areas of resemblance, overlap, and cross-cultural lessons for other peoples will arise out of such particular critical–empirical analyses. Many would like to know more about South Africa's ongoing democratic transformation process, for example. However, such studies are more likely to yield useful results in terms of effective democratic transformative means if they are guided by a search for what Wittgenstein called "family resemblances" amidst differences in democratic transformation processes, rather than by an expectation of discovering universal laws operating within them.

This is not to suggest that no philosophical work at all has been done on this "means" aspect of the philosophy of democratic transformation. Joseph Betz has offered a promising recent example of this kind of critical–empirical analysis of an actual social transformation process in Nicaragua that suggests how other processes might be steered toward democratic goals using justifiable transformative means—and the obstacles such efforts face.[31] Likewise, much of Sara M. Evans's and Harry C. Boyte's work has focused on developing such critical–empirical analyses of actual social transformation processes for the purpose of discovering effective and justifiable democratic means of transformation.[32] As discussed in more detail in Chapter Five, Martin Luther King, Jr., grounded his last prophetic call for worldwide democratic transformation, *Where Do We Go From Here: Chaos or Community?* (1967), in a critical–empirical analysis of the successes and failures of the Civil Rights Movement in America during the 1950s and early 1960s, arguing that transformation processes in various parts of the world are now inseparably interlinked. Likewise, in *Race Matters* (1993), Cornel West draws on the methods of pragmatism and critical theory, as well as on King's life witness, in critically analyzing many African Americans' contemporary experience of racist exclusion compounded with poverty within urban ghettos, and in proposing an activistic "prophetic pragmatism" as his contribution to a comprehensive philosophy of democratic transformation. However, these and related contributions concerning transformative means have been marginalized by the continuing preoccupation of the professional philosophical mainstream with rival methodologies, abstract ideals, and transformatively unproductive cultural criticisms.

Dewey's pragmatist definition of inquiry in his *Logic: The Theory of Inquiry* (1938), which includes critical–empirical social science within its scope, insightfully frames the challenge of developing all of the interconnected elements of a comprehensive philosophy of democratic transformation, defining the project of reflective inquiry as emerging from some problematic situation in ordinary experience that stimulates us to seek both understanding and a practical way to transform that situation in future experience, which in turn provides the context for testing various alternative philosophical elements' critical–transformative adequacy.[33]

> *Inquiry is the controlled or directed transformation of an indeterminate situation into one that is so determinate in its constituent distinctions and relations as to convert the elements of the original situation into a unified whole.*
> (Dewey 1938:108, emphasis in original)

Dewey makes this same point somewhat more clearly in *Experience and Nature* (1925), arguing that a comprehensive process of philosophical inquiry concerning any problem must actively test the adequacy of its analyses and transformative prescriptions in our "primary" experience—by which he does not mean some mythically pretheoretic kind of experience or some totally nonreflective way of living, but our life in the world of daily affairs, with all its theory-influenced, technology-enhanced complexity.

> What empirical method exacts of philosophy is two things: First, that refined methods and products be traced back to their origin in primary experience, in all its heterogeneity and fullness; so that the needs and problems out of which they arise and which they have to satisfy be acknowledged. Secondly, that the secondary methods and conclusions be brought back to the things of ordinary experience, in all their coarseness and crudity, for verification. (Dewey 1925:39)

From a Deweyan perspective, if our experience of democracy did not have problematic aspects, there would be no need for social inquiry concerning it. However, given that we do experience a multiplicity of problematic aspects of "formal" democracies as well as a multiplicity of problems within various nondemocratic societies to which many people worldwide now think democracy may provide solutions, an interlinked set of empirical social inquiries concerning democracy must seek transformative solutions, must actually test the adequacy of our hypotheses about the best ways to transform these problem situations, and must consider these experiences of testing as determinative of the practical meaning of democracy in our era.

The key tests for the adequacy of social inquiry are existential ones, Dewey argues, not some kind of "objective" measures of change thought to somehow stand outside lived experience.

> One fundamentally important phase of *the transformation of the situation which constitutes inquiry* is central in the treatment of judgment and its functions. The transformation is *existential* and hence temporal. The precognitive unsettled situation can be settled only by modification of its constituents. Experimental operations change existing conditions. Reasoning, as such, can provide means for effecting the change of conditions but by itself cannot effect it. Only execution of existential operations directed by an idea in which ratiocination terminates can bring about the re-ordering of environing conditions required to produce a settled and unified situation. . . . The temporal quality of inquiry means, then, something quite other than that the process of inquiry takes time. It means that *the objective subject-matter of inquiry undergoes temporal transformation.* (Dewey 1938:121–122, emphases mine)

Moreover, it is the value-laden aspects or "traits" of our social–natural world of experience that stimulate and should guide our inquiry, and that provide the evaluative criteria for conceptions of democracy and their practical implications, not some artificial and supposedly "independent" statistical measures that detached social scientists could somehow apply disinterestedly.

> If experience actually presents esthetic and moral traits, then these traits may also be supposed to reach down into nature, and to testify to something that belongs to nature as truly as does the mechanical structure attributed to it in physical science. To rule out that possibility by some general reasoning is to forget that the very meaning and purport of empirical method is that things are to be studied on their own account, so as to find out what is revealed when they are experienced. The traits possessed by the subject-matters of experience are as genuine as the characteristics of sun and electron. They are *found,* experienced, and are not to be shoved out of being by some trick of logic. When found, their ideal qualities are as relevant to the philosophic theory of nature as are the traits found by physical inquiry. (Dewey 1925:13–14, emphasis in original)

Our inquiries cannot avoid involving us as participants in the world of experience undergoing transformation—and necessarily as activists, insofar as we seek to change our shared social circumstances in and through the process of inquiry.

Instead of stubbornly clinging to some antecedently hypothesized norm or definition of democracy, we must be prepared to revise our conception of democracy's practical meaning in light of experience if our hypothesis does not produce the results we anticipated. We must continue revising it until we have learned how to satisfactorily transform the problem situations that originally stimulated and continue to fuel our need to inquire.

> Genuine empirical method sets out from the actual subject-matter of primary experience, recognizes that reflection discriminates a new factor in it, . . . makes an object of that, and then uses that new object . . . to regulate, when needed, further experiences of the subject-matter already contained in primary experience. (Dewey 1925:25–26)

Dewey's model does not suggest that a single social inquiry can settle the practical meaning of democracy once and for all. Rather, important problems and projects call for multiple inquiries and new groups of inquirers, especially in differing contexts and when differing concerns are in focus. An adequately formulated critical–empirical philosophy of democratic transformation is in this way humble in its claims and open to correction from others' future experiences in related inquiries.

> Empirical method points out when and where and how things of a designated description have been arrived at. It places before others a map of the road that has been travelled; they may accordingly, if they will, re-travel the road to inspect the landscape for themselves. Thus the findings of one may be rectified and extended by the findings of others, with as much assurance as is humanly possible of confirmation, extension and rectification. The adoption of empirical method thus procures for philosophic reflection something of that coop-

erative tendency toward consensus which marks inquiry in the natural sciences. (Dewey 1925:34)

As this passage suggests, if the conceptual frameworks and the practical solutions they guide within various inquiries about problems related to democracy are actually interlinked by family resemblances, a shared fund of understanding about its practical meaning and transformative possibilities should build up from these efforts. New groups of inquirers should be able to draw on this fund of experience in ways that help their own transformative efforts, even if each moral situation is unique, as Dewey suggests, and thus, even if no universal "cookbook" solution will ever be available that can actually solve new problems without new processes of inquiry.

So understood, a Deweyan conception of transformative social inquiry need not be the work of experts alone—in fact, it is hard to understand how it could be. Rather, as Dewey suggested in his 1948 revised introduction to *Reconstruction in Philosophy,* continuing the project of problem-solving inquiry about deep democracy, understood as a "genuinely modern" way of life, must be the work of many people from all walks of life spanning many generations.

> The genuinely modern has still to be brought into existence. The work of actual production is not the task or responsibility of philosophy. That work can be done only by the resolute, patient, co-operative activities of men and women of good will, drawn from every useful calling, over an indefinitely long period. There is no absurd claim made that philosophers, scientists or any other one. group form a sacred priesthood to whom the work is entrusted. But, as philosophers in the last few centuries have performed a useful and needed work in furtherance of physical inquiry, so their successors now have the opportunity and the challenge to do a similar work in forwarding moral inquiry. The conclusions of that inquiry by themselves would no more constitute a complete moral theory and a working science of distinctively human subject matter than the activities of their predecessors brought the [contemporary] physical and physiological conditions of human existence into direct and full-fledged existence. But it would have an active share in the work of construction of a moral human science which serves as a needful precursor of *re*construction of the actual state of human life toward order and toward other conditions of a fuller life than man has yet enjoyed. (Dewey 1948, in MW 12:273)

In spite of its inspiring brilliance, this passage is peculiar in suggesting that the work of philosophy can be delimited within a larger project of developing a critical–empirical social science, and further distinguished from the actual production of deeply democratic ways of life. These are artificial separations that seem to contradict Dewey's discussion of the complete arc of philosophical inquiry in *Experience and Nature* and in *Logic: The Theory of Inquiry.* Given his clear commitment to the analysis he offers in those places, Dewey should have faced the implication that philosophy's task has no professional boundaries and that it involves both specialists and nonspecialists as cooperating partners in its comprehensive transformative project.

Once we admit the full implications of Dewey's pragmatist analysis of social inquiry, and once we acknowledge that growth of a comprehensive and fully adequate philosophy of democratic transformation must itself proceed by democratic methods, developing in their meaning and adequacy within the process of addressing problems in the world, it becomes clear that the required theoretical methods involve cross-difference negotiation for shared meanings, as needed and revealed within practical cooperation. This means that cross-cultural differences and locational differences within cultures cannot be bracketed until basic definitions and methods have been determined and then themselves treated as problems against this theoretical background. Rather, we must factor group–locational and perspectival differences into critical articulation of the problems we seek to transform through cooperative inquiry. We must also factor our differences into development of operative theoretical definitions and hypothetical transformative methods, which will themselves be tested by the fruitfulness of their results in transforming our variously located experiences and, ultimately, our differently shared forms of life.

Unless a critical–empirical social science is inclusively participatory in this way, its choice and framing of problems, as well as its criteria for and conclusions about results, will be rightly seen by the excluded as arbitrary and biased. They will rightly ask, Whose inquiry? Whose problems? Whose transformative motivations? Whose better life as criterion for results? Deeply democratic participation in transformative social inquiry involves more than letting a few women and members of other previously excluded groups join the priesthood of expert social scientists, perhaps including some of their groups' concerns within the scope of otherwise "normal" processes of scientific inquiry, as some have mistakenly interpreted Sandra Harding's work on democratizing science to suggest.[34] Rather, it requires radical reconstruction of transformative social inquiry as originating, proceeding, and concluding within the larger community, whose member–participants conduct and progressively evaluate the transformative process, assisted in certain ways by consulting specialists whose knowledge and skills allow them to be helpful to various groups who are working on differing problematic aspects of a shared social world.

The foregoing discussion has shown that a critical–reconstructive engagement between Dewey's pragmatism and Habermas's critical theory can be both clarifying and mutually corrective. It has shown that the kind of comprehensive and fully adequate philosophy of democratic transformation toward which both of their projects arc requires *a radically critical perspective* that questions basic assumptions that structure our democratically deficient contemporary experience while drawing on necessary and positive aspects of our forms of life as tools for reconstructing their problematic features. It also suggests that a comprehensive and fully adequate philosophy of democratic transformation is more helpfully guided by completing the "pragmatic turn" toward *a fully pragmatist metaphysics, epistemology, and methodology* like Dewey's, abandoning the pragmatist-influenced but fundamentally neo-Kantian approach Habermas employs within his recent work.

Finally, it has shown that, in the areas in which their gaps and mistakes converge, Deweyan pragmatism and Habermasian critical theory need the help of differing voices at the theory table to further refine the usefulness of their important contributions to a comprehensive philosophy of democratic transformation. Dewey and Habermas agree that all particular solutions to the problem of rebuilding democratic face-to-face communities have certain universal aspects, yet neither offers adequate empirical support for this claim. Both of their conclusions depend on the claim that the democratic ideal is humanly universal, yet neither adequately justifies this claim in light of our actual cultural and social–locational diversity. Both assume that critical and imaginative democratic communication drawing on the resources of a shared symbolic system is a universally necessary and generally effective tool in building and transforming communities, yet neither adequately clarifies or qualifies such an assumption in light of distorted, oppressive, and deeply undemocratic real-world communicative practices. Both call for a new, critical–empirical approach to social scientific inquiry, and both offer important insights about its structure and contents as well as leadings for its development, but neither offers a framework that is democratic enough to be effective in framing diverse problem situations, reflectively incorporating diverse experiences, and carrying out the kinds of experiments within our real lives and times that will open up experience in our democratically deficient, globally interlinked contexts of struggle for human fulfillment.

Fortunately, compatible streams of feminism and cultural pluralism offer additional theoretical resources for filling these gaps. Jane Addams, Alain Locke, and their contemporary inheritors offer more adequate critical–empirical analyses of the basis for universal values, including the twin-faceted ideal of community and democracy both Dewey and Habermas emphasize. Moreover, they democratically correct Dewey's and Habermas's focus on specialists within critical–empirical social scientific inquiry and their inadequate attention to valuable diversity within democratic theorizing. Finally, they offer promising, experience-based strategies for building reasonable trust across presently power-structured differences through cooperative processes that aim to achieve understanding, mutual respect, and effective collaboration within democratic transformative praxis.

Differing Voices at the Theory Table: Feminism and Cultural Pluralism

Jane Addams was both a feminist and a cultural pluralist before the latter term was coined, a close friend and theoretical collaborator of John Dewey's, as well as the founder of Chicago's Hull House, America's first "settlement house" for new immigrants who faced myriad challenges of adjustment to their new social circumstances. Dewey, who quotes almost no one, quotes Addams's *Democracy and Social Ethics* (1903) in the early pages of his own discussion of "The Moral Significance of Social Questions" within the 1932 revised version of the *Ethics* he wrote in collaboration with James Hayden Tufts. Dewey acknowledged the impact of Addams's influence on his theorizing, especially on his psychology and his appreciation of differences, and he reported the value to him of Hull House as a "laboratory" from which he derived vicarious experiential insights.[35] Yet in spite of his brilliance and his democratic sincerity, Dewey seems never to have fully grasped the deeper implications of some of Addams's insights about the lessons of the Hull House experience. Dewey increasingly realized the importance of *culture* as a shaping framework of material practices as well as ideas within experience, going so far as to suggest in his never-completed 1949 revised introduction to *Experience and Nature* that he should have called that work *Nature and Culture*. However, he does not seem to have realized that the Hull House experience revealed the need for a deeper questioning of some of the *cultural presuppositions* that he brought to the project of democratic transformation. Moreover, Dewey does not seem to have realized, as Addams did, that a commitment to democracy requires including *different voices* within processes of social inquiry as well as within the reconstructed institutions it helps to bring into being. Nor does Dewey seem to have shared Addams's realization that such inclusion may be both *deeply disruptive* and *deeply beneficial* in ways that those whose privilege offers them the opportunity to issue such invitations to cooperation may not anticipate.

In her own ability to bring together the cooperating parties that made up Hull House, and to appreciate the radical implications of its lessons, Addams stood on the shoulders of earlier feminists and arm-in-arm with radical women of her own generation. Their self-understandings and life trajectories were reshaped by a passionate commitment to achieving the substantive requirements of justice, positively understood as requiring active social support for the flourishing of all individuals, including those excluded from voice and from growth within power-structured social hierarchies. Some of feminism's most influential British and American contributors to the development of democratic theory and praxis in the eighteenth and nineteenth centuries, such as Mary Wollstonecraft, Margaret Fuller, Elizabeth Cady Stanton, Frederick Douglass, J.S. Mill, Harriet Taylor Mill, and Ida B. Wells-Barnett, pointed out false universal claims within modern philosophy and within the system of gender and race that organized modern social life.[36] These included generalizations about reason, law, and the capacities to contribute to the growth of knowledge and to the direction of community life that were widely said to apply to "all men," but were implicitly understood not to apply to any women, nor to the allegedly "racially inferior" men and women it enslaved.

Although these feminist theorists disagreed among themselves about whether widespread, empirically observable, gender-linked differences in reasoning processes and social capacities were due to nature or to nurture, they agreed that if women were allowed to participate in correcting such false "universals," women's contributions would make a positive difference in every field of intellectual and social endeavor. Their deep moral passion for abolishing great social evils like slavery, which had legally enchained Douglass's clearly extraordinary capacities while justifying the rape, mutilation, and murder of many of their African American sisters, originally led Stanton and a few other middle-class American white women to offend the proprieties and to breach their own narrowly circumscribed, gender-based social role in order to work actively for a practical deepening of America's lofty founding ideal of democracy. When they met refusals to accept women as advocates for such a morally imperative cause, they came to see a change in the gender system, including their own legal and political equality with men, as necessary for efficacy in their moral advocacy. Therefore, they pursued the franchise for women. The Mills pointed out that, contrary to widespread shared norms of positive law in their era, there should be no need to legally prohibit women from doing what they are not capable of doing, and they argued that many additional changes in the laws that enforced the gender system might be beneficial to others as well as to women themselves, including opening up higher education, the professions, and the laws of property to include women as equals.

The Club Women's Movement of the late-nineteenth century provided an organizing framework for educated, middle-class American women's efforts at social benevolence, though its leaders were deeply divided over whether to focus on relatively uncontroversial social uplift projects or on more radical projects like Wells-Barnett's antilynching campaign.[37] By the late-nineteenth century, when Addams came of age, higher education for American women of her race and class was no longer controversial, and though they were still excluded from the franchise, the idea that women like her should contribute to social uplift had become a mainstream norm of her Protestant Christianity. Although Addams was even more ambitious to do good than evolved social conventions regarded as quite proper for a woman like her, she only later realized that these aspirations were unconsciously shaped by her American middle-class experience, expressing a "Lady Bountiful" assumption that she ought to share her various forms of social wealth out of a sense of *noblesse oblige* that implied that she had nothing to learn from her beneficiaries and nothing personal to gain from equal cooperation with them.

Addams discovered the mistake within her "Lady Bountiful" assumption early on at Hull House, thereby bringing into critical–transformative play a richer understanding of the way locations of class and culture work within modern forms of life.[38] There she experienced the existential realization that, like the economically and culturally marginalized people with whom she worked, she was also in need of transformation and rescue from unjust social circumstances, and that a kind of *mutual conversion* that produced new, shared goals and perspectives while preserving much of the participants' original diversity was *the criterial outcome of an effective democratic collaboration.* As Charlene Haddock Seigfried explains in her insightful work of retrieval and creative reconstruction, *Pragmatism and Feminism: Reweaving the Social Fabric,*

> Addams always insisted that settlement workers and others who worked for social change received as much as they gave to those with whom they worked. This deep and abiding faith in the common people grounded her faith in democracy. She saw her role not as deciding what is right for others, but as a trustee of their interests. She sought to replace the leadership ideal of the righteousness of "the great man" with that of "fellowship." (Seigfried 1996:76)

Addams credited one of her fellow women residents of Hull House, Julia Lathrop, with helping her to realize that democratic processes must include participation of Hull House's client–neighborhood in setting its agenda, instead of having it imposed on them (Seigfried 1996:78). Hull House, Addams explained, was founded "on the theory that the dependence of classes on each other is reciprocal; and that as the social situation is essentially a reciprocal relation, it gives a form of expression that has a peculiar value."[39]

Addams's emphasis on mutuality in attitudes, agenda, and activities within effective democratic transformation processes turns on this issue of *trust* as the key to fostering the kind of sincere cooperation that brings forth dispersed knowledge, creative ideas, and committed personal energy. Seigfried relates an example from Hull House resident Mary E. McDowell's account of her experience there that demonstrates that, before cooperative activity within a cross-difference transformative coalition can be initiated, a *basis for reasonable trust* must be demonstrated, and that this requires a *credible interest in genuine reciprocity* rather than patronizing benevolence.

> McDowell had invited to dinner at Hull House a trade-union woman who told her in casual conversation of her feelings of bitterness as a young woman when she could not earn enough to support herself and her invalid mother. She had at first hesitated to accept the offer because she felt it was but another effort "to patronize a working girl." On arriving late, she reported that Jane Addams had risen to greet her just as if she were any other lady, and on seating her said: "I have asked you to come here and see what we could do *with* each other for the girls in your trade." McDowell explained that "she said that little word 'with' took the sting of bitterness out of her soul. If Miss Addams had said '*for* you,'" she continued, "I would have said proudly, 'I want to do for myself,' but when she said 'with,' that made it different. I have been with her ever since.'" (Seigfried 1996:264, emphases mine)

It is not only the choice of a single word that was important to this young woman, but what it revealed about the "grammar" of Addams's and Hull House's whole "form of life"—a transformed, engaged, genuinely concerned, humbly open-minded form of life that disrupted the middle-class American norms that underlay the young woman's well-founded working class suspicions about what such a woman, reputed to be formidably effective in wielding hierarchical power, would be like. Addams's insight that is most important here is that *the social inquiry process must include as equals those affected by its results* if it is to build the mutual trust that makes it possible both to elicit the widely dispersed, necessary *information* only diverse participants can contribute, and to creatively negotiate *shared ends-in-view* that effectively advance the transformative deepening of democracy in that situation. Such a cross-difference collaborative process requires and makes possible *deep changes* in *all of the participating collaborators* that allow and reflect their experience of acting effectively together.

On the basis of her Hull House experiences, Addams theorized that the importance of acknowledging and valuing differences in arriving at the best understanding of and solution to a particular problem includes taking into account *differences in situations* as well as *cultural differences* in *interpretations,* instead of deriving solutions from universal concepts. As Seigfried explains, quoting Addams in the course of her discussion,

> Bringing along those to be benefited as participants in the process often means compromise and a groping toward a good neither group clearly envisioned beforehand. The effort to discover what people really want will most likely slow down progress and limit the goals attainable, but the outcome will be more lasting and worthwhile because it will not be dependent on one person's insights or efforts but will be "underpinned and upheld by the sentiments and aspirations of many others." (Seigfried 1996:230; Addams 1902:121–122)

In her own reconstructive language, Seigfried describes the more insightful epistemological framework that emerges out of this kind of transformative interaction between pragmatism and feminism as follows:

> Although pragmatists deny that any person or group can claim privileged insight into the being of things, they also show that each person's perspective is unique and irreplaceable. *Until each person's perspective on a situation that includes her or him is heard and acknowledged, the complexity of the situation cannot be grasped, and possible relevant insights may be lost.* Claims about what ought to be done based on the truth of any given situation can therefore be justified only in practice. This means that not only should the projected results of acting on such beliefs be evaluated by all those affected but also the actual results themselves. Since effects can be long-term as well as immediate, confirmation is in principle ongoing and subject to revision. Social democracy, as extended from a theory of political governance to a practice of organized life, is thus conceived as a means of guaranteeing the dignity and freedom of persons by its structural incorporation of the widest possible inclusiveness and participation in determining the conditions for our existence. (Seigfried 1996:79, emphasis mine)

Alice Hamilton, who also lived and worked at Hull House, commented that "Hull House was American because it was international, and because it perceived that the nationalism of each immigrant was a treasure, a talent, which gave him a special value for the United States" (Seigfried 1996:76).

As even this preliminary discussion of the wealth of Addams's insights for developing a comprehensive philosophy of democratic transformation shows, an inclusive approach to social inquiry improves the quality of understanding of the problem situation, bringing widely dispersed yet necessary powers of experience-based imagination to bear in finding the right transformative end-in-view and in adequately assessing its success in guiding transformative action. The ordinary women and men that Dewey recognized must be involved in *practical struggles* to realize the best potentials within modernity by deepening democracy must also, as Addams makes clear, be included in *theoretical strug-*

gles for understanding and for transformative direction. In addition, her philosophical works deriving theoretical implications and useful guidelines for future praxis from the Hull House experience model the kind of critical–empirical study of situations with crisis potential that also reveal the deeper social structures and characteristics that both Deweyan pragmatism and Habermasian critical theory regard as so crucial. Addams's theorizing clearly arises out of her activist praxis, revealing her own *changes in character* as well as in *belief* and in *practical modes of engagement* as the challenges, opportunities, successes, and failures of cooperative struggle made these necessary and desirable.

Although it grows out of a different set of social–locational experiences, Alain Locke's philosophical theorizing of the descriptive implications and transformative ideal possibilities of what he called "cultural pluralism" offers insights compatible with those of Addams. Moreover, Locke proposes detailed strategies for cross-difference collaboration in *social inquiry,* in *democratic praxis,* in *communication through the arts,* and in *continuing educational processes* that can critically and creatively reshape individual and cultural self-understandings while cultivating the skills, the knowledge, and the appreciations that a more deeply democratic social life requires in our globalized era. As Leonard Harris has pointed out, in Locke's view, "cultural diversity was inherently desirable," and "a multitude of ways of valuing is characteristic of our being and not a temporal phase of human history."[40] As is discussed in more detail in Chapter Four, some of Locke's most important works focus on how to use inclusive processes of cross-difference democratic conversation and practical collaboration to *empirically reground democratic universal norms* for a globalized *modus vivendi* among culturally differing forms of life that are undergoing creative democratic reconstruction from within.

Although Locke shared Dewey's and Habermas's concerns about the negative influence of value-neutral forms of individual and cultural relativism, he argued, following William James, that *moral and intellectual absolutisms* like those underlying Habermas's construction and use of the "ideal speech situation" do not offer a better alternative for two kinds of reasons. Firstly, they cannot be grounded in a realistic universal psychology and defended by uncontroversial philosophical arguments. Secondly, they cannot win sufficient practical acceptance in a culturally pluralistic world climate marked by significant moral differences and suspicion of Western cultural and economic domination.[41] In terms that have meaning to all parties within our present social and global power-structured hierarchies, Locke argued that, given the perpetually incomplete effectiveness of imperial strategies of cultural domination because of the return influence of the dominated on the dominators, as well as the capacity of the excluded to destroy the peace for all, *rival absolutisms must be abandoned* in favor of a *negotiated, cross-cultural process* of progressive understanding, trust-building, and trust-based democratic collaboration in areas of mutual benefit. Such a process, he suggested, can gradually create the only kind of unity that can have stability: a *cosmopolitan unity* that respects areas of *nonabsolutist value diversity* compatible with those "*common humane values*" that must undergird a democratic peace.[42]

Locke's cross-culturally informed conception of the kind of critical–empirical social science that can foster such a cosmopolitan unity-building peace process by helping to negotiate and to substantively realize "common humane values" offers an insightful, reconstructive correction to Dewey's and Habermas's models. Locke called for *a cross-disciplinary "anthropology in the broadest sense"* that would include philosophical value theorists among its collaborating partners, and that would provide the empirical basis and detailed content for the hypothetical claims about "common humane values" that he believed would eventually become well-warranted.[43] Locke insightfully argued that effective claims about value universals need to be grounded in the kind of critical–empirical awareness of the variety of actual cultural norms that was beginning to emerge from the work of the then-new social science of anthropology, whose direction he helped to influence through his interactions with Franz Boas and some of his students, including Zora Neale Hurston, Margaret Mead, and Ruth Benedict. On a theoretical level, Locke argued, we can *discover* all the common humane values we need for cross-difference, collaborative democratic theory and praxis within the *actual experiences* of differing cultures if our "anthropology in the broadest sense" is guided by *the methodology of "critical relativism,"* which includes three working principles: the principle of cultural equivalence, the principle of cultural reciprocity, and the principle of limited cultural convertibility.[44] Locke's guiding philosophical hypothesis is that cross-cultural differences in values, intuitions, and the moral practices that embody them represent "functional adaptations" to their unique historical situations, including interactive struggle with other cultures under conditions of power inequality. Nonetheless, he argues, these differing functional adaptations seem likely to express deeper value commonalities that could become the basis for actively and effectively promoting *mutual respect, cross-cultural conversation, practical cooperation,* and, eventually, *a democratic peace.* Moreover, Locke suggests, differing functional adaptations of such "common humane values" can be critically understood and evaluated in terms of their past and future usefulness, given changing conditions.

Finally, Locke offers valuable insights about how to redirect and sustain the kind of *committed loyalty* that is necessary to stabilize long-term relationships within cross-difference cooperation, as Habermas has more recently recognized. Offering a practically more challenging but a theoretically more defensible and ultimately more efficacious analysis of the kind of loyalty that is needed, Locke follows Royce in arguing for a broad *"loyalty to loyalty"* as a quality of any good life, rather than for a narrower loyalty to existing, formally democratic constitutions and their dominant interpretations, or to any relatively less significant and less deeply democratic transformative feature of our increasingly globalized and presently problem-riddled forms of life. Locke reminds us that, if the democratic, mutality-fostering ideal values like "loyalty to loyalty" that he believes wise people in differing cultures already affirm are to be more widely and actively realized, our present historically power-structured differences must be acknowledged and gradually overcome. This can best be achieved, in Locke's experience-based judgment, through stagewise, trust-developing collaborative processes that progressively change historically suspicious or arrogant mindsets into appropriately trusting, intellectually democratic ones. Cultural differences about values are real, he argues, expressing imperative feeling-modes that reflect both individual temperaments and shared group history, though they can be revised somewhat through reasoned judgment and the further evidence of experience. Thus, he suggests, it is possible to bring people who hold differing values into productive conversation if they can learn to hold their own culture's values less dogmatically and to regard others' more tolerantly. This can happen over time through working in common cause with one's cultural "others," including former enemies, as long as they are not the kinds of fundamentalists who tend to derail a prospective coalition's mutually transformative negotiations toward mutual understanding and respect.[45]

When it has been broadened and empirically better grounded by the critical and reconstructive contributions of Addams, Locke, and their contemporary inheritors, Dewey's and Habermas's shared ideal of the democratic community can guide the development of a broadly collaborative, highly effective, comprehensive philosophy of democratic transformation. At the same time, such a reconstructed democratic ideal can simultaneously serve as a criterion for the continuing insightfulness and usefulness of feminism's and cultural pluralism's various paths of ongoing development. Historically, a shared critical insight and motivating purpose of both feminist and cultural pluralist theory and praxis has been the need to include all streams and bearers of human experience in the philosophical process of variously articulating the humanly universal, the humanly necessary, and the humanly desirable as guides to imagination, self-understanding, and action in a world in which we are inextricably interconnected across our differences, yet divided by our historically entrenched, deeply undemocratic practices. Thus, rather than rejecting the importance of such a difference-braided understanding of the ideal of the democratic community, both feminism and cultural pluralism should draw upon it, even as they call for a still richer appreciation of diversity in its articulation. The democratic ideal in various family-resemblant articulations can serve as a shared criterion for the insightfulness and transformative usefulness of alternative strands of feminism and cultural pluralism in their ongoing development.

Some Concluding Thoughts: Give Peace a Chance

An appreciative and critical conversation between John Dewey's pragmatism and Jürgen Habermas's critical theory focusing on their shared democratic transformative project shows both that these allegedly competing philosophical methodologies are largely complementary and potentially mutually corrective—and that they are individually and conjointly inadequate to generate the comprehensive philosophy of democratic transformation so urgently needed in our time, unless they are reconstructed in conversation with other philosophical methodologies grounded in and motivated by a richer appreciation of diversity. If we take their shared ideal of the democratic community seriously while interpreting its meaning pluralistically, and if we understand the purpose of philosophy as guiding the quest for humanly fulfilling lives within varying societies in which this ideal has become operative, then philosophy will have four roles to fulfill within the democratic transformation process: (1) to show the need for social transformation and to remove intellectual obstacles to deeper realizations of this twin-faceted ideal; (2) to further develop broadly useful models for collaborative, critical–empirical approaches to social inquiry while actively contributing to case analyses of actual social transformation processes and contemporary situations that have crisis potential; (3) to create effective, value-reflecting tools of democratic social inquiry and citizen-to-citizen communication for real communities to use in their social transformation processes; and (4) to interpret and synthesize insights within and beyond transformative praxis in order to deepen our pluralistic appreciation of the democratic ideal, both for regrounding and reenergizing our self-understandings and for rebuilding democratic processes and relationships within community life. When Deweyan pragmatism and Habermasian critical theory reconstructively collaborate with compatible, diversity-appreciating streams of feminism and cultural pluralism, these differing philosophical frameworks interactively combine the resources to assist in the development of a comprehensive philosophy of democratic transformation that can effectively guide transformative praxis while gaining the empirical resources thereby to democratically deepen philosophy.

The offspring of such critically attentive, empirically attuned, democratically motivated processes of theoretical interaction among Deweyan pragmatism, Habermasian critical theory, and compatible streams of feminism and cultural pluralism is *a radical critical pragmatism* with a cooperative transformative agenda that does not exhaust or dominate their differing separate agendas. Rather, this shared agenda focuses on developing and implementing an urgently needed comprehensive philosophy of deeply democratic transformation that contextualizes their other, differing goals. As the foregoing argument suggests, this project is better served by a pluralistically reconstructed pragmatist approach to metaphysics, methodology, epistemology, psychology, and philosophy of language than by the kind of neo-Kantian approach to critical theory with a "pragmatic turn" at the margins that Habermas currently favors. However, this must be an activist, critical–transformative pragmatism like Dewey's, Addams's, and Locke's, one that recaptures the liberatory commitment of that other great critical theorist, Herbert Marcuse. It must draw cross-culturally on all of the great traditions of liberatory struggle and address itself to important, interlinked contemporary problem situations in Africa, Eastern Europe, Asia, Latin America, and the "formally" democratic West. It must express a "cultivated pluralism" learned through a critical multicultural education that continues in the deeply democratic reciprocity of inclusive, cross-difference liberatory praxis. This is the kind of standpoint that the following chapters express and apply in seeking to contribute to the development of a comprehensive, transformative philosophy of deep democracy.

We know that such collaborative work toward deep democracy is possible because it has already begun. Charlene Haddock Seigfried, Marjorie Miller, Lisa Heldke, Eugenia Gatens-Robinson, Shannon Sullivan, and others have begun the work of expressing a feminist pragmatism that retrieves Jane Addams's passionate, culturally pluralistic commitment to radical social transformation. Angela Davis, James L. Marsh, Seyla Benhabib, Nancy Fraser, Martin Matustik and others have recalled critical theory to retrieve its liberatory commitments while learning from and contributing to the criticisms and the liberatory praxis of feminists, cultural pluralists, and activist pragmatists. Cultural pluralists like Leonard Harris, Blanche Radford Curry, Robert Bunge, Dennis McPherson, and J. Douglass Rabb have made explicit connections between their culture-specific projects and pragmatism while engaging in radical transformative criticism. And many contemporary pragmatists in the classical American stream, including Cornel West, Larry Hickman, Thomas Alexander, Kenneth Stikkers, John Stuhr, and Vincent Colapietro, among others, have recalled pragmatists of all stripes to a radical "recovery of philosophy," drawing on various forms of therapeutic assistance from feminism, cultural pluralism, and critical theory.

Nonetheless, overt hostilities and failures of acknowledgment and inclusion among these once-rival schools of thought continue in the work of many partisans. Such hostilities and failures result in large part from professional philosophical tribalism sustained by ignorance of other intellectual traditions, by parochially inward-focused currying of the texts and terms of one's own tradition's particular academic conversation, and by an insufficiently vital sense of the world's imperative need for practical assistance from—of all people—philosophers. Consequently, perceived rivalries among potential transformative collaborators serve as ballast for the professional philosophical mainstream's focus on debating abstract philosophical methodologies and related ideal principles instead of clarifying real-world conditions and discovering justifiable, effective means of changing them; on detailing formal institutional mechanisms instead of developing inclusive participatory democratic processes; on revising ethical rules instead of rebuilding ethical relationships; and on fighting to maintain educational traditions against the barbarian onslaught of the economic system instead of transforming education to prepare students to transform the system. It is time for these hostilities and failures to cease, and for critically reconstructive conversations among potentially complementary but still-competitive philosophical approaches to become a regular feature of our professional life. Our democratically deficient, conflict-riven world urgently needs our collaborative contributions to the development of a comprehensive, transformative philosophy of deep democracy.

Notes

1. See Steven Seidman's Introduction in *Jürgen Habermas on Society and Politics: A Reader* (1989), 9, italics mine.

2. Kenneth Stikkers coined the term "cultivated pluralism" in his essay, "Instrumental Relativism and Cultivated Pluralism," presented at an Alain L. Locke Round Table at the World Congress of Philosophy in Boston, Massachusetts (August 14, 1998); see Harris 1999.

3. See John Dewey, "The Need for a Recovery of Philosophy" (1917), *John Dewey: The Middle Works*, Vol. 10, 46.

4. See James L. Marsh's essay, "What's Critical About Critical Theory?" presented at a Radical Philosophy Association Conference at Purdue University (West Lafayette, Indiana), November 1996; forthcoming in the *Library of Living Philosphers* Volume on Habermas.

5. This conception of a radical "critical pragmatism" has emerged from conversations with Leonard Harris, Kenneth Stikkers, Martin Matustik, Charlene Haddock Seigfried, and others working within critical theory, pragmatism, feminism, and cultural pluralism who seek to foster effective cross-difference collaboration on deeply democratic transformation of differing contemporary societies, assisted by a reconstructively critical philosophical conversation.

6. All quotations from John Dewey in this chapter are from *The Public and Its Problems* (1927), in *John Dewey: The Later Works,* Vol 2.

7. I am grateful to Larry A. Hickman for clarifying Habermas's adversarial view of modern science and technology in commenting on this part of this chapter at the Central Division Meetings of the American Philosophical Association (Chicago, Illinois), May 1998. See his essay on this subject in the forthcoming *Library of Living Philosophers* volume on Habermas, as well as his *John Dewey's Pragmatic Technology* (1990).

8. See Jürgen Habermas, "Individuation through Socialization: On Mead's Theory of Subjectivity," *Postmetaphysical Thinking: Philosophical Essays* (1992).

9. See Josiah Royce's discussions of community in *The Problem of Christianity* (1918), republished in a critical edition (1968), especially Ch. 1 (81–85) and Chs. 9–12, as well as *The Hope of the Great Community* (1916). See also Jacqueline Ann Kegley's thoughtful discussion of Royce's "absolute pragmatism" in *Classical American Philosophy: Essential Readings and Interpretive Essays* (1987), ed. John J. Stuhr.

10. See *The Essential Peirce* (1992 and 1998), ed. Nathan Houser and Christian Kloesel. For examples of Habermas's acknowledgment of Charles Sanders Peirce's influence, see *The Theory of Communicative Action,* Volume 1 (1984), pp. 276, 387, and 413; and Volume 2 (1987), pp. 3 and 4, as well as "Peirce and Communication" in *Postmetaphysical Thinking* (1992).

11. Robert Bellah and his collaborators also use Royce's phrase, "community of memory and hope," without attribution in *Habits of the Heart* (1985), although in *The Good Society* (1991), they recognize Royce's coinage of the phrase, "the Great Community," as well as his significant influence on both Dewey and Mead. Using very similar language in critically reconstructing Habermas's analysis of communicative action, James L. Marsh links liberatory communities to memory and to "critical" or "rational" hope; see *Critique, Action, and Liberation* (1995), 353–354.

12. See Mead's "The Social Self" (1913) and *Mind, Self, and Society* (1936), as well as Habermas's discussion of Mead in *The Theory of Communicative Action* II, 3ff. See Habermas's discussion of his concept of lifeworld as partially derived from Wittgenstein's "forms of life" in *The Theory of Communicative Action* II, 119. I call Wittgenstein a "proto-pragmatist" because of a passage from *On Certainty* that he wrote a few days before his death: "422. So I am trying to say something that sounds like pragmatism. Here I am being thwarted by a kind of *Weltanschauung*" (54). R.W. Sleeper suggests that "diverted" is a better translation than "thwarted" in his essay, "The Pragmatics of Deconstruction and the End of Metaphysics," in *Philosophy and the Reconstruction of Culture* (1993), ed. John J. Stuhr.

13. See Habermas's discussion of crisis tendencies in modern capitalist societies and the potential they indicate for further social rationalization in *The Theory of Communicative Action* II, 375ff. See also Jane Braaten's helpful interpretive discussion in *Habermas's Critical Theory of Society* (1991).

14. Larry Hickman points out that, unlike Dewey, Habermas includes science and technology within "system"; see my note 7 (above).

15. See Marcuse's *One-Dimensional Man* (1964); but see also his *An Essay on Liberation* (1969), the spirit of which James L. Marsh seeks to revive in his *Critique, Action, and Liberation* (1995). For a related Habermasian critique, see Daniel Hallin's "The American News Media: A Critical Theory Perspective," in *Critical Theory and Public Life* (1985), ed. John Forester.

16. See Robert B. Westbrook's *John Dewey and American Democracy* (1991), 441, and Dewey's "No Half Way House for America" (1934) in *John Dewey: The Later Works, Volume 10,* 289–290.

17. In his pre-1981 works, including *Toward a Rational Society* (1970) and *Legitimation Crisis* (1975), Habermas followed Marcuse in critiquing ideology as the persuasive tool of exploitative elites and the most effective pressure point for transforming late capitalist societies. Thus, *The Theory of Communicative Action* marks an important departure from his earlier work.

18. I am indebted to Edmund F. Byrne for pointing out that some philosophers, including Paul Ricoeur, interpret "ideology" as a positive, constitutive and transformative concept, rather than a negative, critical concept.

19. I am indebted to Frank Kirkland for questioning whether Habermas's view continues to be tied to the ideal speech situation when I presented an earlier version of this discussion at the 1996 Annual Meetings of the Society for the Advancement of American Philosophy at the University of Toronto (Toronto, Ontario), March 1996.

20. See Rawls's development of this concept of "the original position" from *A Theory of Justice* (1971), p. 12ff, to *Political Liberalism* (1993, 1996), p. 304ff.

21. Jürgen Habermas, "Reconciliation through the Public Use of Reason: Remarks on John Rawls's Political Liberalism," *The Journal of Philosophy* 92:3 (March 1995), 110.

22. In this essay and related work on discourse ethics, *Moral Consciousness and Communicative Action* (1990) and *Justification and Application: Remarks on Discourse Ethics* (1993), Habermas acknowledges and tries to factor in social pluralism and deep differences in worldviews.

23. See Wittgenstein, *Philosophical Investigations,* Third Edition (1958), remark 66.

24. "Wide reflective equilibrium" is another key methodological concept Rawls has continued to develop since *A Theory of Justice* (1971), p. 20ff and 49–50. Rawls first made explicit use of the modifier "wide" in his "Independence of Moral Theory" (1974). He developed this concept further in "Kantian Constructivism in Moral Theory" (1980) and in *Political Liberalism* (1993, 1996).

25. Jürgen Habermas, "Struggles for Recognition in the Democratic Constitutional State," in *Multiculturalism* (1994), ed. Amy Gutmann.

26. Wittgenstein, *Philosophical Investigations* (1958), remark 308.

27. On Dewey's activism, see Robert Westbrook's *John Dewey and American Democracy* (1991).

28. See *The Theory of Communicative Action* II, 374–375.

29. See Jane Braaten's *Habermas's Critical Theory of Society* (1991), p. 76.

30. Charles Sherover, "Postmodernism and Democracy," presented at the Annual Meetings of the Society for Phenomenology and Existential Philosophy (Seattle, Washington), October 1994.

31. Joseph Betz, "Sandinista Nicaragua as a Deweyan Social Experiment," Presidential Address to the Society for the Advancement of Social Philosophy at the University of Toronto (Toronto, Ontario), March 1996.

32. See, for example, Harry C. Boyte's *Community Is Possible: Repairing America's Roots* (1984) and *CommonWealth: A Return to Citizen Politics* (1989), as well as his collaborative work with Sara M. Evans, *Free Spaces: The Sources of Democratic Change in America* (1986).

33. I am indebted to Lisa Heldke for drawing my attention to the importance of this passage in this connection.

34. See, for example, Sandra Harding's "Rethinking Standpoint Epistemology: What Is 'Strong Objectivity'?" in *Feminist Epistemologies* (1993), ed. Linda Alcoff and Elizabeth Potter.

35. See Charlene Haddock Seigfried's rich combination of historical retrieval and original theorizing in *Pragmatism and Feminism: Reweaving the Social Fabric* (1996), 73–75.

36. See Mary Wollstonecraft's *A Vindication of the Rights of Woman* (1792); Margaret Fuller's "The Great Lawsuit" (1843), later expanded into *Woman in the Nineteenth Century* (1845), an internationally acclaimed feminist work that influenced Elizabeth Cady Stanton and others to call the 1848 Woman's Rights Convention at Seneca Falls, New York, that produced the "Declaration of Sentiments" for which she is best known, and to which Frederick Douglass was a signatory; J.S. Mill and Harriet Taylor Mill's *The Subjection of Women* (1868), now widely acknowledged to be the coproduction he called it then; and Ida B. Wells's *Crusade for Justice: The Auto-Biography of Ida B. Wells* (1970).

37. See Angela Davis, *Women, Race & Class* (1981) and Carolyn Johnston's *Sexual Power: Feminism and the Family in America* (1992).

38. See Addams's *Twenty Years at Hull House* (1910), which Charlene Haddock Seigfried discusses in detail in *Pragmatism and Feminism: Reweaving the Social Fabric* (1996).

39. See Addams's *Democracy and Social Ethics* (1902), 222.

40. See Leonard Harris's helpful introduction to Locke's philosophy in his edited collection of some of Locke's most important essays, *The Philosophy of Alain Locke: Harlem Renaissance and Beyond* (1989), 17.

41. See Locke's "Values and Imperatives" (1935) and "Value" (1935–47) in Harris, *op. cit.*

42. For Locke's discussion of modern world cultures as "composite and hybrid," see his editor's introduction to a collection of cross-disciplinary essays on cultures and values, *When Peoples Meet: A Study of Race and Culture Contacts* (1942).

43. See Locke's "Pluralism and Intellectual Democracy" (1942) and "Cultural Relativism and Ideological Peace" (1944) in Harris, *op. cit.*

44. See Locke's "Cultural Relativism and Ideological Peace" (1944) in Harris, *op. cit.*

45. See Locke's "The Need for a New Organon in Education" (1950) in Harris, *op. cit.*

Chapter 3

The Deeply Democratic Community: Reconstructing Dewey's Transformative Ideal

> *The end of democracy is a radical end. For it is an end that has not been adequately realized in any country at any time.*
>
> —JOHN DEWEY, "Democracy Is Radical" (1937)

Introduction

The ideal of the democratic community was a touchstone for John Dewey's philosophical thinking and practical activism throughout the first half of the twentieth century. It is the common point of reference in work after work from his middle and later years in which he offers interlinked analyses and prescriptions for transforming problems of lived experience that reflexively require transforming metaphysics, philosophical methodology, the logic of inquiry, philosophy of science, ethics, aesthetics, political philosophy, philosophy of education, philosophy of economics, and philosophy of law. The democratic ideal also guided Dewey's work as a public intellectual writing essays on a wide range of issues of the day for journals and magazines, and helping to organize associations focused on transforming various aspects of the problem situation of his time. In none of these contexts does Dewey attempt to *define* democracy or its twin ideal, community. He expected modern readers already to be familiar with the broad meanings of these concepts as key parts of their languages and their shared forms of life. Rather, his aim was to redirect attention to *unnoticed implications* and *new applications* of the democratic ideal that are called for by the historical unfolding of our shared experience in the societies it helps to shape. For Dewey, this experience shows that our present "formally" democratic political institutions are inadequate fulfillments of the implications of our shared democratic ideal. If we are ever to experience a form of democracy that does not frustrate these implications, he argued, it must be a *deeper democracy* that encompasses the full range of attitudes and institutions of community life.

How we can reconcile our sometimes-divisive diversity with our shared democratic ideal is an urgent question at the beginning of a new millennium. Subsequent experience has shown that Dewey was prophetic in emphasizing the importance of reconstructing various kinds of communities of daily life, not only local neighborhoods but also justice-focused church communities, democratic workplaces, and cooperative networks of people united by a shared, lived concern. The concept of community has become the focus of yearning for many modern people of all races, genders, and classes in recent years. Rival communitarian social movements and related philosophies of the left, right, and center have sprung up to offer leadership to this widespread manifestation of the motivating desire for a more ideal experience of community in daily life. Thus, the questions of how we should understand this ideal of community, how it relates to the ideal of democracy and to our inextricably interrelated issues of diversity, and how we can create local communities that have a sustaining and transformative democratic character within our global reality have become urgent matters for our cooperative critical inquiry.

By highlighting the implications of Dewey's comments about the link between democracy and diversity in community life and rethinking this linkage through the lens of a radical critical pragmatism in light of lessons of the second half of the twentieth century, Dewey's transformative ideal can be reconstructed as *the deeply democratic community*, a not-yet-real possibility within experience that can guide the ongoing cooperative development of a comprehensive and practical democratic philosophy. This reconstructed ideal can, in turn, guide us in appropriating Dewey's helpful leadings about how to answer five crucial questions within contemporary transformative praxis: (1) how to shape educational experiences as key tools and aspects of the ongoing growth of individuals, cultures, and societies; (2) how to build up transformative cross-difference coalitions and diverse self-educating communities amidst the differences that presently divide us; (3) how to develop effective processes of intelligent, cross-difference democratic communication within social inquiry, choice, and action; (4) how to reflectively revise our goals, objectives, and strategies as we learn from our transformative efforts; and (5) how to effectively coordinate and sustain our transformative efforts over the extended time it will take to institutionalize the kinds of progressive changes that will make the deeply democratic community real in our experience.

Diversity within Dewey's Contextualized Discussions of the Democratic Ideal

Dewey's discussions of the twin facets of his guiding ideal—community and democracy—are contextualized within his pragmatic analyses and transformative prescriptions for various aspects of the problem situation of his time, and also for various aspects of philosophy that he believed needed to be reconstructed in order to make it a more effective critical and transformative enterprise. Thus, clarifying how Dewey understood the democratic community and highlighting the place of diversity within it requires piecing together these multiple contexts of its functional significance. An important discussion of the democratic ideal in *Reconstruction in Philosophy* (1920) focuses on the role of education within democratic community life. Dewey argues there in memorable terms that continuing, life-long education for all, unimpeded by the kinds of discriminatory barriers that have limited individuals' access to its self-transforming potential, is the purpose and measure of democracy.

> The test of all institutions of adult life is their effect in furthering continued education. Government, business, art, religion, all social institutions have a meaning, a purpose. That purpose is to set free and to develop the capacities of human individuals without respect to race, sex, class, or economic status. And this is all one with saying that the test of their value is the extent to which they educate every individual into the full stature of his possibility. *Democracy* has many meanings, but if it has *a moral meaning,* it is found in resolving that *the supreme test of all political institutions and industrial arrangements shall be the contribution they make to the all-around growth of every member of society.* (Dewey 1920:186, emphases mine)

Dewey's conception of education, which he had articulated more fully in his earlier *Democracy and Education* (1916) and would continue to develop for the rest of his life, is far from a once and for all indoctrination of children into the traditional expectations of their elders. Rather, it is a continuous process of guided development in response to experience that *progressively reshapes* and *liberates* individuals throughout the course of their lives. This educational process has a widely recognized institutional character within schools during the childhood years in formally democratic societies, but it is also a less recognized, though nonetheless important aspect of adult life as this is shaped within other kinds of social institutions. Dewey's point about the implications of the democratic ideal here is that we should become aware of these aspects of continuing adult education and should become as thoughtful about structuring the institutions that create these experiences as we are about our schools, *not* so as to *control* the continuing reformation of adults or children in conformity to some antecedent cultural norm or the interests of some power group, but in order to *free* them and to *support their flourishing* as interdependent members of deeply democratic communities.

Such deeply democratic communities, as Dewey conceives of them, may continue in varying ways to embody at least some of the differences he mentions— "race, sex, class, and economic status"—but these differences will no longer be allowed to limit individuals' opportunities for development within the *schools,* and also within the *various social institutions* that continuously shape adult minds and personalities—government, business, art, religion, and all the others. This is a far-reaching call for awareness about and reform within the full range of social institutions that structure and determine the quality of our social experience. Such a call challenges the widely echoed libertarian claim that the public purpose of schools, businesses, churches, and other social institutions should be nothing other than to achieve the private purposes of the individuals who happen to own or to control them, an interpretation of the meaning of individual liberty that Dewey argues is *incompatible with the democratic ideal* that contextualizes it. Rather, democracy as a criterion for the adequacy of social institutions requires their positive contribution to the growth of *all* of the diverse individuals that make up the society such institutions exist to serve.

Dewey expressed some of his most provocative and productive insights about the twin facets of his guiding ideal—community and democracy—in the last two chapters of *The Public and Its Problems* (1927). Dewey argues there that *democracy as an ideal* has its place as *a quality within the experience of community life itself,* rather than as just one among various alternative, equally defensible structural forms within which community life might be organized. The development of "formally" democratic political institutions is the result of *a shared desire* that motivated generations of social individuals acting in concert to try to sustain and to expand within community life certain highly valued experiences of conjoint activity that seemed to them good for all. However, because formally democratic institutional structures do not fully satisfy this originary desire, the conception of democracy that grounds them must not be adequate; *a fuller expression of its practical meaning* is needed, and must eventually emerge. The alternative, and the cost of failure to do so, are the frustration of this desire and the increasingly unsatisfying redirection of community life in response to some other desire, most probably the will to power of the few.

Dewey's transformative prescription in *The Public and Its Problems* calls for revitalizing the face-to-face local community, understood as diverse lives interconnected and sustained by full and free communication, because this is the birthing place of the democratic desire, the testing place for social inquiry, and the launching place for a broader, translocally dispersed "Public." Dewey's call is not for a nostalgic and impossible return to times of simpler technologies, narrower aspirations, and more limited opportunities. Rather, it is for development of contemporary, democracy-inspired communities of daily life that dialectically carry forward the memory and the lessons of past partial achievements while critically drawing upon new knowledge and new technologies. Dewey suggests that we need such not-yet-ideally democratic, face-to-face local communities to sustain us as we cooperatively pursue interim goals that will help our communities to develop and to struggle together toward the conditions of lived experience that will more fully satisfy our shared, deeply democratic impulse. Out of a cooperative web of such reconstructed communities of daily experience, a translocal "Public" can grow, linking members' desires and efforts within an effective transformative praxis that harnesses the new technologies to further the practical realization of deep democracy.

Dewey had very little of a general nature to say about how to create such democracy-nurturing local communities or a translocal public that could interlink them, perhaps in part because his attention was focused on urgent questions of national and international policy, and in part because he believed that social problems have a specific and particular character that makes theoretical generalizations about how to solve them largely useless and often invidious. However, in a pithy and suggestive passage from the revised edition of the *Ethics* (1932), written in collaboration with James H. Tufts, Dewey did suggest some *general characteristics and requirements of democracy* that apply to face-to-face communities, as well as to "publics" and to substantively democratic societies. In particular, Dewey stressed that social constructions like poverty, class status, race, and gender must not continue to operate as barriers to individual opportunity. Instead, the institutions and attitudes of democratic social life must actively foster the development of diverse individual potentialities.

> *Democracy signifies,* on one side, that *every individual is to share in the duties and rights belonging to control of social affairs,* and, on the other side, that *social arrangements are to eliminate those external arrangements of status, birth, wealth, sex, etc. which restrict the opportunity of each individual for full development of himself.* On the individual side, it takes as the criterion of social organization and of law and government release of the potentialities of individuals. On the social side, it demands cooperation in place of coercion, voluntary sharing in a process of mutual give and take, instead of authority imposed from above. (Dewey 1932:348–349, emphases mine)

Lest critics suggest that a diverse democratic community so described reflects an unrealistic, utopian, pie-in-the-sky idealism, Dewey argues that it has the deepest possible grounding in strong, valued tendencies and capacities within human nature as these have been embodied within and shaped by human history.

> As an ideal of social life in its political phase it is much wider than any form of government, although it includes government in its scope. As an ideal, it expresses the need for progress beyond anything yet attained; for nowhere in the world are there institutions which in fact operate equally to secure the full development of each individual, and assure to all individuals a share in both the values they contribute and those they receive. Yet it is not "ideal" in the sense of being visionary and utopian; for *it simply projects to their logical and practical limit forces inherent in human nature and already embodied to some extent in human nature.* It serves accordingly as basis for criticism of institutions as they exist and of plans of betterment. . . . Most criticisms of it are in fact criticisms of the imperfect realization it has so far achieved. (Dewey 1932:349, emphasis mine)

An important feature of these general characteristics and requirements is that they imply and support the existence of *diversity* within a democratic community.

Dewey's analysis here goes beyond his earlier remarks in *Reconstruction in Philosophy* about the need to redesign democratic educational opportunities to elude historical barriers tied to race, gender, class, and economic status. Here, he even more insightfully treats what many regard as "natural" differences—"status, birth, wealth, sex, etc."—as a system of unjustifiable, externally structured social arrangements that shape individual lives and personalities in ways that adversely limit the growth of those on the downside of differences. These *harmful difference-creating structures* and the particular kinds of differences they have created must be eliminated if deep democracy is to be realized.

However, *other kinds of differences* cannot and should not be eliminated, including differences in values, viewpoints, and perspectives that reflect desirable and perhaps ineliminable individual and group differences. The democratic community involves ongoing, life-guiding communication among and about differing values in a give-and-take that shapes institutions as well as individual choices. Thus, Dewey's ideal of *deep democracy* necessarily implies *deep, continuing diversity*.

This conceptual link between democracy and diversity within a progressively more satisfying community life has the support of historical experience. Although local face-to-face communities in the dim, disappearing past are often remembered as having been constituted along lines of cultural homogeneity rather than diversity in values and outlook, this sameness—to the extent that it was ever real—implied very limited contact with other cultures and maximal self-sufficiency of the community. What individuals might have gained from such cultural sameness and isolation was *a clear sense of personal identity* and *a sustaining set of life relationships*. What the community might have gained was *stability*. These desirable outcomes from the remembered narrowness of community life in the past are the focus of the nostalgic longings of many contemporary people who seek out the walled fortresses of the privileged, the closed ethnic enclaves of the disadvantaged, or the rural havens of those who regard modern technology as the cause of urban *angst*. However, to the extent that such narrowness and isolation were ever real, what both individuals and communities lost during the era of sameness was the *opportunity to grow* in response to new, fairly presented alternatives, as well as the *opportunity to benefit* from the more extensive material resources that new technologies emerging from the stimulus of cross-difference cooperation can bring. In any case, as is discussed in greater detail in Chapter Four, history shows that the security and stability of communities based on cultural sameness were illusory. Imperial hordes from the Steppes, from China, from Western Europe, and from warrior civilizations in Africa and the Americas swept through self-sufficient, sameness-valuing local communities and transformed their lives forever, not obliterating their cultures, but subordinating them to and hybridizing them with those of the victors. Even before such social cataclysms, mutually beneficial trade relationships introduced the seeds of new ideas and of self-sufficiency–reducing, cross-difference cooperation as normal aspects of community life almost everywhere in the world. This combination of imperialism, trade, new technologies, and the cultural fusions to which they gave rise has shaped the world we live in today and forever closed the door of return to the "pure" and self-sufficient monocultures of the past.

The problem situation in which we seek to realize the democratic impulse today is one in which *cultural diversity* is a basic, unalterable fact of daily life. As Alain Locke pointed out, the lessons of the old empires should discourage those who believe that either cultural dominance or cultural separatism is a workable way to transform this sometimes unpalatable fact. Those who tried to live separately in the past were inevitably swept under the influence of the more powerful. Those who tried to control difference through domination were unable to escape resultant political instability, social unrest, and cultural fusion. Even the solution of genocide has been ultimately ineffective in eradicating the influence of the downtrodden and in preserving dominant cultures from change. Thus, cultural diversity is a fact of our current problem situation that we can neither escape nor eradicate.

As unsettling as it is to those who rest their hopes for a more idealized community life on sameness of beliefs and values grounded in traditional cultural structures, the *best hope today* for preserving what is most insightful and rich in the world's diverse cultures is *deep democracy* of the kind Dewey described. This involves respecting, communicating receptively, and cooperating with those whose values are different than but not unalterably antagonistic to one's own, even as one celebrates one's own cultural memories and renews the rituals that give one's cultural tradition ongoing life in new times and circumstances. Cultures preserved amidst such a conversation with differences will not be uninfluenced, "pure" cultures—but then, no such cultures have ever existed.

Considered from the perspective of our deep social impulses and the ideals that experience and imagination throw before them, deep democracy holds attractions for those who can even partially elude their fears of change and otherness, as well as their unreconciled anger over the limitations of the past. On a relatively external level, many people enjoy and most people constantly experience benefits from cultural diversity. A label-reading excursion through a grocery store or marketplace in most parts of the world today reveals that the material substances on which the habits and pleasures of our daily lives depend are the products of many hands and diverse traditions in far-flung locations. Moreover, many people enjoy the food, clothing, music, dancing, films, books, and handicrafts of other cultures. On the relatively deeper level of the construction of personal identities, these experiences of cross-cultural contact, interdependence, and mutual enjoyment have already influenced who we understand ourselves to be and how we aspire to develop.

Parents have always been anxious about the ways in which change *changes* their children, even when they have recognized that they cannot control the becoming of new beings in the world. Thus, it is understandable that many parents are highly anxious about their children's development in this era of economic globalization, instant communication, and inescapable, often attractive diversity. However, the stimulus to their children's growth and flourishing, as well as the opportunities to escape the limitations of the past and to become cocreators of a new world in which mutual flourishing and valued cross-difference cooperation are realized, are so valuable that they must be seen as good by those who can see clearly—provided that their children have the stabilizing, nutrition-rich medium of a *living community* in which to root their development.

This is the importance of Dewey's insight about the connection between the inseparable ideals of deep democracy and of a supportive, mutually sustaining community life. Without the support of a vital community, individuals can neither develop the capacities nor draw upon sustaining support for the courage, self-respect, and imagination that would allow them to play the active and equal cross-difference role that Dewey's democratic ideal demands for them. Without the shared strength of community life, individuals would not be able to build up and maintain the kind of translocal publics that can effect democratic transformation over an extended period of struggle against those whose resistance to deep democracy is aided by wealth, political power, and control of modern technologies, including the technologies that construct and convey the daily material goods we rely on as well as the information and images that tell us who we are and what we should aspire to become. Thus, we must, as Dewey suggests, reconstruct *communities of daily experience*—not "Smalltown, USA" from the past, but new forms of community life for the world we live in now—if we are to develop and sustain ourselves as the kind of individuals who can bring into being the kind of enduring translocal publics that have the vision and the capacity to create *deep democracy* on national, regional, and worldwide levels. Any more-limited level of transformative aspiration is too limited because of the global connections that now link our lives, because of the realities of power, and because our moral imaginations project this full scope for the meaning of the ideal of democracy, if it is to have any meaning at all.

How are we to build such sustaining communities as hotbeds for deep democracy in these troubled, fast-changing times? *How* are we to raise up a "Public" or "publics" that link them? *How* are such translocal publics to reshape the social and institutional structures of our national protodemocracies to make them supportive rather than antagonistic to the full scope of the democratic project—building Dewey's "Great Community"?

These are the kinds of specific questions about our particular problem situation to which Dewey offered no general answers, believing that these must be discovered through a process of ongoing social inquiry, and agreed upon progressively as the meaning of experience and the results of intermediate transformative efforts unfold. Only such an *experimental method,* he argued, can be effective in guiding the transformation of historically unique and fluid problem situations. To attempt to apply some antecedent, universal set of fixed, noncontextual transformative principles is to assure failure and the frustration of hope. "The alternative to the adoption of an experimental method is not the attainment of greater security by adoption of fixed method (as dogmatists allege), but is merely to permit things to drift: to abdicate every attempt at direction and mastery" (Dewey 1932:350). Again, subsequent experience strongly suggests that Dewey is right about this. Twentieth century transformative struggles in various places—the Civil Rights Movement in the American South, the anti-Vietnam War movement in the United States and elsewhere, the Sandinista experiment in Nicaragua, the anti-apartheid movement in South Africa, the prodemocracy movement in Russia, the international women's movement, the global environmental movement, and countless others—have *valuable lessons to teach* about organization, strategy, tactics, and the difficult challenges of sustaining struggle in the midst of prolonged adversity. However, these lessons—properly understood—are *highly contextual,* and likely to be counterproductive if treated as timeless, abstract, universal tool-bits that can simply be reconnected in new ways, like Lego building blocks. So there is no real alternative to the experimental method for those who are serious about nurturing the growth of deep democracy and who understand clearly from the lessons of past experience that the process of struggle unfolds new challenges at every turn.

Nonetheless, Dewey's comments about various subjects related to an effective transformative agenda for our own times offer *valuable "leadings"* from an earlier stage of our ongoing struggle to actualize the practical implications of our widely shared impulse toward the ideal of the diverse democratic community. As Dewey himself suggested, the continuing philosophical value or "authority" of his or anyone else's ideas should be measured by the transformative energy and guidance they offer: "The authority of thought depends upon what it leads us to through directing the performance of operations" (Dewey 1929:110). Dewey's pragmatic analyses and transformative prescriptions offer valuable guidance concerning *five challenges that must be addressed* within contemporary democratic transformation agendas in all parts of the world, whatever their particular problem focuses may be: (1) educating for democracy; (2) connecting with each other in cross-difference coalitions and democracy-inspired communities; (3) conducting effective democratic social inquiry; (4) continuously redirecting the change process in midstream on the basis of experience; and (5) sustaining our democratic transformation efforts over time. Although Dewey's leadings on these subjects are incomplete and occasionally flawed, they offer important insights for the project of theoretically and practically reconstructing the deeply democratic community.

Democratic Education as Growth of the Individual, Culture, and Society

Dewey rightly regarded education as a key element within and measure of democracy. Rather than conceptualizing it as contemporary liberal theorist John Rawls and communitarian theorist Michael Walzer do—as an apparently external although primary social good that might be compared to and traded off against wealth—Dewey understood education as the *process of formation and reformation of free and flourishing individuals* who are capable of perennially nurturing and actively participating within the dynamic, ongoing development processes of deep democracy.[1] Just as Dewey's democratic ideal has no fixed and final content but rather unfolds its meaning in response to the growth of historical experience and understanding of a people whose form of life creates and is guided by it, so *the content of the educational processes* that serve as means to and measures of the democratic ideal must change in response to past experiences and new needs within emerging problem situations of the present and the foreseeable future. Dewey offers great insight for our contemporary transformative agenda in his treatment of education as a lifelong process shaped by the institutional agencies of business, government, religion, and the arts, as well as by the schools for which it is the acknowledged reason for existence. He wisely emphasizes *values contributed* as well as *received* through the process of social give-and-take in all of these institutional settings, as well as in the daily processes of community life, instead of conceptualizing education narrowly as the development of marketable skills and the mastery of a body of received knowledge. In addition, he offers us an important leading in his acknowledgment of *diversity* within the social contexts that such educational processes must recognize and effectively transform in order to promote individual growth and mutual flourishing.

However, Dewey's comments about the responsibilities of our schools in building democratic societies sometimes seem to suggest that diversity is *a problem to be overcome* rather than *a source of values to be preserved*. This impression or mistake must be reconstructed if we are to effectively and desirably develop our schools, like our other social institutions, as instruments of deep democracy. When Dewey published *Democracy and Education* in 1916, the regional, ethnic, and economic diversity of American society was already so great and so obviously important a factor within the problem situation to be transformed that it was necessarily the initial focus of his analysis of the school environment and of his prescription for democratically transforming it. In an early passage from that work, Dewey rightly recognizes the significance of group memberships in the formative process of individuals, but he seems to suggest that one's social group of origin is primarily a limiting factor that the schools must overcome if they are to fulfill their democratic mission.

> It is the office of the school environment to balance the various elements in the social environment, and to see to it that each individual gets an opportunity to *escape from the limitations of the social group in which he was born*, and to come into living contact with a broader environment. (Dewey 1916:24, emphasis mine)

Dewey's language here could be taken as demeaning to various social groups. However, if so, it is equally demeaning to *all* groups—including socially dominant groups—concerning the adequacy of the learning experience *any one* of them can offer in isolation from other social groups. As Jane Addams learned at Hull House, we all need the kind of *reflective deepening* that *respectful encounters with diverse others* can stimulate, thereby challenging us to overcome personal and cultural limitations in ways that lead to fuller individual development and to cooperative discovery of ways to create conditions for mutual flourishing. Generously reinterpreted in a way that offers a helpful leading, Dewey argues here that effective education requires experiences of *transformative reciprocity amidst diversity*.

In another passage from *Democracy and Education* that similarly requires careful (re)interpretation, Dewey prescribes a response to the fact of diversity that goes beyond broad exposure and balance in his call for creation of a "unity of outlook" brought about by the schools' "assimilative force." This might seem to be a call for the enforced homogeneity and loss of the multiplicity of differences that recent conservative critics of Dewey's democratic philosophy of education have advocated, and that postmodernist and cultural pluralist critics have decried.

In the olden times, the diversity of groups was largely a geographical matter. There were many societies, but each, within its own territory, was comparatively homogeneous. But with the development of commerce, transportation, inter-communication, and emigration, countries like the United States are composed of a combination of different groups with different traditional customs. It is this situation which has, perhaps more than any other one cause, forced the demand for an educational institution which shall provide something like *a homogeneous and balanced environment for the young.* Only in this way can the centrifugal forces set up by juxtaposition of different groups within one and the same political unit be counteracted. The intermingling in the school of youth of different races, differing religions, and unlike customs creates for all *a new and broader environment.* Common subject matter accustoms all to a *unity of outlook* upon a broader horizon than is visible to the members of any group while it is isolated. The *assimilative force* of the American public school is eloquent testimony to the efficacy of the common and balanced appeal. (Dewey 1916:25–26, emphases mine)

Although his choice of terms here like "homogeneity," "unity," and "assimilation" might seem to justify the fears of Dewey's postmodernist and cultural pluralist critics, a closer reading suggests that what he calls for is the growth of commonalities based on *shared knowledge and experience* amidst *persisting valued differences related to group memberships,* addressed in a cooperative, reciprocal way. Dewey calls for a consciously multicultural educational *environment,* if not a critically multicultural *curriculum* of the kind Alain Locke advocated. Nonetheless, the shared subject matter of Dewey's democratic school curriculum need not and should not ignore groups; rather, it should stimulate students to develop a broader outlook than any group has in isolation. Although some might suggest that Dewey's call for "a unity of outlook upon a broader horizon" necessarily implies erasure of diversity, because the school curriculum involves subject matter on which various groups disagree, *unity* of outlook need not mean *identity* of outlook. Instead, it can imply *a practical convergence* of differing, well-informed perspectives that stimulates creative individual thinking within a workable set of common understandings amidst remaining differences, especially concerning subjects in the humanities and social sciences—though the natural sciences, too, have shown themselves to house and to benefit from a range of differences in perspective in relation to shared problems of explanation and practical concern.

Why is *unity* so understood amidst *valued and balanced diversity* a desirable goal for the educative efforts of our schools? Because it prepares students to participate in *a democratic society's cooperative conversation,* which includes desirably differing perspectives and values within shared processes of social inquiry and community building that will democratically reshape the entire range of social institutions in ways that improve the mutual flourishing of each and all. Beyond its facticity, diversity has *epistemological* and *aesthetic* value. Why is it important for both the school curriculum and the school environment to critically acknowledge and sustain the groups themselves—albeit in constantly developing, dynamic forms? Because *group memberships* are a *natural and necessary part* of the formative process of *human individuals,* and because the *differing insights and values* that Dewey rightly treats as resources for the development of deep democracy cannot be *created* or *remembered* or *transformed* by individuals alone. Rather, the growth of individuals who have the creativity and courage to express their own transvaluations of traditional cultural values in response to new situations requires the supportive and cooperative effort of groups.

Dewey realistically acknowledges that students come from and will always live within complex, multigroup environments. Within this context, he understands the school as a special place for supporting the development of the kinds of *well-integrated, resilient individuals* who can cope effectively with and make positive contributions to the development of their complex society.

> The school has the function also of coordinating within the disposition of each individual the diverse influences of the various social environments into which he enters. One code prevails in the family; another, on the street; a third, in the workshop or store; a fourth, in the religious association. As a person passes from one of the environments to another, he is subjected to antagonistic pulls, and is in danger of being split into a being having different standards of judgment and emotion for different occasions. This danger imposes upon the school a steadying and integrating office. (Dewey 1916:26)

Dewey's discussion thus far rightly recognizes the *value discontinuities* among the various group- and institution-structured environments within which any individual must cope in real quasi-democratic societies, and it suggests that the *schools,* perhaps even more than families and churches, must be the place where these differing values and expectations are evaluated and *some working personal integration* achieved, so that an individual can function effectively when crossing the multiple borders of daily life.

Conservative critics would challenge the claim that schools can or should play this role in individual development, arguing that it should be left to families and churches, who are better positioned to replicate group values as integrative forces in personality. If the schools cannot be structured to convey the "right" or dominant cultural norms, in their view, they had better limit the scope of their related activities to teaching democratic tolerance for differences. However, *effective tolerance* cannot be taught without teaching about the *content of the differences* to be tolerated. This content cannot be taught *democratically* without being taught *sympathetically,* and it cannot be taught sympathetically without *acknowledgment and critical evaluation* of the painful confrontations, power-structured lived relationships, and experiences of deeply damaging oppression that these differences have led to historically, continuing into our own times. Thus, the conservative prescription for the development of integrated individual personalities does not include effective preparation for coping democratically with the real and often antagonistic group differences that living in a complex, pluralistic society entails.

Moreover, there is no good reason to think that even formally democratic societies' *present* cultural achievements, including the types of individual personalities they tend to shape, represent the *highest and final stage* of human development and, thus, that mere replication should be our goal for education. Instead, as Dewey suggests, we must realistically recognize the *shortcomings* along with the *achievements* of formally democratic societies; we must structure children's experiences in our schools to reflect both kinds of recognition, as well as our hopes for the future.

> The *reconstruction of experience* may be social as well as personal. For purposes of simplification we have spoken in the earlier chapters somewhat as if the education of the immature which fills them with the spirit of the social group to which they belong, were a sort of catching up of the child with the aptitudes and resources of the adult group. In *static societies,* societies which make the maintenance of established custom their measure of value, this conception applies in the main. But not in *progressive communities.* They endeavor to shape the experiences of the young so that instead of reproducing current habits, *better habits* shall be formed, and thus the future adult society be an *improvement* of their own. Men have long had some intimation of the extent to which education may be consciously used to eliminate obvious social evils through starting the young on paths which shall not produce these ills, and some idea of the extent in which education may be made an instrument of realizing the better hopes of men. *But we are doubtless far from realizing the potential efficacy of education as a constructive agency of improving society, from realizing that it represents not only a development of children and youth but also of the future society of which they will be the constituents.* (Dewey 1916:84–85, emphases mine)

Although both Dewey and his conservative critics recommend that our schools consciously attempt to influence the development of the characters and outlooks of children through the structure and content of the curriculum, an important difference between contemporary conservatives like William Bennett's and Allan Bloom's vision of *tradition-retaining schools* and Dewey's vision of *tradition-transforming schools* is their view of the kind of social future they understand the schools to be tools for shaping. In Bennett's and Bloom's vision, the schools are to be *agencies of cultural preservation of older and better ways of living* against the onslaught of fragmentation and disillusionment brought about by globalization's daily contact with cultural differences and technology's rapid disruption of patterns of doing things in the past. The schools are to reinforce the power of certain social groups, especially traditional two-parent, heterosexual, Christian, Eurocentric families, as well as the churches and sociopolitical organizations they rely on for support in their struggle for continuing economic and cultural dominance in the emerging new pattern of world relationships.[2] In Dewey's vision, the schools are to be *agencies of cultural as well as individual change toward new and better ways of living* that seek to build on, but go beyond, the achievements of the past. New technologies are to be made instruments of progressive social transformation, and the schools are to teach students their mastery so that they can be used as tools for fostering effective and democratic cooperation across group differences in the transformation process. As Dewey rightly suggests, to follow the conservative prescription is to use the schools to reinforce existing patterns of privilege and inequality, an implicit rejection of the feasibility or the desirability of *a deeper democracy* than the expert-administered, dominance-preserving forms the world has achieved in the past, which fail to satisfy the impulse toward individual and mutual flourishing of most of the world's population.

Even the job preparation focus founded on rote instruction in "basic skills" that is widely applauded now by spokespersons for the economically disadvantaged does not go far enough in preparing children to be *equal coparticipants in shaping a more democratic future.*

> *Democracy* cannot flourish where the chief influences in selecting subject matter of instruction are utilitarian ends narrowly conceived for the masses, and for the higher education of the few, the traditions of a specialized cultivated class. *The notion that the "essentials" of elementary education are the three R's mechanically treated, is based upon ignorance of the essentials needed for realization of democratic ideals.* Unconsciously it assumes that these ideals are unrealizable; it assumes that in the future, as in the past, getting a livelihood, "making a living," must signify for most men and women doing things which are not significant, freely chosen, and ennobling to those who do them; doing things which serve ends unrecognized by those engaged in them, carried on under the direction of others for the sake of pecuniary reward. . . . *A curriculum which acknowledges the social responsibilities of education must present situations where problems are relevant to the problems of living together, and where observation and information are calculated to develop social insight and interest.* (Dewey 1916:200, emphases mine)

As Dewey rightly argues here, a formal education that does *not* prepare students to be participants in and builders of deep democracy is an education that *perpetuates the unsatisfactory status quo*—and also deprives students of *the stimulation of the real, the knowledge of the different,* and *the richness of subject matter for lifelong reflection* that the world's diverse cultural traditions have brought into being. Subsequent thinkers about transformative education for deep democracy who have considered this question from the perspectives of variously disadvantaged groups within modern, formally democratic societies, including Alain Locke, Martin Luther King, Jr., Malcolm Shabazz, Paulo Freire, and many recent feminist theorists, have offered insightful arguments complementary to Dewey's concerning the need to *rethink pedagogy* so as to go beyond equal basic education and training for the existing job market to assure *effective preparation for creating new knowledge, new kinds of opportunities,* and *new institutional norms and structures.*

Nonetheless, postmodernist critics might regard both Dewey's allies and his conservative critics as equally wrong-headed in their belief that it is possible to sustain the kind of personal integration both visions call for. They might argue that it is desirable for any social institution to attempt to effect such an integration, because this would seem to require an authoritarian educational program guided by a preset ideological agenda. Dewey rightly replies that *deep democracy* involves *no ideological agenda,* but rather *grows experimentally* out of deep human impulses guided by reflection on experience.

> The development within the young of the attitudes and dispositions necessary to the continuous and progressive life of a society cannot take place by direct conveyance of beliefs, emotions, and knowledge. It takes place through the intermediary of the [social] environment. . . . It is truly educative in its effect in the degree in which an individual shares or participates in some conjoint activity. By doing his share in the associated activity, the individual appropriates the purpose which actuates it, becomes familiar with its methods and subject matters, acquires needed skill, and is saturated with its emotional spirit. (Dewey 1916:26)

Dewey argues that no authoritarian program could develop the kind of individuals who are capable of fostering deep democracy in our complex, fast-changing, pluralistic societies.

> The *deeper and more intimate educative formation of disposition* comes, without conscious intent, as the young gradually partake of the activities of the various groups to which they may belong. As a society becomes more complex, however, it is found necessary to provide a special social environment which shall especially look after nurturing the capacities of the immature. Three of the more important functions of this special environment are: *simplifying and ordering the factors* of the disposition it is wished to develop; *purifying and idealizing the existing social customs; creating a wider and better balanced environment* than that by which the young would be likely, if left to themselves, to be influenced. (Dewey 1916:27)

The last sentence of this passage may raise contemporary eyebrows, even among those who are sympathetic to what has gone before, because it involves *criticism and intentional transformative efforts* within the schools concerning *students' characters and outlooks,* concerning *the customs of the groups of which they are members,* and concerning *the larger environment* that influences their development. Contemporary Americans tend to regard individual personality as sacrosanct, to be shaped by parents if by anyone, and to regard any criticism of groups as necessarily involving disrespect or disloyalty to them. However, in addition to the widely acknowledged facts that many families are dysfunctional and many parents are utterly unprepared for child-rearing, it is important to recognize the facts that no family can or does raise children alone, and that children will inevitably be deeply influenced by their experience in the school environment within which they spend so much of their time, as well as by the larger social environment that unavoidably interpenetrates their experience of home and school.

Moreover, it is impossible to teach children even mathematics or a language without at the same time influencing their development of the personal discipline, critical skills, and creativity that mastery of such subjects requires. Likewise, it is impossible to teach students history or literature well without teaching them both to sympathize with and to critically evaluate the viewpoints of others who live in different circumstances than their own. In the process of undergoing these personal changes required for understanding the subject matter, students begin to develop the capacity and the motivation to analyze and evaluate their own groups' claims and values—although the widespread antidemocratic cultural imperative to uncritical group loyalty may stop them from actually doing so. However, Dewey's implicit suggestion here is that unless this process of *reconstructive cultural criticism* is allowed to *go forward* and is given *mature guidance*, students will not develop the skills and the confidence to apply their studies toward their ultimate purpose of preparing them to live effectively in a complex, fast-changing society while influencing its development in more deeply democratic directions. The alternative to their *coping effectively* is personal misery and despair. The alternative to their *taking an active, democratic role* as citizens is, as Dewey suggested, social drift invisibly steered by those who have the power to shape the future toward their own less-democratic ends.

However, even if these passages from *Democracy and Education* are (re)interpreted to imply that the goals our schools should strive to achieve are *broadened exposure, balanced diversity, constructive convergence in perspectives, guided integration of students' individual characters,* and *thoughtful criticism of group traditions,* Dewey gives us no guidance about *how* our schools are to achieve these worthy goals. Thus, appreciatively yet critically re-reading Dewey reveals another site for contemporary reconstruction of the meaning and practical leadings of his ideal of the diverse democratic community. Without *an effective method for assuring balance and protecting diversity* within unity, the norms of the dominant group in a protodemocracy seem likely to shape a learning environment that aims for homogeneity on the dominant model, even if it is marginally modified by an unspecific call for balance. Moreover, Dewey's concept of educational "assimilation" seems to ignore the importance of maintaining and valuing the *separate, group-focused spaces in community life* within which children can rest and "regroup" at regular intervals as they live through the process by which a society tries to create balanced diversity in its shared schools. It also overlooks the importance of formal and informal educational experiences in such separate spaces for keeping those group experiences alive that are to be brought into balance in the schools. Likewise, Dewey's goal of "purifying and idealizing existing customs" can sound positively dangerous, though what he seems to mean by it is something Alain Locke and like-minded culturally pluralistic democratic theorists would agree with (i.e., transforming absolutisms, parochialisms, and group biases into more reflective, sociohistorically accurate and open-minded attitudes guided by the democratic ideal). Dewey's remarks about the democratic ideal in *Reconstruction in Philosophy, The Public and Its Problems, Ethics,* and elsewhere show that he is aware of these problems and serious about the importance of *cooperative reciprocity* among the differing value contributions of diverse groups within democratic life. However, Dewey proposes no method for achieving *respectful, reciprocal listening and learning amidst diversity* in our schools and our other educative social institutions. This is why Locke's proposal, discussed in Chapter Four, to adopt the method of "critical relativism" in designing school environments, curricula, and teaching methods, is so important.

Perhaps the most valuable leading from Dewey's thinking about democratic education is the insight that the formal education of youth in the schools is just a small, though crucially important, element within *the larger, lifelong process of personal growth* influenced by educative experience within social institutions and relationships of all kinds.

> In its contrast with the ideas both of unfolding of latent powers from within, and of formation from without, whether by physical nature or by the cultural products of the past, *the ideal of growth results in the conception that education is a constant reorganizing or reconstructing of experience.* It has all the time an immediate end, and so far as activity is educative, it reaches that end—the direct transformation of the quality of experience. *Infancy, youth, adult life,—all stand on the same educative level* in the sense that what is really learned at any and every stage of experience constitutes the value of that experience, and in the sense that it is the chief business of life at every point to make living thus contribute to an enrichment of its own perceptible meaning.
>
> *We thus reach a technical definition of education: It is that reconstruction or reorganization of experience which adds to the meaning of experience, and which increases ability to direct the course of subsequent experience.* (Dewey 1916:82, emphases mine)

The educative experiences of adult life, especially those that occur outside schools and universities, are generally ignored in purely formal conceptions of democracy, but they are the most important focus for a transformative theory of deep democracy.

Without the *progressive reformation of adult outlooks, values, habits, and patterns of relationships,* processes will never be set in motion through which the democratic transformation of the wide variety of social institutions, including our schools, will occur. As long as adult Americans and like-minded others hold fast to our "don't try to change me" approach to maintaining our self-understandings and our social locations, we will continue to cling to our ossified cultural and religious norms, our historical patterns of racial and cultural antagonisms, our dysfunctional gender expectations, and our other parochialisms of all kinds. We will fear the future and fight the change process instead of considering how we might make things better and how we might benefit through conjoining our energies with those of others whose efforts create emerging possibilities. We will continue to think, as we have traditionally, that growth is for children, and adult integrity is the ability to remain unchanged in the face of the onslaught of experience: as Frank Sinatra sang, "I did it my way."

Dewey wisely suggests that this conception of adult life rests on a lie that makes it neither feasible nor desirable. We cannot help but change, regardless of whether we acknowledge this process, as we live through the stages of adult life experience with the specific particularities of their slings and arrows. We do not serve ourselves or the future well by refusing to adapt to new times and circumstances in ways that contribute to our own ability to participate in shaping them for the better. The wiser course is to regard ourselves as growing beings throughout our entire lives, to acknowledge the educative effects of the institutions and patterns of relationships that structure our adult experience, and to choose an active role in shaping those educational situations to make them support the development of our best potentials within patterns of mutual flourishing.

Dewey does not advise us in detail about how to be effective in transforming the social institutions of adult life so as to assure that our education within them actually does support the development of our best potentials. His comments on this subject tend to focus on individuals' actions and institutions' effects on individuals, yet twentieth-century experience has shown us that prophetic individuals acting in isolation are unlikely to succeed in changing these institutions, and are more likely to be removed from them as obstacles to their smooth, ongoing operation. However, we can draw on Dewey's lived example, as well as the insights of King, Locke, and complementary democratic change theorists in reconstructing Dewey's leadings to locate effective activist individuals within democracy-inspired, cross-difference coalitions and self-educating transformative communities.

Cross-Difference Coalitions and
Diverse, Deeply Democratic Communities

Jane Addams helped Dewey understand how the educative experience of participating in *democratic transformative communities of lived experience and cooperative effort* offers adults the opportunity to become more fully themselves while transforming their thinking, their habits, and their patterns of relationship in ways that contribute to their capacity to influence the democratic reconstruction of larger social institutions. As Dewey suggests in *Reconstruction in Philosophy,* playing an active role in directing the groups and institutions that deeply influence our lives liberates some of our highest and best human potentials, and thus constitutes the final stage of adult education. Moreover, the democratic participation of diverse individuals with liberated capacities assures the most insightful and effective direction of cooperative efforts.

> The best guarantee of collective efficiency and power is *liberation and use of the diversity of individual capacities* in initiative, planning, foresight, vigor and endurance. Personality must be educated, and personality cannot be educated by confining its operations to technical and specialized things, or to the less important relationships of life. Full education comes only when there is a responsible share on the part of each person, in proportion to capacity, in shaping the aims and policies of the social groups to which he belongs. This fact fixes *the significance of democracy.* It cannot be conceived as a sectarian or racial thing nor as a consecration of some form of government which

has already attained constitutional sanction. *It is but a name for the fact that human nature is developed only when its elements take part in directing things which are common, things for the sake of which men and women form groups*—families, industrial companies, governments, churches, scientific associations and so on. The principle holds as much of one form of associa-tion, say in industry and commerce, as it does in government (Dewey 1920:199–200, emphases mine)

Such diverse democratic communities of lived experience and cooperative effort need not concern or include every aspect of their members' lives, thus being mutually exclusive. In fact, as Dewey's list of examples suggests, we all are members of *multiple groups* that could be transformed into *intersecting, diverse, democracy-guided communities* that reflect differing aspects of our lives: ethnic groups, religious groups, families, neighborhoods, professional associations and unions, cooperative organizations that care for the poor or that restore our natural environment, sports teams, arts collectives, and so on. What is important in the patterns of relationships within and between these differing groups—if they are to operate as *democratic* communities in Dewey's deep sense—is *not* that they somehow operate without functional hierarchy, or that they follow Robert's Rules of Order in their decision processes, but rather that they involve *all* of their diverse members in directing and carrying out their activities in ways that stimulate the development of *each* member's gifts and capacities, building a sense of *deep, satisfying connection* with each other while achieving optimal results from cooperative efforts.

Such diverse, deeply democratic communities have different outcomes for their members and for the larger society than do *cross-difference coalitions* that focus on a narrow set of issues or problems for a limited period of time, though these also can play an important role in the education of their participants as well as in the transformation of the particular unacceptable conditions that brought them into being. Cross-difference coalitions can be very effective ways to achieve *limited public transformational objectives*. One of their desirable features is that they minimize the drain of energy from cooperative effort across unreconstructed historical barriers and power-structured patterns of differences that have created acrimony and ignorance between groups. Coalition-style cross-difference contacts focusing on a common objective offer a way to partially limit their members' exposure to emotional harm. They also can be *educative to a certain degree* for those whose privilege or whose anger has allowed them to remain ignorant and insensitive, although they are prone to involving long-term activists in time- and hope-consuming calls to play the "teacher" in yet another remedial education situation—or equally depressing, to play the "student" yet again for a new "teacher," after one has developed beyond the stereotypical limitations of one's group(s) that rightly call for such remedial education.

However, the *fuller kind of personal growth* Dewey referred to as the measure of democracy and the prerequisite for significant institutional change takes *time, structure,* and the *ongoing support of others.* One of the differences between coalitions and communities is that, though both focus on solving problems in the social environment, *coalitions do not* include ongoing commitment of the members to each others' individual growth as part of their agenda, whereas *communities do.* Because of this, communities have the potential for greater contributions to the liberation of their members' potentials than do coalitions, and their deeper ties give them greater ability to withstand the strains of uncertainty and even outright adversity over a longer period of time. Thus, cross-difference coalitions alone cannot achieve deep democracy; communities of some kind must play an important role in the transformation process. But what role? And what kind of communities?

Howard McGary, Bernice Johnson Reagon, and other democratic coalition theorists have recognized the importance of our human need for home communities that can heal, nurture, and appropriately challenge us, especially if our cross-difference coalition memberships involve power-disadvantaged struggle.[3] This is why they call for participation in both *commonality-focused communities* and *cross-difference coalitions.* It is important to realize, however, that even commonality-focused ethnic communities of lived experience, like the historically embattled African American community in its various manifestations, embody significant differences—class, gender, religion, sexual preference, region, and generational differences—that can become sites for simply replicating other unjust power disparities in the larger society unless they are brought to a level of awareness and respect in reconstructed understandings of the community as formed out of *commonalities amidst diversity.*

Diversity is inescapable today—and in reality, it always has been. What is new is the deeper and more extensive level of our daily exposure to the significance of diversity. Cross-difference coalitions can play a crucial role in preparing individuals and groups to participate in diverse democratic communities. They also contribute effectively to the transformation processes that will make the larger society more hospitable to the birth of *diverse, democracy-inspired, self-educating communities* in a wide range of areas of social life. Such communities must come into being if adult individuals are to achieve the full education of their highest and best powers while building up the soil to support the growth of a "Public" or translocal publics that can democratically redirect present institutional patterns of technology-assisted power and purpose within the national and global institutions whose influence interpenetrates all other levels of our human experience. Therefore, in addition to transitional and limited-purpose cross-difference *coalitions,* progressively more diverse and democratic *communities of daily experience* must become significant elements of our adult educative process if we are to develop our full potentials and, at the same time, to become agents of deeply democratic institutional change.

Some critics might question the feasibility of developing such diverse democratic communities of daily experience, given the power of existing, less than deeply democratic social institutions, group traditions, and personal habits. Dewey argued in *Democracy and Education* that if a society deserves the label "democratic" at all, it allows for the active, equal participation of its members and assures them the lifelong educational opportunities that prepare them to cooperatively effect necessary changes in its institutions, even if it does not yet entirely satisfy the democratic ideal.

> A society which makes provision for participation in its good of all its mem
> bers on equal terms and which secures flexible readjustment of its institu-
> tions through interaction of the different forms of associated life is *in so far
> democratic.* Such a society must have a type of education which gives indi-
> viduals a personal interest in social relationships and control, and the habits
> of mind which secure social changes without introducing disorder. (Dewey
> 1916:105, emphasis mine)

The foregoing argument suggests that a society will be able to meet these tests for everyone only if it supports a certain character and quality of community life (i.e., if it supports the emergence and functioning of diverse democratic communities). Even limited reflection suggests that existing "democratic" societies meet these tests only formally, and not in all areas of social life. These tests cannot be satisfied merely by allowing nonfelon adult citizens to vote for political decision makers whose actions are reported to their constituents by profit-oriented news media, and by assuring their children at least the minimal education that will enable them to participate in the electoral process. In historical context, these are wonderful achievements, but they are not sufficient to justify the claim that such societies are "democratic" even in Dewey's restricted sense. Are our existing, long-term "formal" democracies *sufficiently democratic* to allow the growth of the kinds of diverse, democratic communities of experience in daily life that can progressively transform them into deeper democracies? Experience-based hope suggests that the answer is yes—but it will not be easy, especially in aspects of our shared form of life that involve group relationships within nonlocal government and within major corporations.

The most hospitable environments for the growth of diverse democratic communities are likely to be small, local, and limited in their present social power. Such environments already exist, offering individuals various opportunities for the kinds of personal growth that prepares them to tackle transformative processes in less-hospitable climates by drawing strength from these diverse and democratic local communities. Citizen–activists can cooperatively interlink such local communities into coalitions that can, over time, develop deeper connections. Their task will be formidable, especially as the meanings of deep democracy become more apparent to those who believe they will be disadvantaged by it, changing their current lip service to "democracy" into active opposition.

Even this anticipatible opposition can be overcome, however, if diverse and deeply democratic local communities and their allied cross-difference coalitions can undertake the kind of *cooperative social inquiry* that shows that the *efficiency, stability,* and *mutual flourishing* associated with *a deeper realization of democracy* offers *desirable advantages* over its alternatives, including more limited formal democracy. In addition to its importance for this persuasive task, such cooperative social inquiry is necessary to diverse democratic communities and cross-difference coalitions, both as a source of information for ongoing and prospective democratic decision making, and as a spur to the kind of individual growth that makes intelligent communication across differences increasingly possible. Dewey's comments about the importance of the first of these two rationales for a new, transformative kind of social inquiry offer valuable insights, but his account of how such inquiry should proceed is distorted by his failure to take adequate account of the second: the way in which the participation of ordinary citizens in the processes of a more deeply democratic kind of social inquiry educates them while drawing necessary epistemic contributions from them. Therefore, Dewey's partially insightful leadings on social inquiry must be reconstructed by drawing on both the democratic ideal and the lessons of contemporary transformative praxis.

Intelligent Communication within Democratic Transformative Social Inquiry

Dewey persuasively argued that effective communication of experience can make it shared and thereby available for intelligent use in social inquiry. In contrast with liberal individualists who treat personal experience as ultimately private and unshareable, Dewey argued in concert with William James that our practical connections with others through our shared projects and activities can make our partners' particular experiences, once communicated, part of *a general fund of experience* in which all of us share, though in different ways. Even the experiences of persons remote from us in place and time can become part of our own experience if they are effectively communicated to us. Thus, they can become part of the information and even the evaluative framework we use to assess our own situation and to make choices about it.

> Active connections with others are such an intimate and vital part of our own concerns that it is impossible to draw sharp lines, such as would enable us to say, "Here my experience ends; there yours begins." In so far as we are partners in common undertakings, the things which others communicate to us as the consequences of their particular share in the enterprise blend at once into the experience resulting from our own special doings. The ear is as much an organ of experience as the eye or hand; the eye is available for reading reports of what happens beyond its horizon. Things remote in space and time affect the issue of our actions quite as much as things which we can smell and handle. They really concern us, and consequently, any account of them which assists us in dealing with things at hand falls within personal experience. (Dewey 1916:194)

To the extent that symbolic systems are shared, Dewey argued, experience can be shared, contributing to individuals' growth of understanding and to a community's effectiveness in analyzing, assessing, and making choices about a common future. Dewey draws no important value distinction between direct experience and indirect experience shared through the medium of language. Both become part of the fund of experience on which we can and do draw, and each influences the other. In fact, he argued, without drawing on shared symbolic systems and the wide range of indirect experiences they communicate, one's personal experience would remain very narrow, incomparable, and inarticulable, even to oneself, and we would have virtually no power to shape the conditions of our lives.

> Much of our experience is indirect; it is dependent upon signs which intervene between the things and ourselves, signs which stand for or represent the former. . . . All language, all symbols, are implements of an indirect experience; in technical language the experience which is procured by their means is "mediated." It stands in contrast with an immediate, direct experience, something in which we take part vitally and at first hand, instead of through the intervention of representative media. . . . The scope of personal, vitally direct experience is very limited. If it were not for the intervention of agencies for representing absent and distant affairs, our experience would remain almost on the level of that of the brutes. (Dewey 1916:240–241)

This is why the *development of skills in using shared symbolic systems* at a high level of mastery is such an important element of lifelong democratic education. Likewise, this is why *broad familiarity with texts* that communicate widely differing experiences is so important. Finally, this is why *communication of experience within and between communities* that seek to understand and to transform their shared situation is so important: experience is the basis of *knowledge,* which is an important component of *social power.* Drawing intelligently on a wide-ranging pool of shared knowledge, a community or a coalition can understand the problems it faces and make feasible and desirable decisions together about their course of collaborative action. Social inquiry is the process of filling and sharing that pool of knowledge *intelligently.*

As Dewey uses the concept, *"intelligence" in social inquiry* is an approach to thinking that combines care in observation and analysis with a set of character virtues required for balanced judgment. Because, as was argued previously, the social contexts are constantly changing within which we make choices about what to do to transform our problem situation, to respond to our inner democratic imperative, and to create conditions that allow more individual and mutual flourishing, there can be no prefixed set of moral rules or transformative strategies that we can apply universally to get optimal or even minimally acceptable results without careful analysis and judgment.

> We cannot seek or attain health, wealth, learning, justice or kindness in general. Action is always specific, concrete, individualized, unique. And consequently judgments as to acts to be performed must be similarly specific. (Dewey 1920:175)

Intelligent judgment is the key to responsible and effective action, whether individual or collective, and it requires the kind of *pragmatic processes of inquiry* that reveal and antecedently weigh the consequences of specific choices.

> Let us . . . follow the pragmatic rule, and in order to discover the meaning of the idea ask for its consequences. Then it surprisingly turns out that the primary significance of the unique and morally ultimate character of the concrete situation is to transfer the weight and burden of morality to *intelligence*. It does not destroy responsibility; it only locates it. A moral situation is one in which judgment and choice are required antecedently to overt action. The *practical meaning of the situation*—that is to say the action needed to satisfy it—is not self-evident. It has to be searched for. There are conflicting desires and alternative apparent goods. What is needed is to find the right course of action, the right good. Hence, *inquiry* is exacted: observation of the detailed makeup of the situation; analysis into its diverse factors; clarification of what is obscure; discounting of the more insistent and vivid traits; tracing the consequences of the various modes of action that suggest themselves; regarding the decision reached as hypothetical and tentative until the anticipated or supposed consequences which led to its adoption have been squared with actual consequences. This *inquiry* is *intelligence*. (Dewey 1920:173, emphasis mine)

Intelligence in inquiry, Dewey says, requires a careful process of information gathering and analysis, and its perspective is characteristically guided by *a set of moral and intellectual virtues* that are universal rather than culturally narrow, though the ways in which they operate may vary. The importance of such virtues is revealed by considering why judgment sometimes fails.

> Our moral failures go back to some weakness of disposition, some absence of sympathy, some one-sided bias that makes us perform the judgment of the concrete case carelessly or perversely. Wide sympathy, keen sensitiveness, persistence in the face of the disagreeable, balance of interests enabling us to undertake the work of analysis and decision intelligently are the distinctively moral traits. (Dewey 1920:173–174)

These intelligence-guiding virtues, like practical skills in the processes of information gathering and analysis, are necessary prerequisites for the kind of effective social inquiry that yields insights that can guide coalitions and communities in a democratic transformation process. Developing these virtues and skills, then, must be important goals of the lifelong process of democratic education. *Who* needs to develop and to employ these virtues and skills of intelligence in social inquiry: a few representative, democratically minded expert social scientists, or whole communities? *How* do the participants in social inquiry, whoever they are, need to *communicate* in order to be effective in fulfilling their purposes?

The best answer to these questions is one that reconstructively combines Dewey's and Addams's answers while going beyond them: *any effective approach to social inquiry* guided by the ideal of deep democracy must involve both *expert, democratically minded social scientists* and *the whole diverse democratic communities* of which they understand themselves and are understood as members, communicating fully, freely, and intelligently with each other as they carry out differing roles within the social inquiry process, and communicating their results persuasively yet open-mindedly to others. Dewey's recommendation in *The Public and Its Problems* of expert inquiry combined with effective mass communication, however artistically presented, is a top-down, hierarchical change strategy that does not give adequate expression to Dewey's insight in the *Ethics* that the ideal of democracy requires that each individual contribute as well as receive values in a mutual give-and-take. Although some of Dewey's most pithy and suggestive comments about the need for a new, practical approach to social inquiry that will help us to promote human flourishing seem to suggest that inquirers must be experts, his theoretical description of the new inquiry process itself is fully compatible with participation by a much wider community. In addition, there are good reasons to think that *this wider participation is epistemologically and morally necessary for optimal results.*

In an insightful passage from *Reconstruction in Philosophy,* Dewey explains why general, systematic knowledge of an expert nature about various kinds of problem situations is a valuable but insufficient guide to inquiry and choice of transformative action in problem situations that have a moral dimension, as do all of those in which our interest responds to the democratic impulse.

> *Moral* goods and ends exist only when something has to be done. The fact that something has to be done proves that there are deficiencies, evils in the existent situation. This ill is just the specific ill that it is. It never is an exact duplicate of anything else. Consequently the good of the situation has to be discovered, projected and attained on the basis of the exact defect and trouble to be rectified. It cannot intelligently be injected into the situation from without. Yet it is the part of wisdom to compare different cases, to gather together the ills from which humanity suffers, and to generalize the corresponding goods into classes. . . . But the value of this systematization is intellectual or analytic. Classifications suggest possible traits to be on the lookout for in studying a particular case; they suggest methods of action to be tried in removing the inferred causes of ill. They are tools of insight; their value is in promoting an individualized response in the individual situation. (Dewey 1920:176–177, emphasis in original)

The individual problem situation on which our democratic transformative interest focuses, Dewey suggests here, always calls for new information to help us arrive at its unique transformative solution. General, systematic knowledge about other related situations may suggest what kind of new information we need to look for and what kinds of remedies may or may not be effective. Thus, as Dewey might suggest to Addams, academic social scientific knowledge may be helpful in guiding the particular problem-focused inquiry processes that it should exist to serve. However, general knowledge does not antecedently map particular, specific problems, which always contain new elements, Addams might reply; nor is it an adequate guide to solving them. Rather, new situation-specific information must be gathered, organized, and evaluated. A new solution must be discovered through inductive processes of inquiry that go beyond what academic experts can deduce from general, systematic knowledge.

How to gather and assess the relevant new information and *how to generate a uniquely appropriate solution* are the key methodological questions for practical transformative processes. We need to discover *effective, creative methods of social inquiry,* understood as an art rather than a prescriptive body of general knowledge, as many think of the social sciences.

> Morals is not a catalogue of acts nor a set of rules to be applied like drugstore prescriptions or cook-book recipes. The need in morals is for specific methods of inquiry and of contrivance: Methods of inquiry to locate difficulties and evils; methods of contrivance to form plans to be used as working hypotheses in dealing with them. And *the pragmatic import of the logic of individualized situations,* each having its own irreplaceable good and principle, is to transfer the attention of theory from preoccupation with general conceptions to the problem of developing effective methods of inquiry. (Dewey 1920:177, emphasis mine)

Because the applied context of social inquiry so understood is always within community life, those who participate in the relevant community life will always have something vitally important to contribute, not only as *sources of information,* but also as *participants in inquiry and in problem-solving implementation.* Social scientists' computer modeling cannot replace citizen participation because community members are, among other things, bearers of specific, direct experience as well as particular projects, plans, and preferences that shape their motivations and their actual behavior.[4] Of course, some people must play the role of gathering and coordinating dispersed information from various community members, but the information gatherers alone cannot determine whether they "got it right." Moreover, these human bodies of lived experience and intentions are *interactively dynamic* in the real world. When people broaden their pool of experience with effectively communicated information, they are likely to *reinterpret their direct experience* and to *alter their intentions somewhat* to take into account the fact that they live in relational networks of action and effects. Thus, the invaluable dispersed information that community members offer to the process of social inquiry is not a stable block of data, but rather *a dynamically changing quantum of intellectual and practical energy.*

The only way to gather sufficiently current information and to know what it means, especially in interactive contexts of living experience, is to keep community members actively participating in the inquiry process. Such inquirer–actor participation implies, of course, that disinterestedly "objective" transformative social inquiry is impossible. Nonetheless, *well-informed, multipositional, community-based social inquiry* is desirable and possible if the inquiry process is structured by *effective organization and intelligent communication* among citizen-participants who are supported by "expert" sources of general knowledge.

In addition to its *epistemological* advantages, the *moral* and *political* advantages of community-inclusive social inquiry are clear: by the time they need to reach an action-guiding decision, participants have already broadened their pool of experience to include the shared experience of others, accommodated themselves to one another in a more realistic and more democratic reformation of their direct experience and of their previous plans, and developed a clearer sense of the particular problem and of its feasible solutions. Thus, they are less likely to engage in uninformed, polarized thinking and to form alienated NIMBY ("not in my back yard") groups. Once they make a decision together, they have a shared stake in its success, and thus are likely to act in ways that will promote mutual benefit.[5]

Although academic specialists can make invaluable contributions to the processes of community-based social inquiry that deep democracy requires, they need not direct them, nor need they be passive, "objective" observers. If they try to shape the social inquiry processes to conform to their preset notions of experimental procedure and to control the course of events, they may squeeze out the creative, growth-spurring, directive role of citizen-participants while reasoning without their widely dispersed, experience-based knowledge, which is necessary to any inquiry's effectiveness. However, academic social scientists can play the role of *consultants* who offer the resource of their general, systematic knowledge as well as their suggestions about methods of inquiry that may prove useful. They can help to shape the process without intruding themselves into dominance over it, they can analyze and assess the results, and they can publish the results for the edification of other transformative communities. These are useful and important roles, though they move "experts" from the center to the background of problem-focused democratic social inquiry.

Although Dewey's remarks about democratically reconceptualized social sciences focus on these more traditional academic activities of observation, analysis, and publication of results, and thus seem to imply traditional "expert" direction of inquiry, his prescription for *an alternative experimental methodology* is fully compatible with *a community-based approach to social inquiry* that includes social scientists in the consulting and commenting roles here described.

> When we say that thinking and beliefs should be experimental, not absolutistic, we have then in mind a certain logic of method, not, primarily, the carrying on of experimentation like that of laboratories. First, that those concepts, general principles, theories and dialectical developments which are indispensable to any systematic knowledge be shaped and tested as tools of inquiry. Secondly, that policies and proposals for social action be treated as working hypotheses, not as programs to be rigidly adhered to and executed. They will be experimental in the sense that they will be entertained subject to constant and well-equipped observation of the consequences they entail

when acted upon, and subject to ready and flexible revision in the light of ob-served consequences. The social sciences, if these two stipulations are ful-filled, will then be an apparatus for conducting investigation, and for recording and interpreting (organizing) its results. The apparatus will no longer be taken to be itself knowledge, but will be seen to be intellectual means of making discoveries of phenomena having social import and under-standing their meaning. (Dewey 1927:361–362)

When these remarks are reconstructed to apply to the community-based inquiry processes that the development of deep democracy requires, these leadings from Dewey on experimental method are very helpful. They suggest the importance of *general, systematic knowledge* about the lessons of other inquiry processes as a resource for effective design of *a uniquely appropriate inquiry process* to address a particular community's problem situation—whether this knowledge is supplied by consulting social scientists or retrieved from libraries and the worldwide telecommunications web by educated, interested, and computer-skilled citi-zen–participants. If resultant community-based inquiry processes guided by Dewey's insights about the pragmatic method do not fit some preset assumptions that makes their results mechanically commensurable with each other, and thus easily interrelatable for social scientific analysis that contributes smoothly to the growth of general, systematic social "knowledge" on the traditional model, so much the worse for the traditional model, and so much greater and more interest-ing the challenge to social scientists. Dewey's emphasis on the importance of flexible revision of approaches and strategies that were originally formulated in hypothetical rather than absolute terms is directly relevant to community-based inquiry, and some of the successes to be discussed in Chapters Six and Seven of this book show its importance. Moreover, as is discussed later in this chapter, Dewey offers wise guidance about how to conceptualize ongoing revision within such a flexible, hypothetical approach to social inquiry.

Of course, no one would have the time, interest, and ability to participate in a daily directive role within each of the social inquiry processes that are needed to guide the multiplicity of intersecting communities of which they are a member. However, active participants in a democratic social inquiry process do not all need to play the same role or to be equally active. If trusted leaders and core par-ticipants in a process of democratic social inquiry are representative of a com-munity's diversity, and if they communicate often and effectively with less-active participants, a sense of openness and common cause will be maintained, and these other participants can effectively play a more active role when needed or desired. Moreover, once a decision is made and a course of transformative action is undertaken by a community, most of its members need only do their various agreed-upon parts during the implementation process, leaving someone in the caretaker role of keeping the connections well-oiled and sounding the alarm if "things go off the rails" before the scheduled time to revisit the question of whether the initial solution was effective or must be revised. Thus, one may be a *leader* or a *core activist* in one diverse democratic community as it responds to a particular problem situation by creating a process of conjoint inquiry and decision, while being *a less active but still valuable participant* in the problem-solving social inquiry processes of several other communities that intersect in one's life. By living in this way, one can send down *multiple stabilizing roots* into differing democratic communities of lived experience that engage and support different parts of one's being, while growing in understanding, skills, and Dewey's democratic intellectual and moral virtues. If such processes of social inquiry have even limited success, they can strengthen one's hope in and responsiveness to the democratic impulse, teach one a great deal, and provide the context out of which some of life's greatest comforts and pleasures emerges: *true friendships.*

Only those problem-solving projects that are very limited in scope are likely to have even limited success, however, unless effective communication processes for linking many small communities into *coalitions or larger publics* can be developed. Although Dewey's call in *The Public and Its Problems* for *communicating with a wider audience* through newspapers as well as books and scholarly journals seems to focus on "experts," his remarks imply an active role for other community members within the processes of social inquiry and communication.

> A genuine social science would manifest its reality in the daily press, while learned books and articles supply and polish tools of inquiry. But *the inquiry which alone can furnish knowledge as a precondition of public judgments must be contemporary and quotidian.* (Dewey 1927:348, emphasis mine)

Ideally, the mass media would seem to be highly desirable and optimally effective means for "expert" social scientists to share their general knowledge and their suggestions about problems and methods of inquiry, and also for "inquiring communities" to communicate their results. Dewey, like Marcuse, recognized the difficulty of doing so through conglomerate-owned, for-profit newspapers, at least until this kind of information begins to contribute to their sales. If newspapers, books, journals, and alternative mass-communications media can be so employed, democratic social scientists might make effective "communications officers" to interlink the problems, inquiry processes, decisions, and results of the transformative efforts of multiple communities with one another, thereby broadening their experience and their spheres of influence.

However, Dewey is overly reliant on the communication skills of social science "experts" to shape the form and content of citizen conversations.

> The essential need . . . is the improvement of the methods and conditions of debate, discussion and persuasion. That is the problem of the public. . . . This improvement depends essentially upon freeing and perfecting the processes of inquiry and of dissemination of their conclusions. *Inquiry, indeed, is a work which devolves upon experts.* But their expertness is not shown in framing and executing policies, but in discovering and making known the facts upon which the former depend. They are technical experts in the sense that scientific investigators and artists manifest expertise. *It is not necessary that the many should have the knowledge and skill to carry on the needed investigations; what is required is that they have the ability to judge of the bearing of the knowledge supplied by others upon common concerns.* (Dewey 1927:365, emphases mine)

The only reason for Dewey's reliance on "experts" to conduct social inquiry and to broadcast its results is a lack of confidence in the quality of skills, moral and intellectual virtues, and knowledge base that citizen participants can be expected to bring to and develop within collaborative problem-solving processes. This lack of confidence may reflect Dewey's ongoing conversations with scientists and his interest in redirecting their efforts and revaluing their results. It may also reflect the influence of his ongoing debate with Walter Lippman, which may have shifted him toward a position of "ordinary citizens are educable" instead of the stronger claim that they have valuable experiences to share and the potential to communicate them intelligently.[6] However, there is no good reason for such a lack of confidence today, given rising educational levels, a widespread hunger for community, and the success of some recent experiments in citizen participation in transformative social inquiry that can serve as the basis for future, wider successes, as is discussed in Chapter Seven.

Moreover, *new communications technologies* of various kinds, especially the worldwide web, are now connecting *a broad population of nonacademics,* who may be able to use these technologies to cooperatively communicate the results of community-based social inquiry with each other without the mediation of "expert" social scientists. As Dewey rightly suggested, it is *the quality of citizen-to-citizen conversations* that is of crucial significance in the development of deep democracy, in contrast with *the expert-to-expert conversations* that largely shape public policies in formally democratic countries today. Daily conversations are even more significant in shaping people's attitudes and ideas than is the printed page, and it is those attitudes and ideas that will determine the future of democracy: "formal," deep, or merely a historic memory.

> The winged words of conversation have a vital import lacking in the fixed and frozen words of written speech. Systematic and continuous inquiry into all the conditions which affect association and their dissemination in print is a precondition of the creation of a true public. But it and its results are but tools after all. Their final actuality is accomplished in face-to-face relationships by means of direct give and take. (Dewey 1927:371)

Participation in community-based inquiry processes and in communicating about them can develop in people the kind of intelligence that Dewey, like Emerson before him, regarded as of critical significance in determining whether the democratic impulse will achieve its full realization.

> *That expansion and reenforcement of personal understanding and judgment by the cumulative and transmitted intellectual wealth of the community which may render nugatory the indictment of democracy drawn on the basis of the ignorance, bias and levity of the masses, can be fulfilled only in the relations of personal intercourse in the local community.* The connections of the ear with vital and out-going thought and emotion are immensely closer and more varied than those of the eye. Vision is a spectator; hearing is a participator. Publication is partial and the public which results is partially in-

formed and formed until the meanings it purveys pass from mouth to mouth. *There is no limit to the liberal expansion and confirmation of limited personal intellectual endowment which may proceed from the flow of social intelligence when that circulates by word of mouth from one to another in the communications of the local community.* That and that only gives reality to public opinion. We lie, as Emerson said, in the lap of an immense intelligence. But that intelligence is dormant and its communications are broken, inarticulate and faint until it possesses the local community as its medium. (Dewey 1927:371–372, emphases mine)

Clearly, Dewey shared Emerson's belief that *the potential of democracy* depends upon *the potential of ordinary citizens* to develop their intelligence to a high degree, to communicate effectively with one another within their communities of daily life, and to participate actively in developing wise public policies. He believed that such communities must be given new life and character if individuals are to develop their potential intelligence through their active and directive democratic role within them.

Nonetheless, by the concluding pages of *The Public and Its Problems,* Dewey had reasoned himself into a puzzle: *How are revitalized communities of daily experience to raise up a democratic, effective public with the power and the insight to transform larger social institutions?* This is the same puzzle that, considered from a different angle, continued to perplex Dewey in the early pages of *The Quest for Certainty* (1929): *How can the processes of production and dissemination of practical knowledge be more equitably transformed so that the social and economic power for which knowledge is necessary can be more equitably distributed?*

> There is a genuine and extremely serious problem in connection with the application of science in life. But it is a practical, not theoretical, one. That is to say, it concerns the economic and legal organization of society in consequence of which the knowledge which regulates activity is so much the monopoly of the few, and is used by them in behalf of private and class interests and not for general and shared use. The problem concerns the possible transformation of social conditions with respect to their economic and pecuniary basis. . . . *The practical and social problem is one of effecting a more general equitable distribution of the elements of understanding and knowledge in connection with work done, activities undertaken, and a consequent freer and more generously shared participation in their results.* (Dewey 1929:65, emphasis mine)

The *solution* to this multidimensional puzzle that escaped Dewey is *expert-assisted citizen participation in the processes of social inquiry, decision, and conjoint action.* Within such processes, citizen participants can develop and revise hypotheses about how best to transform particular problem situations toward wider goals. They can intelligently communicate with each other and with other communities, thereby building up problem-focused coalitions that may grow over time into wider, public-like community networks of interest and action. Although such communities and coalitions may initially achieve only limited, local successes, their participatory and communicative processes will develop in their members the skills, the moral and intellectual virtues, the body of knowledge, and the cooperative agency they will need for greater successes in an ongoing transformative process.

A crucial element in these successes and in participants' learning processes is the ability of diverse democratic communities and cross-difference coalitions to *reformulate their goals* and to *adopt new means and strategies for achieving them* on an ongoing basis as experience shows them what does and does not work in their particular situation, and as their knowledge base and cooperative relationships grow through intelligent communication with others. Here again, Dewey's reflections offer valuable leadings on how to make these ongoing evaluative and redirective processes effective.

Ongoing Evaluation and Redirection to Reflect Transformative Experience

Progress in transforming the problem situation on which their attention is focused is, of course, of great importance in keeping alive the hopes of a diverse community's participants in a process of democratic social inquiry, decision, and action. However, Dewey wisely points out that the *original goals* the community initially had hoped to achieve may and perhaps *should undergo revision* during an inquiry process that is conducted in the intelligent, richly communicative, and hypothetical way he recommends. Recognition of the need for such revision, he argues, may indicate an even more significant form of progress than success in implementing the original plans, not only because planning gains *a more worthy object,* but also because it reflects *development in collective self-understanding and skills in social inquiry,* as well as *growth in the intelligence* of the participating individuals.

> Progress is sometimes thought of as consisting in getting nearer to ends already sought. But this is a minor form of progress, for it requires only improvement of the means of action or technical advance. More important modes of progress consist in enriching prior purposes and in forming new ones. (Dewey 1916:231)

What a diverse democratic community will want as their pool of experience becomes deeper and broader will be somewhat different than what they wanted before they began their conjoint transformative activities. In addition, the participating individuals will change epistemically and morally over time in the process, developing greater intelligence and a richer relational awareness.

Dewey insightfully argues that the key to an effective process of social inquiry is its *intelligent guidance,* because the knowledge that the process depends on and produces has reliability and usefulness only if it is the product of intelligence in action.

The worth of any object that lays claim to being an object of knowledge is dependent upon the intelligence employed in reaching it. In saying this, we must bear in mind that intelligence means operations actually performed in the modification of conditions, including all the guidance that is given by means of ideas, both direct and symbolic. The statement may sound strange. But it is only a way of saying that *the value of any cognitive conclusion depends upon the method by which it is reached, so that the perfecting of method, the perfecting of intelligence, is the thing of supreme value.* (Dewey 1929:160, emphasis mine)

If the process of collaborative social inquiry is community-based, *the intelligence in question* must be widely shared, resulting from prior education and previous experience in social inquiry, and also from explicit methods of knowledge sharing and skill development within the inquiry process. It must be *a relational intelligence,* in that it requires skill in reasoning together that is different in kind from that required for reasoning alone. If a community can think effectively together, it has a reasonable chance of formulating hypotheses about past events and the actions required to influence future events that will allow it to act successfully together. "If we can judge events as indications of other events, we can prepare in all cases for the coming of what is anticipated. In some cases, we can forestall a happening; desiring one event to happen rather than another, we can intentionally set about institution of those changes which our best knowledge tells us to be connected with that which we are after" (Dewey 1929:170).

Because events are developing and the problem situation is changing even as a community forms its hypotheses and puts them into action, such relational intelligence must include the ability to *conjointly assess developments in midstream* as well as the shared flexibility to *change goals, methods, and operative assumptions* as the need becomes clear. Dewey realizes that there often is such a need to alter the hypothetical beliefs that a community forms as the result of a careful and intelligent social inquiry process, and experience shows that he is right.

Any *belief as such is tentative, hypothetical;* it is not just to be acted upon, but is to be framed with reference to its office as a guide to action. Consequently, it should be the last thing in the world to be picked up casually and then clung to rigidly. When it is apprehended as a tool and only a tool, an instrumentality of direction, the same scrupulous attention will go to its formation as now goes into the making of instruments of precision in technical fields. Men, instead of being proud of accepting and asserting beliefs and "principles" on the ground of loyalty, will be as ashamed of that procedure as they would now be to confess their assent to a scientific theory out of reverence for Newton or Helmholtz or whomever, without regard to evidence. (Dewey 1929:221–222, emphasis mine)

For a community to cling rigidly to its *hypothetical beliefs* about how to change a problem situation, even as that situation is changing in response to other forces and events, is wrong-headed, creating obstacles to its success and jeopardizing its hopes. However, clinging out of loyalty to the *original formulation of the goals* toward which those hypothetical beliefs suggest *means* is equally foolish if the community is making the kinds of *epistemic and moral progress* Dewey emphasized as the key elements in the transformative endeavor.

As Dewey pointed out, such misguided loyalty and harmful rigidity within a process of social inquiry, choice, and action often result from *a conceptual mistake* about the relationship between means and ends, as well as from *the wrong kind of loyalty* to a cultural vision or a collaborative agreement. Dewey's analysis of the relationship between means and ends as one of *continuity* is helpful in untangling the first mistake.

> Every condition that has to be brought into existence in order to serve as means is, in that connection, an object of desire and an end-in-view, while the end actually reached is a means to future ends as well as a test of valuations previously made. Since the end attained is a condition of further existential occurrences, it must be appraised as a potential obstacle and potential resource. (Dewey 1938:229)

As Dewey suggests, the *broad, general goal* of creating a deeper democracy can guide a community's transformative endeavors to some extent, but its contextual implications emerge only in response to experience, and cannot be antecedently drawn upon to guide action. Instead, *interim goals* of a hypothetical character have to be developed through inquiry and choice. Working to achieve such interim goals is a necessary step in working toward the more general goal. Thus, they serve as *means* to that broader end, but also as intermediate objectives of effort, or *ends-in-view*. A community transforms its problem situation through its efforts to achieve an end-in-view; and though the outcome may not be the one anticipated and desired, analyzing it teaches the community important lessons about its broader goals and also suggests what intermediate objectives should become the new ends-in-view. However, a community that becomes attached to pursuing a particular objective in a particular way out of loyalty to past efforts (and their participants) has misunderstood the point of those efforts and lost the benefit of the experience they offer toward achieving the broader goals that are *a more appropriate object of loyalty.*

This is not to suggest that enduring concepts like democracy are or should be treated as mysterious to a community, or that participants in cooperative social inquiry should assume that none of the transformative techniques applied elsewhere or in the past could be useful to them. *A heritage of struggle* to realize the practical meaning of the democratic impulse contains meanings born of experience, as well as often-useful tools of organization, communication, and action. However, as Dewey points out, it is important to recognize the difference between such practical wisdom and mere habit, and to realize that *even experience-born practical wisdom must be adapted to the particular problem situation.*

> Generalized ideas of ends and values undoubtedly exist. They exist not only as expressions of habit and as uncritical and probably invalid ideas but also in the same way as valid general ideas arise in any subject. Similar situations

recur; desires and interests are carried over from one situation to another and progressively consolidated. A schedule of general ends results, the involved values being "abstract" in the sense of not being directly connected with any particular existing case but not in the sense of independence of all empirically existent cases. As with general ideas in the conduct of any natural science, these general ideas are used as intellectual instrumentalities in judgment of particular cases as the latter arise; they are, in effect, tools that direct and facilitate examination of things in the concrete while they are also developed and tested by the results of their application in these cases. (Dewey 1938:230)

The pragmatic goals and techniques that practical wisdom develops and supplies are not permanently abstract, but only seem so between applications, each of which alters their character to some extent through the lessons it teaches.

Some of the invaluable lessons of experience-born practical wisdom in transformative action pertain directly to the question of *how to appraise ends-in-view and strategies to achieve them in midstream.* Criteria for such appraisals flow directly out of Dewey's analysis of the continuity of means and ends and the roles these play in guiding action.

There have developed, out of past experience, certain criteria which are operatively applicable in new cases as they arise. Ends-in-view are appraised or valued as *good* or *bad* on the ground of their serviceability in the direction of behavior dealing with states of affairs found to be objectionable because of some lack or conflict in them. They are appraised as fit or unfit, proper or improper, *right* or *wrong,* on the ground of their *requiredness* in accomplishing this end. (Dewey 1938:233, emphases in original)

Ends-in-view, which have the double characteristics of means and ends, are to be judged, in Dewey's view, on their *effectiveness* and *necessity* as part of an ongoing process of transforming problem situations by coordinating the actions of the community that develops them.

The attained end or consequence is always an organization of activities, where organization is a co-ordination of all activities which enter as factors. The *end-in-view* is that particular activity which operates as a co-ordinating factor of all other subactivities involved. Recognition of the end as a co-ordination or unified organization of activities, and of the end-in-view as the special activity which is the means of effecting this co-ordination, does away with any appearance of paradox that seems to be attached to the idea of a temporal continuum of activities in which each successive stage is equally end and means. The *form* of an attained end or consequence is always the same: that of adequate co-ordination. The content of involved matter of each successive result differs from that of its predecessors, for, while it is a *reinstatement* of a unified on-going action, after a period of interruption through conflict and need, it is also an *enactment* of a new state of affairs. It has the qualities and properties appropriate to its being the consummatory resolution of a previous state of activity in which there was a peculiar need, desire, and end-in-view. In the continuous temporal process of organizing activities into a co-ordinated and co-ordinating unity, a constituent activity is both an end and a means: an end, in so far as it is temporally and relatively close; a means, in so far as it provides a condition to be taken into account in further activity. . . .

The cases in which ends and means fall apart are the abnormal ones, the ones which deviate from activity which is intelligently conducted. (Dewey 1938:234–235)

Each end-in-view should be an element in a process that links an unacceptable problem situation with a preferable future along an experimental, ideal-guided path. Thus, *whether it contributes to the progress of this dynamic* is Dewey's *principle criterion* for assessing an end-in-view.

Additional criteria are implicit within Dewey's understanding of the transformative process and the ideal of deep democracy as reconstructed here. An end-in-view should also be a stimulus to a community's growth of knowledge, skills, and moral and intellectual virtues, as well as an occasion for the further education of participating individuals. In light of this criterion, an end-in-view that does not turn out to play the originally anticipated and desired role in the projected transformative chain of events still can be extremely valuable, not only in what the community and the participating individuals learn from striving to achieve it, but also in clarifying the meaning of the ideal and indicating a preferable path toward its realization.

Thus, Dewey's criteria for evaluating ends-in-view turn out to be *a set of measures of efficacy within ongoing social transformative processes:* "The generalized ideal and standard of economy–efficiency which operates in every advanced art and technology is equivalent, upon analysis, to the conception of means that are constituents of ends attained and of ends that are usable as means to further ends" (Dewey 1938:235). Within an ongoing transformation process, stages considerably further down the path are not visible at earlier points. This implies *an additional, future-oriented criterion:* that a necessary and effective end-in-view should not become an obstacle to the adoption and achievement of later desirable ends-in-view.

It must also be noted that *activity* and *activities* . . . involve, like any actual behavior, existential material, as breathing involves air; walking, the earth; buying and selling, commodities; inquiry, things investigated, etc. No human activity operates in a vacuum; it acts in the world and has materials upon which and through which it produces results. On the other hand, no material—air, water, metal, wood, etc.—is *means* save as it is employed in some human activity to accomplish something. When "organization of activities" is mentioned, it always includes within itself organization of materials existing in the world in which we live. That organization which is the "final" value for each concrete situation of valuation thus forms part of the existential conditions that have to be taken into account in further formation of desires and interests or valuations. In the degree in which a particular valuation is invalid because of inconsiderate short-sighted investigation of things in their relation of means–end, difficulties are put in the way of subsequent reasonable valuations. To the degree in which desires and interests are formed after critical survey of the conditions which as means determine the actual outcome, the more smoothly continuous become subsequent activities, for consequences attained are then such as are evaluated more readily as means in the continuum of action. (Dewey 1938:235–236, emphases in original)

Dewey argues here that *the combination of existential and substantial materials* that are required for and elements of deliberate action must be factored into the choice of end-in-view. We must realize that *how we use these materials now will affect what materials are available for coordinated activities at later points in the ongoing, unforeseeable transformation process.* If a community makes choices that use up its hope or its ecosystem, later stages will require less desirable and perhaps less achievable choices. Dewey is not suggesting here that the only reason why hope and the environment are valuable is as means for human actors in transforming problem situations. Rather, he is suggesting that coordinated action inevitably affects and is affected by both, so these impacts must be factored in as well as possible when choosing ends-in-view. Such choices should include the realistic recognition that *substantial change takes a long time and involves future actors and events, as well as emergent needs and impacts that are not entirely foreseeable in the present.*

Given this long time frame, the changing casts of characters, and the surprises involved in the kinds of transformative processes that will be necessary if the ideal of deep democracy is to be realized in significant institutional change and in customary habits of the heart, a final related question on which we might wish to seek Dewey's guidance is, *How can we maintain the long-term commitment, the community stability, and the individual growth processes such deep transformations require?* Although Dewey has less to offer on this topic than on the topics discussed earlier, once again, what he does say offers helpful leadings about how to answer this question more fully.

Effective Coordination and Stabilization of Long-Term Transformative Action

Although he does not address this problem directly, Dewey's reconstructed leadings on the previous four topics relate directly to the problem of how to effectively coordinate and stabilize long-term transformative activities. *Education* must be an important part of the solution to this problem, because it involves developing the skills, the funded knowledge, and the characteristic virtues people need in order to participate equally and effectively in intelligent communication within a process of democratic, transformation-focused social inquiry. Such education makes it possible to combine contributions from consulting expert social scientists with the broadly dispersed, grassroots experiences and imaginations of coalition and community members to derive a rolling process of establishing ends-in-view, cooperating in efforts to achieve them, and revising goals and strategies in light of experience. Furthermore, individuals who experience democratic education in the schools and in the conjoint direction of community life, including problem-focused inquiry, will develop the capacity and the desire to be effective participants in the ongoing process of democratic transformation. Through their active membership in multiple, intersecting, diverse, and deeply democratic communities, they will learn the detailed, specific lessons of participation in long-term, ongoing transformative projects.

Even the limited successes of these communities in achieving their flexible, hypothetical ends-in-view will give *hope-building fuel* to the desire to strive for the larger, ideal goals that arise from the democratic impulse as it is expressed in these communities' always-evolving languages and customs. The diverse and deeply democratic communities themselves will be sustained by the hope, the participatory habits, and the emergent transformative skills of their members, so that their increasing effectiveness in the process of problem-solving inquiry, choice, and action over time will allow them to ward off pressures to assimilate to the values and limitations of the larger, less democratic mass society. Their participation in *problem-focused coalitions* with other deeply democratic communities will contribute to their security and their effectiveness in warding off attacks and pressures from the larger society while increasing their transformative influence. Effective coalitions whose member communities and individuals act on the democratic impulse to get to know each other better, to widen their cooperative ties, and to deepen their commitment to each others' flourishing will form new intersecting communities and *"communities of communities"* that have greater endurance and power than the coalitions from which they grew. These communities of diverse democratic communities with deep and enduring commitments to each other, growing social and economic power, and extensive experience in collaborative social inquiry, choice, and action will become *democratic "publics"* in their outward dimension, as they focus their conjoint attention and energies on transforming the institutions of their larger society and of the global political economy so as to diminish their adverse impact and to increase their contribution to the deeply democratic flourishing of diverse individuals and communities.

As Dewey suggests, the *revitalization of diverse democratic communities of daily experience* is the key to the success of this larger transformative process because it is these communities that give their members sustaining relational roots. Moreover, diverse democratic communities can offer their members opportunities to continue their adult education in ways that remediate their experience in less-than-democratic schools and develop their skills, intellectual virtues, pool of knowledge, and self-understanding to new levels. Finally, through participation in diverse democratic communities, individuals can achieve together the initial limited successes that build hope and commitment to the larger, long-term transformative process.

These are helpful basic elements for *a general philosophy of democratic transformation,* a transformation that grows out of experience and that may contribute to our understanding and effectiveness when it is applied to new problem situations with their unique organizational and intellectual challenges. On the subject of how to develop these theoretical beginnings further into a useful tool for shaping effective democratic transformation processes, Dewey offers one last piece of important advice.

> *Theory separated from concrete doing and making is empty and futile;* practice then becomes an immediate seizure of opportunities and enjoyments which conditions afford without the direction which theory—knowledge and ideas—has power to supply. *The problem of the relation of theory and practice is not a problem of theory alone; it is that, but it is also the most practical problem of life.* For it is the question of how intelligence may inform action, and how action may bear the fruit of increased insight into meaning: a clear view of the values that are worth while and of the means by which they are to be made secure in experienced objects. *Construction of ideals in general and their sentimental glorification are easy; the responsibilities both of studious thought and of action are shirked.* Persons having the advantage of positions of leisure and who find pleasure in abstract theorizing—a most delightful indulgence to those to whom it appeals—have a large measure of liability for a cultivated diffusion of ideals and aims that are separated from the conditions which are the means of actualization. (Dewey 1929:224–225, emphases mine)

As Dewey suggests here, *a useful philosophy of democratic transformation* must grow out of experience in transformative activity, just as *effective transformative activity* needs the contribution of the wider, experience-born knowledge that an insightful general theory and consulting "experts" can provide. If they are illuminated by Dewey's reconstructed leadings as discussed here, detailed case studies of the kind Chapter Two called for will make an invaluable contribution to the ongoing development of an insightful general philosophy of democratic transformation. However, unless theorists are guided by some direct participatory experiences of their own, their understanding is likely to be distorted by the love of abstraction Dewey warned against, even if they share in the pool of indirect experience that grows from intelligent communication of the activities and results of others. Thus, to be effective participants in developing a useful general philosophy of democratic transformation, philosophers must also be activists for deep democracy.

Dewey's experience as an activist taught him many of the insights about the meaning and the transformative implications of the democratic ideal that have been discussed in this chapter. However, his is only one of the theoretical standpoints that we must combine in a general theory of democratic transformation that can usefully guide transformative action in our times, not only because it offers an insufficiently participatory model of social inquiry and inadequate guidance about how to build and sustain cross-difference coalitions and diverse democratic communities, but also because it grows out of the needs of an earlier stage of our problem situation, which now must be addressed, as Dewey pointed out, in its evolved specific terms.

As will be discussed in following chapters, the transformative democratic praxis-based standpoints of Alain Locke, Martin Luther King, Jr., Cornel West, and other contemporary philosopher–activists offer insights on these particular theoretical problems that critically complement Dewey's, helping to build up the kind of praxis-guiding philosophy of democratic transformation we need now.

Conclusion

As the foregoing discussion shows, reconstructing Dewey's guiding ideal as the diverse deeply democratic community yields helpful though incomplete leadings about how to democratically transform our problem situation of the present when we focus on five areas in which we need guidance: (1) how to understand and to shape educational experiences as key tools in the process of ongoing democratic reformation of individuals, cultures, and societies; (2) how to build up transformative coalitions and democracy-guided communities of daily life; (3) how to carry out effective processes of action-guiding democratic social inquiry through intelligent communication; (4) how to continuously revise our goals and objectives throughout the transformation process; and (5) how to effectively coordinate and sustain transformative action over time in order to achieve and to institutionalize progressive, more deeply democratic change. As will be discussed in the final chapters of this book, some current transformative efforts that are already working as and toward diverse democratic communities along these reconstructed Deweyan lines have had institution-changing, person-reforming, hope-building results. The successes of these initial transformative efforts show the wisdom of Dewey's democratic vision as reconstructed for our time: "An idealism of action that is devoted to creation of a future, instead of to staking itself upon propositions about the past, is invincible" (Dewey 1929:243).

Notes

1. John Rawls (1971, 1993, 1996) and Michael Walzer (1983) treat education as an "external" good in the sense that they list it among those items that can be "distributed" justly or unjustly, although they disagree about the kinds of basic social principles and structures that justice requires.

2. See, for example, Allan Bloom's *The Closing of the American Mind* (1987).

3. See McGary's "Racism, Social Justice, and Interracial Coalitions" (1997) and *Race and Social Justice* (1998). See Reagon's "Coalition Politics: Turning the Century" (1983).

4. Some economic theorists who use computer modeling have replaced the unrealistic universal assumptions about the motives and behavior of "rational economic man" with more relational assumptions based on evolutionary biology, including some very broad generalizations about the role of cultural differences, but even these assumptions may be too universal to describe human valuing behavior in the public square, especially at the local micro-level where preferences are *interactively* formed and expressed, especially in conditions that are not coercively dominated by macro-level forces of ultrapowerful busi-

ness firms, bureaucratic governments, and profit-motivated mass media. See David L. Wheeler's "Evolutionary Economics: Scholars Suggest that Much of World Trade May Be Controlled by Biologically Based Behaviors," *The Chronicle of Higher Education*, July 5, 1996, A8.

5.   See the developing body of urban and regional planning literature on the importance of citizen participation, including Jane Jacobs' *The Death and Life of Great American Cities* (1961), Peter Calthorpe's *The Next American Metropolis: Ecology, Community and the American Dream* (1993), Anton C. Nelessen's *Visions for a New American Dream* (1994), Anthony Downs' *New Visions for Metropolitan America* (1994), David Woods's "Collaborative Planning for the Lynnwood Legacy: A Successful Alternative to Traditional Planning" (1994), and John Forester's "Beyond Dialogue to Transformative Learning: How Deliberative Rituals Encourage Political Judgment in Community Planning Processes" (1996). I am indebted to David Woods, AICP, for his insights about this emerging body of theory and about the practical requirements for effective citizen participation in urban and regional planning.

6.   On the Lippman–Dewey exchange during the late 1920s over what kind of democracy is feasible and desirable in the emerging conditions after World War I, see Robert B. Westbrook's *John Dewey and American Democracy* (1991).

Chapter 4

Cosmopolitan Unity Amidst Valued Diversity: Alain Locke's Vision of Deeply Democratic Transformation

What is the task which philosophers set themselves to perform; and why do they philosophize at all? Almost every one will immediately reply: They desire to attain a conception of the frame of things which shall on the whole be more rational than that somewhat chaotic view which every one by nature carries about with him under his hat. But suppose this rational conception attained, how is the philosopher to recognize it for what it is, and not let it slip through ignorance? The only answer can be that he will recognize its rationality as he recognizes everything else, by certain subjective marks with which it affects him. When he gets the marks, he may know that he has got the rationality.

—WILLIAM JAMES, "The Sentiment of Rationality" (1879)

Work, culture, liberty,—all these we need, not singly but together, not successively but together, each growing and aiding each, and all striving toward that vaster ideal that swims before the Negro people, the ideal of human brotherhood, gained through the unifying ideal of Race; the ideal of fostering and developing the traits and talents of the Negro, not in opposition to or contempt for other races, but rather in large conformity to the greater ideals of the American Republic, in order that some day on American soil two world-races may give each to each those characteristics both so sadly lack.

—W.E.B. DUBOIS, *The Souls of Black Folk* (1903)

Introduction

On the first page of his poetic and persuasive analysis of the American situation at the beginning of the twentieth century, *The Souls of Black Folk* (1903), W.E.B. DuBois prophetically announced: ". . . the problem of the Twentieth Century is the problem of the color line." At the end of that century of struggle and strife, it is clear that the challenge of the twenty-first century will be to complete the resolution of

95

that problem, more broadly conceived in its global dimensions: to reconcile our antagonistic, power-structured differences in race, culture, gender, and class, as we strive to reconstruct existing, dysfunctional, undemocratic patterns of relationship into diverse, deeply democratic communities. Diversity is a central element of the multidimensional problem situation of our times. We seek the experience of community amidst our differences in order to make a stable and constructive peace in our lives and to fulfill the deeper meanings of the democratic ideal that still has evocative and persuasive power with us. Yet we value and need our group-related identities, which have been adversarially constructed in many ways: as "not this," "better than that," "in control over this," "charged by the faith of our ancestors to defeat that, so as to give meaning to their struggle." Thus we are both fascinated with and fearful of differences now. These feelings are imaginatively extended and symbolized by the swarm of "alien" films and television programs that project the threat of the ultimately "other" onto powerful, conscienceless creatures from outer space. They also are expressed in the frightening revival of narrow nationalisms that aim to exclude, to deny, and even to destroy unwanted "aliens."

Nonetheless, the realities of globalization present us with the need to deal with each other in stable and mutually enriching ways—to collaborate across differences in order to transform injustices and oppressions so that we can get on with our lives and dream sweet dreams once again, or perhaps for the first time. The struggles of the twentieth century have shown us that like-minded and cross-difference coalitions are valuable in this transformative process, but ultimately not enough to accomplish what we need and desire, given the strength of our opponents and of our own history-born antipathies. To generate the power and the persistence to transform our present undemocratic and strife-creating patterns of relationship into more stable and sustaining diverse, deeply democratic communities, we must understand the basic dynamics of our problem situation, and we must develop specific, effective approaches to its transformation.

If it is retrieved and reconstructed to address the problem situation of our own times, Alain Locke's deeply insightful but presently little-known analysis of interrelated economic, political, and cultural aspects of global cross-difference value strife, in combination with his multidimensional prescription for its peace-making transformation, offers us invaluable leadings for this process of struggle toward deep democracy, insightfully conceptualized as *cosmopolitan unity amidst valued diversity*. In spite of the brilliance of his teaching, writing, and public speaking, much of Locke's work was unpublished during his lifetime, and his contribution was largely forgotten after his death in 1954. However, Leonard Harris, Johnny Washington, Jeffrey C. Stewart, and other scholars of African American philosophy and democratic theory began to disinter his philosophical corpus during the 1980s, bringing it fully to life in the 1990s.[1]

A native of Philadelphia, Alain LeRoy Locke (1885–1954) was the first African American to receive the Ph.D. in philosophy from Harvard University, as well as America's first black Rhodes Scholar. Locke combined in his personal history and his philosophical corpus at least two strands of thought and experience. The first is an African American historical, cultural, and intellectual strand that links Locke with forebears in struggle like Frederick Douglass and Sojourner Truth, with older contemporaries like Booker T. Washington and W.E.B. DuBois (who both assisted his early career), with younger contemporaries like Martin Luther King, Jr., and Malcolm (X) Shabazz, and with our living generations of African American public intellectuals. The second strand links Locke's work with acknowledged classical American pragmatist influences like William James and his teachers at Harvard, Josiah Royce, George Herbert Palmer, and Ralph Barton Perry, with his older contemporary and often-complementary philosophical opponent, John Dewey, and with Horace Kallen, his close friend and codeveloper of a world-minded, "culturally pluralistic" theoretical and praxical transformation of classical American pragmatism.

In reality, such a two-strand analysis is inadequate to capture the richness of Alain Locke's critical yet sympathetic engagement with a globe-ranging multiplicity of diverse streams of thought and experience. These include the lifelong influence of friends from all corners of the declining British Empire he met during his studies as a Rhodes Scholar at Oxford University (which he called "the Imperial Training School"), as well as during his subsequent studies at the University of Berlin, where, like DuBois, he encountered German historicism, emerging schools of sociology and anthropology, and new friends from Eastern Europe. In addition, Locke's work shows the influence of serious engagements with Marxism, with diverse religious and spiritual traditions including, among others, Christianity, Buddhism, and Bahá'í, and with struggles in various parts of the globe for liberation from colonialism and its economic, political, and cultural aftermath.

Although he chaired the Department of Philosophy at Howard University for many years, Locke first came to the attention of a diverse intellectual public as "the dean of the Harlem Renaissance" because of the acclaim and influence he gathered for its African American authors and artists through influential publications he wrote and edited, especially *The New Negro* (1925). His greatest intellectual achievement, however, is an original and insightful, difference-embracing reconstruction of the pragmatism of James and Royce that is complementary to Dewey's. Locke's *culturally pluralistic critical pragmatism* draws on his own diverse formative influences, deepening the cross-cultural empirical grounding for a democratic transformative philosophy and praxis to guide the development of habits of the heart and of social institutions that express cosmopolitan unity amidst valued diversity.

Grounded in an acutely insightful analysis of global power-structured cultural differences, Locke's analytical and transformational vision links *intra*personal processes of valuation to group-structured *inter*personal patterns of kinship and struggle. A tendency toward absolutism about our worldviews is natural for human persons, Locke argues, but problematic in leading to conflicts. In order to gain relief from the *internal conflicts* this absolutist tendency leads to, we must and generally do learn to overcome it through flexible interconversion among our own "value feeling-modes." This widely shared experience, Locke argues, gives us hope that we can gain relief from *social conflicts* by broadening our learning to disrupt group-related absolutisms, to teach ourselves emotional and conceptual flexibility on the interpersonal level, and then, in progressive stages, to *build democratic cooperation* grounded in and fostering those *"common humane values"* that make for lasting peace and the mutual growth of inextricably interlinked but valuably differing world cultures.

As chapter two suggested, Locke's guiding democratic ideal of cosmopolitan unity amidst valued diversity offers a complementary, much-needed corrective to Dewey's and Habermas's insufficiently diverse and inadequately justified universalisms while interconnecting his rich and varied contributions to a transformative philosophy of deep democracy. In combination with his Jamesian epistemological pluralism, his Roycean ideal value of "loyalty to loyalty," and his experience-based commitment to pursuing the kind of understanding that makes for a just and lasting peace across the various "color lines" that presently divide us, Locke's conception of deep democracy motivates the development of the reconstructed pragmatist philosophical methodology for which he is chiefly known, "cultural pluralism," as well as his model of a critical, cross-disciplinary, value-committed social science, which he called "anthropology in the broadest sense." Locke's tripartite value theory combines democratic ideal values with social scientific methodological values and an empirical anthropology of values, which itself includes three interactive levels: common humane values, culturally specific values, and individual transvaluations of values. Applying and further developing this culturally pluralistic value theory, Locke contributed insightful criticisms and promising reconstructions in the fields of race theory, economics, the arts, politics, and education, all of them grounded in his experience within democratic transformative praxis.

Like those of Dewey, Habermas, Addams, James, DuBois, and many others, Locke's valuable contributions to a transformative philosophy of deep democracy are neither wholly original nor final. They build on others' contributions and add important new insights, yet they require reconstruction in light of subsequent historical experience and collaborative criticism. Even when reconstructed as a culturally pluralistic critical pragmatism, Locke's contributions constitute only some of the elements of a comprehensive philosophy of deep democracy. They require additional theoretical insights from other experiential standpoints about gender, class, and other social–locational differences, and also about the human place in nature. They also require more detailed strategies for transforming our era's complex, powerful, and radically undemocratic global political economy. This is to be expected, of course, because *a comprehensive and transformatively effective philosophy of deep democracy* is *necessarily collaborative, perpetually reconstructive,* and *never final.* Nonetheless, as the following discussion will show, when Alain Locke's contributions to a philosophy of deep democracy are reconstructed as insights and tools for transforming the problem situation of our own times, they offer us invaluable guidance.

Race Contacts, Cultural Imperialism, and the Transformative Power of the Arts

Contemporary American controversies about race, African American liberation, and the arts echo those of the early years of this century, when Alain Locke was an undergraduate at Harvard, a Rhodes Scholar at Oxford, a postgraduate student at the University of Berlin roving Eastern Europe in his spare time, and a young scholar beginning his career at Howard University.[2] A series of nineteenth- and early twentieth-century books of great influence had argued that race is a fixed biological characteristic that inevitably leads to racial hierarchies, as several contemporary conservative scholars have claimed again in recent years. In light of counter-claims from the new social science of anthropology, some leading African American scholars of the early twentieth century argued that race as a concept is scientifically bankrupt, harmful to the cause of African American liberation and, therefore, to be jettisoned, as K. Anthony Appiah and Naomi Zack have argued in recent years.[3] Against this background, Locke offered an eloquent and still-resonant series of public lectures on "Race Contacts and Interracial Relations" in 1915 and again in 1916, his third and fourth years as a junior member of the Howard faculty. In these lectures, Locke constructed an argument to show that *race is a social category* that, once stripped of false claims about a static, essential, biological basis of unique racial characteristics, has *great explanatory and transformative usefulness,* as Charles Mills, Lucius Outlaw and Amy Gutmann have recently argued.[4] This series of lectures allows the reader to appreciate the subtlety, boldness, and restraint Locke displayed ten years later in the 1925 work that made him famous, his manifesto-like editor's introduction to *The New Negro.*

This "New Negro Manifesto" introduced the cross-cultural intellectual world to the explosive energy and uniqueness of Harlem-centered African American voices and visions in the arts, emerging with all the noise and power of a rebirth of a suppressed people taking that place on the stage of world cultures W.E.B. DuBois had prophesied for them:

> After the Egyptian and Indian, the Greek and Roman, the Teuton and Mongolian, the Negro is a sort of seventh son, born with a veil, and gifted with second-sight in this American world. . . . This, then, is the end of his grieving: to be a co-worker in the kingdom of culture, to escape both death and isolation, to husband and use his best powers and his latent genius. (DuBois 1903:2–3)

Like those of DuBois, Locke's comments in *The New Negro* were prophetic rather than purely descriptive. Ironically, the vision he articulated there was rejected within a few years by some of the very artists whose work his comments purport to explain. Nonetheless, read against the background of his more expansive, less strategically calculated 1915–1916 lectures, Locke's vision of *the personal and social transformative power of the arts* shines forth with continuing usefulness and hope. As Locke insightfully argues in the "New Negro Manifesto" that gave a visible shape to the Harlem Renaissance, the arts offer *an effective radical middle path of self-creation and cultural liberation* between imitative appeasement at one extreme and a separatist anti-aesthetic at the other. Now, as then, the arts so conceived can help to transform conditions of cultural imperialism into respectful and mutually beneficial interracial relations.

Although Locke's earlier lectures on "Race Contacts and Interracial Relations" that provide the necessary interpretive background for his manifesto-like introduction to *The New Negro* were never published during his lifetime, they were brought to the attention of the wider audience they deserve in 1992, when they were finally published due to the herculean efforts of their editor, Jeffrey C. Stewart, to clarify the transcriptions and to track down Locke's many references to scholarly works and debates of the time.⁵ Without this background, Locke's "New Negro Manifesto" might seem to have a peculiarly idealist ring to it that is strangely out of joint with the violent and uncertain times of riots and lynchings that preceded and followed its articulation. It might also seem peculiarly deferential and carefully nonthreatening to the white monied elite who formed one of its primary intended audiences. However, the 1915–1916 lectures offer a fuller understanding of Locke's culturally pluralistic critical pragmatist analysis of the dual aspects of race imperialism that motivates his reconstructive and communicative strategies in his "New Negro Manifesto," including an understanding of *the transformative power of culture* as an important aspect of what John Dewey was soon to characterize as a second, moral–communicative engine of history.⁶

A key element of Locke's earlier analysis of race contacts and cultural imperialism is his non-biological, historical definition of *race* as a group characteristic in which *color* plays no necessary role. Drawing upon and eventually influencing some of the major anthropological developments of the first half of the twentieth century, Locke argued that *race has no fixed basis at all*—neither biological nor social—but rather is *a highly adaptable, environmentally influenced* characteristic of groups who are defined by their shared historical experience, of which they may have no shared consciousness. Nonetheless, *group feeling*—defining ourselves as members of particular groups—is part of *our shared nature* as social animals, in Locke's view, tracing back in ancient times to kinship relationships and continuing on in various reformulations of in-group vs. out-group, us vs. them, and sameness vs. difference throughout history. What a race of people shares, Locke argued, is *a historically dynamic and relational culture,* rather than a set of fixed and essential biological or social characteristics. As the pioneering anthropologist Franz Boas demonstrated, such a culture (and its biological basis) is always changing in response to contacts with other races, which *mutually influence* one another's development in ways that are necessary stimulants to the positive growth of civilizations.

However, race contacts are not always as equals, and not always mutually enhancing; often, though not always, they have the character of *cultural imperialism.* Empires and empire-mindedness have been with us since ancient times, Locke argued, but the aspirations and strategies of the imperial peoples of the modern era are radically different than those of old. What ancient Rome sought from most of the elements of its far-flung empire was limited money tributes and the kind of military security that makes for peace at home. What the Anglo–Saxon imperialists of the modern era seek is far more extensive: it is *cultural conversion* that assures large, growing markets for costly finished goods produced by the conquering culture—markets biased in their operation by coercive trade policies backed by military might. In Locke's view, the *fundamental impulse* underlying modern political colonialism is *economic.* Cultural imperialism has the role of strategic adjunct to economic imperialism in the modern era, though it is also deeply satisfying in its own right to peoples whose cultural consciousness is shaped by a desire to dominate others and a history of doing so successfully.

An important element of such modern cultural imperialism, Locke points out, is an ideological justification that allows the dominators to ignore certain facts and to interpret others as indicative of their right to rule. It is especially helpful to the dominant group if the subordinate group also accepts this ideological justification. Thus, *cultural imperialism has a psychological aspect with a normative dimension,* in addition to its economic and political aspects. This psychological aspect involves more than fear of the repercussions of violations of the imperial cultural hierarchy; it also involves the conviction that one culture is superior to others and, thus, that cultural conversion of the inferior and dominance by the superior are right and desirable. Locke draws a contrast between *two patterns of imperial psychology* in the modern era, one typical of *imperial homelands* like England, and one typical of *colonial or postcolonial constituent nations* of the Anglo–Saxon empire like his own United States of America. In England, Locke claims, members of a subordinated culture are accepted to the extent that they exhibit cultural conversion: thinking, valuing, and acting like the English. In the United States and other postcolonial appendages of Anglo–Saxon imperial culture, by contrast, increasing cultural convergence tends to be threatening to those whose cultural superiority will always be derivative rather than originary.

This helps to explain why, Locke argued, racial prejudice increased in America during the era following the end of slavery and what he calls the "historically premature" enactment of the Fourteenth and Fifteenth Amendments to the U.S. Constitution, so that Jim Crow laws came to seem a necessary protection of the dominant culture.[7] Color, he argued, which is the apparent focus of segregation, plays some role in exacerbating intergroup tensions by symbolically making intergroup differences visible and apparently unconvertible. However, *the real source of racial tension,* in Locke's view, is *intergroup economic rivalry* and *the now-imperiled desire of the culturally dominant group to remain dominant.* The irony is that the biological and cultural purity that the Jim Crow laws sought to preserve had already been eroded in ways that would have been regarded as natural and even desirable in the ancient Roman empire. *Biological commonalities* had been increased through sharing an environment, as Boas demonstrated, as well as through interrace sexual contacts; simultaneously, *deep mutual influences* in language, world view, and the material culture of productive activity had already transformed both cultural groups.

In contrast with Derek Bell's despairing diagnosis of racism as a permanent and unalterable feature of American society, Locke argued that *racism waxes and wanes* in relationship to changing conditions, with a significant role being played by interested elites in manipulating the race feelings of others to their own advantage.[8] How races see themselves and others is highly variable, Locke argues, and thus, to some extent within human control, though the impulse to think in group terms is natural and somewhat automatic. Like other impulses on the continuum between fully automatic and fully chosen, *race feelings can be cultivated, redirected, or allowed to wither* to a great extent, as history shows. Moreover, dominant groups tend to seek out a *modus vivendi* with those subordinate groups they can neither fully absorb nor fully obliterate, and such subordinate groups have some cultural power in shaping what this working arrangement will be, in addition to whatever political and economic power they also may be able to exercise.

The key to *effective exercise of cultural power* on the part of a subordinate group in the ongoing renegotiation of a *modus vivendi* with a dominant group, Locke argues, is the development of *a positive race consciousness.* One of the important therapeutic aspects of such a positive race consciousness is that it undercuts the unconscious cultural conversion process in the hearts and minds of the economically, politically, and culturally oppressed group members by undercutting the seductive effectiveness of the ideological justification of group subordination by the cultural imperialists. A second vital aspect is its stimulus to the reconstruction of a semi-autonomous path of cultural development that reflects the contributions of members of the oppressed group, and thus, gives those members something to bring to life's multiple, daily negotiating tables as a dialectically alternative vision. A third significant factor is that a group that has a positive race consciousness must be treated differently by an imperialist culture than one that lacks such group self-definition. Neither the casual, unreflective assumption of cultural superiority nor its correlative unquestioned, benevolent, but patronizing direction of others' affairs is possible when dealing with a group that asserts a cultural counter-consciousness that explicitly or implicitly challenges the dominant group's normative ideological assumption of the right to rule.

Locke does not claim that such a positive race consciousness can achieve an oppressed group's liberation from cultural imperialism *all by itself.* Rather, it is *one* of the necessary elements in ongoing negotiations toward the various forms of psychological and practical freedom and empowerment that can change the dynamic of race contacts toward mutual respect, appreciation, and equality over time within the multicultural cosmopolitan world civilization he believed was already beginning to emerge in the early years of the twentieth century. *Economic and political transformations* in intergroup relations must accompany such *cultural transformations,* Locke insisted, but these cannot be achieved independently of the *reconstruction of cultural semi-autonomy,* and this requires a *positive race consciousness.* Moreover, as a cultural pluralist, Locke agreed with DuBois that there are incommensurable and precious aspects of each culture's uniqueness that should be preserved *for their own sake* and developed along the lines of their own semi-autonomous trajectory. In his concluding lecture on *Race Contacts and Interracial Relations,* Locke argued that *the arts* are important for both kinds of reasons: because they can make powerful contributions to a positive race consciousness, thus helping to fire up the second, redirective, moral–communicative engine of history; and for their own sake, as the expression and communication of a race's unique, incommensurable, and precious cultural experience and the particular kind of creative energies to which that experience gives rise. Here, again, Dewey was later to agree with Locke: in addition to its expressive significance within experience, the arts provide "the only media of complete and unhindered communication between man and man that can occur in a world full of gulfs and walls that limit community of experience" (Dewey 1934:110).

Locke's 1915–1916 lectures provide the background argument for the *strategically unstated main thesis* of his 1925 manifesto-like introduction to *The New Negro:* the artistic achievements of Harlem-centered African American artists are to be celebrated and announced to the world at large for these same two reasons. First, they hopefully and effectively express *an emerging positive race consciousness* that requires a reassessment on the part of members of the dominant culture as well as members of the subordinate culture. Secondly, they represent *a new, historically unique aesthetic vision* that offers something wonderful and precious to an emerging, multi-strand, cosmopolitan world civilization. His strategic purpose in the "New Negro Manifesto" is to *translate* the self-revelatory and communicative symbolic systems being created and deployed by African American artists—or, if necessary, to *reconstruct* their meanings in ways that he regarded as historically necessary and salutary to the cause of overall liberation from the American variant of Anglo–Saxon cultural imperialism.

Locke's first task in his "New Negro Manifesto" is to demonstrate that the powerful, explicitly African American creative achievements of Harlem-centered artists are but the first fruits of an emerging positive race consciousness that has been a long time in coming. Although whites and blacks alike were bemoaning "the race problem," an unnoticed parallel development in history was occurring: the Old Negro, who had always been largely a myth, was being replaced by the development of *a New Negro consciousness* that had now burst forth from "the chrysalis . . . achieving something like *a spiritual emancipation*."[9] Changing conditions had transformed a problem into a task because "the vital inner grip of prejudice has been broken" (Locke 1925:4). With the unchaining of this second engine of history and its firing up with the energy of Harlem's new young voices, Locke argued, *a new historical era had already begun* (Locke 1925:4-5).

> With this renewed self-respect and self-dependence, the life of the Negro community is bound to enter a new dynamic phase, the buoyancy from within compensating for whatever pressure there may be of conditions from without. The migrant masses, shifting from countryside to city, hurdle several generations of experience at a leap, but more important, something happens spiritually in the life-attitudes and self-expression of the Young Negro, in his poetry, his art, his education and his new outlook, with the additional advantage, of course, of the poise and greater certainty of knowing what it is all about. From this comes the promise and warrant of a new leadership. As one of them has discerningly put it:

> We have tomorrow
> Bright before us
> Like a flame.

> Yesterday, a night-gone thing
> A sun-down name.

And dawn today
Broad arch above the road we came.
We march!

The militant tone of Langston Hughes's poem sets the background beat for
Locke's smooth surface language in the rest of the manifesto. As Locke smiles,
the New Negro shows his teeth. How they will be used depends upon the dominant culture's uptake of their message, which will influence what channels are
available for the pent-up energy of a reviving culture too long subordinate.

Great changes have been happening in America, and more are coming, Locke
argues, but the challenges to be met are not the old race problem, but rather *how
a democracy will adjust itself to accommodate cultural differences,* now that the
spell of the old master–slave ideology has worn off.

[T]he problems of adjustment are new, practical, local and not peculiarly
racial. Rather they are an integral part of the large industrial and social problems of our present-day democracy. (Locke 1925:5)

The great migration from the South to the North and from the country to the city
has occurred because of "a new vision of opportunity, of social and economic
freedom, of a spirit to seize, even in the face of an extortionate and heavy toll, a
chance for the improvement of conditions" (Locke 1925:6). This process has
formed Harlem, "not merely the largest Negro community in the world, but the
first concentration in history of so many diverse elements of Negro life" (Locke
1925:6). What has grown out of this unplanned convergence is a conscious recognition of group unity amidst diversity: "a race sympathy and unity have determined a further fusing of sentiment and experience . . . a great race-welding"
(Locke 1925:6–7). This development, in Locke's view, is the beginning of a positive new race consciousness that has the potential to assert a counter-thesis
within history: "Harlem, I grant you, isn't typical—but it is significant, it is
prophetic" (Locke 1925:7). This beginning of a new race consciousness that has
grown out of convergent conditions has begun to express itself in the artistic
voices of the Harlem Renaissance—voices speaking the new awareness of
masses of African Americans, and not just the hopeful rantings of the agitator.

These voices of the Harlem Renaissance powerfully and beautifully express a
unique cultural vision growing out of a shared historical experience, and they also
communicate an initial statement of terms for a new multicultural *modus vivendi*
that a revitalized culture demands from its long-time imperial oppressor.

Mutual understanding is basic for any subsequent cooperation and adjustment. The effort toward this will at least have the effect of remedying in large
part what has been the most unsatisfactory feature of our present stage of
race relationships in America, namely the fact that the more intelligent and
representative elements of the two race groups have at so many points got
quite out of vital touch with one another. (Locke 1925:8–9)

The time for *a new round of cross-cultural renegotiations for terms of democratic cooperation* has arrived, and the artists of the Harlem Renaissance have begun to articulate some of the terms of a new counter-consciousness that must be dealt with.

However, the cross-cultural renegotiation process itself is long familiar, and the parties have already made countless accommodations on both sides, many of which have been helpful to the growth of *a peculiarly American civilization.*

> The Negro mind reaches out as yet to nothing but American wants, American ideas. But this forced attempt to build his Americanism on race values is a unique social experiment, and its ultimate success is impossible except through the fullest sharing of American culture and institutions. . . . The racialism of the Negro is no limitation or reservation with respect to American life; it is only a constructive effort to build the obstructions in the stream of his progress into an efficient dam of social energy and power. Democracy itself is obstructed and stagnated to the extent that any of its channels are closed. Indeed they cannot be selectively closed. So the choice is not between one way for the Negro and another way for the rest, but between American institutions frustrated on the one hand and American ideals progressively fulfilled and realized on the other. (Locke 1925:11–12)

Because "constructive channels" are opening for "the balked social feelings of the American Negro," the prospects for *a peaceful renegotiation* of the terms of cross-cultural cooperation are good (Locke 1925:13–14). Such renegotiations of terms—*peaceful or otherwise*—are occurring between dominant and suppressed peoples around the world. While Locke is careful to reassure the monied white intellectuals who had become materially invaluable patrons of the arts in support of the Harlem Renaissance that he anticipates a peaceful, civilization-building renegotiation process, his suggestion of the image of the African American mind as having "leapt, so to speak, upon the parapets of prejudice and extended its cramped horizons . . . link[ing] up with the growing group consciousness of the dark-peoples and . . . gradually learning their common interests" (Locke 1925:14) presents *the alternative to negotiated agreement—the teeth* within the smile.

The conception of the emerging African American arts that Locke argues characterizes the Harlem Renaissance is thus carefully and strategically calculated to illuminate *an effective middle path* of self-creation and positive race consciousness that can play a crucial role in a multilaterally negotiated cultural liberation. Locke was no revolutionary. He did not believe that a violent rising of long-suppressed and practically disempowered African Americans against their Anglo–Saxon imperial oppressors had any chance of succeeding. Even if he had believed a violent revolution had a chance of succeeding, it could not be expected to achieve the multilateral transformations in self-consciousness, values, and practical competences that are necessary for an equal, respectful, and mutually enhancing cooperation in building a culturally pluralistic, cosmopolitan civilization. Julius Nyerere made the same point in the 1960s about the limited transformative power of violent revolution, based on his experience of the Tanzanian struggle for liberation from the Anglo–Saxon colonial empire.[10] The nonrevolutionary alternatives to Locke's middle path are equally doomed to failure. Imitative appeasement of the dominant culture's art forms is not culturally liberating, and will predictably encounter an increase of opposition from America's postcolonial, imperially derivative dominant culture. Likewise, a separatist anti-aesthetic like that expressed in contemporary "gangsta" rap is reactive and culturally self-destructive, rather than originative; it does not draw deeply enough on the unique and particular African American historical experience, and it does not project a positive, semi-autonomous cultural future that grows out of and builds upon that experience.

Thus, Locke's radical middle path offers *an effective and genuinely self-creative model for the cultural dimension of social transformation* that offers helpful illumination of a powerful potential *the arts* offered during the Harlem Renaissance, and offer again with fresh vitality during our own global millennial era. Although our times are not Locke's times, and the specific forms of cultural resistance, intervention, and transformative renegotiation that our times call for must be and have been somewhat different than those Locke celebrated as the Harlem Renaissance, our problem situation is a successor generation of his own. Within our continuing quest for the realization of deep democracy, unreconciled racial divides and tragic emergences of drug- and despair-related black-on-black violence reflected in "gangsta" rap are counteracted by the best of hip-hop's appropriations of new creative and communicative technologies and its fusions of earlier art forms.[11]

In turn, these positive, new cultural developments substantively combine with hope-sustaining continuities through gospel music, jazz, the novel, the essay, and the resurgence of African American poetry in clubs, in concerts, and on street corners in urban centers of African American creative energy, crossing and connecting generations while linking them back to roots in African cultural remainders and in the history and hopes that have guided the American struggle for democracy.[12] Toni Morrison and Alice Walker are brilliant and influential contemporary examples of positively race-conscious African American novelist–essayists whose works seek to express African American experience in ways that contribute to the renegotiation of a cross-cultural and an intra-cultural *modus vivendi* that is more deeply democratic than those of the past and of the present. In their activist intellectual social commentaries as well as their art, both women have had a profound impact in aiding the revival of a semi-autonomous African American cultural trajectory that lovingly transforms the self-contempt and the imitative oppression of women arising from chattel slavery and its insufficiently reconstructed aftermath, pointing toward liberation in new ways that have already helped to deepen the experience of democracy for people of all colors and cultures.[13] Likewise, in "Blood on the Fields" (1994), Wynton Marsalis's soul-stirring jazz oratorio, these elements of history, hope, self-expression, cultural voice, and democratic renegotiation of the terms of cross-cultural and intra-cultural engagement combine.[14] As the wise man Juba advises Jesse, the enslaved former prince with freedom on his mind:

One you got to love the land, forgive it for its sin
You'll never get your freedom if the land is not your friend
Two, you've got to sing with soul so Indians will dance
If no one helps you run then you haven't got a chance
Three, what will you call yourself if you become free?
If a man is a prince then he too a slave can be.

As these contemporary examples suggest, Locke's insights about the transforma-tive power of the arts offer invaluable guidance for our own era's struggle. The arts can express a positive group consciousness that can stimulate the reemergence of a semi-autonomous cultural trajectory in daily, negotiated interactions with other cul-tural groups within an imperially power-structured field of social forces. In this way, the arts can empower a once-suppressed people to play a significant role in steering the second, redirective engine of history toward a more deeply democratic future.

Locke's Culturally Pluralistic, Feeling-Focused Theory of Valuation

Motivated by the reality of widespread, deeply destructive social strife flaring in the twentieth century into two World Wars and countless civil blood baths—and by a resultant, widely shared imperative sense of the necessity of a lasting demo-cratic peace that has been deeply felt among those who have experienced its hor-rible alternative—Alain Locke sought to develop an accurate diagnosis of the root causes of such disastrous social strife and an effective transformative pre-scription for resolving it into a stable dynamic of mutuality and cooperation amidst continuing valued differences. Two central aspects of the empirically grounded value theory Locke developed for this double-sided purpose may seem strikingly discomforting and initially wrong to many Western democratic theo-rists of diverse philosophical orientations. First, though Locke continues to rec-ognize the importance of economic and political dimensions of struggle, his attention focuses on a third dimension—culture—that tends to be ignored in Marxist, liberal, and earlier pragmatist theories. And second, Locke emphasizes feeling more than reason, both in his analysis of social strife and in his proposals for its solution. As his analysis of modern imperialism in his 1915–1916 lectures on *Race Contacts and Interracial Relations* show, Locke was well aware of the economic causes of strife Marx emphasized, as well as of modern nation–states' competing political and military interests in the kind of self-serving dominance that Machiavelli, Hobbes, and van Clausewitz theorized. However, Locke be-lieved there is *an additional cause of social strife* that partially includes and helps to explain these economic, political, and military causes—*value strife,* in which *cultural differences* play an inescapable role.

In this dimension of his thinking, Locke is distinctively post-Nietzschean. Al-though he realizes the importance of "will to power" in human motivations and in human history, Locke shifts from an individual analysis to a group analysis of its origin and its operation. Moreover, he does not celebrate its adversarial triumph, but rather emphasizes the possibility that the conflict to which it leads may be redirected to play a constructive role in advancing the development of a cosmopolitan world civilization, eventually leading to *mutual realization of diverse conceptions of the good life* within respectful, cross-difference cooperative contexts.

However, this cannot be achieved, in Locke's view, without understanding and educatively reorienting the *central feeling dimension of practical valuing activities,* taking into account their inescapable cultural locations as well as their habitual configuration by cultural loyalties—which are so invaluable to us, but also so dangerous in their traditional and current adversarial formations. Therefore, Locke's *tripartite normative, methodological, and empirical analysis* of practical valuing activities treats individuals as culture members and culture transformers, geopolitically located in historically power-structured relationships with members and transformers of other cultural groups. Based on this analysis, his *multistage peacemaking prescription* gives important knowledge-gathering and reflective roles to reason, but his central emphasis is on *reorientation of feeling* as the key to the cooperative struggle toward the kinds of economic and political transformations that a lasting democratic peace ultimately requires.

Locke's initially surprising and discomforting but highly insightful analysis of value strife and his promising prescription for its peaceful transformation are conveyed in a series of short essays, book introductions, and speeches from the period between 1935 and his death in 1954, many of them written in a dense, highly technical style. Fortunately, this rhetorical lump is leavened by a number of more accessible essays and speeches intended for the broader audience Locke addressed in his role as an organic public intellectual.[15] In writings of both kinds, Locke acknowledges his debts to William James and Josiah Royce while suggesting at least some of the other philosophical voices that create an interpretive context for his work.

Alain Locke's lifetime of experience as a multidimensional "problem" within a diverse, culturally hierarchical America made the importance of *group memberships*—especially race and associated culture—painfully apparent to him. Perhaps this helps to explain why Locke goes beyond James and Dewey in emphasizing the importance of such differences, specifically the inescapable and largely positive role of *culture,* in both the derivation and the directionality of moral orientations and other modes of valuation. The dominant dynamic of the value strife that has shaped and repeatedly riven human experience in the twentieth century has been *cultural, not individual,* Locke argues, though individuals can and must play a role in transforming it toward peace. In Locke's view, *diversity* in cultural values must be both acknowledged and appreciated within the quest for the kind of cosmopolitan unity within diversity that a deep and lasting peace requires.

"Values and Imperatives" (1935) is the densely argued, theoretically demanding, yet provocative, innovative, and insightful essay with which Locke announced his culturally pluralistic approach to value theory. Echoing yet historicizing William James, Locke begins this essay with a bold claim that lo-

cates his theoretical stance within the stream of Jamesian pragmatism and in opposition to Kantian attempts to ground values in acts of transcendental reason.[16]

> All philosophies, it seems to me, are in ultimate derivation philosophies of
> life and not of abstract, disembodied "objective" reality; products of time,
> place and situation, and thus systems of timed history rather than timeless
> eternity. They need not even be so universal as to become the epitomized *ra-
> tionale* of an age, but may merely be the lineaments of a personality, its tem-
> perament and dispositional attitudes projected into their systematic
> rationalizations. (Harris 1989:34)

However, Locke immediately differentiates his culture-related conception of valuation from James's overly individualistic one, implicitly linking it instead with
Dewey's social approach to ethics and epistemology, especially Dewey's criticisms of the Cartesian "quest for certainty" and of the reductively relativistic
stance concerning value claims put forward by then-ascendant logical positivism
and its offshoot, ethical emotivism.[17] Their relativistic stance has been eerily
echoed and even carried further by postmodernist philosophers at the end of the
twentieth century, and Locke's critique of the earlier forms of value reductivism
is still relevant to them.

> [N]o conception of philosophy, however relativistic, however opposed to ab-
> solutism, can afford to ignore the question of ultimates or abandon what has
> been so aptly though skeptically termed "the quest for certainty." To do that
> is not merely to abdicate traditional metaphysics with its rationalistic justifi-
> cation of absolutes but also to stifle embryonic axiology with its promising
> analysis of norms. Several sections of American thought, however, have
> been so anxious to repudiate intellectualism and escape the autocracy of cat-
> egoricals and universals that they have been ready to risk this. Though they
> have at times discussed the problems of value, they have usually avoided
> their normative aspects, which has led them into a bloodless behaviorism as
> arid as the intellectualism they have abandoned or else resulted in a com-
> pletely individualistic and anarchic relativism, which has rightly been char-
> acterized as "philosophic Nihilism." In de-throning our absolutes, we must
> take care not to exile our imperatives, for after all, we live by them. We must
> realize more fully that values create these imperatives as well as the more
> formally super-imposed absolutes, and that norms control our behavior as
> well as guide our reasoning. . . . Man does not, cannot, live in a valueless
> world. (Harris 1989:34)

In opposition to such positivist, emotivist, and postmodernist approaches to de-
throning Kantian absolute value universals by rejecting the meaningfulness or the
interpersonal significance of ethical, aesthetic, and religious valuations, Locke
regards these and other valuations as supremely significant human activities that
call for an empirically based normative account.

However, in contrast with Dewey's normative emphasis in the 1932 *Ethics* on
the central role of cognitive reflection in reconstructing values, Locke stresses the

nearly insuperable significance of *imperatives of feeling* in the valuation process, and at the same time, suggests that flexible reorientation among value feeling-modes and normatively preferable reperception of values are possible. ". . .[W]e must realize that not in every instance is this normative control effected indirectly through judgmental or evaluational processes, but often through primary mechanisms of feeling modes and dispositional attitudes" (Harris 1989:34). Although Locke credits reason with playing a significant supportive and corrective role in clarifying, validating, and reorientating values, "the primary judgments of value are emotional judgments" (Harris 1989:39). Nonetheless, in proposing his own functional, radically empiricist approach to developing a theory of valuation in relation to a transformative democratic praxis, Locke concurs with Dewey that valuation as a set of activities is broad and fluid, including in the scope of his theory a wide range of religious, logical, scientific, and aesthetic dimensions, in addition to the specifically moral or ethical. He also concurs with Dewey's analysis of valuational activities as *ongoing processes in time*—dialectical processes interactively combining reflective uses of reason with feeling-laden perception, action, and re-perception—rather than as merely momentary appraisals.

Locke argues that a Jamesian pluralism unmediated by a set of comparative and normative principles has not resolved the problem of how differing values are to be understood and justified; and though pragmatism has helpfully shifted theoretical value questions from a focus on ends to a focus on the active processes of value creation, it has not settled the historically wide range of evaluative issues, but only succeeded in connecting their appraisal with a functional criterion of truth (Harris 1989:34–35). Still-unresolved theoretical issues about how to preferably transform value absolutisms and their related implications for praxis are enormously important, in Locke's view, because *most people are absolutists in practice,* and this is why their differing values lead to value strife, with all its profoundly tragic consequences.

> The common man, in both his individual and group behavior, perpetuates the problem in a very practical way. He sets up personal and private and group norms as standards and principles, and rightly or wrongly hypostatizes them as universals for all conditions, all times and all men. Whether then on the plane of reason or that of action, whether "above the battle" in the conflict of "isms" and the "bloodless [battle] of ideas" or in the battle of partisans with their conflicting and irreconcilable ways of life, the same essential strife goes on, and goes on in the name of eternal ends and deified ultimates. The blind practicality of the common man and the disinterested impracticality of the philosopher yield similar results and rationalizations. Moreover, such transvaluations of value as from time to time we have, lead neither to a truce of values nor to an effective devaluation; they merely resolve one dilemma and set up another. And so, the conflict of irreconcilables goes on as the divisive and competitive forces of our practical imperatives parallel the incompatibilities of our formal absolutes. (Harris 1989:35–36)

In search of *a remedy* for this real and destructive problem of everyday absolutism in practice that does not duplicate and compound its tendencies, Locke proposes to articulate *a realistically group-conscious, radically empiricist theory of commonalities and differences in valuation,* mediated by a set of cross-cultural, experience-based, comparative and normative meta-level principles. He offers *specific hypotheses* about how valuation actually occurs that can effectively guide the kind of *research* that will either confirm his generalizations or suggest the need to revise them.

> To my thinking, the gravest problem of contemporary philosophy is how to ground some normative principle or criterion of objective validity for values without resort to dogmatism and absolutism on the intellectual plane, and without falling into their corollaries, on the plane of social behavior and action, of intolerance and mass coercion. *This calls for a functional analysis of value norms and a search for normative principles in the immediate context of valuation. It raises the question whether the fundamental value modes have a way of setting up automatically or dispositionally their end-values prior to evaluative judgment.* Should this be the case, there would be available a more direct approach to the problem of value ultimates, and we might discover their primary normative character to reside in their functional role as stereotypes of feeling-attitudes and dispositional imperatives of action-choices, with this character reenforced only secondarily by reason and judgment about them as "absolutes." We should then be nearer a practical understanding of the operative mechanisms of valuation and of the grounds for our agreements and conflicts over values. (Harris 1989:36, emphasis mine)

Locke frames his theoretical claim *hypothetically,* although he clearly believes that research will bear out the value of his emphasis on feeling rather than cognition in the valuation process, both in its realism and in its efficiency at getting at the aspect of consciousness that is most powerful in the production of value strife, and thus, most in need of transformative reorientation. Such an empirical and normative study of valuation activities as he proposes will provide the basis for a *well-warranted and effective prescription for desirable transformations* in the plasticity of feeling orientations through respectful, democratic social processes of *critical education, conversation, and cooperation* in pursuit of more desirable experiences, reconstructed institutions, and ideal goals.

Within "Values and Imperatives" and subsequent essays, Locke outlines *a hypothetical theory of the universal human valuing process* that he believed would be richly born out by an empirical "anthropology in the broadest sense" while giving an effective direction to it by occupying a helpful and insightful "middle ground" between objectivism and subjectivism (Harris 1989:38). This middle ground is *a negotiated, experience-based intersubjectivity with an explicitly normative dimension* that proceeds by historical analysis, contemporary observation, cross-difference conversation, reflective reconsideration, hypothetical proposal, and the experiential test of ideal-directed transformative action. Drawing explicitly on Franz Brentano's empirical categorization of value types, as well as on Carl Jung's insights about inward vs. outward directionality in valuing activities, Locke constructs his own difference-regarding, feeling-focused, radical empiricist theory of valuation. He pairs this theory with *a model of value-transformative praxis* that reflects his own personal experience (direct and imaginatively expanded) in grappling with differing, oppositional, culture-linked values while struggling to renegotiate a preferable intergroup *modus vivendi* that fulfills the prerequisites for a democratic, cross-cultural peace.

According to Locke, *we as human beings experience values as a primary element of our original perception of situations and objects,* rather than as a separate and secondary redescription of an originally value-free experience. Reconstructing Brentano and Jung, Locke hypothesizes that we immediately categorize our experience in terms of a set of *four feeling-modes* (exaltation, tension, acceptance, and repose or equilibrium), each of which maps a *cognitive value form* (religious, ethical/moral, logical/scientific, and aesthetic, respectively), and each of which has both a *variable valence* (positive or negative) and a *directional focus* (inward or outward).[18] Thus, we operate within a stable *framework* of value feeling-modes and associated cognitive forms, but the situational or object-focused *contents* of our valuing activities are changeable, and we can experience the same object or situation through the lens of *more than one value feeling-mode,* with associated change in our cognitive valuing experience.

An example may illustrate Locke's point. In a solitary moment high up in the Rocky Mountains or the Himalayas, in an alpine meadow filled with the first flowers of early summer, one might pass from a positive, originally outward-focused aesthetic perception of soul-satisfying beauty to a brief, outwardly focused scientific sense of the surprisingly interactive order of the whole, to an experience of being struck by a positive, inward perception of one's own elevating unity with a holy place within a larger living universe (a feeling of religious awe). A leisurely celebration of this feeling might lead, by a train of associations, to an inward sense of less-positive contrast with one's ordinary obliviousness to nature, giving rise to a sense of inward conflict between that larger body of experience and this special moment, and, through a series of interactions between this ethical feeling-mode and cognitive reflection, to a feeling of discontentedness with the flatness and the insignificance of one's usual preoccupations. Finally, the contrast between this special experience of elevation and one's more typical flatness of aesthetic, religious, and moral feeling might lead to a resolution to refocus one's life purposes and to reform one's daily habits so as to continue this elevated and peace-giving mode of inward experience through a responsible reorientation to nature.

Locke suggests that the value feeling-modes themselves are the source of the *psychological urgency* about particular values we feel, although cognitive judgment and experiential testing can make an imperative feeling more explicit.

> These modes co-assert their own relevant norms: each sets up *a categorical imperative* of its own, *not of the Kantian sort* with rationalized universality

and objectivity, but instead *the psychological urgency (shall we say, necessity?) to construe the situation as of a particular qualitative form-character.* It is this that we term a functional categorical factor, since it operates in and through feeling, although it is later made explicit, analyzed, and validated by evaluative processes of judgment and experiential test. (Harris 1989:41, emphases mine)

If Locke's empirical hypothesis is correct, the categorical imperative we need to attend to is *not* the Kantian rationally validated (or rationalized) motive of will, but rather *the underlying imperative of feeling* that strongly inclines us to act on a certain perception of a situation. Each of Locke's four kinds of value feeling-modes has this imperative character about itself in particular, so that we experience that value feeling-mode as tending toward the absolute, even in competition with the other kinds of value feeling-modes we experience within ourselves. Moreover, we experience each of the basic value feeling-modes within a particular characteristic pattern of *habitual attitudinal stances,* the "stereotyped and dispositional attitudes which sustain them," again, each in competition with the others (Harris 1989:42). Thus, we are generally inclined to a certain rigidity and absolutism within ourselves on behalf of whatever value feeling-mode frames our original perception, even to the exclusion of our own other value feeling-modes that also call for our attention, and within which we could alternatively and autonomously frame our perception of the same thing or situation. On occasion, at least, this leads to *internal value conflicts.*

Locke's analysis allows us to explain both how such internal value conflicts develop within us and how normal, widely shared processes of resolving them work by reframing the contents of our experience through the differing lenses of our own alternative value feeling-modes. "Once a different form-feeling is evoked, the situation and value-type are, *ipso facto,* changed. Change the attitude, and irrespective of content, you change the value-type; the appropriate new predicates automatically follow" (Harris 1989:44). What Locke is saying here is that, although originally, perhaps by habit and preference, we may tend to perceive an object or situation through the lens of one of the four particular kinds of value feeling-modes, we have some perceptual autonomy to re-choose our value mode or attitude, even after the mode of our original perception strongly suggests a particular evaluative response. Thus, we can to some extent *consciously, reflectively choose* to adopt a different attitude or mode of feeling-laden perception toward the object or situation. In addition, as is often the case, a train of associations within a relaxed mind, or the jolt of a new experience, may *immediately change* the way we perceive and feel about the object or situation, and consequently, what we are prepared to think and say about it. The kind of *normal urgency* Locke suggests we typically feel about *ending our internal value conflicts* may arise from a regulative desire to feel *James's peaceful "sentiment of rationality"* within our own stream of experience. This urgency may be aided in fulfilling its peace-seeking purpose by the *acquired knowledge* that the stimulus of another's differing evaluative stance, or a relaxed inner round of reorientations across alternative feeling modes, or a consciously chosen change in one's attitude toward a particular object or situation, will give rise to a different value feeling-mode, to the extent that one has the *personal self-directive skills* and the *habitual character virtues* to support this knowledge by flexibly adopting an alternative attitude.

This ability to adopt a different attitude and thus to move ourselves away from the absolutism of our own original value feeling-mode is an essential skill Locke thinks each of us must, and generally does learn in order to resolve *the value conflicts that naturally and inevitably arise within ourselves.* He regards its broader extension to include *at least some* of others' expressed and evinced absolutes within its scope as an invaluable skill for resolving *interpersonal and intercultural value conflicts.* Locke suggests that interpersonal conflicts may arise even between people who share a dominant value feeling-mode, such as the exaltation that gives rise to religious values, if they differ in their habitual and preferred directional orientations of those feelings (e.g., inwardly toward mystical ecstasy vs. outwardly toward reformist zeal) and, thus, in the cognitive attitudes and actions to which the differing directionalities give rise (Harris 1989:45). Certain value feeling-modes tend to become *dominant though never universal* among people who share a form of life within a relational economic and geopolitical situation. Because shared habits of initial perceptual orientations, related loyalty-building cognitive rationalizations growing out of shared experience, and shared habitual patterns of resultant action are important elements of what we mean by *shared culture,* these inner tendencies toward absolutism within all human individuals can also be seen to have a distinctively sociocultural dimension.

> [A]s each of these attitude-sets becomes dispositional and rationalized, we have the scientific clue to that pattern of value loyalties which divides humanity into psychological sub-species, each laying down rationalizations of ways of life that, empirically traced, are merely the projections of their predominant value tendencies and attitudes. (Harris 1989:46)

If they are allowed to, the differing attitudes associated with these differing preferred directional orientations relative to a shared dominant value mode may be cognitively rationalized into warring cultural and personal absolutes whose "taproot" is, in Locke's view, "will to power." (Harris 1989:46)

We can do little on the rational level, he suggests, to reconcile such warring absolutes once they have arisen. Instead, the solution lies in *understanding and reeducating the natural dynamic of our feeling-modes.*

> Little can be done toward their explanation or their reconciliation on the rational plane. Perhaps this is the truth that Brentano came near laying hands on when he suggested a love-hate dimensionality as fundamental to all valuation. Certainly the fundamental opposition of value modes and the attitudes based upon them has been one of the deepest sources of human division and conflict. The role of feeling can never be understood nor controlled through minimizing it; to admit it is the beginning of practical wisdom in such matters. (Harris 1989:46)

We can draw on our *learned understanding* of how to use our *internal mechanisms of reconciliation* between our own incompatible absolutes by shifting from one value feeling-mode to another in experiencing different dimensions of a situation (e.g., from religious exaltation to scientific acceptance or aesthetic repose), applying this *intrapersonal* understanding *interpersonally* in order to achieve a "truce of imperatives" based on a recognition of these stances' functional "reciprocity."

> Without doubt many value attitudes *as separate experiences* are incompatible and antithetic, but all of us, as individuals, reconcile these incompatibilities in our own experience when we shift, for variety as often as for necessity, from one mode of value to the other. *The effective antidote to value absolutism lies in a systematic and realistic demonstration that values are rooted in attitudes, not in reality, and pertain to ourselves, not to the world.* Consistent value pluralism might eventually make possible a *value loyalty not necessarily founded on value bigotry,* and impose a *truce of imperatives,* not denying the categorical factors in valuation, which, as we have seen, are functional, but *by insisting upon the reciprocity of these norms.* There is not necessarily irresolvable conflict between these separate value modes if, without discounting their emotional and functional incommensurability, we realize *their complementary character in human experience.* (Harris 1989:46, emphases mine)

By stressing the "reciprocity" of differing modes of experienced values, Locke is not suggesting that all of our warring absolutes actually amount to the same thing, or that we can compromise them interpersonally and somehow "meet in the middle," but rather that *sometimes* these incommensurable differences are the result of looking at the same object or situation through the *differing lenses of different preferred feeling-modes.* If this is the case, trying on the other's preferred lens may allow us to see the object or situation approximately as the other sees it, which will bring a certain appreciation of the resultant value perception, even if we continue to prefer our own original feeling-mode as an evaluative stance.

Locke is *not* suggesting, however, that *all* differences in valuation can be understood and appreciated in this way. *Some valuations will and must continue to seem simply wrong and harmful.*

> At the same time that it takes sides against the old absolutism and invalidates the *summum bonum* principle; this type of value pluralism does not invite the chaos of value-anarchy or the complete *laissez faire* of extreme value individualism. It rejects equally trying to reduce value distinctions to the flat continuum of a pleasure-pain economy or to a pragmatic instrumentalism of ends-means relations. (Harris 1989:47)

Thus, for example, the more than two hundred years of chattel slavery in America's not-yet-fully resolved past, like the Nazi genocide during the Holocaust that was still to come when Locke wrote this passage, were *deeply wrong and harmful,* in spite of the fact that they had some kind of cultural endorsement during their time.

Rather than trying to make such categorically absolute appraisals of culture-located feeling and reflection go away, Locke aims to provide the basis for demonstrations of their *cross-cultural validity* in terms of *a set of empirically grounded, meta-level normative value principles* that grow out of the overarching imperativeness of *a democratic peace* and its practical corollaries.

> Should such a view become established,—and I take that to be one of the real possibilities of an empirical theory of value, we shall then have *warrant* for taking as the *proper center of value loyalty* neither the worship of definitions or formulae nor the competitive monopolizing of value claims, but *the goal of maximizing the value-mode itself as an attitude and activity.* This attitude will itself be construed as the value essence. . . . *Social reciprocity for value loyalties* is but a new name for the old virtue of *tolerance,* yet it does bring the question of tolerance down from the lofty thin air of idealism and chivalry to the plane of enlightened self-interest and the practical possibilities of effective value-sharing. *As a working principle, it divorces proper value loyalty from unjustifiable value bigotry,* releases a cult from blind identification with creed and dogma, and invests no value interest with monopoly or permanent priority. (Harris 1989:48, emphases mine)

When Locke's advocacy of *democratic tolerance* is thus understood, it is very different from the dangerous form of value-neutral, ahistorical, unreflective tolerance with which his otherwise sympathetic interpreter, Johnny Washington, has charged Locke.[19] If Washington were right, Locke's principle of tolerance would block the possibility of any well-warranted evaluation of racism within the historical dynamic of American democracy, including chattel slavery, the sabotaged failure of Reconstruction, and its legacy of continuing inequalities, exclusions, and resentments as *real and wrong.* Thus, it would remove the *normative ground* for any interpersonally, cross-culturally significant call for *institutional and attitudinal reconstruction,* as well as for *restitution* to the survivors of those harmed by chattel slavery and the Holocaust.

However, more carefully interpreted, Locke's approach to value theory would have opposite implications from those Washington fears. It would call America's insufficiently deep democracy as well as Germany's so-called "national socialism" to account for violating what Locke, with Josiah Royce, calls *"loyalty to loyalty"*—a concern to support the possibility of others' experiencing loyalty, one of the great goods of human experience, that frames and limits particular loyalties. Locke's approach would also criticize both nations for violating many of the *"common humane values"* that the globally catastrophic events of World War II led representatives of widely differing cultures to cooperatively express in solemn and mutually significant terms within the United Nations Declaration of Human Rights.

> *Loyalty to loyalty* transposed to all the fundamental value orders would then have meant, reverence for reverence, tolerance between moral systems, reciprocity in art, and had so good a metaphysician been able to conceive it, relativism in philosophy. (Harris 1989:49)

Royce argued that *"loyalty to loyalty" as a democratic ideal value has an empirical basis,* that mature members of a variety of world cultures have long recognized the value of others' culturally differing modes of attachment to their families, faiths, people, lands, traditions, and hopes for the future, and have honored each other for this.[20]

In calling for a "cultural relativism" in philosophy guided by Royce's principle of loyalty to loyalty, Locke is not concurring with the reductive relativists he had so pointedly criticized at the beginning of "Values and Imperatives." Rather, he is suggesting that *a plurality* of group-derivative, creatively and reconstructively harmonized value stances, habitual patterns of preferential employment of the diverse feeling-modes, and related patterns of socially coordinated action are likely to turn out upon empirical investigation and cross-difference negotiation to be *cognitively warrantable,* and perhaps part of the full story of the Jamesian pluriverse.

> What over a century ago was only an inspired metaphorical flash in the solitary universal mind of a Goethe,—that phrase about civilization being a fugue in which, voice by voice, the several nations and people took up and carried the interwoven theme, could in our day become a systematic philosophy of history. . . . (Harris 1989:48)

The best way to live peacefully in a world shaped by such culture-related value differences, Locke argues, is to *strive for agreement when agreement is necessary*—as is shared, perpetual opposition to chattel slavery and genocide—and to *"live and let live"* in appreciation of one another's differing group-related value loyalties when agreement is not necessary.

History has taught us that we must *reduce our ordinary, everyday value conflicts* wherever we can, not only because of their own urgency, but also because *we must be able to stand together cross-culturally in opposition to cataclysmic violations of value* that we collectively understand must never again be tolerated. Locke's proposal about how to prepare ourselves to resolve interpersonal and cross-cultural value conflicts is to learn and to teach others to *broaden the scope of our familiar skills of internal peacemaking and to project them outward,* interpersonally and across group-related value differences, drawing on his principle of *critical social reciprocity.* Many people today, adults as well as children, may need remedial assistance in developing such internal self-management skills and related character virtues in order to lessen the univocal grip of a totalizing absolute of feeling by learning to flexibly use perceptual reorientation and attitude readjustment to make room for their own other feeling modes. We must all learn to do this if we are ever to become able to broaden the scope of such skills and virtues to include the differing feelings, attitudes, and norms of others. Locke's hope is that, through effective formal and informal education, many of us can develop these internal and interpersonal skills to their broadest extension, so that we can flexibly adopt widely differing alternative attitudes that encompass diversity and *make peace within our own inner worlds, as well as in interaction with people of other cultures* whose preferred value modes, directional orientations, valences, attitudes, and customary modes of action are significantly different from our own.

Critical–Empirical Social Science: "Anthropology in the Broadest Sense"

In order to provide an empirical basis for his quest for a cosmopolitan unity amidst diversity, Locke calls for and makes insightful contributions to the development of a critical, cross-disciplinary, transformation fostering *"anthropology in the broadest sense."* Rather than retilling the same ground that he believed James and DuBois had already effectively analyzed, Locke called other laborers to join him in cultivating growth of knowledge about the values of various cultures and the fruits thereof by empirically testing his hypothetical value theory. Locke himself employed this approach effectively in studying and transvaluing values within his own special sector of cultural experience, the uniquely African American cultural fusion. This was possible because Locke's "anthropology in the broadest sense" is not a disinterested, nonparticipatory, "purely objective" approach to studying humanity's differing group-based experience of beliefs, values, and institutional practices. Following James, Locke did not believe that such a nonparticipant social science is possible, since we are ourselves always active, belief-directed "x-factors" in James's complete world formula, "M + x."[21] Moreover, extensive human experience, including the twentieth century's cataclysmic events of civil and international value strife, have already given us an extensive evidential basis for focusing our empirical search. Finally, the need to satisfy *our own inner sentiment of rationality,* relating as it does to *our own future directionality,* motivates adoption of *a hypothetical belief* that this *cooperative, cross-disciplinary "anthropology in the broadest sense"* will allow us to discover and to validate *a set of common humane values* within our valued diversity that can become *our basis for peace.*

In his discussion within "Cultural Relativism and Ideological Peace" (1944) of the implications for social science of his culturally pluralistic reconstruction of James's pragmatist value theory, Locke lists a set of *three methodological "working principles"* for a critical, peace-seeking "anthropology in the broadest sense" that are derived from his ideal values of loyalty to loyalty, democratic tolerance, and peace, and thus, that combine descriptive and normative aspects.

> 1. The principle of *cultural equivalence,* under which we would more wisely press the search for functional similarities in our analyses and comparisons of human cultures; thus offsetting our traditional and excessive emphasis upon cultural difference. Such functional equivalences, which we might term *"culture-cognates"* or *"culture-correlates,"* discovered underneath deceptive but superficial institutional divergence, would provide objective but soundly neutral common denominators for intercultural understanding and cooperation;
>
> 2. The principle of *cultural reciprocity,* which, by a general recognition of the reciprocal character of all contacts between cultures and of the fact that all modern cultures are highly composite ones, would invalidate the lump estimating of cultures in terms of generalized, *en bloc* assumptions of superiority and inferiority, substituting scientific, point-by-point comparisons with

their correspondingly limited, specific, and objectively verifiable superiorities or inferiorities;

3. The principle of *limited cultural convertibility,* that, since culture elements, though widely interchangeable, are so separable, the institutional forms from their values and the values from their institutional forms, the organic selectivity and assimilative capacity of a borrowing culture becomes a limiting criterion for cultural exchange. Conversely, pressure acculturation and the mass transplanting of culture, the stock procedure of groups with traditions of culture 'superiority' and dominance, are counterindicated as against both the interests of cultural efficiency and the natural trends of cultural selectivity. (Harris 1989:73)

The first of these principles as Locke explains it here, *cultural equivalence,* seems intended to discourage a theoretical focus on the unique or exotic, instead preparing the way for discovery of *"common humane values"* by focusing attention on differing functional adaptations by means of which various cultural groups in their particular historical, geographic, and geopolitical locations have attempted to meet their *common human needs* in response to their reflectively considered value feeling-modes. We share a form of embodiment, a social species nature, an evolutionary history, and a set of evolved cognitive–emotional structures that frame our experience within nature, as well as complex linguistic capacities and a telos-seeking approach to our individual and communal projects. These give rise to a large set of interconnected needs that can be prioritized, conceptualized, pursued, and ritualized in various ways, depending on environment, invention, choice, chance and the influence of other cultures. Thus, we can expect to find *differing but functionally equivalent ways* of meeting these needs among various cultural groups. Locke's second methodological principle, *cultural reciprocity,* emphasizes that differing cultures share the planet and have influenced one another's development to such an extent that none of them can be accurately understood as "pure" or superior overall to the rest. Instead, their specific features must be analyzed and critically evaluated in terms of the functional impacts they have on members of their own and other cultures. Locke's third methodological principle, *limited cultural convertibility,* is a difference-acknowledging descriptive principle with normative implications, such that *democratically tolerable forms of cultural diversity are to be valued as contributive to the evolution of civilizations, and to be taken seriously in effective, democratic processes of specific, culturally located institutional transformations.* This principle suggests, for example, that policies of the International Monetary Fund (IMF) and the World Bank concerning post-Soviet societies, Latin America, Asia, and Africa need to be culture-specific rather than based on some theoretically universal, economistic model of capitalism that hides its historical and cultural origins as well as the interests it most effectively serves.

Some of the important contributions Locke's comments about his three methodological concepts can offer to our contemporary controversies about the possibilities and prerequisites of "unity in diversity" are expressed in his insights that not all cultural differences are equally deep and important, that all modern cultures are highly composite rather than pure and distinct, and that there are limits to the desirable scope of cross-cultural interchange of values and their institutional forms that we must respect in equitable cross-cultural collaborations. Locke's methodological values suggest *a social scientific approach for a critical, cross-disciplinary "anthropology in the broadest sense"* that would be *validated by its progress* in fostering the deepened realization of the democratic ideals that motivate it. Investigating and evaluating relationally contextualized, culturally specific values would be its primary focus as it seeks to discover both *common humane values* and *unconvertible cultural differences*. As Locke persuasively argued, the kind of *cross-cultural democratic unity* such an empirically warranted value theory and practice would help to achieve does *not* require *uniformity*.

> It is a *fluid and functional unity* rather than *a fixed and irrevocable one,* and its vital norms are equivalence and reciprocity rather than identity or complete agreement. (Harris 1989:71)

Understood in this way, rather than as Jacques Derrida, Iris Marion Young, and other postmodernist critics analyzed the concept, *unity* is fully compatible with *diversity,* and the quest for unity so understood need *not* lead to *oppression* of the less powerful or repress differences in interchanges within or between cultures.

This evaluatively descriptive information would be invaluable to *peace-building processes* of fostering democratic cooperation across historically contested differences. It could also contribute curricular materials to *democratic educational processes* that will develop the understanding and the skills we need in our global millennial era in order to realize cosmopolitan unity amidst valued diversity. However, nothing in the model as thus far explained allows us to make the evaluative move from common *human* values to common *humane* values that is the key to its democratic peacemaking potential. This requires *a further evolution of cultural values within actual cross-cultural negotiation processes,* including imaginative transvaluation of values.

Taken as a whole, Locke's empirically grounded, culturally pluralistic value theory, which he began developing in *Race Contacts and Interracial Relations* (1915–1916) and his "New Negro Manifesto" (1925), which he outlined in "Values and Imperatives" (1935), and to which he continued to add detail in *When Peoples Meet* (1942) and a series of essays, especially "Pluralism and Intellectual Democracy" (1942) and "Cultural Relativism and Ideological Peace" (1944), involves *interactions among three kinds of values* that, working together and interpersonally across differences, have the potential to end intrapersonal, interpersonal, and cross-cultural value strife and to replace it with democratic peace. These three kinds of values include: (1) *democratic ideal values* that motivate the effort to resolve interpersonal and cross-cultural value strife, including democracy, peace, and loyalty to loyalty; (2) *methodological values* to guide the work of a cross-disciplinary, critical–empirical, transformation-fostering "anthropology in the broadest sense," including cultural equivalence, cultural reciprocity, and limited cultural convertibility; and (3) *empirical values* on three levels that interlink individuals within and between cultures, including (a) those *common humane values* whose family resemblant, functionally equivalent character Locke believed this new critical–transformative social science would confirm and foster, (b) *distinctively differing cultural values* relationally understood, and (c) *individual transvaluations of values* that reflect, yet have the potential to creatively transform the cultural values from which they originally derive.[22]

In their actual operations, Locke seems to rightly suggest that values of all of these kinds and levels would *dynamically contextualize and critically correct one another.* For example, one might reflect on a previous, feeling-based valuation in light of democratic ideal values or common humane values. Or one might draw on Locke's methodological values as well as shared culturally specific values in order to teach another member of one's culture how to develop intrapersonal or interpersonal skills in ending value conflicts. Or one might draw on all three kinds of values to transform traditional, power-structured cross-cultural relations through conversation, negotiation, and the development of cooperative democratic projects.

The life and writings of Martin Luther King, Jr., offer an example of these three kinds and levels of values operating interactively and reconstructively to good effect: *creative and culturally reconstructive individual transvaluations of cultural values* are communicated as new interpretations of struggle-born, African American values within the larger American cultural fusion, combined with a historically specific liberation theology within the Judeo–Christian prophetic stream, yet drawing upon *common humane values* including justice, the Golden Rule, and human dignity–respecting provisions for access to opportunities and basic goods for those who have been marginalized by the imperfect operations of institutional systems or by bad luck. These draw upon *cross-cultural appropriations of the Biblical justice traditions* of leaving the edges of fields to be gleaned by widows and orphans and of revising property relations during the Jubilee Year, interactively warranted and being warranted by the *democratic ideal values* King rhetorically evokes, including peace, loyalty to loyalty, reciprocity, and a kind of critical relativism about interpersonal and cultural values.[23]

In grounding his "culturally relativistic" value theory in a set of democratic ideal values, Locke is *not* focusing on *how we originally acquire* our values or how members of a particular culture *typically justify* their shared values, e.g., how faithful inheritors of Islam, Confucianism, Hinduism, Buddhism, Christianity, or Native American spiritual traditions learn to think and act within their cultural value frameworks, and why they regard these value systems as justified. Rather, the focus of Locke's value theory is twofold. First, Locke seeks to describe the *mature processes of reflective, experiential reinterpretation or transvaluation of values* that are necessary and desirable within each of these differing cultural traditions. Second, he hopes to explain *how we must and can learn to understand and to work with value differences across diverse cultural value frameworks* if we are to achieve a just and dignified peace. Such a peace, Locke suggests, must be based on *common humane values* of the kind the United Nations Declaration of Human Rights attempts to express, as well as on *respect for differences in responsible interpretations* of these rights and for their *differing roles* in the ways differently situated communities of memory and hope imagine and struggle to realize the good life.

Significant differences in value stances, processes, and outcomes correlated with culture, class, and gender that subsequent historical developments have made highly visible show why the aspects of valuation and of the peacemaking processes Locke emphasized are so important, and why they must precede the aspects of reflective reason Dewey emphasized within *a democratic transformative ethics that includes interpretive, reflective, and evaluative elements.* A broader, more democratic, postcolonial dispersal of cultural power means that no one dominant group is in a position to summon or compel all the other groups to listen submissively and attentively to its teachings on universal value commonalities. If such *commonalities* are to matter, they cannot be *stipulated,* but must be *discovered* or *negotiated* through *a cooperative, cross-difference process* of information-seeking and understanding-building that results in a *cultivated pluralism* that will change some customary self-understandings and destabilize some existing, power-structured relationships with others in the process.[24]

Mutual willingness to enter into such processes must be *carefully nurtured* in a suspicious, power-structured world within which communities of memory have some major past and present problems with each other to overcome if their trust is to be elicited and their hopes are to be progressively intertwined. The imperative quality of feelings that are connected with such memories of past harms and such suspicions of present motives should not be passed over too quickly as theorists attempt to design processes for creating *cross-difference cosmopolitan moral convergences* in praxis. Any hint that "cosmopolitan convergence" is code language for the same old self-serving "cultural conversion" that Locke has so insightfully shown imperial peoples to have practiced in the past would undermine the tentative trust upon which cooperative negotiation processes must be built.

Surely it is true that any hope for a cosmopolitan unity of values expressed in cooperative interaction amidst recognized and valued diversity relies on the willingness and developed capability of representative and leading members of differing groups to sensitively listen and learn, to share their experience honestly and with the confidence that it will be respected, and to reflectively reconsider their memories, their past valuations, and their hopes, as Dewey suggests. However, the kinds of relational contexts within which such renegotiations are likely to occur cannot be created by simple exhortation of differing, historically divided peoples to be reasonable according to Dewey's hypothetically universal model. They must develop out of realistic recognition of characteristic, group-correlated differences in the value feeling-modes with which reflective reason interacts, perhaps in varying ways. If it is empirically confirmed, Locke's suggestion that each of us has already attained some degree of mastery of sophisticated processes of interpersonal interconvertibility in value feeling-modes offers hope that, if this skill is used in combination with cultivated interpersonal respect, more information about culturally differing others, and more deeply democratic, ideal-guided approaches to reflective moral reasoning, we can overcome present suspicions that loyalty to one's own group values is incompatible with development of the kind of loyalty to loyalty that Locke persuasively suggests is necessary to sustainable intergroup peacemaking.

Democratic Cooperation across Historically Contested Differences

Guided by Locke's "critical relativism" in progressive processes of cross-cultural conversation and negotiation, we can recognize or create functional value commonalities amidst our acknowledged and valued diversity, and then employ both aspects of this recognition to direct democratic decision making and collaborative action. In "Cultural Relativism and Ideological Peace" (1944), Locke projects that there will be *step-wise stages of development* in the practical capacity of differing groups to engage in *cross-difference conversation, negotiation, and collaboration* with each other.

> [Cultural] Relativism, with no arbitrary specifications of unity, no imperious demand for universality, nevertheless enjoins a beneficent neutrality between divergent positions, and, in the case of the contacts of cultures, would in due course promote, step by step, from an initial stage of cultural tolerance, mutual respect, reciprocal exchange, some specific communities of agreement and, finally, with sufficient mutual understanding and confidence, commonality of purpose and action. (Harris 1989:71)

Locke's suggestions in "Pluralism and Intellectual Democracy" (1942) about how to employ this process in *developing cross-cultural relationships into a deep and lasting peace* following the cultural value clashes that led to and sanctioned the violent brutality of World War II have relevance for us today, as we seek ways to end specific ethnic conflicts and to achieve *the full, cooperative meaning of democracy.*

> A reasonable democratic peace (like no other peace before it) must integrate victors and vanquished alike, and justly. With no shadow of cultural superiority, it must respectfully protect the cultural values and institutional forms and traditions of a vast congeries of peoples and races—European, Asiatic, African, American, Australasian. Somehow cultural pluralism may yield a touchstone for such thinking. Direct participational representation of all considerable groups must be provided for, although how imperialism is to concede this is almost beyond immediate imagining. That most absolutistic of all our secular concepts, the autonomous, sacrosanct character of national sovereignty, must surely be modified and voluntarily abridged. Daring reciprocities will have to be worked out if the basic traditional democratic freedoms are ever to be transposed to world practice, not to mention the complicated reconstruction of economic life which consistent reciprocity will demand in this field. One suspects that the practical exigencies of world reconstruction will force many of these issues to solution from the practical side, leaving us intellectuals to rationalize the changes *ex post facto.* Out of the crisis may yet come the forced extension of democratic values and mechanisms in ways that we have not had courage to think of since the days of

democracy's early eighteenth century conception, when it was naively, but perhaps very correctly assumed that to have validity at all democracy must have world vogue. (Harris 1989:62–63)

Locke suggests here that a cease-fire enforced by military might is not the same as *peace,* which can only be developed by transforming the conflicting value systems that lead to war from absolutisms and fundamentalisms into pluralistically held value loyalties.

The best way to bring about this *peacemaking democratic transformation* is by *stage-wise progression,* starting with *bringing together on just terms the representatives of all the conflicting groups who recognize that they have an interest in peace,* even though some (perhaps most) of them will still be understanding their loyalty to their own culture's values in absolutist and perhaps fundamentalist terms. Because differing groups are so closely interconnected and so mutually influential in our modern world of complex cultures and global interchange, these representatives will already have some awareness of each other's cultures, but they may not understand each other's historically rooted perspectives. So the first thing they must do is to *talk to each other as tolerantly as they can* in order to learn about the other's experience and concerns, to discover their functional commonalities, and to learn a deeper respect for each other as individuals and as group representatives. On this basis, *specifically appropriate reciprocal exchanges* can be arranged, which, if well-handled by all involved, may lead to *recognition of some areas of agreement, the beginnings of well-founded trust, and the willingness to undertake some collaborative projects for their groups' mutual benefit.* Of course, individuals and groups who persist in their absolutisms and fundamentalisms will be impediments to this process, but Locke expects that these stances will have difficulty enduring in the face of *the scholarly evidence* and *the lived experience of just interaction with others* who embody both group value differences and humane value commonalities (Harris 1989:70). As an Irish constable said about an underground program of retreat-style weekend meetings that he and his Belfast-based priest–brother were operating, through which they were bringing together in a safe and secret place Catholics and Protestants who had never really talked with a member of the other, "enemy" group relative to which they held an oppositional identity, "At least they learn that the other is not the devil with horns." Such strategies as Locke proposed and the Irish brothers employ might also bear fruit in seeking peace in Bosnia, Rwanda, and South Central Los Angeles.

It is important to remember the *hypothetical, contextual character* of Locke's theory-implicating prescription for transformative praxis in order to realize that, in a particular set of circumstances, it may offer invaluable guidance, but in circumstances in which its *contextual conditions* are not yet met, it must be *supplemented by other methods,* such as those King helped to develop. Locke's transformative prescription focuses on conditions in which culturally differing parties to power-structured historical conflicts have become persuaded by their own reflection-endorsed imperatives of value-feeling that it is time to come to the negotiating table and to bracket the previously absolutistic character of their own culturally located values as well as their narrowly adversarial cultural loyalties, so that they can more open-heartedly encounter as equals those who have been their enemies, their competitors, even their oppressors or imperial subordinates. Such *an overcoming of powerful, past-regarding, oppositional feelings* is only possible, Locke suggests, when former adversaries are motivated by *an even more powerful, future-regarding hope* that reflection helps to bring forth from them. Such a hope may move them to *attempt to negotiate that set of relational conditions* that is prerequisite to their hearts' mutual and varying deepest desires, which experience has shown them cannot be attained by dominance, control, violent sabotage, subversion, or in any other way: *the conditions of a just, lasting, and democratic peace.*

After a second world war within thirty years, during which countless lives were lost, innumerable hearts were broken past repair, cultural treasures were intentionally blown to pieces by both sides, and a variety of culturally cherished illusions were destroyed, the various warring parties were finally prepared to negotiate. Locke urged the importance of their *negotiating inclusively and as equals,* and making the *goal* not just the end of war but *a just and lasting democratic peace.* History shows that these conditions and goals were *not fully met* at the time, nor in the fifty years that followed the declaration of "peace." A "Cold War" continued, and many of the struggles for liberation from continuing colonialism had just begun. Nonetheless, the United Nations was founded, and the 1948 U.N. Declaration of Human Rights stands as a lasting reminder of two years of noble effort to listen to each other respectfully that resulted in a still-controversial yet still-useful statement of "common humane values" that has become a basis for further efforts to build a cooperative peace that is more than the end of global war.

In its subsequent employments, as in its context of development, the U.N. Declaration of Human Rights reflects the fact that Locke's hypothetical conditions for peacemaking have not been fulfilled. At the same time, it serves as a tool for bringing the still-warring absolutes of unreconciled cultural, economic, and political adversaries to both inner and practical, cross-difference negotiating tables. It played this background role within the American Civil Rights Movement of the 1950s and 1960s in both of its alternative, ultimately complementary branches: one led by Malcolm X (El-Hajj Malik El-Shabazz) and the Organization for Afro-American Unity he guided too briefly from the time of his conversion of heart and change of name in Mecca until his culturally and politically motivated assassination in 1963, and the other led by Martin Luther King, Jr., and the Southern Christian Leadership Conference (SCLC) until his 1968 assassination in still-unclear circumstances. In his poetic and persuasive *Letter from Birmingham Jail* (1963), King makes it clear that the nonviolent direct action campaign he and the SCLC had been conducting, which led to his incarceration with many other activists, had been adopted as a tactic only because their adversaries had refused to negotiate. Its goal was to bring about the kind of crisis of incompatible imperatives of feeling that would require their white Southern opponents to reorient their feelings, to reconsider their absolutes, and to recognize the necessity of meeting face to face in order to renegotiate the terms of cross-difference cooperative social life. The continuing significance of King's writings and his life witness, like those of Malcolm Shabazz and of other leaders and activists within the American Civil Rights Movement, have been widely attested to by leaders of related struggles in Europe and Africa, including South Africa's Nelson Mandela, as well as by liberation leaders in very different contexts of struggle in Asia and Latin America, all of them also seeking to bring their adversaries to the negotiating table in order to seek a cooperative path to conditions that fulfill the U.N. Declaration of Human Rights.

Thus, Locke's culturally pluralistic transformative prescription may need to be *supplemented* by those of King, Shabazz, Mandela, and others *in order to bring about the kind of conditions for which it is proposed as hypothetically applicable: conditions in which cross-cultural opponents have found a common interest in negotiating a new, positively peaceful modus vivendi.* Nonetheless, even in contexts where this precondition for the applicability of Locke's model has not been satisfied, it serves to indicate a crucially significant end-in-view that must be achieved in order for further transformative peacemaking processes to be fruitfully undertaken.

Intellectual Transformation and Critical Multicultural Education

The *practical role of intellectuals* in promoting a positive peace has two aspects, in Locke's view: *scholarship* and *teaching.* On the one hand, he argues in "Pluralism and Intellectual Democracy" (1942), collaboratively building up an empirical "anthropology in the broadest sense" requires learning enough about varying specific cultures to understand their unique functional adaptations to the conditions of their lived experience, and through that process, discovering the humane value commonalities that may become the basis of democratic cross-cultural bridges.

> *The intellectual core of the problems of the peace,* should it be in our control and leadership, will be the *discovery of* the necessary common denominators and the basic equivalences involved in a democratic world order or democracy on a world scale. (Harris 1989:62, emphases mine)

However, as Locke points out, the importance of this responsibility does not imply that intellectuals have already learned to *think pluralistically.* Rather, we must struggle to overcome our own absolutisms, fundamentalisms, and suspicions of the prospect of unity in diversity if we are to fulfill our portion of responsibility within the peace process.

> What intellectuals can do for the extension of the democratic way of life is to *discipline our thinking critically into some sort of realistic world-mindedness.* Broadening our cultural values and tempering our orthodoxies is of infinitely more service to enlarged democracy than direct praise and advocacy of democracy itself. For until broadened by [critical] relativism and reconstructed accordingly, our current democratic traditions and practice are not ready for world-wide application. Considerable political and cultural dogmatism, in the form of *culture bias, nation worship, and racism,* still stands

in the way and must first be invalidated and abandoned. In sum if we refuse to *orient ourselves courageously and intelligently to a universe of peoples and cultures*, and continue to base our prime values on fractional segments of nation, race, sect, or particular types of institutional culture, there is indeed little or no hope for a stable world order of any kind—democratic or otherwise. Even when the segment is itself a democratic order, its expansion to world proportions will not necessarily create a world democracy. *The democratic mind needs clarifying for the better guidance of the democratic will.* (Harris 1989:63, emphases mine)

Unless scholars and intellectuals develop this kind of *"realistic world-mindedness"* ourselves, we cannot insightfully understand cultural differences and discover humane value commonalities on which we can reconstruct a global vision of the processes, institutions, and deeper values of democratic community life appropriate for our time. If we can develop Locke's kind of culturally pluralistic perspective and bring it to our value research and theorizing, our scholarship may be able to *constructively influence and support the practical peacemakers* who need to come together around the table in the next twenty years. Of course, consulting scholars also have a great deal to learn from these cross-cultural actors in the inner circles of peacemaking transformative praxis. Though it is expressed in the same kind of misguidedly expert-focused language of social inquiry that Dewey employs, Locke's overall value theory clearly implies *creative participation of all walks of life,* because diverse transvaluative powers and forms of expertise are widely distributed.

If this kind of culturally pluralistic perspective and the scholarly research to which it gives rise can direct our teaching as well, we can hope to influence the way future generations understand others' group loyalties and shape their own. Thus, one of the important transformative objectives Locke prescribes that we need to undertake now in order to achieve this kind of peaceful, multicultural collaborative future is *transformation of the curricula* of our schools, colleges, and universities into broad cross-cultural encounters guided by what he called "critical relativism." In "The Need for a New Organon in Education" (1950), Locke argued that what is needed is not just extension, revision, or inclusion of new curricular elements, but *transformation of methods of thinking and teaching.*

> A more fundamental methodological change both *in ways of teaching and in ways of thinking* is necessary, if we are to achieve the objectives of reorientation and integration so obviously required and so ardently sought. (Harris 1989:266)

Students need to learn to *critically evaluate information* about the world's cultures, including their own, *in the historical context of the power-structured interaction of* those cultures. Clearly, Locke's "critical relativism" is very different from the simplistic forms of individual and cultural relativism in our schools and America's mass media today. All too often, these leave students "too polite" to comment about others' values and too intellectually insecure to take a normative stance, even about broadly humane values, except in the rare cases of students whose worldviews and characters are undergirded by religious fundamentalism or some other absolutism.

Locke's "critical relativism" is also very different from simply adding more non-Western information to the standard curriculum.

> Let us suppose, for example, that we have extended the study of history of man and his cultures from the conventional Western hemispheric to a global range and setting, have we automatically exorcised parochial thinking and corrected traditional culture bias? As I see it, not necessarily. It is surely a patent fallacy to assume that a change in the *scope of thinking* will change *the way of thinking*. To convert parochial thinking into global thinking involves *meeting head on their issues of conflict, realistically accounting for their differences by tracing the history of their development, and out of a process-logic of this development, bravely to take a normative stand.* (Harris 1989:268, emphases mine)

The alternative Locke proposes requires reeducating our teachers, and in turn, our students, away from traditional philosophical claims about the separateness of facts and values, instead preparing them to see how *values and their functional embodiment arise out of experience and serve certain needs.* Against this background of understanding their costs and who pays these, as well as their benefits and who receives these, their consequences for war or for peace can be assessed, and *empirically based value judgments* can be made.

> [T]he only practical alternative is to discover a way of projecting into the study of social fact a normative dimension objective enough to be scientifically commensurable. Though difficult, such a development is methodologically feasible. It could stem from a broadly comparative and critical study of values and their historical and cultural backgrounds. By so regarding civilizations and cultures as objective institutionalizations of their associated values, beliefs, and ideologies, a realistic basis can be developed not only for a scientific comparison of cultures but for an objective critique of the values and ideologies themselves. Study and training in such analyses and interpretations should develop in students *a capacity for thinking objectively but critically about situations and problems involving social and cultural values.* (Harris 1989:270)

In contrast with the curricular guidance of the kind of *traditional Eurocentrism* William Bennett and Allan Bloom have advocated in recent years, and also in contrast with the kind of *uncritical cultural relativism* that their opponents have too often posed as its only alternative, *Locke's "critical relativism"* would: (1) interpret values realistically in relation to backgrounds; (2) interpret values as "functional adaptations" to particular backgrounds, evaluating them pragmatically in terms of their "functional sufficiency and insufficiency"; (3) "claim . . . no validity for values beyond this relativistic framework"; (4) assess ideologies as "adjunct rationalization[s] of values and value interests"; (5) "trace value development and change as a dynamic process"; and (6) substitute this "realistic value dynamics" for "traditional value analytics, with its unrealistic symbols and over-generalized concepts" (Harris 1989:273–274). The kind of *intracultural critique* feminists have called for is implied within this kind of *critical cross-cultural pedagogy.* It can be further enriched by *decentering the teacher and even the classroom* to bring *active student-centered, community-based service learning* into the educational process.[25]

Many who advocate educational multiculturalism today simply recommend the addition of representative works from different voices and a greater range of world cultures than the traditional curriculum includes, teaching them as all equal in clarity and insight, or teaching that there is no basis for judging their merit that does not merely reflect either cultural power or advocacy for the disinherited. In contrast, Locke called for *a historical, relational expansion of the curriculum and a critical yet practical, problem-solving focus and measure of student learning.*

> It could stem from a broadly comparative and critical study of values and their historical and cultural backgrounds. By so regarding civilizations and cultures as objective institutionalizations of their associated values, beliefs, and ideologies, a realistic basis can be developed not only for a scientific comparison of cultures but for an objective critique of the values and ideologies themselves. Study and training in such analyses and interpretations should develop in students a capacity for thinking objectively but critically about situations and problems involving social and cultural values. (Harris 1989:270)

Although its aspects and implications need further development before we can use it to guide an insightful and democratically useful multicultural transformation of our curricula, Locke's "critical relativism" suggests *the middle path* so many teachers of ethics have been seeking between a universalized rational value absolutism that is dangerously blind to cultural differences, on the one hand, and skeptically limited forms of individualist and cultural relativisms that are dangerously antinormative, and thus useless as weapons against absolutist and fundamentalist embodiments of the will to power, on the other.[26] If we can develop and teach others the relevant *intrapersonal skills and character virtues,* Locke's recommended approaches to *critical multicultural education* can help to build the *interpersonal skills and character virtues* we need. It can shape the *relational knowledge base* and *practical experience* to guide these skills, while at the same time making the world a safer place in which to exercise them.

Transformative Cultural Democracy and the Neocapitalist Empire

Although such education-guided human development may reduce and eventually help to end cross-cultural value strife, it could *never* lead to *a global uniformity of values,* in Locke's view, even if economic, political, and military contributions to strife were resolved. Thus, he argued in "Values and Imperatives" (1935), we must learn to live with significant, but *democratically tolerable, cross-cultural value differences,* instead of trying to force differing peoples to adopt a uniform set of values and institutions, such as those that characterize "formal" democracies and capitalist global organizations. Locke offers *a prophetic, non-Marxian alternative* to the kind of value monopoly and cross-cultural institutional control that neocapitalist economists have guided the International Monetary Fund (IMF) in attempting to extend to a global basis since Soviet-style communism failed and the "Iron Curtain" in Eastern Europe came down in 1989.

> One way of reform undoubtedly is to combat the monopolistic tradition of most of our institutions. This sounds Marxian, and is to an extent. But the curtailing of the struggle over the means and instrumentalities of values will not eliminate our quarrels and conflicts about ends, and *long after the possible elimination of the profit motive, our varied imperatives will still persist.* Economic classes may be absorbed, but our psychological tribes will not thereby be dissolved. So, since there may be *monopolistic attitudes and policies with respect to ends and ideals* just as well as *monopolies of the instrumentalities of human values*—(and of this fact the ideological dogmatism of contemporary communism is itself a sad example), it may be more effective to invoke *a non-Marxian principle of maximizing values.* (Harris 1989:49, emphases mine)

The non-Marxian principle Locke had in mind was Royce's "loyalty to loyalty," which he thought has the transformative power to reframe diverse, historically clashing cultural perspectives in ways that make for a positive, cooperative peace.

Nonetheless, as Locke also argues in various places, cross-cultural value strife can never be ended without *global transformation in economic and political relations*—transformation away from the kind of multidimensional cultural imperialism he critiqued in his 1915–1916 lectures on *Race Contacts and Interracial Relations,* and toward *the substantive, systemic implications of deep democracy.* What he suggests here is that both the democratic transformative process and the goal of cosmopolitan unity amidst valued diversity that can only emerge through it have irreducible, cultural dimensions that will always imply *some areas of incommensurability in values.* Cultural differences are not simply the result of early isolation and differing adaptations during a mythical "Asiatic" period in economic development of the kind Marx theorized, nor are they simply the result of differing geopolitical power locations created and maintained by modern imperial capitalism. *Culture-specific differences* have always had and—barring total genocide—will always continue to have *a semi-autonomous character and potential trajectory,* though this is, of course, influenced by other forces as it develops within a power-structured network of cross-cultural relations. Thus, even if Marx is correct in his analysis of *a powerful economic engine within history,* and Dewey is also correct that there is *a second, moral-communicative engine,* the *linkage* between the two, Locke argues, has a *distinctively cultural character* that is not fully subsumed by either of them. Thus, though Locke's analysis shows an appreciation of Marx's, its focus is distinctively non-Marxian.

Critics of this non-Marxian dimension of Locke's analysis might argue that *global capitalism at the end of the twentieth century* has broken outside of the cultural boundaries Locke emphasized as an irreducible aspect of its operations at the beginning of the century. Instead of being culturally contained, they might say, *it now stands, vampire-like, outside all cultural, legal, political, and military systems, gobbling up all other value feelings and forms, and reducing them to a monetarily measurable, flat intersubstitutability.* Locke might reply that they are mistaken to believe that this transnational capitalist monster is anything other than the full-grown form of the less-developed Anglo–Saxon cultural imperialism he analyzed in the 1915–1916 lectures, having effectively extended acceptance of its rationale for dominance to a global level. *This is the same Leviathan grown up,* not only in its ideological control of national decisions and its functional control of financial markets through its individualistic propertarian logic, but also in the structural design of the IMF as well as in the enforced content of international law. *The cultural specificity and locatedness of global capitalism* is what Enrique Dussel points to in his claim that late-twentieth-century global capitalism must be understood as a strategically organized and rationalized domination of "the South" by "the North," and must be remedied with a comparable geopolitical and cultural specificity.[27]

As Locke and Dussel both suggest, to ignore this specifically cultural character of global capitalism—and who it serves—is to fail to grasp its actual, perverse motivational structure and, thus, to fail to understand *how it can be defeated and transformed.* The value cannibalism of mature global capitalism has *a specifically cultural character,* as do the values it feeds upon. What is lost to the world by its predations is *the cultural depth and diversity that human persons need in order to live fully human lives.* At the same time, this self-serving appetite for subversion of other cultures' values can be satisfied only at the expense of *a reductive flattening and homogenizing of its native culture's traditionally dominant value framework.* This inevitably leads to the derivative experience Cornel West has described as "existential nihilism": *a life of meaninglessness and anomie* even for successful members of the dominant culture, as well as for those it marginalizes, accompanied by *a hunger* felt by all but the most cynical and corrupt for *a life-giving value infusion of the existential elements they have been missing.* If the dominant culture is to reconstruct these lost cultural elements, and if other peoples are to regain the resources for effective individual, cultural, and cross-cultural resistance, they must regain their rootedness and semiautonomous trajectory within *dynamic, value-affirming cultural communities of memory and of hope,* while at the same time working for the kinds of *transformations in the global network of political and economic relationships that will allow these communities to flourish.* As Locke argues, working to positively transform intrapersonal, interpersonal, and cross-cultural value strife is a necessary aspect of working effectively for such democratic economic and political transformations—and also important in its own right when one values the cultural values at stake.

Thus, the key to the kind of *cultural democracy between cultures* that can resist and transform imperial neocapitalism is *personal growth in value-mode flexibility* combined with *democratic cultural revitalization, critical multicultural edu-*

cation, and *democratic cross-difference negotiation.* Such a deeply democratic, four-strand initiative will teach and instantiate creative self-knowledge, loyalty to loyalty, appreciation of differences, and cooperative struggle. At the same time, it will undercut the kinds of warring nationalisms that have resurfaced so violently in our times, and that tend to destroy *democracy within cultures.*

As Locke argued in his 1915–1916 lectures, we need to realize that *we who resist the global neocapitalist empire have power,* if we will claim it and develop it. Our sources of transformative energy will include not only *limited economic power,* but also *flexible strength of character, cultural resources for life sustenance and joie de vivre, experience-based transformative intelligence and creativity,* and *moral–communicative power*—especially at a time when the global capitalist empire's cultural inability to support a sense of meaning and purpose in life has left so many of its apparent beneficiaries gasping for existential air. *We need to claim these various forms of power, to multiply them, and to use them well.* This means we must pursue *lifelong educations in* personal development of attitudes and character that will wean us away from our own absolutisms, replacing them with value-mode flexibility, critical appreciation of our own and other cultures, adaptive histories of struggle, and loyalty to loyalty. It means we must develop *a critical multicultural approach to value inquiry and the education of our young people that will prepare them to participate in deep democracy and to accept nothing less.* And it means that we must continue to build on our successful experiences of *cross-difference conversation and cooperative struggle,* so that we can multiply our effectiveness and begin to realize "cosmopolitan unity amidst valued diversity" as a *transnational, multicultural community.* If we are successful in pursuing these strategies of deep democracy, the future meaning of the currently dominant empire will be nothing more than past-generated obstacles to the good life—obstacles we are already overcoming.

Notes

1. A series of books have brought Alain LeRoy Locke's work back to influential life, stimulating the founding of the Alain L. Locke Society, which supports further scholarship on the themes and concerns of Locke's work. See Leonard Harris's invaluable edited collections, *Philosophy Born of Struggle: Anthology of Afro-American Philosophy from 1917* (1983), *The Philosophy of Alain Locke: Harlem Renaissance and Beyond* (1989), and *The Critical Pragmatism of Alain Locke: A Reader on Value Theory, Aesthetics, Community, Culture, Race, and Education* (1999); Johnny Washington's *Alain Locke and Philosophy: A Quest for Cultural Pluralism* (1986) and *A Journey into the Philosophy of Alain Locke* (1994); Jeffrey C. Stewart's editor's introduction to and reconstructed text of Locke's *Race Contacts and Interracial Relations* (1992); and Arnold Rampersad's introduction to the republication of *The New Negro* (1992). I am grateful to members of the Society for the Advancement of American Philosophy, the Society for the Study of Africana Philosophy, and the Alain L. Locke Society for inviting me to present sections of this chapter to them, and for offering many stimulating and helpful comments.

2. I am grateful to J. Everet Green, organizer and moderator of the Third Annual Philosophy Born of Struggle Conference focusing on "The Harlem Renaissance and the Black Enlightenment" (October 1996), where I had the opportunity to present an earlier version of this section of this chapter and to benefit from the comments of my fellow panelists and conference participants.

3. See K. Anthony Appiah's half of the conversation in *Color Conscious: The Political Morality of Race* (1996) and Naomi Zack's *Race and Mixed Race* (1993).

4. See Charles Mills's *The Racial Contract* (1997), Lucius Outlaw's *On Race and Philosophy* (1996), and Amy Gutmann's half of the conversation in *Color Conscious: The Political Morality of Race* (1996).

5. See Locke's *Race Contacts and Interracial Relations*, edited with an introduction by Jeffrey C. Stewart (1992).

6. See Dewey's *The Public and Its Problems* (1927), in *The Later Works*, Vol. 2.

7. Here Locke reflects the historical analysis and transformative prescription of Booker T. Washington, as expressed in his 1895 "Atlanta Exposition Address," to which W.E.B. DuBois stood in lifelong opposition.

8. See Derek Bell's *Faces at the Bottom of the Well: The Permanence of Racism* (1992).

9. All citations in this chapter of Locke's manifesto-like editor's introduction to *The New Negro* (1925) are to the 1992 Atheneum edition. This passage is from *The New Negro*, 1925:4.

10. See Julius Nyerere's *Uhuru na Ujamaa: Freedom and Socialism* (1968).

11. For a well-researched, thoughtfully written discussion of the range and significance of rap music as a mode of cultural self-expression and cross-cultural renegotiation, see Tricia Rose's *Black Noise: Rap Music and Black Culture in Contemporary America* (1994).

12. On the multiple venues for the resurgence of African American poetry from street corners to concert halls, including multigenerational poetry festivals, see Jon Pareles's "Out of the Mouths of Black Poets," *The New York Times,* February 11, 1997, C11.

13. See Toni Morrison's powerful *Beloved* (1987), her insightful essays in *Playing in the Dark: Whiteness and the Literary Imagination* (1992), as well as the influential collection of essays she edited, *Race-ing Justice, En-gendering Power: Essays on Anita Hill, Clarence Thomas, and the Construction of Social Reality* (1992). See Alice Walker's novels *The Color Purple* (1982) and *The Temple of My Familiar* (1989), as well as her influential collection of essays, *In Search of Our Mothers' Gardens* (1983). In *The Future of the Race* (1996), Henry Louis Gates, Jr., argues that, in recent years, the arts have shown themselves to be the most effective vehicle for and dimension of African American liberation as well as a broader democratic deepening within and beyond American culture.

14. On the quality and significance of Wynton Marsalis's "Blood on the Fields," as well as the value of his retrieval of the multicultural roots of jazz history through his leadership of the Lincoln Center Jazz Orchestra, see Theodore Rosengarten's "Songs of Slavery Lifted by a Chorus of Horns," *The New York Times,* February 23, 1997, H1.

15. "Organic public intellectual" is a descriptive phrase that Cornel West, following Antonio Gramsci, has revived. It refers to the kind of socially engaged scholar Locke was, one whose work reflects awareness of ongoing cultural developments and problem situations, and who writes at least some essays for journals that reach a broad audience of nonspecialists, thereby having a significant effect on the developments of the times.

16. All cited essays by Locke are included in Leonard Harris's edited collection, *The Philosophy of Alain Locke: Harlem Renaissance and Beyond* (1989).

17. See Dewey's *The Quest for Certainty* (1929) and his *Theory of Valuation* (1939). In my view, Locke's critique of the Western philosophical "quest for certainty" allies him broadly with Dewey, contrary to Leonard Harris's suggestion that Locke rejected Dewey's approach as well as Kant's. Contra the view of Ernest Mason that Harris reports, I also read Locke's value-critique of metaphysical absolutism as incompatible with Derridean deconstruction (Harris 31–33).

18. This is a summary of Locke's discussion (Harris 1989:39–43), which is displayed visually in a chart on p. 43.

19. See Washington's "Alain L. Locke's 'Values and Imperatives': An Interpretation," in Leonard Harris's edited collection, *Philosophy Born of Struggle: Anthology of Afro-American Philosophy from 1917* (1983).

20. See Josiah Royce's chapter on "Loyalty to Loyalty" in his *The Philosophy of Loyalty* (1908).

21. See William James's "The Dilemma of Determinism" (1884), later included in *The Will to Believe and Other Essays in Popular Philosophy* (1897).

22. In suggesting that Locke's functionally equivalent common humane values have a "family resemblant" character, I mean to evoke Ludwig Wittgenstein's analysis of commonalities amidst diversity in uses of a concept or language-game in *Philosophical Investigations* (1958). In *On Certainty* (1969), the book he was writing in the last months before his death in 1951, Wittgenstein expresses his general sympathy with some developments in pragmatism and cultural anthropology; see remark 422.

23. See King's "Letter from Birmingham Jail" (1963) in *A Testament of Hope The Essential Writings and Speeches of Martin Luther King, Jr.* (1986), ed. James M. Washington. See also Taylor Branch's Pulitzer Prize–winning discussion of King's life and work in *Parting the Waters: America in the King Years, 1954–63* (1988).

24. "Cultivated pluralism" is Kenneth Stikkers's term, stressing the creative, developmental aspect of the process that Locke's more descriptive language hides. See his "Instrumental Relativism and Cultivated Pluralism" in Harris (1999).

25. On feminist pedagogy, see *Gender and Academe: Feminist Pedagogy and Politics* (1994), ed. Sara Munson Deats and Lagretta Tallent Lenker, and Johnnetta B. Cole's "She Who Learns Must Teach" in her *Conversations: Straight Talk with America's Sister President* (1993). An insightful, widely influential work that stresses the importance of decentering the teacher in order to activate students' agency, creativity, and responsibility is Paulo Freire's *Pedagogy of the Oppressed* (1970). On community-based service learning, see *Beyond the Tower: Philosophy and Service Learning*, ed. David Lisman.

26. I have proposed a critical multicultural educational model that draws on Locke's and Dewey's suggestions about how to deepen democracy in my "Educational Multiculturalism, Critical Pluralism, and Deep Democracy," in *Theorizing Multiculturalism: A Guide to the Current Debate* (1998), ed. Cynthia Willett.

27. See Dussel's *Ethics and Community* (1988).

Chapter 5

Prophetic Pragmatism: King, West, and the Beloved Community

> *If great new undertakings enter into the lives of many men, a new community of hope, unified by the common relations of its individual members to the same future events, may be, upon occasion, very rapidly constituted, even in the midst of great revolutions.*
>
> —JOSIAH ROYCE, *The Problem of Christianity* (1918)

Introduction

How can we motivate ourselves and our fellow citizens to risk our hopes as well as our time, effort, and resources in working to transform our democratically deficient societies? How can we sustain ourselves in struggle over the long time period it may take to achieve and to institutionalize deep democracy's habits of the heart and ways of community life, especially in the face of entrenched and powerful opposition? A prophetic pragmatism that struggles and builds toward the Beloved Community offers promising answers to these key questions of democratic character, and of the character of effective transformative movement toward deep democracy.

In the last chapter of his brilliant and highly influential book, *The American Evasion of Philosophy: A Genealogy of Pragmatism,* Cornel West prophetically called for a reengagement of American philosophy with the practical work of democratic social transformation. "Prophetic pragmatism" is the label West chose for the kind of theoretical and practical political engagement he believes America and the world need now. Although West does not specify its elements in that context, his conception of prophetic pragmatism seems to combine a pragmatic approach to transformative theory, a significant role for guiding ideals, and a motivating personal sense of the moral urgency of democratic change-making action. After five chapters of critically discussing the distinctively American genealogy and character of pragmatism as a transformative theoretical approach, West's surprising choice of a patron saint for prophetic pragmatism is the brilliant Italian communist theorist, Antonio Gramsci.

> Prophetic pragmatism is inspired by the example of Antonio Gramsci principally because he is the major twentieth-century philosopher of praxis, power, and provocation without devaluing theory, adopting unidimensional conceptions of power, or reducing provocation to Clausewitzian calculations of war-

fare. Gramsci's work is historically specific, theoretically engaging, and politically activistic in an exemplary manner. His concrete and detailed investigations are grounded in and reflections upon local struggles, yet theoretically sensitive to structural dynamics and international phenomena. He is attuned to the complex linkage of socially constructed identities to human agency while still convinced of the crucial role of the ever-changing forms in class-ridden economic modes of production. Despite his fluid Leninist conception of political organization and mobilization (which downplays the democratic and libertarian values of prophetic pragmatists) and his unswerving allegiance to sophisticated Marxist social theory (which is an indispensable yet ultimately inadequate weapon for prophetic pragmatists), Gramsci exemplifies the critical spirit and oppositional sentiments of prophetic pragmatism. (West 1989:231)

Although West expresses great appreciation for Martin Luther King, Jr.'s historical contribution to the legacy on which West himself draws in calling for a new and more deeply democratic social transformation movement, West regards King's contribution as *practical* rather than *theoretical.*

The social movement led by Martin Luther King, Jr., represents the best of what the political dimension of prophetic pragmatism is all about. Like Sojourner Truth, Walter Rauschenbusch, Elizabeth Cady Stanton, and Dorothy Day, King was not a prophetic pragmatist. Yet like them he was a prophet, in which role he contributed mightily to the political project of prophetic pragmatism. His all-embracing moral vision facilitated alliances and coalitions across racial, gender, class, and religious lines. His Gandhian method of nonviolent resistance highlighted forms of love, courage, and discipline worthy of a compassionate prophet. And his appropriation and interpretation of American civil religion extended the tradition of American jeremiads, a tradition of public exhortation that joins social criticisms of America to moral renewal and admonishes the country to be true to its founding ideals of freedom, equality, and democracy. King accented the antiracist and anti-imperialist consequences of taking seriously these ideals, thereby linking the struggle for freedom in America to those movements in South Africa, Poland, South Korea, Ethiopia, Chile, and the Soviet Union. (West 1989:234–235)

Somehow, although Gramsci was not a pragmatist, he offers theoretical inspiration to prophetic pragmatism as West conceives of it, but King does not: "the social movement led by Martin Luther King, Jr., represents the best of what the *political* dimension of prophetic pragmatism is all about," but "King was *not* a prophetic pragmatist."

Why is this? Perhaps West does not regard King as a prophetic pragmatist because he believes King was *not a pragmatist.* In other words, perhaps West believes King was committed to fixed and unchanging antecedent political, moral, and spiritual ideals to be realized by platonic successive approximations in transformative praxis, rather than open to the kind of protean and dynamically developing guiding ideals that emerge from John Dewey's theorizing of pragmatist transformative praxis.[1] Such an interpretive claim has been made by some King scholars who point to his earlier self-description as their basis for interpreting him as a lifelong *personalist,* which implies to them both an antimaterialist metaphysics and an antecedently given and divinely originating set of moral ideals that somehow do not require creative human interpretation. This may be what West intends in part by his comment about King's "appropriation and interpretation of *American civil religion,*" a concept employed by Robert Bellah and others to explain the continuing public persuasive power of intertwined themes from Judeo–Christian prophecy and Enlightenment political theory, perhaps with special reference to King's recurring evocation of justice in the biblical prophetic tradition: "Let justice roll down like waters, and righteousness like an everflowing stream" (Amos 5:24).[2] Or perhaps West's comment is intended to suggest an interpretive and evaluative conclusion that King's theoretical contribution was as *an interpreter and practitioner,* rather than as an originator. Or perhaps West does not regard King as a moral and political theorist at all, remembering instead King's stirring speeches and life witness, the most visible and best-known aspects of his galvanizing transformative leadership, as King's greatest contribution to the struggle for deep democracy, toward which prophetic pragmatism aims.

However, implicit in King's last writings, especially *Where Do We Go from Here: Chaos or Community?* (1967), are the structural elements for a model of democratic transformative theory and praxis that is *pragmatic* as well as *prophetic,* that is *original,* and that has *all the virtues* West attributes to Gramsci's work without the liabilities. That is, King's last writings are "historically specific, theoretically engaging, and politically activistic in an exemplary manner," with theoretical claims based on "concrete and detailed investigations . . . grounded in and reflections upon local struggles, yet theoretically sensitive to structural dynamics and international phenomena"; they are also paradigmatically "attuned to the complex linkage of socially constructed identities to human agency while still convinced of the crucial role of the ever-changing forms in class-ridden economic modes of productions"—all within *a deeply democratic model of the change process,* rather than the Leninist one that restricts the usefulness of Gramsci's analysis as a guide to political transformation in the United States or anywhere else in the world at the present time. If any *one* person deserves to be described as "*the* major twentieth-century philosopher of praxis, power, and provocation without devaluing theory, adopting unidimensional conceptions of power, or reducing provocation to Clausewitzian calculations of warfare," it is Martin Luther King, Jr. Not only did he play a leadership role within the coalition-based American Civil Rights Movement of the 1950s and 1960s, the most effective democratic change movement of the twentieth century, which continues to have worldwide impact as inspiration and model; he also shaped a *prophetic and pragmatic* theoretical model of political transformation, evolving through a large corpus of speeches, sermons, interviews, letters, essays, and books, and emerging in final though still incomplete form in his last book, *Where Do We Go from Here: Chaos or Community?* (1967).

As West's litany of invaluable historical contributors to our activist heritage shows, the imperative project of developing a "prophetic pragmatist" theory and praxis of deeply democratic social transformation, to which he prophetically recalls American philosophers, intellectuals, and grassroots activists, can draw on the theoretical contributions and life witness of more than one "patron saint" from the past. West clearly recognizes that the kind of urgently needed rethinking and reconstruction of democratic political, economic, and cultural processes and institutions that can save America and our larger world from chaos must attract new commitment from large numbers of those who are ready, willing, and able to become collaborators in the development of a new transformative theory and praxis. If prophetic pragmatism remains just "Cornel West's thing," it is doomed. A plurality of patron saints that model a cosmopolitan unity within their diverse backgrounds, theoretical emphases, and lived contributions is far more likely to attract the kind of diverse new "collective grassroots leadership" West rightly regards as needed now, in part as a corrective to the excessive hero worship of both Martin Luther King, Jr., and Malcolm X that led many to despair of the possibility of making significant democratic change after their lives were taken. Thus, not only does prophetic pragmatism need more patron saints from the past than the single, somewhat confusing, though noble example of Antonio Gramsci, it also requires more diversity in theoretical and praxical role models than even the additions of Martin and Malcolm to its "cloud of witnesses" can offer.

My purpose here is to show that Martin Luther King, Jr., left a theoretical legacy of great usefulness in developing *a comprehensive philosophy of deep democracy,* in addition to his more widely acknowledged historical legacy of *prophetic moral leadership.* West's own theorizing would gain greater depth, consistency, and directiveness from repositioning his post-Deweyan thinking farther away from the influences of Gramsci and Richard Rorty, and closer to the more compatible, prophetic and pragmatic model of deeply democratic theory arising out of praxis that we can retrieve from King's final theoretical work when it is understood against the ground of two of his greatest influences: Josiah Royce, the great "absolute pragmatist" teacher of his teachers, and Malcolm X (El-Hajj Malik El-Shabazz), his greatest adversarial partner. More importantly, a critical reconstruction of King's final pragmatic philosophical insights and his prophetic life witness offers a unifying common ground for coalescing the kind of *interracial, gender inclusive, class-mediating, cross-cultural, international movement toward deep democracy* West so rightly understands our torn, tattered, dangerous, meaning-hungry, and hope-deprived world desperately needs now.

King's Prophetic and Pragmatic Transformative Framework

One of King's great insights as a democratic transformation theorist was his awareness that *significant and lasting social change requires extensive and deep social consensus,* not just the limited and superficial agreement expressed by the liberal social contract model that John Rawls and Jürgen Habermas continue to attempt to articulate. Instead of consensus merely about *negative values,* understood as setting limits between the rival domains of government and of private life, and between citizen and citizen, King realized the necessity of at least a partial consensus about the *positive values* that will guide both public and private life. To be stable, the terms of change must be able to bring almost everyone concerned into the bargain on the level of *personal commitments and personal values,* especially the significant stakeholders who have the power to veto change. King realized that there is generally less deep agreement in American political life about specific goals to be achieved than about the unacceptability of specific present realities. Therefore, King's most successful *organizational work,* which was always the pragmatic basis and focus of his *theoretical work,* aimed to persuade a critical mass of social agents to regard a specific reality as unacceptable, and on that basis to struggle to democratically transform the hearts and minds of others as well as the reality-administering and reality-enforcing institutions that depend upon their continued support.

Thus, like Dewey's, King's transformative focus is always on *the problematic historical present within a specific cultural context,* located at the midpoint on a time line between *the past,* which gave birth to current problems but also to resources for overcoming them, and *a preferable future,* when today's well-chosen actions will have had their beneficial effect on the institutions, the attitudes, and the characters that are presently obstacles to free and equal human flourishing. Both the past and the present can be interpreted in more than one way, of course, and how one interprets them will deeply influence one's choice through action between the alternative futures toward which King gestured as "chaos" or "community." Thus, *which interpretation* of the past and of the present a critical mass of community members shares will determine the practical significance of their future-directed actions. I have coined the paired terms *dystopian* and *eutopian* to express the alternative characters of two kinds of evaluative judgments about the specific characteristics of shared, concrete social patterns and institutions people experience within their past-created present geopolitical "place" (*topos*) in history. Through his rhetoric and his life witness, King sought to persuasively model evaluative processes that would lead people to judge specific social and institutional characteristics as either bad, harmful, undesirable, and provoking resistance (*dystopian*), or good, healthy, desirable, and motivating struggle to expand their sphere of influence (*eutopian*), subsequently generalizing these latter characteristics as aspects of their guiding ideals.[3]

Although his use of prophetic language throughout his writing and speeches might tempt one to regard King as a utopian ideal theorist who, like a platonic philosopher–king, sought to generate and direct power in order to approximate a preexisting, reason- or spirit-derived ideal vision of the best republic, *King's use of ideals was originally critical,* serving to heighten popular awareness of and discomfort with dystopian realities, and *secondarily transformative,* evoking shared ideals as symbolic guides to suggest a eutopian direction for preferable reconstruction processes. This second use of ideals was less detailed in King's theory and less effective in his practice, perhaps because of theoretical gaps in his method, and also because of the historically greater difficulty of achieving consensus about the specific and concrete, positive meaning of shared ideals within American society that King himself points out. Thus, in theory as well as in practice, King's model of democratic social transformation is fundamentally pragmatic rather than idealist, bringing not only "intelligence" but also moral commitment to bear in achieving preferable solutions to social problems that are experienced as real and significant. What King adds to Dewey's pragmatic model of political transformation, in addition to an enhanced affective dimension similar to Alain Locke's, is the concept of the *democratic acceptability*—in fact, the *prophetic imperativeness*—of using historically rich, ideal-directed reformulations of the meanings of shared concepts within our philosophically laden language to influence people to experience a specific social problem as real, significant, and calling for their personal transformative commitment.[4]

A single example shows the continuing practical significance of King's theoretical location of transformative action in the time and place of realizable opportunities, that near-future historical space on the time line between present dystopian realities and a realistically hoped for eutopian future. Many who oppose affirmative action argue on ideal theoretical grounds that race is an accidental difference (or not a biologically well-founded concept at all, and thus, not a real difference).[5] Therefore, these critics argue, race should never have played a historically significant role and, thus, should not be employed in righting historical wrongs. Rather, each person should now be treated as each person always should have been treated, as an embodiment of mind and personality of moral worth equal with all others. Thus, in their view, affirmative action diverges from the transformative line linking the present to the ideal through progressive stages of approximation. In contrast, the line in King's theoretical approach leads away from a dystopian historical origin of brutal racism through a progressive series of historically attainable, less dystopian stages: from slavery to *de jure* institutional segregation to *de facto* legalized discrimination, to private but not public discrimination to . . . racial neutrality, otherwise known as "color blindness"? No, not in this society, at least not anytime soon.[6] *Attainable midpoints* on the line toward King's *attainable but eutopian goal of racial inclusiveness* include cross-cultural education, cross-cultural artistic and social appreciation, cross-cultural political participation, and cross-cultural economic empowerment, and all of these require the strategy of affirmative action. "Race," for King, is neither a fundamentally biological concept nor a merely logical concept, definable in terms of a set of necessary and sufficient conditions. Rather, it is a largely sociohistorical concept that has played a significant symbolic role throughout American history and that has shaped Americans' hearts and minds, the institutions they support, and the value-laden story they continue to transmit of who we are as a people, toward what we should aspire, and what kind of larger reality locates and conditions our striving and our aspirations. To refuse to face the real meaning and power of the concept of race within the ordinary, historically conditioned, philosophically laden language-games of American society is to refuse to accept responsibility for the still unredeemed failures and obligations that have descended

from the past to our present times, and that will be transferred to the future regardless of whether we acknowledge them—unless we face and transform both
the meaning of "race" and the race-related deformities in our attitudes, characters, institutions, and distributions of basic social goods during our present era.
Does the distant future hold a stage of American life in which race—as distinguished from culture—is so unimportant that we can afford to be neutral or blind
to it? Only the distant future can tell, and future gazing is the role of a fortune
teller, not a prophet, though Martin King did say, "I have a dream."

Nonetheless, implicit in King's last book, *Where Do We Go from Here: Chaos
or Community?*, is *a historically located, future-oriented pragmatic theoretical
model of social transformation,* which can be organized into *eight elements* that
can be expressed in very general terms, although they have variable specific content, not only from situation to situation, but also for different groups of participants in a single change struggle. The elements of King's transformative
framework we can reconstruct from his last work include:

- *Dystopian concepts*—What intolerable aspects of our lived reality must we
  change?

- *Eutopian concepts*—What are the best aspects of our lived reality that we
  can draw upon for guidance in projecting an ideal direction for our transformative struggle?

- *Basic focuses of interest*—What key things do the various parties (democratic change agents and their opponents) believe they must gain or retain?

- *Transformative barriers*—What obstacles do we need to overcome?

- *Transformative tactics or means*—Given the preceding elements, what
  change strategies are feasible and desirable in achieving objectives that help
  us advance in our ideal direction?

- *Characteristics of successful change agents*—Who do we need to be or to
  become in order to make feasible and desirable changes in this way?

- *Characteristics of a successful change organization*—How do we need to
  organize ourselves in order to bring about, maintain, and extend such a
  process of eutopian transformation in our real, lived circumstances?

- *Change heritage*—What relevant examples and evidence from related experiences can we draw upon to guide us in the situation or struggle at hand?

King's theoretical articulation of a democratic transformative praxis that uses
and, in turn, informs each of these elements of a prophetic and pragmatic theoretical framework can be illustrated through a close reading of *Where Do We Go
from Here: Chaos or Community?*[7]

Chapter One, "Where Are We?," is devoted to a concrete and specific historical analysis of the situation of the American civil rights struggle during the 1950s
and 1960s, including dystopian concepts, eutopian concepts, transformative barriers, and transformative means as these relate both to the democratic change activists and to their opponents in struggle. It begins with an analysis of the
differing dystopian concepts organizing the differing perceptions by diverse co-

participants in the situation at various points in time. *White segregationists* in the South were the forces of tradition and institutional power; their dystopian conceptual structure is not explained in detail, but clearly, integration and racial equality were dystopian concepts for them. Among civil rights activists, King divides his analysis in terms of white *liberals' dystopian concepts* and *Southern blacks' dystopian concepts* within two phases of the movement's development. As King analyzed then-recent history, the dystopian concepts of these two allied groups of change activists were *in agreement in the first phase* of the Civil Rights Movement, but *diverged as it moved toward a second phase.* In Phase One, liberal whites and African Americans agreed in both their opposition and determination to end various wrongs: unwarranted violence, such as that displayed by the police against nonviolent marchers in Selma, Alabama (King, 1967:1); "brutality and coarse degradation" (p. 3); "cruelties" (p. 3); "unregenerate evil" and "barbaric conduct" (p. 4); "injustice" (p. 8); and the institutionalized practices of "prejudice, discrimination, and bigotry" (p. 13) expressed in race-based segregation (p. 17). During Phase Two, African American activists deepened their dystopian analysis to include "economic inequality" (p. 17), including "exploitation" (p. 3), calling for massive government investment to fight "poverty, ignorance, and slums," without which America could expect "further deterioration of the cities, increased antagonisms between races and continued disorders in the streets" (p. 6). However, most liberal whites were not willing or able to revise their dystopian conceptual analysis in this way, perhaps, King suggests, because the government did not adequately inform them about the scope of the problems and the imperative need for such publicly funded, citizen-supported antipoverty programs (p. 6).

In each case, King's analysis of dystopian concepts is followed by an analysis of *operative eutopian concepts,* again differing by group and by phase. King's insights suggest that democracy itself ceased to be a eutopian concept for *segregationists* if it entailed racial equality. *Liberal white and African American activists* agreed in their eutopian concepts during Phase One, according to King's analysis. These eutopian concepts included what some theorists have called "negative rights" (rights of nonintervention) and "civil rights" of equal political participation, as well as the basic values and attitudes to support their effective assertion that are validated by America's intertwined biblical and Enlightenment democratic traditions: "voting rights" (p. 1), "full rights as citizens" (p. 2), "freedom" (p. 2), "decency" (p. 3), "justice" (p. 4), "fair play" (p. 4), and "righting wrongs" (p. 8). King suggests that many white liberal supporters of the first phase of the movement may have thought that legally reaffirming African Americans' full civil rights so understood would bring about "a middle class utopia embodying racial harmony" (p. 4–5). However, the scope of the moral and political vision of equality affirmed by many liberal whites did *not* include the *more extensive eutopian concepts* that inspired the second phase of the Civil Rights Movement: "social equality" (p. 3–4), "brotherhood" (p. 4, 9), and "comradeship" (p. 9). Like Abraham Lincoln (p. 77), William Lloyd Garrison, and many abolitionist activists a century earlier, many white liberals of the 1950s and 1960s advocated an end to specific injustices, but did not desire or believe in full social integration as King conceived of it; some *de facto* separatism, if no longer *de jure* segregation, especially in the economic hierarchy, in residential patterns, in social associations, and above all, in marriage and family relations, still claimed the allegiance of their hearts, if not their minds (p. 8).[8] As King reflects on the successes and the incomplete achievements of this second phase of the Civil Rights Movement, he reveals some of *his own additional eutopian concepts.* "Internal integration" has been achieved (p. 16), by which King means a consistent conversion of hearts and minds among participating African Americans that allowed them to actively believe in their own "somebodiness," a necessary prerequisite to the still-unachieved goal of full social integration; thus, a "spiritual undergirding" has been created, if not yet a great deal of "material progress" (p. 16). Nonetheless, through these achievements, African American activists "have now accumulated the strength to change the quality and substance of their demands" (p. 17), so that they now can focus on the necessary conditions for upward mobility, which is still "sharply restricted" (p. 19). These additional eutopian concepts express some of the "positive" rights (i.e., the substantive entitlement claims) that the U.N. Declaration of Human Rights also validates, as well as the values and attitudes to support them, but King's second-phase eutopian concepts prophetically point beyond that recently coalesced, cross-cultural documentary affirmation of what Alain Locke called "common humane values" to suggest *a deeper conversion of hearts and minds* that is necessary if now deeply divided peoples are to share a way of life that is deeply democratic.

A *flaw* in King's analysis of both dystopian and eutopian concepts as geopolitically located both in the first phase of the Civil Rights Movement and during the time of his writing *Chaos or Community* was his tendency to speak of "Negro" perspectives generically, without sufficiently taking into account *the actual plurality of perspectives* that reflected such differences as North vs. South, urban vs. rural, middle-class vs. working class and "underclass," Christian vs. Muslim, and male vs. female. Thus, *his transformative prescriptions* failed to achieve their full intended scope in part because *his analysis of the reality they were intended to transform* was insufficiently rich. The first four of these differences were forcefully brought to King's attention by Malcolm X, who spoke for the polar opposition on each of them in an adversarial way until his conversion experience in Mecca the year before his death, after which he, too, tried to speak in more inclusive ways that drew upon broader ideals like human rights, without giving up the specificity of his location and the particular work to which he felt called.

King's discussion of *operative transformative barriers* that block further development in this eutopian direction is interspersed within his discussions of the change situation, analyzed in terms of the previous elements of his transformative framework. Here the list is long. "Traditions" (p. 1) that date back to before the Civil War and that constitute what President Lyndon Johnson called "fierce and ancient bonds" (p. 2) were the basis of one type of barrier that included the various aspects of institutionalized segregation and the attitudes that supported it, including "bigotry, prejudice, half-truths and whole lies" (p. 2), "white violence followed by swift and easy acquittals" (p. 2), and segregationist "obstruction" of the transformative legislation that, once adopted, was "evaded, substantially nullified, and unenforced" due to the "equivocations and retreats of government" (p. 10). Another type of transformative barrier arose among whites who were neither civil rights activists nor avowed segregationists, but who eventually became part of the "white backlash," thus giving practical ballast to the segregationist position (p. 3). This barrier was built up out of white resistance to what seemed to many a too-rapid change process, expressed by the belief that "the Negroes had gained so much it was virtually impudent and greedy to ask for more so soon," a view that was devastating to the hopes of African Americans, who felt "cheated, especially in the North" (p. 4). This resistance to the pace of change combined with "apathy and disinterest" (p. 5), "bonds to the status quo" and resistance to change as such (p. 5), white psychological commitment to maintaining a racially based social and economic gap in America, so that "equality is a loose expression for improvement" (p. 8), "complacency" (p. 9), "racial ignorance" (p. 9), and a tendency to confuse change in the law with change in real conditions (p. 5). These change-obstructive attitudes underlay Northern institutional policies of tokenism and substitution (p. 21) in response to the new legal and social requirements that arose from the early successes of the Civil Rights Movement.

Inheritors of King's legacy who remember primarily its moral and inspirational aspects may be surprised to learn that the next major type of transformative barrier King discussed in detail in his first chapter of *Where Do We Go from Here: Chaos or Community?* is a sophisticated nexus of the social, the political, and the economic. This aspect of the growth of King's democratic vision clearly shows the influence of Malcolm X, especially after his return from Mecca in 1994 as El-Hajj Malik El-Shabazz, when he publicly revised his previous views on race, founded the Organization for Afro-American Unity, and expanded his efforts to transform the economic basis of urban African American community life.[9] In King's 1967 view, *the American political economy* constitutes *a specific type of transformative barrier.* Our basic social, political, and economic institutions, especially as they operated in the South, had yielded a predictable, patterned result for African American communities that King characterized as "poverty, ignorance and slums" (p. 6). According to King's analysis, these structural aspects of America's intertwined political and economic systems include the "menial jobs" that are "a structural part of the economic system in the United States" (p. 7), which interact in predictable ways with the continuing effects of long-term legal and traditional economic discrimination in the South (p. 7), as well as discriminatory attitudes (p. 8), second-rate education for Negro students (p. 7) often amounting to no more than "crude vocational training" (p. 9), the cohesive political structure of the South that allowed the region disproportionate power in Congress (p. 14) as well as an "alliance of Southern racism and Northern reaction" (p. 14), resulting in unequal laws and unequal enforcement of the laws (p. 1ff). The operation of this system produced the resultant transformative barriers of actual conditions within African American communities: substandard housing and low incomes (p. 6); high unemployment; high infant mortality; a disproportionately high rate of Vietnam War deaths (p. 7); lagging performance in the elementary grades; and a lower rate of college attendance, with half of these most successful students attending ill-equipped Southern institutions (p. 7). Moreover, as King pointed out, *the accumulated real cost of changing these dystopian conditions* resulting from structural aspects of the American political economy was expertly assessed in 1966 at three trillion dollars. Both King himself and the expert on whom he relied for this figure, then-Assistant Director of the Office of Economic Opportunity, Hyman Bookbinder, regarded such an expenditure as "comfortably possible," given the growth of the nation's gross domestic product (GDP): "The poor can stop being poor if the rich are willing to become even richer at a slower rate" (p. 6). Subsequent events (including the fiscally devastating costs of fighting the Vietnam War in the following eight years as well as the continuing Cold War in the 1980s, which gave rise to a conservative-led taxpayer revolt in the 1980s, followed by contagious, widespread sentiment for budget-balancing in the 1990s) have made it clear that the costs of remedying this dystopian backlog constitute *a third, continuing type of transformative barrier,* even if the social, legal, and economic institutions that gave rise to it are themselves changed.

Like Douglass, DuBois, and Locke before him, King regarded *the social psychology of the historically shaped African American community* as another twofold transformative barrier, one aspect of which had been positively transformed by participation in the Civil Rights Movement, while the other aspect remained a problem.[10] The aspect of this social psychology that had been *changed for the better,* the lingering effects of generations of "servitude" and "solitude" (p. 15), had been transformed into *"internal integration"* (p. 16). The troublesome aspect of this shared social psychology—*the old mood of frustration and despair* among some African Americans who were once hopeful about the prospects for success of the Civil Rights Movement but who had since come to the conclusion that the movement had failed—had been *reinforced* by their response to the difference in eutopian conceptions of "equality" between blacks and whites who were allies in the first stage of the Civil Rights Movement (p. 8). This difference had led to disunity about strategies and objectives, internal struggle, loss of belief on the part of many in the potential fruitfulness of cross-racial coalitions, and widespread disenchantment, depression, and despair that themselves became further barriers to revitalizing the American struggle for deep democracy. This reaction resulted, in King's opinion, from *a misunderstanding of the nature of progressive historical development*—that is, from a failure to understand that progress is dialectical and cumulative of many small and partial victories (p. 11–12). Even if King is correct, however, this widespread ignorance of the developmental patterns of social change processes constitutes another transformative barrier.

A final element in the chapter, interspersed within the foregoing ones, is King's discussion of *transformative means,* again analyzed in strategic terms relative to the goals of the different phases of the Civil Rights Movement. During the first phase, *legal challenges in the courts* focusing on civil rights (pp. 10–11) played an important role, as did *demands for new federal legislation* (p. 2). However, the single most effective strategy during this period was *nonviolent direct action,* including mass marches (p. 1) as well as sit-ins and boycotts (p. 17), all leading to confrontations with dystopian oppressors under the gaze of the national news media, thus creating public awareness and public indignation. Black–white unity among activists during these actions was important to their success (p. 4), not only to create the appearance of psychological identification on the part of the nonactivist white viewing audience, and thus to open up their hearts and minds, but also to support activists' hopes that such an occasional experience of identification and concern could become daily reality. *The overriding objective* of this period was *legal change,* and registration of Negro voters (p. 14) and election of Negroes to public office in the South (p. 15) were essential means to that end.

Writing during the period shortly before his death, King argued that continuation of the second phase of the Civil Rights Movement called for *different, additional transformative means* to achieve its less widely supported goal of substantive economic and social equality. Some of these transformative means had already begun to be employed, including *job training* for African Americans (p. 8), dissemination into African American homes of books and periodicals that *build appreciation of African American culture* (p. 9), and the introduction of courses in schools that *lead black students to college and beyond* (p. 9). Here again, Malcolm's influence on King is obvious, as is the influence of proponents of "Black Power" of whom King is highly critical in the book's second chapter. Other transformative means King argued needed to be undertaken include *mass efforts by whites* to educate themselves out of racial ignorance (p. 9), *targeted struggles* to achieve *incremental structural changes* in the basic institutions of American society (p. 12), and *particular strategies for transforming inferior schools, poor neighborhood economies,* and *the other real transformative barriers* to substantive equality that he outlines in greater detail in Chapter Five, "Where We Are Going," and in the book's appendix.

A final visionary Chapter Six, "The World House," calls for *transformation toward a humanely democratic global economy* while rejecting revolutionary replacement of capitalism by an antecedently specifiable, context-independent, universal "cookie cutter" model of socialism—although King, like Malcolm X, Dewey, and West, sometimes uses the term 'socialism' as a gesture in this alternative, humanely democratic direction while treating capitalism-as-it-is as a key problem to be overcome. Unlike Angela Davis, King never saw Soviet-style communism as the answer. Instead, like Malcolm X, who pointed to emerging, context-specific African socialisms as models to suggest how a people might reconstruct a situationally and culturally appropriate set of economic institutions for themselves, and like Dewey, who argued for stagewise ameliorative transformations in America's historically emergent economic institutions, King called for *a revolution in values* to guide *specific transformations in our interconnected key public institutions.* He believed this process could and should be actively influenced by *nongovernment agencies within civil society,* including churches, businesses, African American cultural organizations, and interracial coalitions.[11]

Perhaps the single most important element in King's transformative framework that we must retrieve for transformative struggle in our own global millennial era is *his ideal conception of the Beloved Community* as *the location and goal of transformative struggle,* guiding as it does his analysis of the characteristics of successful change agents and of successful change organizations in relation to a shared change heritage. Although he does not explain his conception of the Beloved Community, King evocatively illustrates it by describing a visionary moment within a prosaic aspect of civil rights struggle, when people from very different, once-antagonistic backgrounds who were drawn together and drawn out of themselves by a shared hope waited patiently together for return transportation to their far-flung homes and their differing daily lives.

> After the march to Montgomery, there was a delay at the airport and several thousand demonstrators waited more than five hours, crowding together on the seats, the floors, and the stairways of the terminal building. As I stood with them and saw white and Negro, nuns and priests, ministers and rabbis, labor organizers, lawyers, doctors, housemaids, and shipworkers brimming with vitality and enjoying a rare comradeship, I knew I was seeing *a microcosm of the mankind of the future* in this moment of *luminous and genuine brotherhood.* (p. 9, emphasis mine)

In the prophetic final chapter of *Chaos or Community,* "The World House," in which he brings together all of the elements of his democratic transformative framework reconceptualized for a worldwide struggle, King argues that in our closely interconnected global reality, which has been created by *a scientific revolution* and is now going through *a freedom revolution,* we will all be destroyed by chaos unless we consciously undertake a *revolution of values* guided by the cross-cultural ultimate value of love. Working through nonviolent exercise of power in strategies focused on transforming structures and habits of racism, poverty, and militarism, King calls us to struggle toward the justice and peace of a democratic community. Thus, this third revolution is to have *three transformative focuses* (racism, poverty, and militarism) with *a single motivating ideal* (love), *one general strategy* (nonviolent exercise of power), and *a two-sided criterion for evaluation* (justice/peace).[12] King argues that even if one's interest in preventing chaos is self-interested, only the other-regarding motive of love, with its related criterion of justice/peace, can achieve this. Given historically marginalized peoples' real needs and their inner sense of worth that has been brought to consciousness by the worldwide freedom revolution, racism and poverty have become intolerable, especially given their knowledge that a better life is now possible. Given the kinds of arms the scientific and technological revolution have brought into existence, military might is no longer a safe and sure way to prevent chaos, and has become a threat in its own right, because we have not yet overcome our traditional tendencies to try to resolve conflicts with force. Therefore, our transformative problems need to be understood as including racism, poverty, and this militaristic tendency that leads to the choice of highly dangerous and ultimately ineffective strategies that aim for control by force, but direct our attention and our resources away from the first two explosive issues, and from discovering the very different kinds of strategies that would resolve them.

Love, King argues, understood both as *the distinctive ideal quality of the Beloved Community* and as *a criterion inseparable from justice* for evaluating transformative strategies and ends-in-view, is *a substantive experience that is necessary for human survival,* now more than ever. Wise people of all cultures and faiths have always understood the importance of love, regarding it as a real and powerful force that sustains and transforms.

> When I speak of love, I am speaking of that force which all the great religions have seen as the supreme unifying principle of life. Love is the key that unlocks the door which leads to ultimate reality. This Hindu-Moslem-Christian-Jewish-Buddhist belief about ultimate reality is beautifully summed up in the First Epistle of Saint John:
>
> Let us love one another: for love is of God: and every one that loveth is born of God, and knoweth God. He that loveth not knoweth not God; for God is love. . . . If we love one another, God dwelleth in us, and his love is perfected in us.
>
> Let us hope that this spirit will become the order of the day. We can no longer afford to worship the God of hate or bow before the altar of retaliation. The oceans of history are made turbulent by the ever-rising tides of hate. History is cluttered with the wreckage of nations and individuals who pursued this self-defeating path of hate. As Arnold Toynbee once said in a speech: "Love is the ultimate force that makes for the saving choice of life and good against the damning choice of death and evil. Therefore the first hope in our inventory must be the hope that love is going to have the last word. (p. 190–191)

Thus, in addition to its *ethical* dimension, *love* as King understands it has a *metaphysical* dimension, an *aesthetic* dimension, a *spiritual* dimension, and a *historical* dimension, because love connects people transformatively in ways that allow for new beginnings in history. *Love changes reality for us all the way down,* from the core of our sense of self-worth, to our location within a network of relationships, to the direction and meaning of the stream of history that interconnects our communities to the larger metaphysical whole within which we experience, interpret, feel, reflect, choose, and act.

Thus, *action guided by love and for the sake of the Beloved Community* gives King's pragmatic transformative framework its prophetic energy and urgency. Within the present phase of South Africa's daunting struggle to build *a multicultural democracy* out of years of racist apartheid, official as well as insurgent violence, postcolonial economic distortion, and radical social inequalities, Bishop Desmond Tutu has bravely led *a world-historic experiment* to see whether public communication about past hatreds and injustices through the work of a Truth and Reconciliation Commission can give former enemies who have all lost so much the new beginning King prophesied—*a better beginning,* perhaps, than the purely punitive justice–focused Nuremberg Trials gave the world after the Holocaust, bringing out truth but not reconciliation, so that Nazism is still with us, though in mutated forms and largely driven underground.[13] King inherited key aspects of this prophetic, experience-grounded ideal concept of the Beloved Community from the great absolute pragmatist, Josiah Royce, whose views deeply influenced King's graduate professors at Boston University. *Royce's conception of the Beloved Community,* which combines memory and hope, and which helps its members to fulfill their best human potentials through shared struggle, also offers *still-valuable insights for retrieval,* both to deepen our interpretation of King's prophetic pragmatic vision, and to guide our development of the kinds of desirable and effective transformative communities than can support and direct our own struggle to deepen democracy.

The Beloved Community as Location and Goal of Transformative Struggle

The nuanced richness of Royce's conception of *the transformative interpretive community of memory and hope* that shaped the visionary power and practical effectiveness of King's conception of the Beloved Community can be more deeply appreciated by contrasting it with a recent, highly influential, but relatively powerless and despairing conception of *the ethnocentric interpretive community,* that of Richard Rorty. Ironically enough, Rorty is often portrayed as the contemporary inheritor of the Deweyan mantle, and he certainly has played a leading role in the revival of widespread contemporary interest in pragmatism. However, Rorty's conception of pragmatism is greatly at odds with those of Dewey, Royce, and King at key points, including the role and content of the democratic ideal, the origin and purpose of interpretive communities, the function of language, and the justifiability of transformative social movements guided by a positive conception of democratic social ethics. In all of these dimensions, Rorty's pragmatism has been corroded and misled by his encounter with postmodernism. Because of Rorty's influence, the power of Cornel West's vision of prophetic pragmatism has been diffused to some extent. It can be clarified and strengthened by a fresh philosophical encounter with King and King's teachers' teacher, Josiah Royce.

In his widely anthologized essay, "Solidarity or Objectivity?," Richard Rorty argues that the continuing human ethical quest for community-validated meaning in life has arrived at a fork in the road in our era, so that *a choice* must be made between *two very different kinds of interpretive and evaluative frameworks,* both of which seem unattractive to his critics.[14] The first framework, which Rorty calls *"objectivity,"* was originally shaped in Plato's day by belief in the possibility of a timeless, universal, impersonal, and culture-free standpoint and ideal standard for judgment that could unite the loyalties and activities of a community of knowers, led by philosopher–kings who could transform the misguided world by progressive approximations in order to bring it into correspondence with the ideal. Those who sketched the original outlines of this framework were motivated by the *desire to escape* the narrow parochialism of the kind of tradition-bound cultural community that could kill a Socrates—not in order to live as hermits, but to re-found *a better kind of community* on the highest truths. In the centuries since Plato, Rorty suggests, this *always-sketchy framework* has become *shaky* in its ability to bear our ethical hopes for meaning in life because it has come under successful critical attack accompanying the growth of science.

Thus far, Rorty follows Dewey in *Reconstruction in Philosophy, The Quest for Certainty,* and other late works in which Dewey critically attacks the kind of epistemological framework that is structured by the correspondence theory of truth, showing that the quest for certainty that motivates its construction is both hopeless and misdirected, arising as it does out of the attempt to defend reified, rigidified, and increasingly brittle traditional conceptions of moral values against challenges coming out of the rapid and increasingly more powerful development of the methods and models of modern science. Such rigid moral conservatism, Dewey argues, represents poor understanding of the hard-won wisdom of experience-based moral insight, because it leads to a conception of values that is radically out of joint with a world of lived reality that reflects the reductive transformations in worldview and the material reorganizations wrought by modern science without the balancing influence of an equally powerful, contextually relevant moral vision. In Dewey's view, this challenge to the moral dimension of life expressed in our inheritance of meaning-illuminating, goal-directing, and limit-setting values might better be met by abandoning the traditional metaphysical bulwark of separate material and spiritual spheres that underlies the correspondence theory of truth. Instead, Dewey argued, we must bring to the moral problems of contemporary life the kind of *progressive, consequence-focused, hypothetical problem–solving approach* that has developed over time within the sciences and has led to their growth in knowledge and transformative power.

Here, Rorty's postmodernism leads him to part ways with Dewey, in that he rejects such a collaborative hypothetical approach as *naively scientistic* and tending to *suppress the development of creative individual life experiments* for the sake of *a futile attempt to create positive mutuality conditions* for the good life. What we have already attained in liberal democracies, and must struggle to defend, Rorty argues, is *purely negative mutuality conditions* for the good life: We have learned the importance of leaving one another alone in important ways. This is the kind of framework of *Western liberal individualist "ethnic solidarity"* Rorty suggests is *a preferable alternative* to continuing to try to shore up the brittle and indefensible framework of universal epistemic objectivity—an ethnic solidarity that prizes "our own" limited, negative liberal values that have emerged from the West's bitter and bloody struggle to develop a shared interpretive framework within which each of us can live a life that is meaningful to us personally as well as respected to some minimal extent by others. Rorty is no cultural pluralist; he makes no claim about the value of other ethnic solidarities, and sees no reason why "we" should even attempt to understand them unless their interpretive frameworks are somehow useful to and appropriable within "our own."

However, Rorty's analysis of the meaning-saving moral and epistemic potential of "ethnic solidarity" so understood is *fatally flawed by four kinds of unrealism.* First, as Alain Locke argued, differing ethnic communities *must* pay attention to one another in our global millennial era in order to *keep peace,* which depends on mutual informed recognition of and respect for differing experience-based evaluative standpoints while seeking common humane values as a basis for cooperation, or at least noninterference. Second, what Rorty calls "our" values, like the values of other cultures, are *under threat* in their practical influence, and thus their tenability, from *globalized economic forces* that increasingly control and contextualize the meaning and the impact of environmental, political, and ethical values and institutions. Only effectively organized counterpower can protect and expand the influence of these moral values and institutions, yet Rorty's minimalized, negative democratic ideal does not contain any conceivably effective "early warning system" to alert atomized individuals who are pursuing their purely private life experiments, however creative, so that they will recognize this common threat to their differing and disengaged life projects. Nor does it have the attractive gravity to bring these individuals together in common hopes and concerns to organize effective resistance. Thus, realistically, Rorty's vision offers "us" the alternatives of *denial* of "our" real situation or *despair* over the possibility of realizing the individual dreams whose pursuit is supposed to give "our" lives meaning. Third, many of us who are Rorty's readers are *not "one of us"* as he casts the net and draws the boundary of the ethnic solidarity he attempts to defend. Instead, we are critics of his elitist negative liberalism that leaves all of the "old" problems of American history and more broadly Western history unacknowledged and untransformed—problems of injustice and oppression along lines of gender, race, class, and those unacknowledged, embattled, yet valuable and emotionally powerful cultural differences within his melting pot over which we continue to "stew." These differences have *explosive potential* to create the *chaos* of which King warned if the larger society of which we are members by right as well as necessity is not progressively and positively transformed into a diverse, deeply democratic community. Fourth, given the *real existential challenges to meaning and hope* in our global millennial era that repeatedly slap the faces of all of us, not just the most marginalized among us, *the interpretive resources of Rorty's thin ethnic solidarity are insufficient* to frame inspiring life projects of the kind that can motivate us to exert our best efforts, to reflect on the results, and to grow thereby. Rorty's thin ethnic solidarity is insufficient to knit us together into the kind of *active community of fellow interpreters and Aristotelian "friends of the mind"* that can give one another valuable feedback grounded in both caring and common cause, and that can lift up whichever one of us is depressed and in danger of despair when too many of those all-too-common blows have hit especially hard.[15] Thus, Rorty's "ethnic solidarity" around a purely negative conception of the democratic ideal is *naive, elitist, unrealistic,* and *existentially too shallow* to support human growth and a sense of life-sustaining, community-enhancing purpose in our global millennial times.

Instead of *backing away* from the positive dimensions of Dewey's formulation of the democratic ideal, as Rorty has, we need to follow Royce, Locke, and King in *expanding them even farther,* beyond Dewey's *practical ideal of democratic community life* to the *spiritually richer, transhistorical ideal of the diverse*

Beloved Community. Although an ideal of this kind is impossible to realize literally, as Dewey pointed out, such an ideal does not actually function within our form of life as an endpoint for progressive realization by successive platonic approximations. Rather, it serves to express *a comprehensive diagnosis* of the widely shared ills of our age and to suggest the kind of *cooperative remedial response* that will improve our practical situation while creating a larger, life-interpretive context that can make experience rich and motivating for us.

As a *desirable middle way* between the two unattractive epistemic alternatives Rorty considers, Josiah Royce proposes a conception of "objectivity" very different from the mythically extra-historical, linguistically unmediated conception Rorty describes, an *objectivity* that can be *the basis for historical community solidarities that are not arbitrary, blinkered, solipsistic, or closed.* During Royce's final years of living and writing as what he called an "absolute pragmatist," he produced a series of works on the problems and transformative ideals of community life: *Race Questions, Provincialism, and Other American Problems* (1908), *The Philosophy of Loyalty* (1908), and *The Problem of Christianity* (1918). These works inspired King, like Alain Locke before him, and they continue to offer powerful insights for diagnosing and healing our contemporary ills. Royce's alternative metaphysical, epistemological, and moral interpretive framework expresses *a transactionally mediated objectivity* that reflects our experience that, just as we participate within and contribute to the shape of reality through an inescapable interpretive and transformative process, reality also pushes back. As Royce suggests, we can learn more about these dimensions of reality that limit, contextualize, and suggest criteria for our own interpretive and transformative processes through the sciences, and also through constructing *a shared, interactively developing, interpretive phenomenology of our lived experience* as individual members of historical and cultural communities of memory and of hope.

In *The Problem of Christianity,* Royce offers a persuasive analysis of how our *individual identities and interpretive processes* emerge within *the context of community life*—whether rich or relatively barren—that provides a larger framework for our experiences, including *time processes of memory and hope* (understandable in postmodern language as experiences of "absence" that give shape and value to a protean "presence").[16] Flaws and omissions in the way a community keeps its memories tend to be passed on to its new members, thus perpetuating flaws in the structures and processes of contemporary life. *What a community does not acknowledge in its memory-guided present awareness it cannot cooperatively transform.* In *Race Questions,* Royce discusses examples of such memory-perpetuated flaws and omissions, including the shameful treatment of immigrant Chinese laborers he witnessed growing up in the nineteenth century in California gold rush country, and of white Americans' transgenerationally cultivated ideological blindness concerning black Americans. The *"loyalty"* that binds people to their particular interpretive communities, which Royce understands as a humanly natural disposition to love and to serve those to whom one feels closely connected, is one of the keys to solving the perennial ethical problem of meaning in life on which Rorty focuses. Despite differences in and between the communities of memory and hope that attract the loyalty of their members, Royce argues, *the loyal are "essentially kin"* (Royce 1918:84). The historically traceable developmental process of expanding the scope of that loyalty moves in the direction of the ideal of a universal community of the loyal—*"the Beloved Community"*—guided by the ideal of *"loyalty to loyalty"* that so deeply influenced Alain Locke's democratic transformative theorizing. Thus, *to act as if one is already a member of the Beloved Community* is, in Royce's view, the universal ethical ideal goal of individual life, though individuals whose development continues to be hampered by a barren or seriously flawed experience of community life, in which memory is selective and hope is based on denial, may not fully understand or feel the attraction of this ethical imperative. Many members of "our" elite Western liberal intellectual community Rorty calls to "ethnic solidarity" have been *developmentally hampered* in this way, so that they claim a self-createdness and an atomic separateness of life projects that simply flies in the face of the empirical realities of daily life that Royce, following Wundt and concurring with Mead and others, points out to show that there is *a kind of "oneness,"* however impoverished, that must be taken into account.

This oneness of community life includes both *a backward-looking, historical dimension* and *a forward-looking sense of future consequences* for which one hopes as one acts. Communities are the product of socially contextualized, self-constituting individuals who share events, deeds, and a language, thus creating shared dimensions of their life experience as *"communities of memory"* and *"communities of hope"* (Royce, 1918:248). Moreover, this sharing is not merely coincidental, but rather the result of *intentional interpretive interactions* by means of which persons make such links with one another. In a reconstruction of Charles Sanders Peirce's view, Royce argues that interpretation is a nonsymmetrical, triadic relation linking interpreter, object interpreted, and the persons to whom an interpretation is addressed (pp. 286–288). It is through such interpretive processes that we establish and maintain the time processes of memory and hope that are essential parts of the life experiences of each of us in our ongoing self-creative processes (p. 294). Any interpretation of a sign, Royce suggests, is a new sign that calls for further interpretation, always seeking a "spiritual" object, a possibility that is encoded within the situation, but not yet real. Thus, interpretive discoveries are constantly renewed in social relations, ideally demanding mutual interpretation to fulfill their experienced potential (pp. 290–294). Interpretation so understood is "the main business of philosophy," Royce argues (pp. 297, 319), thus agreeing with Rorty that the epistemological quest has an ethical core. The aim of *the will to interpret* is to make an *interpretive community,* and every ideal good attainable through human social cooperation depends upon such loyalty-bound interpretive communities (pp. 312–318).

The ideal circumstance of the realization of all our ideal goods conjointly is *the community of those who are loyal to loyalty itself,* to which we are attracted by the inner logic of our own language-based understanding of ideal goods, as well as by our practical experience of differences among particular interpretive communities of memory and hope. This community of the loyal to loyalty itself is *the Beloved Community,* which is also an ideal interpretive community (p. 318). It affords the communicative location for interconnecting individuals and communities whose memories are incomplete, and perhaps antagonistic, into a *community of shared hopes* that allows them to communicate with one another on a basis of trust across past differences and with a lively recognition of their continuing valuable diversity, so as to direct cooperative actions in the direction of shared hopes, and to guide and support the ongoing self-recreation of its members toward their shared and yet deeply personal ethical goals. As Royce writes in a passage that must surely have struck King like a thunderbolt, " . . . if great new undertakings enter into the lives of many men, *a new community of hope,* unified by the common relations of its individual members to the same future events, may be, upon occasion, very rapidly constituted, even in the midst of great revolutions" (p. 249, emphasis mine).

To Royce's conception of the Beloved Community of memory and hope, King adds the importance for the historically oppressed of *attaining "somebodiness"* through *membership in a deeply democratic transformative community* (King, 1967:122–123). Others' self-respecting respect serves as a mirror to reflect back a sense of one's own worth—George Herbert Mead's "me" interacting with the "I" within the experience of acting together in freedom as the Beloved Community. Such a community makes it possible for its members to undertake *self-transforming personal risks* in the nonviolent exercise of power to realize democratic ideal values in transformed social institutions and cross-difference community relations, developing and exhibiting the virtues of commitment, patience, and active courage, while *making peace between differing communities' memories and hopes* through *revolutionary transvaluations of values* made possible by the transformative impact of *a lived ethic of love.* Because this interactive dynamic multiplies energies through personal growth, mutual commitment, and shared memories, it generates much-needed spiritual sustenance to *stabilize hope and courage over the long period of struggle* that deeply democratic transformation actually takes.[17]

What does this tell us about *effective transformative change agents* for deep democracy? Their inspiration, role models, interpretative context, and source of sustenance all derive from the *communities of memory and hope* into which they are drawn, in addition to the educational and character-reforming of participating in such communities Dewey and Locke stressed. To the extent that the *ideals* that guide these communities are *realistic* (i.e., well-grounded in experience, reflecting open-eyed awareness of tragic as well as joyful moments), *well-focused* (drawing on the best aspects of experience in ways that can be recreated, sustained, and expanded in the future), and *effectively expressed* (drawing deeply and imaginatively on a culture's shared language-games to combine the emotive powers of memory and of hope)—and to the extent that their *role models* are able to *exemplify these ideals* in their lived witness and not just in their words—to that extent, the kinds of characters and understandings these communities help to shape and to sustain will tend to be *loyal to those ideals* and *sturdy* in their ability to withstand the shocks and setbacks of transformative praxis.

These invaluable insights nonetheless reveal *two areas of insufficient development* in King's transformative prescription at the point when an early and violent death tragically cut off further growth in his transformative insight and in his prophetic life witness: the *insufficient realism and effectiveness* of his expression of the transformative ideal of the Beloved Community relative to the *great diversity of group experiences* whose hopes it must link, and a related *insufficient diversity in visible role models* who could be observed and learned from in their collaborative interaction. A more complete realization of prophetic pragmatism that goes beyond King's transformative vision requires *full inclusion of women* as partners in leadership with men, *full grassroots participation in transformative inquiry and strategic decision making* as well as in implementation, and *full inclusion of those who have been further marginalized by differences* in class, religion, disability, sexual preference, prison, and "priors." Septima Clark, one of the most effective and influential women activists in the Civil Rights Movement, bravely and lovingly called King and the Southern Christian Leadership Conference (SCLC) to account for refusing to include women in the core leadership, recounting more than one incident in which the all-male SCLC leaders criticized her for supporting grassroots initiatives without consulting them first.[18] King's reasoning on this subject is suggested by his comments in Chapter Four of *Chaos or Community,* "The Dilemma of Negro Americans," in which he reflects on how slavery and its unreconstructed aftermath have led to the disintegration of the African American family, echoing the then-recent Moynihan Report (1965) in tracing current problems in African American families to the artificial construction of impoverished African American matriarchies. King argued that women-dominant social structures should be replaced by stronger family units in which men have regained their rightful places as leaders and effective breadwinners: "To grow from within, the Negro family—and especially the Negro man—needs only fair opportunity for jobs, education, housing and access to culture" (pp. 106–108).

Malcolm X was originally even more suspicious of the power of women, relegating them to secondary, supportive roles, both on religious grounds and because of his adverse experiences with women during his days as a pimp and street hustler prior to his incarceration and his initial conversion to Islam. However, after his deeper conversion experience culminating in Mecca and his broadening African travels and consultations with African revolutionary leaders, Shabazz rejected his previous attitude toward women as well as his demonizing of whites, recognizing a potential human "brotherhood" and that *women play key roles in transformative struggle and serve as indicators of cultural progress* (Shabazz, 1970:179). Thus, Shabazz was able to attract the internationally acclaimed poet and formidable activist Maya Angelou to his new leadership core. He also invited the brilliant and highly effective civil rights activist Fannie Lou Hamer to speak at a rally for his newly formed Organization of Afro-American Unity, which had but a few months to coalesce before the world's loss of the incalculable potential of his transformative leadership to the bullets of those who feared the implications of his independence and his democratic deepening.[19]

A second important aspect of Shabazz's final, more deeply democratic vision in which his development went beyond King's was his *rejection of traditional top-down hierarchical leadership models* in favor of *a model that stressed full and equal participation* reflecting participants' differing gifts and differing so-cial–epistemic locations.[20] Shabazz regarded such participation as necessary to the transformative empowerment of racially and economically oppressed indi-viduals and their larger communities. He had earlier criticized King for propos-ing radically inappropriate general transformative strategies for situations beyond his experience, especially for violent black ghetto communities in Northern cities, many of which lacked the African American civic institutions, social struc-tures, and partial accommodations with the white power elite that empowered African American struggle in the Jim Crow South.[21]

As Chapter Four of *Chaos or Community* shows, King took these criticisms very seriously, moving his whole family to the poor, violent black ghetto commu-nity of Lawndale in South Chicago during the summer of 1966 in order to broaden their experience as he struggled to organize and to uplift his neighbors there. Al-though King gives his account an upbeat spin, it is clear that the experiment was largely unsuccessful; he sent his family back to Atlanta after several miserable months and stayed only a few months longer himself. This seems to have been a chastening time of realization that *deep differences make a difference,* even among those who share the American stigma of race and the insufficiently reconstructed inheritance of chattel slavery. Yet King does not seem to have realized that no one of us can encompass all of the differing relevant epistemic locations that must be brought together to achieve an adequate understanding of where we are, where we need to go from here, and how we can get there. Only *broadly participatory, co-operative processes of social inquiry and transformative leadership* of the kind Shabazz was beginning to understand are epistemically encompassing enough, as well as character-transforming and energy-multiplying enough, to generate feasi-ble and desirable strategic insights for guiding real-world processes of deepening democracy.

In critiquing errors and retrieving insights from both Shabazz and King, James H. Cone points to *dangerously hierarchical, "messianic" leadership structures,* as well as *failures of inclusiveness on lines of gender and class* in both of their origi-nal visions, which both were overcoming when their lives and leadership were cut short, but whose incomplete transformation led to *a widespread sense of radical disempowerment* when they were gone. Cone's own promising transformative vi-sion calls for a *broad inclusiveness* that carries forward these complementary, con-verging dynamics within King's and Shabazz's visions. Yet even here, there is more to retrieve from their final visions than Cone has yet made explicit, espe-cially *democratic inclusion of the marginalized among the marginalized,* such as those Malcolm Shabazz deeply understood who previously had sought meaning, acceptance, and economic sufficiency through gangs and the "alternative econ-omy" of drugs and violence, some of whom eventually seek to be part of building something better.[22] We need *an even fuller surrender of traditional hierarchies of power within democratic change movements* today to make room for and to ener-gize processes of deeply democratic reconstruction of characters and institutions. As Cornel West and bell hooks have cooperatively theorized, we must raise up "a *shared, grassroots leadership"* within the kinds of *cross-difference "solidarities"* that can transform hearts and minds as well as the public square.[23]

West and the Future of Prophetic Pragmatism

As the foregoing argument attempts to show, King's philosophical and experiential trajectory led him by the end of his too-short life to become a pragmatist in the classical Roycean–Deweyan stream, enlivened and deepened in his democratic understanding of the significance of diversity and injustice, as was Locke, by the African American intellectual inheritance and tradition of struggle. No one questions King's prophetic credentials, rich and rolling as his speeches and writings are with the language of the ancient Hebrew prophets, and astute as his critical diagnoses are concerning the sources and implications for the future of the moral failings of contemporary American social institutions and habits of the heart. Thus, West's "prophetic pragmatism" is a direct descendant of King's in its *pragmatist democratic theory* as well as its *prophetic transformative practice—* though any child has more than one parent, and some of any family's forebears can hardly be called good influences, as with the postmodernist aspects of Rorty's influence on West. If he reclaims King's *philosophical* legacy, West's work can shed light on, extend, and critically correct King's, combining Roycean "loyalty to loyalty" with Deweyan appreciation of the interpretive philosophical difference a later historical context makes and King's own prophetic urgency to get on with the work of justice. Moreover, King's pragmatist transformative framework offers a structure for ordering West's sometimes scattered philosophical insights in a way that clarifies their power while raising questions and revealing gaps still to be addressed within a *"prophetic framework of moral reasoning"* activated as a *"politics of conversion"* guided by a *"love ethic."*

These are three of the extraordinarily promising concepts West uses to organize his analysis and prescription in *Race Matters* (1994), one of the most important contributions in recent years to a transformative philosophy of deep democracy for our global millennial times.[24] In sharp contrast with Rorty's shallow, negative conception of democracy, West's analysis focuses on the 1992 Los Angeles riots in order to demonstrate the converse of Dewey's and King's more deeply democratic claim that *the good life for any of us depends upon satisfying the democratic mutuality conditions for the good life for all of us:* "If we go down, we go down together" (West, 1994:8). As a prophetic, peaceful demonstrator's sign read on the periphery of the chaos, "No justice, no peace." Like Alain Locke, West focuses on *moral emotions* as the key to understanding and transforming the conditions that led to the riots. They expressed, West argues, *justified social rage* (p. 3), by which he seems to mean a widely shared, publicly expressed, strongly felt, and morally appropriate emotion of anger, distress, and imperative urgency about righting a wrong that people experience in response to an action, event, or institution that violates important ethical values they hold dear. Although he endorses social rage as justified by the racism, poverty, and overall social marginalization of daily life in South Central Los Angeles, West does *not* endorse rioting and looting behaviors as expressions of that rage, because these fail to meet the standards of "a prophetic framework of moral reasoning" that he sketches later in the book, and because in many, perhaps most cases, they actually expressed "the nihilistic threat" he fears.

West diagnoses *four interconnected material and spiritual causes of the justified social rage* that was expressed by at least some participants in the 1992 Los Angeles riots, for which he seeks a more socially constructive, less self-destructive form of expression. The first cause is a "widespread mistreatment of black people, especially black men, by law enforcement agencies" (pp. 8–9) that still continues in many American cities, as witness the 1997 near-murder and brutal sodomizing with a toilet plunger of Abner Louima, a Haitian immigrant, by police officers of Brooklyn's 70th Precinct, and the 1999 doorstep execution of Amadou Diallo, a Ghanaian immigrant, by four Bronx police officers, to which outraged citizens have thus far responded with peaceful demonstrations and nonviolent civil disobedience.[25] The second cause was "the 'silent' depression ravaging the country" (p. 9), an unacknowledged economic depression in central cities that continues to generate deep anxiety, even for those residents who still have jobs, because their real incomes have fallen, in spite of America's overall healthy growth in gross domestic product. This location-specific economic depression denies many residents adequate wage-earning opportunities, thereby forcing them into the "informal economy" (legal, semilegal, and illegal) to pay the rent and feed their families, especially since a new paradigm for welfare assistance has limited the availability of government support. The third cause of the justified social rage, the one on which West focuses his attention without ignoring the others to which it is connected, is "a pervasive spiritual impoverishment," by which he means "the collapse of meaning in life—the eclipse of hope and absence of love of self and others, the breakdown of family and neighborhood bonds" that leads to "rootless, dangling people with little link to the supportive networks—family, friends, school—that sustain some sense of purpose in life" (p. 9). The fourth and final cause, which exacerbates the previous three by blocking the relief from them to which endangered communities are entitled, is "a political atmosphere in which images, not ideas, dominate, where politicians spend more time raising money than debating issues" (p. 10).

An adequate transformative prescription must effectively respond to all four of these still-untransformed causes of justified social rage in the African American communities of our central cities, West argues. It must *combine ethics and politics, economics and spirituality* far more insightfully than do either of the distortedly one-sided, currently dominant political frameworks: "liberal structuralism," which seeks to solve the problem by well-financed institutional reconstruction alone, and "conservative behaviorism," which sees a necessary and sufficient solution in the reconstruction of poor people's characters, guided by the Protestant work ethic, to make them more hardworking, more self-reliant, and thereby more successful. Echoing analyses offered by DuBois, Locke, Shabazz, and King in earlier generations, West argues that further *cultural reconstruction* is needed in order for *institutional reconstruction* and *character reconstruction* to be possible and well-directed: "We have witnessed the collapse of the spiritual communities that in the past helped Americans face despair, disease, and death and that transmit through the generations dignity and decency, excellence and elegance," so that many people live lives of "'random nows,' of fortuitous and fleeting moments preoccupied with 'getting over'—with acquiring pleasure, property, and power by any means necessary," in ironic contrast to what Shabazz meant by this phrase (pp. 9–10). These *four real causes of justified social rage*—police mistreatment of black people, economic distress in central cities, spiritual impoverishment, and political unresponsiveness, which together violate a widely shared sense of justice and destroy our shared social peace—are *West's dystopian concepts* and *the transformative barriers to be overcome*. In addition, they suggest the *shared interests* that West hopes to persuade his readers can only be advanced by democratic transformation.

West sums up his transformative prescription equally quickly, including the *eutopian concepts* that express the goals of struggle and a remedial transformative focus, his *characterizations of successful change agents and organizations*, and the *change heritage* or fund of experience on which he believes they can most profitably draw now. First, " . . . *We must admit that the most valuable sources for help, hope, and power consist of ourselves and our common history*" (p. 11). Second, " . . . *We must focus our attention on the public square*" (p. 11), "the common good that undergirds our national and global destinies," by meeting the needs of children and rebuilding the public infrastructure through "some form of large-scale public intervention to ensure access to basic social goods—housing, food, health care, education, child care, and jobs"—through a combined effort of "government, business, and labor that does not follow any existing blueprint" (p. 12). Third, we need to generate *new, prophetic, grassroots-based leadership* that is both moral and effective.

> Our ideals of freedom, democracy, and equality must be invoked to invigorate all of us, especially the landless, propertyless, and luckless. *Only a visionary leadership that can motivate 'the better angels of our nature,'* as Lincoln said, and activate possibilities for a freer, more efficient, and stable America—only that leadership deserves cultivation and support. This new leadership must be *grounded in grass-roots organizing* that highlights *democratic accountability*. Whoever *our* leaders will be as we approach the twenty-first century, their challenge will be to help Americans determine whether *a genuine multiracial democracy* can be created and sustained in an era of global economy and a moment of xenophobic frenzy. Let us hope and pray that the vast intelligence, imagination, humor, and courage of Americans will not fail us. Either we learn a new language of empathy and compassion, or the fire this time will consume us all. (p. 13, emphases mine)

These are *West's transformative elements:* self-reliant grassroots community organizations guided by a shared history of struggle, focused on transforming the public square in coalition with other interested parties, and organized by accountable visionary leaders with their eyes on building a genuine multiracial democracy—prophetic leaders who are able to teach the language of empathy and compassion and to evoke the imagination, humor, courage, and vast intelligence Emerson and Dewey saw as latent within the American people. These are *the right transformative elements,* West suggests, because they *respond realistically and effectively to all four causes* of the problem situation that has turned central cities into "black holes" that rapidly gobble up energy and material resources from the entire social system that is affected by the massive gravity of their desperate conditions of lived experience.

This attractive yet destructive power of active despair—this *"nihilistic threat"* West alluded to as a kind of pervasive spiritual impoverishment—is the greatest danger now to the possibility of realizing the mutuality conditions of the good life for all and any Americans as partners in "a genuine multiracial democracy." This nihilistic threat is a danger to personal and social well-being because it combines "psychological depression, [a sense of] personal worthlessness, and social despair" (p. 20). West's focus here is not on the philosophical claim that no rational grounds for ethical standards or political authority can be given, but rather on "the lived experience of coping with a life of horrifying meaninglessness, hopelessness, and (most important) lovelessness" that leads to "a numbing detachment from others and a self-destructive disposition toward the world," a "loss of hope and absence of meaning" (pp. 22–23). Nihilism so understood is "a disease of the soul" (p. 29), and a contagious, life-threatening disease at that, because "life without meaning, hope, and love breeds a cold-hearted, mean-spirited outlook that destroys both the individual and others" (p. 23). This is a disease to which humans have always been vulnerable, and many Americans today of both genders and all classes, races, and geopolitical locations experience it to various energy-sapping and character-distorting degrees. However, its most virulent forms are found in locations where the lack *of material means* to change one's intolerable and morally unjustifiable life situation collides with the *loss of hope* that one's situation can ever be changed. Many central city neighborhoods have become such nihilism-breeding locations, though recent research suggests that not all of them are, as is discussed later in this chapter.

Prior to the early 1970s, West argues, urban African American communities very effectively defended themselves against this nihilistic threat by means of *powerful traditional buffers* of "cultural structures of meaning and feeling" embodied in and transmitted by African American civil society, especially religious and civic institutions that sustained familial and communal networks of support, and that worked as a kind of "cultural armor" by teaching and reminding people of shared "ways of life and struggle that embodied values of service and sacrifice, love and care, discipline and excellence" (pp. 23–24). However, these traditional cultural buffers have been *shattered* in recent years. A multiplicity of forces have contributed to this destructive work, West acknowledges, but he focuses his diagnosis and transformative prescription on "two significant reasons" why the nihilistic threat is more powerful now: *"the saturation of market forces"* and *"the present crisis of black leadership"* (p. 24).

West's analysis of the first of these factors is acute, insisting, as did Alain Locke's analysis, on identifying *a cultural dimension of economic imperialism and of effective modes of resistance to it.* In their various modes of exerting culture-destroying influence through profit-motivated television, films, popular music, magazines, and advertisements for products and services, capitalistic market forces attempt to reduce the meaning of the good life to pleasure, understood as "comfort, convenience, and sexual stimulation" (p. 26). They "stigmatize others as objects for personal pleasure or bodily stimulation" and undermine "traditional morality in order to stay in business and make a profit," bombarding consumers with "seductive images [that] contribute to the predominance of the market-inspired way of life over all others and thereby [edge] out nonmarket values—love, care, service to others—handed down by preceding generations" (p. 27). In using their communicative powers to substitute *profit-promoting, pleasure-focused ideal values* for *traditional African American democratic cultural values of faith, solidarity, and struggle,* they help to create a "jungle ruled by cutthroat market morality" in locations in which this pervasive message about what kind of life is worth living comes up against a hopeless lack of cash to purchase such pleasures legally. When West calls such jungles "*the tragic response of a people bereft of resources* in confronting the workings of U.S. capitalist society"— spiritually as well as materially bereft—he means this as a partial explanation of resultant criminal behavior, not as an excuse.

> Saying this is not the same as asserting that individual black people are not responsible for their actions—black murderers and rapists should go to jail. But it must be recognized that the nihilistic threat contributes to criminal behavior. (p. 25)

The lack of material means to meet one's own and one's family's basic human needs (much less such infinite consumer desires), as well as the lack of "cultural armor" and community support to resist such manipulative, profit-motivated, pleasure-focused messages in favor of the claims of an alternative, democratically hopeful, and morally responsible conception of the good life, makes such doubly poor people vulnerable to claims that traditional democratic values are for suckers, and that one should experience available moments of dominance and pleasure because that's all there is or ever will be: "The predominance of this way of life among those living in poverty-ridden conditions, with a limited capacity to ward off self-contempt and self-hatred, results in *the possible triumph of the nihilistic threat in black America*" (p. 27, emphasis mine).

This *possible triumph,* this *very real threat* created by such two-dimensional poverty and exacerbated by "ontological wounds and emotional scars inflicted by white supremacist beliefs and images permeating U.S. society and culture," can be averted, West argues, only by a *constructively thoughtful, equally passionate,* but *much more effective* and *morally more appropriate expression* of the same justifiable social rage that the 1992 Los Angeles riots expressed: "*a politics of conversion*" (pp. 27, 29). This politics of conversion requires new models of collective African American leadership that can help people to believe "there is hope for the future and a meaning to struggle" (p. 29). *Effective transformative leadership* requires intellectual understanding of the problem situation that can guide a choice of transformative tactics and means, including insightful analyses of what justice requires, and of "how racism, sexism, [and] class subordination operate." However, even more importantly, it requires a demonstrable, lived understanding that "Any disease of the soul must be conquered by a turning of one's soul," and "This turning is done through one's own affirmation of one's worth—an affirmation fueled by the concern of others." Thus, "*a love ethic* must be at the center of a politics of conversion" (p. 29).

West only sketches what he means by such a love ethic, the transformative heart of his remedy, through gestures that link his thinking to that of the great contemporary African American novelist Toni Morrison, as well as implicitly to King and to Royce before him. The kind of love ethic he has in mind is "*a last attempt at generating a sense of agency among a downtrodden people*" (p. 29, emphasis added). Because West shares Dewey's and Mead's relational view of the self, a *transformation in self-conception,* and in its inseparable dimension of self-valuation, must depend on an *a change in the message* being dialectically exchanged between the inner voice of the "I" and the social appraisal inwardly absorbed as the "me," the result being outwardly expressed in one's words and behavior toward others, whose response leads to new inputs to the "me."[26] Although West does not explain, as King and Royce attempt to do, what he means by "*love*" or how it is absorbed into one's self-conception and conveyed to others, clearly it is more than a cognitive attitude or belief. It is what Alain Locke describes as *a reflectively shaped, culturally supported, action-directing organization of one's various feeling-modes* that has *a potentially universal scope,* combining Roycean "loyalty to loyalty" with Locke's "common humane values," and given a culturally specific, transformative mode of expression that sustains what King calls the sense of one's own and others' individual "*somebodiness.*"

> Self-love and love of others are both modes toward increasing self-valuation and encouraging political resistance in one's community. These modes of valuation and resistance are rooted in a subversive memory—the best of one's past without romantic nostalgia—and guided by a universal love ethic. (West 1994:29–30)

An overarching moral emotion of love so understood empowers individual and collective resistance to threats to the integrity and preciousness of persons, as well as to a community's shared, memory-rooted way of life and the hopeful vision of the good life that normatively guides it. Such an affirmation of the sustaining power of love is not an antirealistic, panglossian claim that this is the best of all possible worlds and that we are all growing better and better. Rather, it is a historically and empirically grounded Jamesian claim about *the possibility of influencing an indeterminate future,* an experience-nuanced claim that reflects the tragic realities one seeks to transform.[27]

Moreover, as West suggests, *a normative ethical stance toward life* grows out of such an individually experienced, historically and culturally rooted but culture-transcending and future-transforming moral emotion of love. An *ethic of love* that combines feeling with reflection into commitment and relational action can motivate and empower an effective, nihilism-defeating *politics of conversion* that can realistically connect people into *transformative communities of memory and of hope,* as well as *coalitions* of such communities. Given the nature and causes of the nihilistic threat, such a politics must focus initially on rebuilding face-to-face communities, as Dewey suggested, through individual-reaching and transforming participatory processes that bring together people with dispersed knowledge and diverse insights to create locally effective remedies that respond specifically to experienced problems, needs, and opportunities. With Dewey, West suggests that *there are no generic solutions.* With Locke, he emphasizes that *effective solutions must reflect culture,* not in some stereotyped essentialistic sense, but rather in their attunement to the dynamic, hybridized, composite character of particular cultural streams of experience in their localized variants, within which real people can *ground love and hope in a shared sense of meaning and purpose.* The *leaders* of such a collective politics of conversion will be those who are able to *live* a reflective and critical love ethic that sustains them and embraces others in an expanding network. They will be those whose gifts of character and intelligence, and whose *demonstrated trustworthiness,* cause others to respond by *entrusting their hopes* to these leaders' democratic guidance within committed, cooperative action. This trust will include supporting their representative role as *liaisons to other communities* that share at least some of these hopes and ideals and, thus, that may become appropriate partners within more powerful and effective *transformative coalitions.* Thus, *local, face-to-face communities of democratic struggle* are the heart of a politics of conversion.

> The politics of conversion proceeds principally on the local level—in those institutions in civil society still vital enough to promote self-worth and self-affirmation. It surfaces on the state and national levels only when grassroots democratic organizations put forward a collective leadership that has earned the love and respect of and, most important, has proved itself accountable to these organizations. This collective leadership must exemplify moral integrity, character, and democratic statesmanship within itself and within its organizations. (p. 30)

Within West's transformative framework, these are the *characteristics of successful change agents and change organizations* working to overcome the nihilistic threat, to transform the oppressive political and economic conditions that intensify it, and to build a genuine multiracial democracy.

What are the *transformative tactics or means* of such a politics of conversion? What should be its *ends-in-view* and its *approach to social inquiry?* Although its transformative tactics or means will be localized to specific situations while broadly drawing upon a shared, culturally attuned change heritage, West's analysis suggests that, to the extent feasible, *effective strategies* will involve those *institutions of civil society* that continue to serve effectively as sources of hope and love, and as buffers against the nihilistic threat. Where such institutions are absent or moribund, or worse yet, where they hang on vampire-like, sapping energy and blocking the growth of new transformation-minded organizations fueled by justifiable social rage as well as by love and hope, how is the building of a transformative community to proceed? *Suggestive general strategies* for effective transformative organizing in such real and anticipatible circumstances in a badly damaged civil society must be part of the general framework for an effective politics of conversion. Furthermore, if West's diagnosis is adequate and insightful, the *ends-in-view* of successful democratic change organizations in America must guide transformative efforts in two areas compatibly and simultaneously: *efforts to create new cultural armor* that will protect individuals and communities against spiritual dimensions of the nihilistic threat, and *efforts to democratically transform the political and economic conditions* that create social and material barriers to the development of a genuine multiracial democracy, including *transforming the messages of a capitalist market system* that are presently wreaking cultural havoc. How are the relevant ends-in-view of these two dimensions of the deeply democratic transformation process within a politics of conversion to be effectively coordinated?

Effective answers to these questions about ends-in-view and about the transformative tactics or means to achieve them through an effective politics of conversion must result from *an approach to social inquiry* guided by a collective prophetic leadership that is *democratically inclusive and respectful of internal diversity,* and that keeps constantly in mind both the *particular characteristics* of the problem situation to be transformed and *the larger ideal goal* of transformative activity. Thus, it must successfully substitute what West calls "*a prophetic framework of moral reasoning*" for the presently dominant "framework of racial reasoning," an approach to reasoning about the public square based on restrictive criteria for black authenticity, a closed-ranks mentality, and black cultural conservatism (pp. 42–43). This failed approach contrasts sharply with a prophetic approach encouraging and growing out of *a mature African American identity* that assesses the past and present responses to racism in terms of moral qualities, that respects differences of opinion among African American people instead of trying to impose uniformity, that stresses dignity and decency, and that avoids "deifying and demonizing" entire groups of people. Such a prophetic approach adopts *a coalition strategy* that "solicits genuine solidarity with those deeply committed to antiracist struggle," and that actively embodies an African American cultural democracy that rejects patriarchy and homophobia. West regards the presently dominant framework of racial reasoning as self-defeating and immoral, in contrast with such a prophetic framework of moral reasoning, which he regards as expressing a love ethic with the potential to direct an effective politics of conversion, and building on that, to contribute to cooperative transformation of the public square guided by the ideal of multiracial democracy.

Where there is no *vision,* the people perish; where there is no *framework of moral reasoning,* the people close ranks in a war of all against all. The growing gangsterization of America results in part from *a market-driven racial reasoning* that links the White House to the ghetto projects. In this sense, George Bush, David Duke, and many gangster rap artists speak the same language from different social locations—only racial reasoning can save us. *Yet I hear a cloud of witnesses from afar*—Sojourner Truth, Wendell Phillips, Emma Goldman, A. Philip Randolph, Ella Baker, Myles Horton, Fannie Lou Hamer, Michael Harrington, Abraham Joshua Heschel, Tom Hayden, Harvey Milk, Robert Moses, Barbara Ehrenreich, Martin Luther King, Jr., and many anonymous others who championed the struggle for freedom and justice in *a prophetic framework of moral reasoning.* They understood that *the pitfalls of racial reasoning are too costly in mind, body, and soul*—especially for a downtrodden and despised people like black Americans. The best of our leadership recognized this valuable truth—and more must do so in the future if America is to survive with any moral sense. (pp. 48–49, emphases mine)

Although West's cultural critique is acute, and his general characterization of an effective and morally desirable prophetic framework of moral reasoning is wisely responsive to the needs and resources of the problem situation, his articulation of the ideal goal of an effective, democratic politics of conversion requires greater visionary precision and evocative power, in that it must both reflect and insightfully transcend the characteristics of the problem situation. The ideal goal, West says, is *"a genuine multiracial democracy,"* but it might be better articulated in cultural terms that capture West's accurate diagnosis of the heart of the problem—terms that move transformative visioning past the old American conception of race as color toward Locke's *"cosmopolitan [cultural] unity amidst valued diversity."* After all, many of the local communities West has insightfully argued are most endangered by the nihilistic threat, in part because of their poverty, are already *multicultural communities,* many of whose residents may also share the *multiracial designation "people of color"* in a historically color-conscious American society. Although it is certainly possible for West, with Alain Locke, to interpret "race" as referring fundamentally to culture rather than to color, this is not what "race" means to most of the people he seeks to organize and others he hopes to convert. Thus, *an articulation of the transformative ideal that emphasizes the values that politics of conversion seeks to affirm* might be preferable to one that emphasizes the present problem to be overcome. Yet even Locke's "cosmopolitan unity amidst valued diversity" is not emotively rich enough as an ideal concept to engage the hope and activist energies of those who must struggle together long and hard against economic, political, and cultural opposition and across historically power-structured differences to transform our democratically deficient, value-reductive global political economy and the habits of the heart that accept and sustain it. Rather, infusing prophetic pragmatism with the motivating visions of Royce and King, we must persuasively interpret our guiding ideal of *the diverse, deeply democratic community* as *the Beloved Community of memory and of hope.*

Conclusion

The insightfulness of prophetic pragmatism's cultural critique and transformative "big picture" has been given *recent empirical support* by the preliminary findings of "the largest study ever undertaken of the causes of crime and delinquency," the Project on Human Development in Chicago Neighborhoods. This study has focused on all areas of Chicago since 1990, under the direction of Dr. Felton Earls of the Harvard University School of Public Health, with support from the MacArthur Foundation, the National Institute of Justice, the National Institute of Mental Health, and the United States Department of Education.[28] The authors have reported that "by far the largest predictor of the violent crime rate was *collective efficacy*," by which they mean "a sense of trust, common values, and cohesion in neighborhoods." The most important characteristic expression of this collective efficacy was "willingness by residents to intervene in the lives of children" in order to stop "truancy, graffiti painting, and street-corner 'hanging' by teen-age gangs." The study shows that this sense of community cohesion is not directly correlated with kinship or strong personal ties, though home ownership or long-term residence is a significant contributing factor. The most important element of this collective efficacy that results in low crime rates, the study suggests, is "*a shared vision . . . a fusion of a shared willingness of residents to intervene and social trust, sense of engagement and ownership of public space.*" Although this study shows that poverty, unemployment, single-parent households, and racial discrimination are contributing factors in crime, some of the Chicago neighborhoods studied, such as Avalon Park on the South Side, "are largely black and poor, yet have low crime rates" correlated with high levels of such social cohesion. The authors acknowledged that poverty makes it "harder to maintain" community cohesion, but their study shows that *collective efficacy is possible in spite of poverty.*

This suggests that the kind of *grassroots-based, transformative politics of conversion* that West outlines may be *an effective intervention* in supporting the emergence of this kind of local collective efficacy, even in areas that are very poor, racially oppressed, and otherwise most vulnerable to the existential nihilism that expresses itself in violent crime and in the gangs and the drug trade so often associated with it. *Further study* of the evolved characteristics and the organized methods of building collective efficacy that have worked in Chicago neighborhoods of varying racial compositions, including mixed-race Hyde Park and largely white Norwood Park as well as largely black Avalon Park, will be of incalculable value in giving further strategic detail to a prophetic pragmatist politics of conversion and coalition building. Communities that can *build collective efficacy* of this crime-preventing, child-saving kind by *revitalizing shared values and individual interventionary agency* may at the same time be creating the basis for the kind of *transformative efficacy* that will allow them to *work with interested parties to rebuild other aspects of the public square,* including schools and the local economy, and to begin to transform that international economic Leviathan that West acutely suggests is gnawing away at the cultural institutions upon which people everywhere depend for armor against the nihilistic threat.

For *the nihilistic threat is a global threat,* at work within communities everywhere in the world, affecting the lives of women and men of all ages, races, classes, and cultures. No one is so rich, so powerful, or so culturally dominant as to be immune to the rootlessness, loss of meaning, and loss of love that accompanies the reductive flattening of all values to material values, the uprooting of face-to-face communities by economic forces, and the loss without replacement of the deeper and bigger stories that contextualize individual lives within historical communities of memory and hope. In America, members of so-called Generation X and the generation that follows them seem especially vulnerable now, regardless of their class, ethnic, and religious background, because so many of them approach life from a "spectator" standpoint, having never lived "inside" a community of memory and hope. Their parents and grandparents, the "Baby Boomers" who may have had such experiences in their youth, now feel frustration and fatigue as they struggle to hold onto the memories and hopes that shaped their life trajectories, seeking in midlife a new experience of community within which they can find life-interpretive conversation, emotional sustenance, and a realistic new sense of shared ends-in-view worth pursuing in the next phase of their lives. Worldwide, people express an urgent need for faith, hope, and charity: for the life-reviving experience of guiding ideals within functioning communities inspired with a prophetic sense that the day of justice will come, and that advancing toward that day together in friendship gives meaning and joy to our lives now. Thus, *the time is ripe for a prophetic pragmatism* that can offer a transformative framework for assessing the problem situation of the present, for cooperatively discovering desirable and effective strategies for rebuilding the public square, for democratic deepening of our hearts and minds, and for shaping our diverse lives within and toward the Beloved Community.

Notes

1. I am grateful for the insights and encouragement of Leonard Harris, my commentator on a discussion of King's final view that I presented to the 1992 Annual Meeting of the Society for the Advancement of American Philosophy at Xavier University (Cincinnati, Ohio), and also to a number of members of that audience, especially Robert Corrington, Larry Hickman, Thelma Lavine, Evelyn Shirk, Ralph Sleeper, John McDermott, Beth Singer, and Kenneth Stikkers. I am also grateful to the late Eric Hill, my commentator on that same paper at the 1992 Eastern Division Meetings of the American Philosophical Association (Washington, D.C.), who later wrote to me with additional insightful suggestions, including the importance for our contemporary retrieval of King's views of bringing them into this critical and creative tension with those of Malcolm X. Eric Hill died too young, but he left a legacy that continues to influence many of us.

2. See, for example, Robert N. Bellah, *The Broken Covenant: American Civil Religion in Time of Trial* (1975).

3. Both of these historically specific, existentially located evaluative judgments contrast with Thomas More's concept of *"utopian"* (*no* place or *without* place), which was used critically by Marx and others to express their evaluative judgment about the lack of such an experienced sense of concrete "place" or historicity in most ideal theories that leads to their theoretical obscurantism and practical unrealizability. For the original location of this coinage, see my "King's Pragmatic Philosophy of Political Transformation" (1994).

4. For a more detailed discussion and defense of the way King used history-laden concepts like "race," see my "King's Historical Location of Political Concepts," *The American Philosophical Association Newsletter on Philosophy and the Black Experience,* 91:2 (Fall 1992), 12–14.

5. For examples of the argument that race is not a biologically well-founded concept, thus not a real difference, and should be abandoned from liberatory discourse, see Naomi Zack's *Race and Mixed Race* (1993) and K. Anthony Appiah's *Color Conscious: The Political Morality of Race* (1996). I agree with Albert Mosley that this is a poltically dangerous argument that plays into the hands of opponents of affirmative action, and with Charles Mills (1997), Lucius Outlaw (1996) and Amy Gutmann (1996) that race is a significant concept in America even if it is a social construction whose continuing evolution we must try to guide through critical and reconstructive public communication.

6. See Bernard Boxill's "The Color-Blind Principle" in *Blacks and Social Justice* (1984) and Howard McGary's "Affirmative Action: A Review and Commentary" in *Racism and Social Justice* (1999).

7. King's *Where Do We Go from Here: Chaos or Community?* (1967) is cited hereafter by page number only. For a brilliant and beautifully written analysis of the originality and significance of King's philosophical contribution, especially the transformative power of love operating on conscience through nonviolent direct action, see Greg Moses, *Revolution of Conscience; Martin Luther King, Jr., and the Philosophy of Nonviolence* (1997).

8. On Lincoln, see King 1967:77. On Garrison, see Philip Foner's introduction to his invaluable short collection, *Frederick Douglass: Selections from His Writings* (1945).

9. See *The Autobiography of Malcolm X* as told to Alex Haley (1964) and *By Any Means Necessary* (1970), ed. George Breitman, a collection of Malcolm X's (El-Hajj Malik El-Shabazz's) speeches, interviews, and letters from 1964–1965.

10. See Foner's *Frederick Douglass: Selections from His Writings* (1945), especially "Why Reconstruction Failed," and W.E.B. DuBois, *The Souls of Black Folks* (1903), especially his discussion of "double-consciousness" and "the veil" (2–3). Cornel West (1989) argues that DuBois was profoundly influenced by the work of William James during his studies at Harvard University. See also Bernard Boxill's (1976) persuasive analysis of the relative insightfulness of DuBois's transformative model in comparison to that of his contemporary, Booker T. Washington.

11. James H. Cone reports that King read Marx as a student in 1949, expressed "anti-capitalist feelings in a Crozer Seminary paper, and was deeply impressed by the Swedish model of socialism"; see Cone's *Martin & Malcolm & America: A Dream or a Nightmare?* (1991), 285–286. For Shabazz's final view of political economy, which reflects the influence of diverse emerging African socialisms, see *The Autobiography of Malcolm X* (1964) and *By Any Means Necessary* (1970).

12. Of course, Malcolm was never to agree that a nonviolent, universal love-based strategy was sufficient in dealing with real conditions, even though after his return from Mecca he expressed support for King and the SCLC's nonviolent efforts in the South, offering to cover their backs by slipping in a few OAAU brothers who understood the meaning of "by any means necessary" (see Shabazz 1970:66). For a persuasive analysis of Shabazz's understanding of "by any means necessary" as compatible with the Western natural law tradition of John Locke, see Jill Gordon's "By Any Means Necessary: John Locke and Malcolm X on the Right to Revolution" (1995).

13. See Mark Gevisser's "The Witness," *New York Times Magazine,* June 22, 1997, 32–38: "Day after day the Truth and Reconciliation Commission in South Africa listens to the pain of apartheid's victims and offers amnesty to its villains. But the jury is still out on whether truth is the same as justice." The Commission's report was issued October 29, 1998.

14. Richard Rorty, "Solidarity or Objectivity?" in *Post-Analytic Philosophy,* ed. John Rajchman and Cornel West (1985).

15. bell hooks and Cornel West develop this Aristotelian concept of "friends of the mind" and apply it in explaining the possibility and the importance of personal cross-gender solidarities in struggle in their collaborative conversation, "Black Women and Men: Partnership in the 1990s" (1990). One of their key sources of shared inspiration is Toni Morrison's novel, *Beloved* (1987).

16. Royce discusses "loyalty to loyalty" in more detail in his *The Philosophy of Loyalty* (1908), and uses it as a key concept within *The Problem of Christianity* (1918), republished with an introduction by John E. Smith by the University of Chicago Press (1968).

17. See George Herbert Mead's classic essay, "The Social Self" (1913).

18. See Septima Clark's *Ready from Within* (1986), which bell hooks (1990) cites as giving her courage to speak.

19. James H. Cone analyzes the interactive growth in King's and Shabazz's perspectives, as well as their lasting legacies and some flaws in their visions, in his *Martin and Malcolm and America: A Dream or a Nightmare?* (1991). On Shabazz's transformation on the "women question" and his growing collaboration in leadership with Maya Angelou and Fannie Lou Hamer, see Cone (1991:254, 279). For a persuasive critique of the widespread view that was reinforced by the Moynihan Report that slavery and its aftermath distorted traditional African family structures into black matriarchies, see Angela Y. Davis's "The Legacy of Slavery: Standards for a New Womanhood" in *Women, Race and Class* (1981). I am indebted to Mark Chapman for clarifying Shabazz's double conversion process.

20. See George Breitman's introductory comments as well as the texts of Shabazz's speech at the Founding Rally of the OAAU in Harlem (June 28, 1964); his letter from Cairo (August 29, 1964), where he was recognized as an observer at an annual conference of the Organization of African Unity; and his speech at a Homecoming Rally of the OAAU after his further travels to Africa and Europe (November 29, 1964), in Shabazz 1970.

21. See *The Autobiography of Malcolm X* (1964).

22. See, for example, the discussion of attempts by New York's Latin Kings and Queens to rethink and rebuild on the basis of their gang solidarity, away from drugs, violence, prison, and "priors," and towards sobriety, mutual respect, nonviolence, and economic self-sufficiency, in Barry Bearak's *New York Times* article, "Man of Vision or of Violence? Where Gang Leader Talks Peace, Police Just See Talk" (November 20, 1997).

23. See bell hooks and Cornel West, "Black Women and Men: Partnership in the 1990s" (1990). For a related discussion of how to build solidarities among women amidst historically power-structured differences, see hooks's "Sisterhood: Political Solidarity among Women" in her *Feminist Theory: From Margin to Center* (1984).

24. See West's brilliant, best-selling essay collection, *Race Matters,* originally published in 1993, republished with a new epilogue and new pagination in 1994, cited hereafter by page numbers only.

25. See John Kifner's article in the *New York Times* (August 30, 1997), "Thousands Call on City Hall to Confront Police Brutality," about a peaceful display of righteous indignation on the part of demonstrators who marched to New York's City Hall to protest Abner Louima's police beating, which they characterized as a human rights' violation. Similarly, thousands have responded to Amadou Diallo's killing by engaging in civil disobedience and inviting arrest at New York's One Police Plaza. See Jodi Wilgoren, "Diallo Rally Focuses on Call for Strong Oversight of Police," *N.Y. Times,* (April 16, 1999).

26. See Mead's "The Social Self" (1913) and Dewey's *The Public and Its Problems* (1927) and *Ethics* (1932).

27. See William James's essay, "The Dilemma of Determinism" (1884).

28. See Fox Butterfield, "Study Links Violence Rate to Cohesion in Community," *New York Times* (August 17, 1997), A27.

Chapter 6

Transforming World Capitalisms through Radical Pragmatism: Economy, Law, and Democracy

The greatest obstacle that exists to the apprehension and actualization of the possibilities of experience is found in our economic regime. One does not have to accept the doctrine of economic determination of history and institutions to be aware that the opportunities of men in general to engage in an experience that is artistically and intellectually rich and rewarding in the daily modes of human intercourse is dependent upon economic conditions. As long as the supreme effort of those who influence thought and set the conditions under which men act is directed toward maintenance of the existing money economy and private profit, faith in the possibilities of an abundant and significant experience, participated in by all, will remain merely philosophic.

JOHN DEWEY, "What I Believe" (1930)

What is denounced as 'Utopian' is no longer that which has 'no place' and cannot have any place in the historical universe, but rather that which is blocked from coming about by the power of established societies.

HERBERT MARCUSE, *An Essay on Liberation* (1969)

I do not think that the triumph of capitalism means its assured long and happy life or that the defeat of socialism means its ignominious exit from history. The collapse of centralized planning shows that at this moment socialism has no plausible economic framework, but the word has always meant more than a system of economic organization. At its core, it has stood for a commitment to social goals that have seemed incompatible with, or at least unattainable under, capitalism—above all, the moral, not just the material, elevation of humankind. However battered that conception may be from the designation of bloody and cruel regimes as "socialist," the vision has retained its inspirational potential, just as that of Christianity has survived countless autos-da-fe and vicious persecutions.

ROBERT HEILBRONER, "Reflections on the Triumph of Capitalism" (1989)

Introduction

These are times of interlinked crises on a global scale—cultural crises, environmental crises, and crises in political economy. World Bank statistics show that approximately one-fifth of the world's population—1.3 billion people—now spend their lives in absolute poverty, unable to obtain adequate food, clothing, and shelter. Meanwhile, the richest 20% of the world's people consume 80% of the world's income. Per capita incomes in the richest nations are forty-five times greater than in the poorest nations, and the gap is growing as whole locations and their peoples are swept away in an instant by global economic actors whose measures of success and loss consider only marginal return on invested capital.[1] Air quality is dangerous to human health in many heavily populated industrial locations worldwide, and the quality of Earth's atmosphere as a whole is threatened by emissions of chlorofluorocarbons (CFCs) and other destabilizing gases, 70% of which are created by wealthy member nations of the Organization for Economic Cooperation and Development (OECD).[2] Urban growth controls have failed to work, and socially and environmentally unsustainable "hyper-cities" are emerging worldwide, encompassing four billion people in 1995 and twenty billion people by 2025 if present trends continue, as the poor and dispossessed of rural areas uproot themselves from the familial and cultural networks that once sustained their lives, flooding into overwhelmed cities where they seek the safety and happiness these places cannot provide. More than eight million children die each year from preventable diseases. Billions of people live without clean water, clean air, and adequate sanitation.[3]

We cannot protect our global environment without economic development that effectively reaches the poor, because, in the words of Ismail Serageldin, "the poor will consume the planet unless we build bridges that give them means and hope."[4] Poverty is a visible and growing problem, even within the ultrawealthy United States of America. However, instead of making just, caring, and ultimately cost-saving national investments in education and creative experiments in economic development that might provide interlinked opportunities for economic, political, and social participation for residents of our poor, racially marginalized, and increasingly violent urban ghettos, we build prisons: as Phillip Thompson suggests, "prisons have become warehouses for men who lack economic value and will always be poor."[5]

These interlinked crises have been created in part by ultrapowerful neocapitalist national political economies, by the transnational corporations to which they have given birth, and by international organizations like the International Monetary Fund (IMF) that promote their interests while coercing other countries to conform to Western institutional models. Economic change alone will not solve all of these problems, but they cannot be solved without economic change, because currently dominant institutional frameworks of political economy multiply differences in existing distributions of economic power and magnify adverse social and environmental impacts while masking many important problems and blocking many desirable interventions. Ironically distorting Dewey's transformative prescription that "the cure for the ailments of democracy is more democracy," contemporary neocapitalist economists claim that the universal solution to the problems Western-style neocapitalism has helped to create is more Western-style neocapitalism. Many neocapitalist economists have argued that the world's diverse nations presently writhing in interlinked cultural, environmental, and economic crises must transform their governmental, legal, and banking institutions, norms, and processes to conform to the pattern set by economically powerful Western "formal" democracies, so that "geography is erased" in making financial transactions within other nations "transparent" to global capitalists who control the flow of the one scarce resource they claim every nation needs most: global investment capital for economic development.[6] Treating Poland's partially successful post-totalitarian struggle to democratically reform its political economy as a model for other nations in Eastern Europe, neocapitalist economist Jeffrey Sachs has warned that, "If instead the philosophy were one of open experimentation, I doubt that the transformation would be possible at all, at least without costly and dangerous wrong turns."[7]

If the thesis of this book is correct, this prescription is dangerously wrong, and transformative processes of deep democracy that reconstruct the capitalist political economies of the Western "formal" democracies, as well as their controlling relationships with other nations' political economies, are urgently needed as part of the solution to interlinked global crises. In this transformative process, as Dewey argued, "The alternative to the adoption of an experimental method is not the attainment of greater security by adoption of fixed method (as dogmatists allege), but is merely to permit things to drift: to abdicate every attempt at direction and mastery" (Dewey and Tufts 1932:350). Responsibly advancing this thesis in such perilous times requires careful, multileveled argumentation as well as extensive empirical support based on the most reasonable interpretation of the evidence. Unless experimental democratic transformations in political economy from the local level to the global level are *possible,* deep democracy as a guiding social ideal is simply nostalgic or unachievably utopian, and in either case harmful in times like these. Thus, the pivotal questions we need to ask now concerning economy, law, and democracy are: (1) What practical crisis interventions and institutional changes will allow us to respond well enough, soon enough, and sustainably enough to this threefold global crisis? and (2) Given the failures of the now-dominant, neocapitalist model of political economy, what new theoretical approaches and econometric instruments do we need to develop in order to assess our human and environmental needs and to evaluate our progress in order to assure that our crisis interventions are appropriate and sustainable? The thesis of this chapter answers both of these questions: We need to transform world capitalisms and to assist in the progressive, liberatory development of other models of political economy through radical pragmatism.

Why the World Needs a New Approach to Political Economy

The severity and global scope of our interlinked crises in culture, natural ecology, and political economy call for carefully targeted transformative interventions, rather than romantic calls for revolution, or simply waiting for "systemic self-corrections" as might seem to be an appropriate response to the cyclical character of "normal" times. However, *what kinds* of interventions? Answering this question requires understanding what produced and sustains these crises and then effectively addressing each crisis without worsening the others. Our understanding of each of these three areas of inquiry and practical action depends upon the guidance that theories offer to our thinking. Yet the theories that seemed to offer good guidance in "normal" times are themselves rightly called into question in times of crisis, especially if their past guidance may have helped to cause the crisis.[8] This is the situation of neocapitalism, the currently world-dominant model of political economy. Instead of guiding "normal" times of global peace and prosperity that would seem to confirm its hypothetical adequacy, neocapitalism reigns in a time of interlinked global crises that it seems to have helped to create, and offers transformative prescriptions that seem to worsen matters. Thus, the times themselves call the neocapitalist model of political economy into question at a deeper level of seriousness than the long history of methodological criticisms concerning its unrealistic assumptions about human nature and values could ever achieve as long as the theory seemed to have great predictive power and, thus, transformative usefulness for promoting human welfare.

Many said that "capitalism" triumphed when the former Russian-dominated Union of Soviet Socialist Republics (USSR) fragmented and its former member states as well as postcommunist Eastern European nations and even still-communist China began to experiment with introducing capitalist markets. Francis Fukuyama, Jeffrey Sachs, and other influential libertarian and neocapitalist commentators have linked these developments with a recently accelerated, cross-cultural historical trend toward extending a "formal," institutional model of democracy to a global scope.[9] They have analyzed recent world-historic events, such as Germans swinging sledge hammers to break down the Berlin Wall, Boris Yeltsin and a crowd of unarmed civilians facing down Red Army tanks outside the Russian parliament building, and South Africans standing in long lines for days to vote peacefully for Nelson Mandela's leadership of a multicultural democracy, as symbolic of this democratic trend. They have pointed to misleading economistic indicators that link "formally" democratic institutions to a projected increase in the wealth of nations, or at least to an increased willingness of global investors to risk their capital in nations that were once beneath their notice. Virtually equating capitalism with democracy, they have argued that these recent historical developments demonstrate that the "formal" model of democracy typified by the United States and the wealthy nations of Western Europe is objectively preferable, not only to recently overthrown, autocratic, state-control models of political economy, but also to any alternative, deeper conception of democracy.

However, as Robert Heilbroner pointed out in 1989, world capitalisms face uncertain alternative paths of future development, and the ethical spirit that once motivated widespread support for socialism lives on.[10] Although the memorable events that neocapitalist triumphalists point to clearly *do* symbolize democratic aspirations, they *do not* show that "formally" democratic institutions coupled with neocapitalist economic formations express the *full meaning of democracy*, or that they create the *social* and *environmental* as well as the *material prerequisites for the good life*. In fact, in many parts of the world, this capitalist partnership in political economy is contributing to serious environmental harms and the expansion of human misery at levels and in locations "below the radar screen" of the theoretical models and instruments that guide the governmental activities of Western "formal" democracies, as well as the transnational business firms to which they have given birth and international organizations like the IMF that respond disproportionately to their influence. According to interlinked neocapitalist and formally democratic theoretical models, a "normal path of development" for less wealthy and powerful nations involves opening up markets as well as ownership and control of firms and agricultural lands to "investors" from other places—individuals and transnational firms with no loyalty to their "host countries" whose self-interested choices and economic power typically force local firms and their employees out of business, move subsistence farmers off the land without offering them a preferable mode of making a living, destroy habitat for other-than-human life forms, damage air and water quality for all, and undercut the meaning-giving power of indigenous cultures. They achieve this culture-destroying impact by sweeping people away from their home places into "labor flows" that take them wherever a job beckons while seductively introducing them to the endless material desires and shallow measures of success that capitalist advertising promotes. Ignoring adverse cultural and environmental impacts, the standard transformative prescription for solving resultant economic and political crises in various parts of the world that the neocapitalist IMF has coercively imposed as the price of assistance is the requirement that radically differing societies immediately adopt Western-style, formally democratic models of law, politics, and economy that make global investors' assets more secure. This transformative prescription has backfired in virtually all cases, failing to end these nations' economic and political crises while adding loss of hope and of cultural pride to their growing troubles.

As Lipsey and Lancaster's now-classic work on "The General Theory of the Second Best" suggests, even if it were *possible* to persuade decision makers in all of the world's societies to ignore the differing historical, cultural, and practical factors underlying their actual forms of political economy, and to work toward a single, theoretically preferable, ideal version of capitalism, a platonic strategy of attempting to approximate the ideal in real conditions that differ significantly from the ideal's background assumptions is likely to result in *significantly worse outcomes* than those that might be attained by adopting a different model and a different transformational approach.[11]

> It is well known that the attainment of a Paretian optimum requires the simultaneous fulfillment of all the optimum conditions. The general theorem for the second best optimum states that if there is introduced into a general equilibrium system a constraint which prevents the attainment of one of the Paretian conditions, the other Paretian conditions, although still attainable, are, in general, no longer desirable. In other words, given that one of the

Paretian optimum conditions cannot be fulfilled, then an optimum situation can be achieved only by departing from all the other Paretian conditions. The optimum situation finally attained may be termed a second best optimum because it is achieved subject to a constraint which, by definition, prevents the attainment of a Paretian optimum. (Lipsey and Lancaster 1956:11)

"The General Theory of the Second Best" suggests that attempting to approximate a single real or ideal model of capitalism across significantly differing social, economic, cultural, environmental, and geopolitical conditions *assures suboptimal outcomes* for each national capitalism, and for all of them collectively. Worse yet are the anticipatible outcomes of employing capitalist models of political economy that are based on the history and cultural conditions of the West in *radically different contexts*.

Consider the impact on Russia's efforts to democratically transform the multiple aspects of its postcommunist political economy while coping with the IMF's coercive conditions for assistance under the direction of Western neocapitalist economists like Jeffrey Sachs. These neocapitalist economists who called for something even more unrealistic than a platonic, stage-wise approximation of their theoretically ideal model of capitalism—a "jump to the market economy" or a "Big Bang" through immediate, centrally directed changes in property law, industrial ownership, tax regulation, and banking policies that copy those of Western capitalist political economies. The imposition of such ahistorical, essentialist requirements for the development of ideal-form monetarist capitalism has constituted a Procrustean bed for a country emerging into conditions of national near-bankruptcy after seventy-five years of Cold War, with the resultant exclusions, shortages, and angers one might expect. Moreover, the neocapitalist transformative prescription ignores Russia's centuries-long history of centralized totalitarian command and control of the national political economy from the tsars through the communists, which has had such a profound shaping impact within the national culture, reaching deep into the self-creating processes of social psychology, that it caused Jean-Jacques Rousseau, in writing *The Social Contract* (1762), to despair of the possibility that Russians would ever be capable of democratic self-governance. The neocapitalists also ignored the actual levels and locations of experience-based skills, the maldistributions of productive tools and infrastructures, the long-term shortages of basic goods and services, and the deep-seated attitudes toward life that have emerged out of these historical and cultural processes, cavalierly treating the enormous adverse impacts and displacements such abrupt changes have caused as "necessary pain." The inability of ordinary people to pay for food, clothing, and shelter with the almost-worthless rubles they earn for their labor has led to a dangerously unstable political situation in which "democracy" ironically has become a dirty word to many citizens, and some of the old centralist–elitist communists who used to run things better, however repressively and inefficiently, have regained wide popular support.

If this disaster-producing, top-down, outsider-controlled approach to making decisions about the shared conditions of social life is rightly called "democracy," then the Russian people are right to be skeptical of it. The transformative challenges Russia now faces are specific and unprecedented, very different from the conditions out of which Western capitalist formal democracies emerged. Thus, as "The General Theory of the Second Best" has warned political economists for many years, enforcing a transformative approach that implicitly assumes conditions very different from those that actually exist assures a suboptimal outcome. In the context of interlinked crises as severe as those Russia will face for the foreseeable future, other nations' coercive insistence on a transformative prescription based on radically unrealistic assumptions about operative conditions may be a prescription for disaster.

However, *if not neocapitalism and formal democracy, then what?* In spite of the increasingly loud rumblings of popular support in Russia and Poland for unreconstructed communists, it seems clear that the "soviet socialist" vision is no longer a live political option. However, it may be that the neocapitalist triumphalists have misread the twentieth century, and perhaps the whole modern era, as ultimately a struggle for dominance between two abstract, universal models of political economy—"capitalism" and "communism"—on the assumption that one or the other of them could offer an "end of history" and the beginning of a new era in which a single, globally uniform model would optimally promote mutual human flourishing. What the world needs now may be neither the "loser" nor the "winner" of such a historical struggle, but rather *a democratically reconstructive approach to political economy* that learns from the technical and ethical achievements and failures of both of its major predecessors—an approach that can guide crisis intervention experimentally through locally sensitive, democratic participatory processes, collecting these lessons into a fund of empirical experience that can reshape theory in order to make future crisis interventions more effective as we attempt to steer a cooperative course toward global survival and better times.

Any adequate reconstructive approach to political economy must offer a feasible and desirable transformative path for dealing with real problems that emerge within our increasingly globalized sphere of legal, political, and economic interaction. It must recognize the present dominance of the family of wealthy, neocapitalist formal democracies and guide us in transforming them toward a deeper democracy, both in their internal affairs and in their uses of power internationally. At the same time, it must assist those who are presently dominated and culturally threatened by them in liberating themselves to find the right institutions of politics, law, and economy to assist them in finding their own path of development toward deep democracy.

Radical pragmatism is such an approach. If it is the *best* approach, the challenge of its supporters is to show both *how* radical pragmatism guided by the ideal of deep democracy within critical–empirical social theorizing and transformative processes yields *realistic and desirable solutions* to the problems of our times, and *why* ongoing practical transformation toward social and environmental sustainability requires *new approaches to theorizing political economy*.

Radical Pragmatist Transformative Praxis:
Economy, Law, and Democracy

When properly interpreted, both successful and unsuccessful crisis-interventionary efforts since the late 1980s at local, national, and international levels offer powerful lessons. They show that the only *sustainable transformations* in our interlinked crises of culture, environment, and political economy involve at least *proto-democratic change processes* with *more deeply democratic implications.* They show that neither top-down nor grassroots strategies alone combine sufficient economic and political power, institutional support, technical skill, local knowledge, and stakeholder commitment to bring about such sustainable transformations. Rather, sustainable and potentially deeply democratic transformations that can effectively resolve these interlinked crises require *a consciously coordinated, mutually supportive, effectively interactive combination of efforts at local, national, and international levels,* with an ultimate focus at the *local levels* at which most real human actors live their daily lives. They require not only rescuing "less developed countries" from the shocks of an increasingly globalized market economy, but also transforming ultrapowerful world capitalisms' internal and international institutions and processes—*if* their adverse impacts on our shared environment and on various world cultures are to be reversed in time to *restore and strengthen the fragile, dynamic equilibrium* of this still potentially person-nurturing, cultural–natural world that thousands of years of human effort within diverse civilizations as well as a much longer period of development within nature's myriad niches of biodiversity have interactively built up.

If these coordinated transformations toward more deeply democratic sustainability were not possible, then calling for them would be either nostalgic or utopian, but in any case dangerously undesirable in times of global emergency. In a broadly insightful analysis that offers criteria for antecedently assessing the potential of alternative approaches to crisis-interventions at all levels, Carl V. Patton and David S. Sawicki argued that *successful social planning processes must effectively coordinate four factors:* technical feasibility, economic and financial possibility, political viability, and administrative operability.[12] When the successes of recent interventionary experiments that use the deeply democratic methods of radical pragmatism in transforming economy, law, and government at local, national, and international levels are compared with the dangerous failures of interventions based on top-down, "universal recipe," neocapitalist methods, application of Patton and Sawicki's criteria suggests that, far from being unrealistic, *radical pragmatism may guide the development of the only kinds of transformative crisis interventions that can work well enough, soon enough, and sustainably enough.*

In the interconnected spheres of economy, law, and government, the practical meaning of radical pragmatism is exemplified by problem-solving interventions at local, national, and international levels that deeply democratize hearts and minds as well as institutions. Such interventions call forth shared visions, building practical skills and networks of efficacy while more widely dispersing participatory and substantive power. They focus region-specific, people-empowering attention at local levels through networks of micro-entrepreneurs, cooperatives, collectives, democratically owned and operated firms, appropriate support institutions, and coordinating strategies that require and elicit new policies and institutions at national and international levels.

Some promising recent experiments that keep a local focus on the poor while transforming support institutions and generating interlinked interventions with wide-ranging "trickle up" implications reflect the deeply democratic vision of Bangladeshi economist Mohammed Yunus, founder of the Grameen Bank, which offers micro-loans as well as networks of practical training and assistance to poor rural entrepreneurs that help them to start up self-supporting small businesses that have proved to have broad transformative impacts. The efficacy of Yunus's approach has been demonstrated through the successful efforts of more than 1.6 million micro-entrepreneurs—more than 1% of Bangladesh's population—who have borrowed and generally repaid almost one billion dollars, which they have invested in small businesses. These interlinked micro-entrepreneurs—many of them women—make small items for which there is a domestic or international market, such as string, cookies, baskets, and toothpicks, often starting with themselves as the only employee and an initial capitalization of ten to fifteen dollars.[13]

Grameen Bank developed in 1976 out of Yunus's efforts as an American-trained economics professor to bridge the gap between what he was teaching in his home country's classrooms and the situation of the nearby poor—for example, the woman making bamboo stools for two cents per day because she lacked the twenty cents in capital to buy bamboo and to choose her market. Forty-two people in her village needed a total of $27 in capital to start the small businesses that would allow them to achieve a life-transforming return on their primary investment of dedicated, skilled labor. "How easy and cheap it is to bring happiness," Yunus exclaims, but his challenge was to find a way to continue and to expand such transformative economic support. The campus banker said that poor people are not credit-worthy according to standard banking principles and rules, and the hierarchy agreed. When Yunus offered himself as a guarantor for the village's initial loan, the campus bank granted it, but warned that he would not be repaid—yet he was. So Yunus persuaded the bank to loan more and somewhat larger amounts, though they said that poor people would not repay such loans, and that such a program would not work in more than one village. Within the next two years, Yunus expanded his experiment to include the whole district and began to think, why not set up a bank especially for this purpose? The Bangladeshi government initially hesitated to license such an unconventional bank, but two years later, Grameen Bank had 2.1 million borrowers, 96% of them women, with a 98% repayment rate. By 1997, Grameen Bank had more than $1 billion in active assets working in 36,000 villages, with an average loan size of $150. Grameen now offers ten-year housing loans in amounts of $300–$600 as well—300,000 such loans in 1997.

Since Grameen Bank's founding, its general model has been situationally adapted in fifty-six countries, including Vietnam, the Philippines, India, China, Norway, France, Canada, and the United States, and "it has worked every time." The World Bank has undertaken responsibility to organize donor programs to fund micro-lending in additional countries, with a goal of reaching 100 million people worldwide by 2005, assisting people who have been denied credit, especially women. Thus, Yunus suggests, "we can dream of creating a poverty-free world soon."

On the basis of twenty years' experience, Yunus asks *not* whether the poor are *credit-worthy,* but whether the traditional capitalist banking system is *people-worthy.* Poverty is created by the banking system, Yunus argues, which practices a kind of *financial apartheid,* creating two classes of people for no good reason, because it is the rich who have shown themselves unwilling or unable to repay loans. *Credit is a human right,* he argues, because it allows people to use creativity to improve their life prospects. We should not tolerate poverty, Yunus insists— the question is *what economic level we should strive to assure for all* between presently widespread absolute poverty and the top levels of wealth and income. Differences in incomes are good, he suggests, but these should be *commensurate with abilities and contributions,* and institutions can be created that will do this. One-third of Grameen borrowers have already crossed the poverty line, typically between the fifth and the thirteenth years of their participation. Grameen Bank's next goal is to help its borrowers to realize this achievement between the third and the eighth years. In Bangladesh, both the nationalized banks and the private banks are problems, in Yunus's view, so the question is *how to manipulate the system* and, ultimately, *how to transform it.*

Credit is a key to transforming poverty, but it needs other accompaniments and many other steps, addressing all dimensions of life. Grameen Bank is creating co-operative spinoffs in agriculture and fisheries organized from the angle of the poor, as well as a cellular phone company that can transform the speed of information while creating new entrepreneurs, and an electricity generating company specializing in environmentally sustaining, renewable sources like solar and wind energies. Grameen Bank's work has helped to keep rural areas attractive to the poor, and some actually have returned from the cities. Although Grameen is prohibited by charter from urban work, some related urban institutions are developing. Grameen continues to give priority to women, offering staff incentives for approaching them because banks traditionally have been antiwoman. There is now no real difference in their male vs. female repayment rates, but women have shown themselves to be more careful about money and more self-sacrificing, with a longer vision for the family, so that children benefit. Screening is less a problem for Grameen Bank now, Yunus says, than is finding the real poor, who do not believe anyone will lend them money and who must grow into the belief that they can change their situation instead of focusing on avoiding risk.

This *"trickle-up" economic strategy* of people creating their own jobs and improving the quality of life for all through their productive contributions is well-founded in human history, Yunus argues—in fact, the way economy began. Furthermore, people can create their own jobs better than someone else can, but they need money and know-how, and traditional banks will not lend money to micro-entrepreneurs unless they have "the three Cs": character, capacity, and collateral, with the last being the most important to banks and the great stumbling block for poor people. In contrast, the Grameen Bank exists to loan money to poor people who have character and capacity to succeed as micro-entrepreneurs. It assures their success and its own by organizing them into borrowing groups that give them supportive feedback and teach them the "tricks of the trade." When asked why, if investing in micro-enterprises is a real business opportunity, American banks almost universally forego it, Yunus replies that bankers are "brainwashed in the business schools" into accepting the empirically false belief that banking can be done only on the basis of collateral and that poor people are poor risks; if they had grown up with the Grameen Bank, he says, they would think differently.[14]

Like Bangladeshis, financial analyst Paul Solomon suggests, "Americans on the economic margins can parlay their particular skills into entrepreneurial success . . . with new attitudes, money, and know-how." During its first five years of operation, the State of Arkansas's Good Faith Fund, one of two hundred experiments in applying the Grameen Bank's experience within significantly differing American contexts, loaned more than $380,000 to more than 140 borrowers, averaging $2,700 per loan (up to a limit of $25,000) at 13.5% interest. In the Good Faith experiment, training and peer support are key elements. Prospective borrowers must attend what Solomon calls a "business boot camp," must join a borrowing group in which members share experiences and a borrowing limit, and must approve each others' loan applications as cosigners, thus sharing in each others' successes or failures. However, unlike the Grameen Bank, which is growing, the Good Faith Fund raised its initial capital from private benefactors and the Small Business Administration (SBA), and it has not yet met its expenses.

Although it may be still too early to assess the success of the Good Faith Fund, this difference in experience suggests that it may be important to create the right conditions for its success and that of related experiments in other parts of America and in other countries by striving to *consciously coordinate* transformative efforts in the realm of *business and economy* with those in the realm of *law and government.* What specific institutions and processes are likely to be most feasible and desirable is likely to vary somewhat from region to region and country to country. In the United States, the best strategy may combine *regulatory transformation* (e.g., requiring traditional banks to offer a portion of their loans through programs secured on an alternative basis, given the discriminatory impact of "the three Cs" in terms of class, race, gender, and geographic location) *with transformation through incentives to experiment* (e.g., funding many additional Good Faith Funds through the SBA and private donors, within flexible legal guidelines that encourage differing, locally sensitive experiments with micro-entrepreneurial networks and other democracy deepening micro-structures from which we can learn about the shared and differing characteristics of successful and unsuccessful programs in American contexts). If introduced with artful use of the mass media to communicate a new perspective based on better information, this micro-lending strategy might become a culturally acceptable way to empower citizens who live in both urban and rural "pockets of poverty."

In combination with cooperatives, democratic collectives, democratically owned and operated firms, appropriate support institutions, and coordinating strategies, micro-entrepreneurial networks might also play a role within more comprehensive but decentralized national economic restructuring processes in Russia and in other countries struggling to transformatively reenergize post-totalitarian political economies, as well as in wealthy Western formal democracies.[15] Such strategies may offer avenues for talented, experienced farmers as well as midlevel managers and industrial workers who are presently losing their jobs due to corporate downsizing, industrial closings, and technological changes to reemploy themselves while flexibly locating and filling emerging business niches. Such opportunities and successes will lift up the self-esteem and practical productive capacities of their direct beneficiaries while creating good jobs that are widely distributed, including rural people, middle-class suburbanites, and residents of presently desperate, violent, and apparently unreachable urban ghettos like South Central Los Angeles. Like the Grameen Bank, such locally focused efforts in the United States and elsewhere can include ecosystemic integrity among their goals and side constraints, giving targeted support to enterprises that practice *environmental sustainability*, especially those that aim to create new and practical environmentally sensitive technologies and those that employ workers who are losing jobs in areas like America's Pacific Northwest forests because of government-mandated changes to environmentally sensitive resource management techniques.

Such localized, deeply democratic economic interventions also may offer opportunities for American women who, like Bangladeshi women, are an underpaid and generally underutilized source of economic energy who may flame into transformative activity if special efforts are made to include and to empower them. On average, full-time American women workers earn one-third to one-fourth less than their male colleagues and find fewer opportunities for promotion to top positions. At the same time, the largest segment of America's poor are single mothers with children who are limited in their job opportunities by their location, child-care responsibilities, and inadequate education. As futurist-economist Hazel Henderson puts the problem with traditional approaches to economic planning, "If you refuse to look at half of your economic sector, how are you going to make policy?"[16] The publicly valued and supported efforts of American women to generate household income from democratically owned and operated business enterprises could have profound impacts for their families and for their communities, especially as they are progressively able to hire additional workers. Eventually, many small, coordinated local efforts could have a geometrically dynamic "trickle-up" significance of national and international scope.

If American women micro-entrepreneurs, linked together in Good Faith borrowing groups as well as cooperatives and democratic collectives, are like their Bangladeshi sisters, they will practice entrepreneurship with a heart, "lifting each other as we climb," in Mary McLeod Bethune's prophetic phrase. They will analyze each others' business plans carefully and critically in order to help each other to succeed, understanding what needs, fears, and dreams drive each others' behavior. In addition, because of the daily lessons many of them teach children about how to think and act, they will be able to influence micro-transformation of prevalent habits of the heart that presently make the kinds of economic participation that can transform self, situation, and institutions so difficult.

The lessons of these multifaceted, situation-sensitive, radical pragmatist experiments in transforming local and national political economies have global significance. Their implications interlink personal identity with practical agency and a sense of self-esteem that allows one to claim basic human rights, including rights of political participation. In turn, active experience of political participation includes cross-difference encounters that can further one's education, focus one's efforts, and fire up one's transformative imagination. Thus, locally focused experimental interventions in *radical pragmatist economics*, in combination with *democratic citizen participation in rebuilding the public square*, and the related processes of *education, communication, self-transformation, and community-building* both kinds of initiatives entail, can raise up a Deweyan "Public" that can help to create the conditions for and play a decisive role within processes of democratic institutional transformation at national and international levels. Such grassroots, "trickle-up" processes *alone* will *not* allow us to transform world capitalisms and other forms of political economy *well enough and soon enough* to deal with our interlinked crises in political economy, culture, and the environment. However, we cannot address these crises *well enough, soon enough, and sustainably enough without* such grassroots, "trickle-up" processes.

We also need to *make changes in our crisis-intervention approaches* within *international organizations,* within *ultra-powerful Western capitalist formal democracies,* and within *other kinds of political economies,* and each of these change projects requires these grassroots, "trickle-up" processes. On a global level, we need to support and to encourage the recently adopted *experimental, participatory, location-sensitive approach* of the World Bank, as compared to the coercive, top-down, "cookie-cutter" approach of the IMF, which has been unsuccessful in solving the critical problems that have prompted its interventions while dangerously dividing the world's nations into "the defiant, the drifters, and the dutiful."[17] Both World Bank and IMF economists would agree at least in part with Mancur Olson's empirical claim that "the poor are poor because of misgovernment," and that tangible capital would flow to poor countries where return might be highest if they were well-governed. What separates Olson's evidence-based, proto-pragmatist transformative prescription from that of the IMF neocapitalists, however, is his suggestion that *"the right reforms* would make a great difference, but *these do not follow any particular ideology."*[18] Pointing to the unacknowledged cultural aspect of IMF's neocapitalist guiding vision, which seems to be invisible to proponents who regard it as social–scientifically universal and, thus, culture-free, Richard Miller has noted that interventionary policies that the United States has insisted on as reflecting "best economic practice" have been evaluated by Japan and other nations as narrow and culturally Anglo-Saxon. Miller argues that *cultural appropriateness,* including cultural tolerance of a particular intervention as well as the skilled bureaucracy to implement it, is necessary for any intervention's success. "There is no magic bullet" for killing economic problems, in Miller's view. Instead, the right approach is *an eclectic, experimental approach,* grounded in market operations but with a government role that leads to policies that will be *embraced* by "less-developed" countries—policies that promote the kinds of growth that benefits the poor—instead of being *imposed* on them.[19]

Concurring with Miller while drawing especially on his experience in Latin America, Andres Solemano argues that *reforms in political and economic institu-*

tions that promote sustainable growth must reduce poverty, and that privatization *per se* is not an income-equalizing policy: "Market-based reform mechanisms need to address inequality as well as growth, since they must consider *political sustainability* as well as moral and economic factors"[20] Situation-sensitive economic policy is important in reducing poverty through sustainable growth, Solemano agrees, but *"the deeper question is social requisites in policy formation."* Thus, it is not enough for government policies that will promote sustainable growth in Latin America to be market-friendly. They must also promote education, a high savings rate, and the growth of a middle class in societies that traditionally are sharply divided between the very poor and the ruling elite. This requires, he argues, *"improving popular representation and renewal in power in creative ways, especially in ways that expand citizen participation."* Moreover, Alice Amsden adds, "Many national problems in political economy may derive more from *lack of domestic investment in human capital* than from lack of foreign investment."[21] If so, a key feature of situation-sensitive transformative strategies for building sustainable national political economies is that they *draw on international support in developing human capital,* stressing education, training, information, and citizen participation in combination with meeting basic needs like shelter, health care, and nutrition, rather than allowing themselves to be externally reshaped by intrusive, foreign capital–focused interventions like those the IMF has undertaken in recent years.

Some have argued that global economic and political forces have made the nation–state outmoded, and that we should swiftly relocate its present functions, responsibilities, and authority both *upward* (toward international organizations and regional transnational unions) and *downward* (toward local political economies). However, the IMF's dangerous mistakes show that, especially when supported and interlinked by international organizations that focus and maximize their resistant and transformative influence, *nation–states continue to provide important locations of protective leverage against misuses of power within the shifting plate tectonics of the family of global capitalisms.*[22] Although both the IMF and the World Bank attempt to influence our shared global situation by intervening in national crises, in contrast with the economic stability–promoting role of the IMF, the World Bank is designed to be transformative: to *fight poverty* in ways that *meet basic human needs while creating opportunities for more meaningful, self-liberatory participation* within national political economies that are *just* as well as *successful* in aggregate terms.

In recent years, according to Kyu Sik Lee, the World Bank has adopted a collaborative, democratic participatory approach toward sustainably transforming particular locations and aspects of poverty within its member nations, whose cultural frameworks of political economy are necessarily self-transformatively implicated in the required processes of documenting that those who are supposed to benefit from the projects described in particular funding proposals are likely to do so and have been consulted in the course of designing the projects.[23] This new approach emphasizes "ownership of the project," which means that *funded projects must be demand-driven, municipal in origin, participatory in structure, and accompanied by an environmental impact statement.* To promote sustainable development, in Lee's view, these poverty-transforming municipal development programs must *effectively address four kinds of constraints* that tend to limit the success of local political economies: (1) weak local political and financial institutions; (2) inappropriate and costly regulations; (3) poor access to financing combined with low tax revenues; and (4) infrastructure deficiencies. "Once institutions are set right," Lee predicts, "people will respond, but they need strong local leadership, and sequencing of development programs rather than a single Big Bang." Successful local transformative projects often include nongovernment organizations (NGOs) as well as the informal institutions of civil society among their collaborating participants. In Lee's experience, *locally focused transformative efforts* are more likely to be successful in promoting sustainable economic development than are national models because of their greater effectiveness in implementation.

However, as Ismail Serageldin argues, *the environmental aspect of sustainable economic development* requires active roles for nations and international organizations, working through a combination of information-gathering, regulation, and market mechanisms.[24] The World Bank first created a department of environmental issues in 1987, and environmentally sustainable development for human persons (including clean air, clean water, and fertile soil) is its basic focus. To achieve this goal, Serageldin argues, we need to *change the way we think about meeting human needs*—to do this with dignity and in a way that works for the future by being financially, environmentally, and socially sustainable, the latter requiring equity, participation, and human rights. Since the 1992 Earth Summit, the World Bank has been committed to *a four-part environmental agenda:* (1) first, do no harm; (2) offer proactive support for environmental transformation; (3) look for win–win areas of investment in human development, including education, health, and empowerment, especially for women and girls; and (4) address global problems and seek cooperation among nations in addressing shared problems, such as those concerning shared rivers.

The solutions to these problems must go beyond market mechanisms, because "public goods cannot be captured through markets—we need *a consensus-based regulatory framework* that captures real costs and sets limits globally." As a basis for such a consensus, Serageldin argues, "*we need to change the way we measure progress*" so as to internalize "externalities" like the costs of air and water pollution, to factor in social inequities in adverse impacts as well as benefits, and to transform our conception of knowledge and education to make it serve the many. In building "*bridges of means and hope that will keep the poor from consuming the planet,*" we need to focus on *three key areas:* (1) transforming agriculture at the level of the small holder–farmer (the bulk of the world's poor) while increasing food security and protecting biodiversity; (2) reducing carbon dioxide production, to which carbon-offset trading is one possible answer; and (3) reducing energy and water consumption through right pricing. Achieving these three goals will require the kind of collaboration between government and civil society that, in Serageldin's view, can be most effectively promoted by *devolution of power to local authorities* (nations and municipalities) and by *strategies that "change behavioral signals,"* including tax policies.

Environmental racism needs to be at the center of our concerns in finding sustainable transformative solutions, Serageldin argues, because it affects most of the humans on the planet. We need to address attitudes that allow the rich to turn their backs on the poor, continuously asking, "Who pays, who benefits, and how do we protect the marginalized?" Echoing Alain Locke, Serageldin argues, "This is a matter of *practicing our common humanity.*" In promoting this practice, Serageldin suggests, the information media carry an important responsibility and can play a key role. Graciela Chichilnisky adds that there is no innate contradiction between economic development and protecting the environment—this is a tragic misunderstanding. *"Destroying our own niche is unwise,"* she argues, yet "Third World countries house most of the remaining biodiversity and most of the environmental destruction."[25] *Knowledge rights* and *environmental use rights* are crucial in achieving a sustainable global transformation process, in her view, and we may be able to use competitive markets to assure best enforcement of these universal rights by seeing that they are paid for locally. For example, emission rights can be used as flexible taxes that "internalize" economic costs while assuring that those who are directly harmed by emissions are economically benefited.

Partnerships will shape and implement *the most sustainable solutions* to our interlinked global crises, in the view of Aliye Pekin Celik—partnerships that include NGOs, political authorities at all levels, women's groups, universities, and business people.[26] The key to developing *sustainable human settlements* in our era is developing sustainable linkages between rural settlements and cities, in Celik's view. Education is the first need, but we also must focus on protecting rural environments while connecting increased food production to increased rural income. To reverse dangerous processes of rural flight that lead to "hyper-cities," we need to stimulate rural development, education, health care, nutrition, housing, sustainable agriculture, and infrastructure, while creating private wholesale-based food markets with equitable access and promoting rural products in urban areas. In doing all this, we must *follow the best examples,* including gender balance, empowering differing social groups while promoting partnerships, and working to improve both urban and rural quality of life.

Such insightful thinking and such promising experiments show that *the prevailing international system needs to be "fixed,"* in George Cabot Lodge's words, by "being realistic instead of lingering with old assumptions, upgrading existing international institutions and creating some new ones, and recognizing the developing communitarianism of world thinking, instead of applying an outdated individualist language."[27] Democratically effective international organizations would strengthen the collective power of other nations and locales to push back against the value cannibalism of ultra-powerful global capitalisms. Using the *leverage* provided by *shifting pressure points* in the plate tectonics of complex, multilayered relationships within the family of world capitalisms, the *economic, legal, and cultural support* such international organizations could offer would help nations and municipalities to selectively affect the financial feasibility of alternative projects and approaches, thereby influencing *self-transformation within the internal regulative processes of world capitalisms.*

Just as "The General Theory of the Second Best" warns us, radical pragmatism suggests that *if* there is an effective way to develop democratic forms of political economy in the former USSR and the nations it dominated for fifty years, it is not by incautious imposition of a historically ill-fitting abstract ideal model. Rather, *stable and workable democratic political economies* for Russia, its partners in confederation, and the newly autonomous nations of Eastern Europe are more likely to develop out of *transformative collaborations* among those representative individuals who are close to specific local situations and who can coordinate their insights concerning local history and cultures within cooperative efforts to *remedy recognized problems, remove particular barriers, and develop the people's skills as self-directed, cooperating agents of change.*

Likewise, *ultra-powerful capitalist regimes* like the United States are not likely to achieve even their presently narrowly conceived goals of social stability and overall economic growth by approximating abstract ideal models of national currency manipulation, diplomatic and military international arm-twisting, and local police containment of violent displays of civic dissatisfaction. Rather, as the placard of one insightful, nonviolent demonstrator during the 1992 Los Angeles riots read, "No justice, no peace." *The operative American understandings of both capitalism and democracy must change* at the local level as well as the national and international levels. *But how?*

In the spheres of law and government, the answers to how to transform operative American understandings of capitalism and democracy must be *situation-specific* yet *broadly coordinated,* and they must emerge through *collaborative conversations* in which well-informed, mutuality-minded, realistically hopeful, nonabsolutist individuals representing diverse social locations with related specific concerns meet and work together with the consulting assistance of relevant "experts" to craft solutions that they regard as both feasible and desirable. They must take the time to listen respectfully to each other and to come to understand each others' differing experiences and value perspectives. Spurred on by their shared broadly humane values, they must study the situation in its various dimensions together. On this basis, they must find the courage to propose specific changes, to explain them to their constituencies, and to actively support their implementation and subsequent reevaluation. They will be challenged and changed in the process, and with their ongoing efforts, so will others with whom they share a form of life and a regime of political economy.

The courts must become sufficiently committed to radical pragmatism to *accept* and to *aid these changes,* even though they may entail reconceptualizations of individual and corporate property rights, government's role in protecting the community's health, safety, and welfare, and the entitlements of individuals, families, and communities. Radical transformation of world capitalisms toward more egalitarian political economies that facilitate the flourishing of variously situated persons differing in culture, gender, race, class, geography, and access to technology may require transformation of property rights and relations, but not necessarily "worker ownership of the means of production" as Marx and Engels understood that concept. Rather, *sharing in the various other elements of property* that C.B. Macpherson (1973) and Lawrence Becker (1977), citing A.M. Honore (1961), analyze within the property rights bundle may be more transformatively significant. For example, the right to share in use, the right to share in management, and the right to a share of the income from use may be more important than the right to control and the right to destroy, which will in any case need to be more strictly limited for everyone in the future.

It is ironic that the United States of America, the nation that combines the world model of "formal democracy" with the world's most powerful economy, has recently played a largely counterproductive, obstacle-creating role within cooperative international efforts to sustainably transform the conditions that have created our interlinked global crises. Yet it cannot be surprising to anyone who knows John Dewey's prophetic critique of "money capitalism" in the 1930s, as well as the contemporary culture–power of the peculiarly American form of capitalist ideology: its chauvinistic boosterism, its invocation of "the invisible hand" operating within capitalist markets to assure that all will be better off than they could be within any other system of political economy, its sense of manifest destiny, of divine providence for the worthy and hard-working, and, in its most extreme manifestations, its apocalyptic religious disregard for our natural environment and for the sin-flawed creatures of "this world." In recent years, politically successful "centrist liberals" have "bought into" neocapitalist economic theory, and also into partnership with ultra-powerful capitalist business firms, in the belief that these firms have the capacity to take down others with them, if not to heal.

However, as Dewey rightly reminded us, *American culture has other strands* that have great potential counterpower within our understanding, our imagination, and our motivating desires. Thus, *a culture-liberatory revival and deepening of our democratic aspirations,* as well as of convergent *justice-seeking* aspects of the differing religious strands of our multicultural fusion, may have powerful impacts on American government, law, and civil society, as well as our practices of daily life. And these, in turn, can *prod capitalist business firms and our capitalist formations of political economy toward self-transformation* by progressively reframing the terms within which economic markets and actors operate.

Within all of the wealthy Western "formal" democracies, we must promote *intracultural* as well as *intercultural conversations* about the meaning and positive transformative potential of the democratic ideal, accepting *mutual conversion* to a more deeply democratic way of life as necessary to civil peace and transformative effectiveness in resolving our interlinked cultural, environmental, and economic crises. We must draw upon the *existing resources of formal democracy* as well as on *our memories and hopes* for a mutually optimal quality of community life in order to focus and energize *cooperative, cross-difference coalition-based, grassroots-led projects of rebuilding the public square.* We must carefully assess these projects and learn from their results in building up *a general fund of democratic transformative experience.* We must emphasize *education* that will prepare people for this kind of deeply democratic participation and help them to learn and to teach others through its processes, thereby shaping democratic attitudes and skills as well as gaining general and technical knowledge. We must institute the use of *more locationally and culturally sensitive measures of human welfare* so that the situation of regions and subgroups is not hidden within national aggregates, and so that the cultural assumptions underlying current, seemingly culture-neutral indicators of human welfare can be unmasked and critically-empirically

reshaped to reveal impacts of political–economic transactions in terms that are in-
traculturally meaningful while expressing what Alain Locke called "cognate
forms of common humane values." We must *seek out or create local economic
niches* that can be desirably developed by economically marginalized people with
cooperative assistance from fellow citizens and various levels of government. We
must support and participate in those *transnational NGOs* that promote socially
and environmentally sustainable transformative projects of deep democracy
within and between nations. Finally, we must use the *resources of environmental
law* along the lines of the ancient "Public Trust Doctrine" so effectively revived
by Robert F. Kennedy, Jr., on behalf of the Hudson Riverkeepers and the National
Resources Defense Council.[28]

These are *the methods of radical pragmatism,* and *no other transformative
method* will guide wealthy and powerful capitalist political economies—as well as
precapitalisms, communisms, and postcommunisms that must integrate their national political economies into a presently capitalism-dominated world economy—in the *self-transformations* that will allow them to revise and then to
achieve their currently narrower goals while progressively embodying those
broader, shared ideal values that will hold the faith of their citizens: *peace, justice,
ecosystemic integrity, and human flourishing.* The successes of such examples of
radical pragmatist transformative praxis have already shown that ordinary citizens
as well as less powerful countries need not wait for deliverance, either through an
epiphany of deeply democratic consciousness among the powerful or through a
global revolution of the oppressed. Rather, change will come through a combination of *grassroots experiments and self-empowering initiatives* that bring some
immediate relief on local levels that show what can be done differently, interacting on national and international levels with *a critical–empirical reformulation of
economics, politics, and law* driven by awareness of the inadequacy of the
presently dominant neocapitalist model of political economy to predict and to positively influence world events, including the deep damage world capitalisms are
doing to our cultural lifeworlds and our global ecosystems.

Influentially placed economists who understand the urgency of transforming
ultra-powerful world capitalisms, and who can see the IMF's recent actions as
countereffective and undemocratic despite their justificatory rationale, must
bring the full weight of their professional credibility to bear in publicly critiquing
and attempting to rein in their misguided colleagues. As James D. Wolfensohn,
President of the World Bank, recently argued:[29]

> We must address the issues of long-term equitable growth on which prosper-
> ity and human progress depend. We must focus on the institutional and struc-
> tural changes needed for recovery and sustainable development. We must
> focus on the social issues. We must do all this. Because *if we do not have the
> capacity to deal with social emergencies, if we do not have longer-term plans
> for solid institutions, if we do not have greater equity and social justice, there
> will be no political stability. And without political stability, no amount of
> money put together in financial packages will give us financial stability.*
> (Sanger 1998:A6)

Moreover, as Serageldin would remind Wolfensohn, *political sustainability* also requires *environmental sustainability.* Those of us who have professional credibility and responsibility as philosophers, as environmental scientists, as democratic theorists, and as social leaders who have learned these lessons of transformative praxis must add the strength of our voices to these economists' critique, and we must cooperatively assist them in discovering *democratically deeper models of political economy.* Having learned within transformative praxis what kinds of tools, measures, and critical–empirical generalizations we need in order to more effectively and more democratically intervene in various aspects of our urgent, multidimensional, situation-specific global crisis, we can now bring the right focus and the right questions to the necessarily cooperative, cross-disciplinary project of transforming neocapitalist economic theory through radical pragmatism.

Transforming Neocapitalist Economic Theory through Radical Pragmatism

In his original theorizing of capitalist political economy, Adam Smith never adequately spelled out the meaning and the implications of *the central ethical value* he thought should guide political economy—*human welfare*—though this is the value he argued is most effectively promoted by linking capitalist markets with "formally" democratic political institutions. Yet the econometric indicators and analytical tools that have since come into use in capitalist economic theorizing have continued to depend for their justification and presumed explanatory power on the implicit claim that they gather and interpret descriptive and predictive information that relates to human welfare. In the middle and late years of the twentieth century, a set of positivist methodological claims about human welfare were defended by Milton Friedman and other "Chicago School" libertarian economists who dominated capitalist economic theorizing: first, that we do not need to specify what "human welfare" means, because people deeply disagree about it, so that it is ultimately a matter of individual specification within the minimal legal framework of a formally democratic society; and second, whatever human welfare might mean in social terms is adequately indicated by "objective" aggregate economic indicators of national wealth, productivity, and the basic material prerequisites to individual choice, because capitalist economic theory predicts outcomes so well. These claims are *no longer tenable* in times of interlinked global crises that clearly place human welfare at risk. Moreover, we have since realized that human welfare is inseparable from another central value: *environmental sustainability.*

In order to guide *transformative crisis interventions* that are both *technically effective* and *ethically desirable,* we need to develop *better critical–empirical indicators* relative to a more specific yet pluralistic analysis of the double-sided goal we now seek to achieve through the workings of political economy. This requires that we find ways to wrestle together across our differing cultural, ecosystemic, geopolitical, and geo-economic locations to clarify and specify what human welfare and care for the Earth mean to us. In present times of interlinked global crises, we need to do this cooperative wrestling for the meaning of these basic values *well enough and soon enough* to effectively and desirably intervene in the particular problem situations that engulf us. At the same time, we also need to initiate the kinds of ongoing democratic processes of cross-difference conversation and cooperation that eventually will allow us *to rebuild the public square on all levels* in order to *enhance and sustain* the global realization of these interlinked central values.

"The General Theory of the Second Best" should have put an end in 1956 to the one-model, Procrustean-bed approach to economic theory that the Chicago School continued to perpetuate, largely on ideological rather than empirical grounds. In evolving a more effective and desirable approach to transformative political economy, we need to recognize that currently dominant models and power formations of capitalist political economy theoretically ignore while actively cannibalizing other values that are necessary to human flourishing and ecosystemic integrity. We need to critically challenge the dominant, "formal" conception of democracy as appropriately uncommitted on ends, and to reinstate *a guiding teleological role* for the central values of *mutual human flourishing* and *care for the Earth*. We need to *conceptually decouple* democratic models of law and politics from dominant, neocapitalist models of economy, and then to use the resources of the first two to *reconfigure interrelationships* within political economy on a more deeply democratic conceptual and institutional basis, *relocating political economy* as *a domain of means for embodying lifeworld values*. We need to *characterize additional lifeworld values* that are *necessary to human flourishing and ecosystemic integrity,* and to appropriately factor these into reconceptualized models of political economy that can guide assessment and policy development on global, transnational, national, and local–regional levels. We need to develop *more accurate critical–empirical generalizations about the "plate tectonics" among global capitalisms,* revealing the pressure points and leverages for transformative legal and political interventions, as well as the processes by which actual actors of various kinds affect these shifting macro-relationships. We need to discover niches within various economic formations that can be developed in ways that *increase the economic power of the oppressed while enhancing their democratic will and capacity.*

Effective and desirable international crisis interventions need *a new model of the "expert" transformative actor.* Instead of the neocapitalist model of heroic "corporate raiders" who take over for the good of the business, enforcing market discipline by ignoring nonmarket values and unloading countercompetitive costs and inefficiencies, we need a new "medical" model of "transformative healers" who help to restore assistance-requesting patients from life-threatening crises or general "dys-ease" to health, and then cooperatively develop with them specifically appropriate programs for maintaining and enhancing the various dimensions of health. This new model of transformative healing needs to be based on the realization that, although empirical generalizations may offer invaluable suggestions, every "body" of political economy is unique, and diagnosis and curing is an art requiring synthetic imagination and creativity. The kinds of critical–empirical generalizations that may help diverse political economies in crisis are not standard rules to be enforced, but rather *general principles* to be followed within *respectful, situation-specific processes of diagnosis and curing.* We lack many of the critical–empirical generalizations we need now because the dominant neocapitalist theoretical model has not been asking many of the right questions, committed as it is to *unrealistic assumptions of fundamental uniformity* across economic situations that are incompatible both with "The Theory of the Second Best" and with the practical teachings of common sense.

Economistic aggregate indicators like gross domestic product (GDP) inadequately indicate quality of life for human persons, even when they are nuanced in terms of per capita income. They do not express the wide range of differences in practical economic power between the very rich and the poorest of the poor within a society, nor the range of life choices that are linked to such great differences in economic power. At a deeper level, such economistic indicators ignore most of the *humanly crucial aspects of lived existence* on which structures and processes of economy, law, and politics have a profound impact:

1. whether people have adequate food, clothing, shelter, health care, socially basic education, transportation, means of communication, water quality, air quality, and an uplifting, renewing biophysical environment;
2. whether people feel safe in their homes and on the streets;
3. whether people have secure and personally meaningful work that affords them income, cooperative social connection, and a sense of accomplishment and contribution, as well as opportunities for growth in mind, spirit, and character;
4. whether people have meaningful and sustaining cultural roots that connect them to a larger history that contextualizes their own story and that offers ethical guidance and resources for the spirit;
5. whether people are valued and effective members of diverse communities of daily lived experience whose cooperative practices shape a sustaining social ecology that meets their broader social needs;
6. whether persons' specific individual needs for intimate understanding and caring are met by a network of families and friends;
7. whether persons' particular located voices, experiences, and visions of various aspects of a common good life carry significant weight in shaping public policies that influence outcomes within and through shared political and economic institutions.

The abstract analytic indicators of neocapitalist economic theory are premised on a model of the *"rational economic man"* that treats all of these aspects of human need, human motivation, and experienced human personhood as irrelevant in explaining and predicting economic activities in terms of consumer choice, labor flows, and investment strategies, in measuring outcomes in purely monetary terms, and in assessing economic welfare as the basis for public policies, whether national or international.[30] Yet these *cross-culturally shared human needs,* which must be *prerequisite to any realistic and reasonable conception of human flourishing,* have been well-documented and further detailed by anthropologists, sociologists, and other researchers in the social sciences—in fact, we seem to share many of these needs with other animal species.

To suggest that human persons could be made *"better off"* by a pattern of living within an institutional framework that requires us to *forego* some of these needs for the sake of a greater abstract material potency is *existentially, if not logically, contradictory.* An institutional framework that encourages or requires us to forego such basic human needs may be rationally justifiable if the outcome of the only alternative institutional framework in a real situation is starvation or death by violence, but this is only to claim that its outcomes are *better than the worst imaginable outcomes, not* that they constitute the *best imaginable* or even *generally the best attainable* outcomes, and thus, that the institutional mechanisms that produce maximal abstract material potency at the expense of basic human needs *generally* constitute necessary means to human flourishing. To say that the good life is characterized by *maximal material potency, even at the cost of meeting some of our basic existential needs,* is like saying that we would be happier because of having more time for tennis if we gave up sleeping. It is as existentially contradictory as saying, as did Aristotle and the leaders of America's antebellum South, that some human beings can achieve the highest happiness of which they are capable only if they are deprived of *practical liberty* and subjected to the will of others for their entire lifetimes.

Like practical liberty, *a rich, supportive cultural nexus* also is necessary to human flourishing. It is prerequisite to the personal development of existential liberty, or "agency" as Cornel West calls it, and to the ongoing connection of one's personal life "script" to a larger historical and interpretive framework. For related reasons, *a deep and reliable network of particular intimate relationships* sustained over time is necessary in early childhood for physical health and flourishing, as well as for the development of a sense of personal identity and preciousness. Such a reliable network of intimacy continues to be important throughout the human lifespan, a key factor in weathering midlife crises and surviving in health and happiness as one becomes truly old.

Therefore, the neocapitalist claim that an abstract, purely aggregative, market-driven model of capitalist political economy, including the formally democratic "universal" framework of law and politics it justifies and requires, actually *improves human welfare* when it *destroys the cultures and networks of intimacy on which human flourishing demonstrably depends,* is not only *false,* but also *existentially self-contradictory,* whereas the harms its institutional employment creates are *real* and *humanly devastating.* Moreover, as we come to have a deeper sense of the generally still-unacknowledged *positive existential importance* for humans of *lived relationship with a particular geo-biotic terrain,* in addition to the *already clear and dangerous aggregate significance of abusing our ecosystems* through forms of daily life and "business as usual" guided by a shallowly democratic institutional framework and the economic processes it permits and even dictates, we will begin to realize that the relocative and environmentally distancing lived impacts of a shallowly democratic neocapitalist ideology are *existentially "dys-locative."*

The project of rebuilding the public square in ways that fulfill each of the crucial existential needs of human persons and, thus, genuinely promote the good life for all, does not reject a role for *aggregate measures* as such, but rather insists that such measures *meaningfully indicate effectiveness in meeting our shared human needs.* Simplicity in expression and operation is not the first criterion of adequacy for such indicators, nor can existential aspects of real human lives and shared situations be insightfully inferred from easily observable and quantifiable behaviors alone. The economistic approach that relied primarily on aggregate national measures like GDP has fundamentally misled us by focusing our attention on *abstractions that are ultimately unconnected with human experience*. To assess the extent to which real human persons are actually experiencing the good life as well as the effectiveness of various social interventions in contributing to the achievement of that goal, we must employ *different kinds of aggregate indicators* that reflect processes of interpretation based on humanly shared experiences that makes at least partial cross-difference existential understanding possible.

One of the first things we must take into account in developing more adequate aggregate indicators of the humanly experienced quality of life is that *human persons are attached to particular places on the planet*. It is certainly true that we live in an era in which a large proportion of workers within various world economies relocate many times in their lives, but there are *humanly good if economistically irrational reasons* why many people do not wish to relocate, even if they could earn a higher income in another place. These include familial responsibilities and an existential commitment to a particular place. Moreover, the reasons for the high rate of actual relocations cannot be so easily explained, and their actual human costs in many cases are hidden by an assumption about human location that treats us more like *potted plants,* who can live anywhere as long as we are fed, watered, and given our quota of photons, instead of like *trees,* who need to put down deep roots in a compatible kind of soil in order to gain the stability and the diverse forms of nutrition we need. Even this tree metaphor is inadequate, however, in that it leaves out the unique particularities on which the quality of our individual lived experience depends: *the particular family members and friends* with whom our ongoing lives and the roots of our very beings are richly intertangled, *the particular culture, the particular communities, the particular profession, and the particular geo-biotic terrain* that locate our lives. None of these can be replaced with generic others without fundamental change to us as persons at the core of our being.

When our home location of origin is perverse in some aspects of its formation, or does not offer us as individuals enough room to grow, then we must leave our formative nexus and try to find some other more congenial place in which to reroot our lives—although this process is difficult, takes time, and is not always completely successful. Many people who take up their roots and move to new locations these days do it willingly in order to "get ahead" in economistic terms, in order to "get away" from something toxic in their home location, or in order to "get a life" when some aspect (perhaps relational or professional) could not be satisfied where they were. However, *the difficulty and the human costs of such relocations* are often underappreciated when people first undertake them. With a second or third relocation, these existential elements often become key factors in painful tradeoffs that are simply obscured by the economistic assumption that relocations are "freely chosen." Thus, in our meta-theoretical approach to developing the kinds of aggregate indicators that will allow us to assess the quality of human life in our present situation and, on that basis, to analyze the causes of our problems and to plan transformative strategies that are likely to bring about improvements, we need to *replace humans in nature* and to *relocate particular human persons in particular places on the planet in relation to particular others.* Our theoretical approach must be *locational* as well as *relational.*[31] Such a locational relational approach to human welfare reveals patterns among the manifest and manifold symptoms of contemporary social and existential "dys-ease" that are caused by *failings of democracy in the public square* that can be corrected only by *deepening democracy* in the United States and in other parts of the world.

According to neocapitalism's economistic measures, the quality of life in the United States in the last years of the twentieth century has been getting better and better. This *"success"* offers the rationale for semicoercively imposing America's shallowly democratic public institutions, and the neocapitalistic economic model that increasingly guides them, on other nations that fall within the purview of American *"interests"* (narrowly defined in terms of military security and continuing increases in American GDP), or that somehow arouse America's *humanitarian concern* (expressed through interventions directed by the general principle that only the institutions of an American-style capitalist formal democracy can assure a permanent cure). However, if the welfare of human persons, in the United States and elsewhere, is assessed in light of *different indicators*—those that express the humanly crucial aspects of lived existence outlined previously—in a way that preserves locational differences instead of subsuming and homogenizing them into national and global outcomes, and if *deeper causal patterns and existential outcomes* are sought behind and beyond quantifiable, monetarily expressible behavioral data, *a different picture emerges.*[32] It shows local and regional pockets of poverty, violence, and despair, widespread insecurity and ontological rootlessness, dissatisfaction with the quality of working experience, alienation from political processes and institutions, all-too-common family breakdown and personal loneliness even in wealthy, "democratic" America. In other countries it highlights interrelated but locally specific existential problems for political economy: Bosnia–Herzegovina, Rwanda, and Israel experience seemingly irresolvable civil conflicts; Russia experiences widespread poverty even among the well-educated, as well as continuing political instability and the growth of an indigenous mafia; and Korea, until recently regarded as the leader of the "Asian Tiger" economies, is now regarded as a carrier of the "Asian Flu," and therefore experiences cultural humiliation as the price of rescue by the IMF.

Such a new set of indicators will show that a global environmental crisis interlinks all the world's peoples, yet national and international obstacles created through the use of "formally" democratic institutional mechanisms are blocking a timely and effective collective response. If such *qualitative aspects of human experience* are the *true indicators of individual and general welfare* (rather than abstract marginal monetary activities, the ease of "flow" of labor across locations and occupational categories, and gross and per capita domestic product), then "formally" democratic legal and political institutions and the capitalist economic institutions and firms that increasingly drive them are *not* displaying the efficacy in promoting the good life their proponents claim demonstrate their adequacy and finality. We must *retheorize political economy* in ways that start with and continuously return to our specific existential prerequisites for human flourishing within the context of a flourishing geo-biotic whole.

Conclusion

The seriousness of capitalism-linked global crises within valuably differing world cultures, our shared natural environment, and our increasingly interlinked political economies suggests that Western capitalist, "formally" democratic nations do *not* exemplify a final, universally applicable model of political economy. Nor is there some alternative universal model that can offer rapid, desirable, and sustainable relief. Rather, the history of these crises, including the successes and failures of alternative crisis-intervention strategies, suggests that we need *a new, reconstructive approach to political economy* that will allow us to transform existing institutions and their impacts *well enough, soon enough, and sustainably enough.* This approach is a *radical pragmatism* that is critical, experimental, culturally pluralistic, and reciprocally participatory, finding locally effective solutions to interlinked problems while facilitating the transformation of institutions of political economy as well as the habits of the heart that sustain them through collaborative democratic processes. As we learn the lessons of these crisis-interventionary efforts and discover the need for *new intellectual tools* to help us guide them, radical pragmatism also offers the best approach to *transforming neocapitalist economic theory and "formally" democratic legal and political theory* in order to create more realistic, existentially sensitive indicators of human welfare and ecosystemic health, as well as technically more effective, experience-based strategies for transforming current crises into sustainable and flourishing deeply democratic futures.

Notes

1. Cited by Dr. Mohammed Yunus of the Grameen Bank (January 1997), Dr. Aliye Pekin Celik of the United Nations Centre for Human Settlements (April 16, 1997), and Dr. Ismail Serageldin of the World Bank (April 30, 1997) at Reuters Forums at Columbia University (New York, New York).

2. Cited by Dr. Graciela Chichilnisky, UNESCO Chair of Mathematics and Economics, and Director of the Program on Information Resources (April 30, 1997) at a Reuters Forum at Columbia University.

3. All of these statistics and related analyses are from Dr. Aliye Pekin Celik and Dr. Graciela Chichilnisky, *op. cit.*

4. Dr. Ismail Serageldin, *op. cit.*

5. Dr. Phillip Thompson of Barnard College's Political Science Department (April 16, 1997) at a Reuters Forum at Columbia University, who also predicted: "A majority of African American men will serve a term in prison, nearly all in certain neighborhoods."

6. Dr. C. Michael Aho of Columbia University's Economics Department (April 2, 1997) at a Reuters Forum at Columbia University.

7. Dr. Jeffrey Sachs, *Poland's Jump to the Market Economy* (1993), 5.

8. My analysis here broadens and emphasizes normative aspects within Thomas Kuhn's highly influential analysis of processes of theoretical development in the physical sciences in *The Structure of Scientific Revolutions* (1962).

9. See Francis Fukuyama's *The End of History and the Last Man* (1992) and Jeffrey Sachs's *Poland's Jump to the Market Economy* (1993). Speaking for many others in *Specters of Marx* (1994), Jacques Derrida challenged their triumphal celebration of the capitalist "new world order" as premature, suggesting that "specters of Marx" haunt their dance of denial of expanding human misery and portend a renewal of the international struggle for social justice.

10. See Heilbroner's "Reflections on the Triumph of Capitalism," originally published in *The New Yorker* (1989), reprinted in *Moral Issues in Business, Fifth Edition* (1992).

11. See R.G. Lipsey and Kelvin Lancaster, "The General Theory of the Second Best," *Review of Economic Studies,* XXIV:63 (1956), pp. 11–32. I am grateful to Kurt Nutting for bringing this study to my attention.

12. See Carl V. Patton and David S. Sawicki, *Basic Methods of Policy Analysis and Planning* (1986), 37.

13. Dr. Mohammed Yunus, Managing Director of the Grameen Bank of Bangladesh (January 27, 1997), speaking at a Reuters Forum at Columbia University.

14. Paul Solomon, "Bootstrap Economics," *The McNeil–Lehrer News Hour,* February 17, 1994.

15. For an empirically supported argument that firms that are owned and run democratically by their workers can be equally efficient in a suitable institutional setting as nondemocratic firms, in addition to their other advantages, see Samuel Bowles and Herbert Gintis, "A Political and Economic Case for the Democratic Enterprise" (1993).

16. See Hazel Henderson, *Paradigms in Progress: Life Beyond Economics* (1991).

17. See David E. Sanger, "Policy Means Nothing if the Shelves Are Bare," *The New York Times,* September 27, 1998, Section 3, 4.

18. Prof. Mancur Olson, Economics Department, University of Maryland (February 12, 1997), speaking at a Reuters Forum at Columbia University.

19. Richard Miller, Reuters's Chief Economics Correspondent (February 12, 1997), speaking at a Reuters Forum at Columbia University.

20. Andres Solefano, Executive Director for Chile and Ecuador at the Inter-American Development Bank (February 12, 1997), speaking at a Reuters Forum at Columbia University.

21. Prof. Alice Amsden, Department of Politics and Economics, Massachusetts Institute of Technology (February 12, 1997), speaking at a Reuters Forum at Columbia University.

22. See Prof. Omar Dahbour's "Globalization and the Contradictions of Liberal Nationalism," presented at a Radical Philosophy Association Conference at Purdue University, November 1996.

23. Dr. Kyu Sik Lee, Principal Evaluation Office at the World Bank (April 16, 1997), speaking at a Reuters Forum at Columbia University.

24. Dr. Ismail Serageldin, Vice President for Environmentally Sustainable Development at the World Bank, *op. cit.*

25. Dr. Graciela Chichilnisky, *op. cit.*

26. Dr. Aliye Pekin Celik, Director of the New York Office of the United Nations Centre for Human Settlements (April 16, 1997), speaking at a Reuters Forum at Columbia University. See also *The Habitat Agenda: Goals and Principles, Commitments and Global Plan of Action*, adopted at the United Nations Conference on Human Settlements (Habitat II), at Istanbul, Turkey, June 3–14, 1996.

27. Prof. George Cabot Lodge, Harvard University Business School, speaking at a Reuters Forum (April 2, 1997), summarizing his key recommendations in his *Managing Globalization in the Age of Interdependence* (1995).

28. Robert F. Kennedy, Jr., Chief Prosecuting Attorney for the Hudson Riverkeepers, Senior Attorney for the Natural Resources Defense Council, and Clinical Professor and Supervising Attorney in the Environmental Litigation Clinic at Pace University School of Law, explained this ancient Western legal concept and the transformative strategy he derives from it (April 30, 1997) at a Reuters Forum at Columbia University. See also Michael Brint and William Weaver, eds. *Pragmatism in Law and Society* (1991).

29. James D. Wolfensohn, President of the World Bank, speaking to the finance ministers and central bank governors from 182 nations at a joint meeting in New York of the World Bank and the International Monetary Fund (October 6, 1998), as reported by David E. Sanger in "Dissension Erupts at Talks on World Financial Crisis: I.M.F.'s Austerity Policies Draw Criticism," *The New York Times,* October 7, 1998, A6.

30. The dominant model of "rational economic man" has been challenged by feminist economist Julie A. Nelson of Brandeis University as leading to overreliance on game theory and insufficient empirical field research, including failure to investigate the economic implications of our interdependent human needs, motivations, and life structures. See her "The Masculine Mindset of Economic Analysis," *The Chronicle of Higher Education,* June 28, 1996, B3, as well as her *Feminism, Objectivity and Economics* (1996).

31. See my "Retrieving the Human Place in Nature," *Environmental Ethics,* 17:1 (Winter 1995).

32. Marc L. Miringoff, Director of Fordham University's Institute for Innovation in Social Policy, annually publishes an alternative aggregate index of human welfare in America, "The Index of Social Health," that includes some of the elements of analysis I call for here.

Chapter 7

Deepening Democracy: Rebuilding the Public Square

The genuinely modern has still to be brought into existence. The work of actual production is not the task or responsibility of philosophy. That work can be done only by the resolute, patient, co-operative activities of men and women of good will, drawn from every useful calling, over an indefinitely long period. There is no absurd claim made that philosophers, scientists or any other one group form a sacred priesthood to whom the work is entrusted. But, as philosophers in the last few centuries have performed a useful and needed work in furtherance of physical inquiry, so their successors now have the opportunity and the challenge to do a similar work in forwarding moral inquiry. The conclusions of that inquiry by themselves would no more constitute a complete moral theory and a working science of distinctively human subject matter than the activities of their predecessors brought the [contemporary] physical and physiological conditions of human existence into direct and full-fledged existence. But it would have an active share in the work of construction of a moral human science which serves as a needful precursor of reconstruction of the actual state of human life toward order and toward other conditions of a fuller life than man has yet enjoyed.

> JOHN DEWEY, Introduction to
> *Reconstruction in Philosophy* (1948)

Introduction

Our focal challenge during these times of threefold global crisis in culture, ecology, and political economy must be deepening democracy by rebuilding the public square. "The public square" is Cornel West's gathering concept for "the common good that undergirds our national and global destinies."[1] West's use of this concept is more suggestive than specific, but the public square clearly must include a built infrastructure, a cooperative framework of social institutions, and a set of daily practices that structure interactions within our environment and that interconnect us through communication, transportation, and exchanges of goods, services, and information, thereby giving our individual efforts efficacy. Rebuilding the public square so understood is crucial for us now because its present democratically deficient state has helped to create and has blocked effective responses to our interlinked crises. Moreover, participating in such cooperative projects offers us the best opportunities to deepen the democratic character of our diverse hearts and minds.

The public square is no singular place. Rather, it is shaped by many social actors in many places, including government agencies at all levels, large-scale economic actors operating at a distance, and participants in the kinds of localized voluntary organizations Sara Evans and Harry Boyte call "free spaces," where people develop civic skills and virtues as well as a sense of "somebodiness" within cooperative, democratic, cross-difference efforts through which they aim to solve problems, to improve their lives, and to realize at least some of their hopes.[2] Government grows out of, depends upon, and influences the operation of many other aspects of community life that shape the life context of individuals, families, groups, and semi-autonomous cultures. When the public square functions well, it is the dimension of our lives in which we are most inclusively "we"—but when it fails, we feel threatened, vulnerable, and alone. Its real, historical failures lead West to remind us that, "If we go down, we go down together" (West 1994:8).

We must rebuild the public square for our global millennial era and the beckoning future in ways that create a context for each human person to experience "the good life" that satisfies our shared existential needs in individually specific, culturally connective ways within an institutional framework and a set of related cooperative practices that are socially and ecologically sustainable. Because of the very character of our shared existential needs, as well as the dispersed knowledge and coordinated action from which adequate transformative solutions must emerge, we all must participate in the problem-solving, future-shaping process. Fortunately, diverse philosopher–activists' recent experiences in transformative praxis, including my own, suggest how we can do this: through collaborative participation of local citizens and other stakeholders in planning for their community's future, with consulting assistance from "public philosophers" who have particular relevant skills and who draw upon a broader transformative framework in helping participants to tailor and to communicate their own locally appropriate transformative solutions to others.

In addition to effectively addressing local problems, creating locally desirable futures, and re-educating local participants' hearts and minds in the ways of deep democracy, such a collaborative approach allows citizens to contribute widely dispersed knowledge and differing embodiments of values to a fund of deeply democratic experience upon which others' transformative efforts can draw. Although cross-difference coalitions will be the initially best attainable character of such locally focused transformative collaborations, my experience suggests that, in order to be successful over time, and as they become progressively more successful, the developmental dynamic of cross-difference coalitions arcs toward *deeply democratic communities* within which participants can experience *cosmopolitan unity amidst valued diversity,* expressed in the mutual personal support and caring that allows the shared memories and hopes that make them *beloved communities* to emerge, to stabilize long-term commitments, and to give meaning to shared struggle.

Symptoms, Causes, and Solutions
of Our Problems in the Public Square

Our American middle-class lives preponderantly in *"suburbs"* now—placeless locations lacking both civic traditions and a distinctive "look" that are politically independent from the major cities that spawned them, as well as existentially distanced from both these cities' problems and their cultural resources. At the same time, our suburbs voraciously encroach upon rural lands without gaining the benefits of a life closer to the rhythms of nature. The individualistic American ideology that urges us to follow the flow of the labor market to our "optimal location" also suggests that the nuclear family is the largest circle of human relationships we should consider or count on in framing our lives—and even that only when children are small and their parents' cooperative relationship seems fully voluntary and still activated by romantic love. This worldview regards as immature, unseemly, or irrational the adult who fails to separate—to "individuate"—around the age of majority, who continues to seek the active presence of parents and other kinfolk in daily life. Equally unseemly is the parent who fails to "let the children go" so that they, too, can follow the flow of the labor market to their own "optimal location," where they, too, are expected to make the economistic best deal possible on real estate, appraised in its potential as shelter and investment while calculating in the quality of relevant social services like schools and various "lifestyle amenities" like views and nearby recreational facilities.

This widely shared worldview guides many people to the better housing "values" and better-funded schools of our various functionally interchangeable suburbs, building no particular relationship to a specific place on the planet other than a real estate title, typically accompanied by a too-heavy mortgage and a recurring demand for payment of local property taxes. Choosing such a placeless location for one's impermanent "home" often commits suburban Americans to a long commute to a workplace where the continuity of their employment is increasingly insecure and, thus, to which they now tend to make only a shallow and provisional commitment. For this reason, interpersonal relationships in the workplace increasingly tend to lack the depth of friendship or collegiality, in spite of a currently fashionable employer emphasis on "teamwork." The amount of time and energy suburbanites spend on work, commuting, and life's various necessary errands leaves little for their nuclear families, let alone for finding cultural and spiritual support, for earning a valued place within the local community, and for discovering deeper relationships with the land. Perhaps equally important is the sense or fear that it hurts more to relocate again if one puts down the kind of roots that create locational attachments that allow community life to offer "too much to lose."

Thus, it should not be surprising that *generalized insecurity* and *ontological rootlessness* are widespread in America's suburbs today, existentially blighting the lives of many dys-located and directionless suburban members of the so-called Generation X and the younger one that follows. These two dys-eases also affect their "Baby Boomer" parents, who are running out of socially prescribed "script" in midlife as their children leave the nest, and who are finding themselves frantically wondering what will connect them deeply to other people now, what will give their lives meaning in the future, and how they will cope with the needs of their own aging parents, who typically live at some distance. Family breakdowns are common in these placeless locations in which rootless adults whose vital needs are unmet try to be all to each other and enough to their children in the scraps and margins of their time—without the daily surrounding support of an extended family and intimate friends, without significant cultural and spiritual infusions of energy, guidance, and inspiration, and without the sense of personal identity, efficacy, and nonmarket value that comes from the experience of being a person to be counted in and relied upon in shaping and operating local institutions that serve present needs and create a legacy for the future. So go the lives of many "fortunate" middle-class Americans—rootless, lonely, starved for meaning and purpose, longing for support, and angry to have so little control over all the things that might let them feel that they "have a life."

These are but the *symptoms* of suburban existential distress. The *background causes* include not only existentially poor though socially "normal" personal choices that fail to factor in the human importance of location and relation, but also the lack of democratic depth in contextualizing institutions and in the dominant ideology that guides so many Americans to make such choices. *Adequate solutions* must remedy these institutional and ideological failures in ways that support people in making different choices—more locational and relational ones—by deepening our understanding and realization of democracy into a shared, mutually committed way of life.

Meanwhile, many of the losers within America's economic lottery, especially those who also are members of racial minorities, have been left behind in *our central cities*—locations that have become places where nobody wants to be. People who live in these history-burdened, economically and politically under-funded locations must cope on a daily basis with the racist cultural subscript within our official, shallowly democratic institutional and ideological "script" of equality of American opportunity, even as they cope with many of the same symptoms of existential dys-ease as their economically more fortunate suburban fellow citizens. Cornel West powerfully evokes how all these factors come together to weigh down the lives of many African Americans in some of our most hopeless urban locations. Poverty, lack of jobs, and racism combine with the collapse of resistance-sustaining cultural and civic institutions under the systematic assault of mass media that seductively teach individualist ideology and materialist values. These factors combine with poor schools, inadequate housing, environmental blight, and the alternative attractions of gangs, drugs, and violence to produce widespread *existential nihilism,* "a pervasive spiritual impoverishment" that creates "rootless, dangling people" trying to cope with "a life of horrifying meaningless, hopelessness, and (most important) lovelessness" that leads to "a numbing detachment from others and a self-destructive disposition toward the world."[3] West's deeply insightful transformative solution is *a "politics of conversion"* guided by *"a love ethic."* This means collective, democratic, grassroots struggle focusing a community's transformative energies "principally on the local level—in those institutions in civil society still vital enough to promote self-worth and self-affirmation," with accountable leadership that can "exemplify moral integrity, character, and democratic statesmanship," while drawing upon "a subversive memory—the best of one's past without romantic nostalgia" (pp. 29–30).

West's promising transformative prescription can be extended and further specified with the realization that *sustainable transformation requires the development of a deeper democracy.* America's race-specific, shockingly deep pockets of urban poverty and despair are caused by two kinds of democratic failures— racism and exclusion (both participatory and substantive)—that have damaged the cultural and civic institutions that play key roles in the shaping of individual self-image, aspiration, and agency. The transformation of such deeply damaged urban neighborhoods into locations that can increasingly support their residents' existential needs will require *situation-sensitive interventions with a local focus* guided by democratically inclusive local leadership that effectively invites participation of other stakeholders who are affected by the outcome and who are in a position to contribute various valuable resources. These other stakeholders will include people who originally came from that particular neighborhood or other neighborhoods like it who have "made it" economically and educationally, who may now live in more comfortable surroundings, and who are animated by the spirit of "Them that's got must give" to offer time, energy, and personal resources to the neighborhood's civic and cultural institutions. They can serve as role models to young people as well as consultants and fund raisers in support of local leadership. They also may be able to provide planning and investment support for the development of local "Good Faith Funds" modeled on Mohammed Yunus's Grameen Bank, which can provide capital, advice, and organizational structure for small business start-ups as well as cooperatives and collectives in the neighborhood that are collateralized on the basis of managerial capacity, character, and the cooperative support of a loan-sharing group that has been trained in successful small business techniques. They also may be able to assist the local leadership in attracting appropriate business investments from outside firms who are prepared to hire, train, and employ local residents for family-wage jobs with a future, the only kind of "public–private partnerships" that are actually likely to have transformative existential significance for the people who presently live in our desperately poor, "minority majority" urban locations.

Such a two-pronged, deeply democratic, locational–relational approach to economic and political transformation already begins to address and transform the root causes of the existential nihilism West describes, though more cooperative rebuilding of the public square will be needed to reach to a deep and intimate level within the lives of individuals. Given generations of disintegrative pressure on the family as well as on the cultural and civic institutions that support them, locally controlled, culturally specific training in effective parenting will be an essential intervention in helping children to grow roots in our central cities, as it is an increasingly needed intervention in our suburbs, as well.[4] Localized support for the arts also will be very important, both as a mode of personal therapeutic self-expression and life-mirroring, and as a mode of interactive visioning that can lead to the kind of cooperative reiteration of a semi-autonomous cultural trajectory Alain Locke theorized. Excellent, lifelong multicultural education with both broadly humane and specific career–skill aspects also will help to root individuals' memories, hopes, and personal visions in ways that defuse existential nihilism. Working through and thereby revitalizing existing civic and cultural institutions, neighborhood residents and other supportive stakeholders can create new green spaces, cafes, arts organizations, and athletic facilities in which people of all ages can gather to exchange ideas, to celebrate, to grow, and to cooperate in making all things new. Such life-saving transformations cannot be achieved through "Disneyfication" by outside forces that simply move current residents out, level the built environment, and replace it with something different. This only relocates human misery. Only a deeply democratic approach can transform people's lives in ways that are existentially satisfying and humanely problem solving while making our central cities existentially supportive, vital, good places to be.

In a complementary but differently situated analysis, Daniel Kemmis poignantly and powerfully describes the *existential inadequacies* of contemporary life in a third kind of American location: *rural lands with their small towns and cities* like his own Missoula, Montana, which structure economic, political, and cultural aspects of life for the people who live in the region.[5] Drawing on his experience as mayor of Missoula, Kemmis focuses on a sustained political impasse among rival groups who use "formally" democratic processes in attempts to coercively impose their preferred responses to various interactive problems of economic marginalization, environmental degradation, and cultural stagnation. These long-term adversarial struggles have come to the point where "anybody can stop anything," and typically does. This impasse leads to civic frustration and suboptimal outcomes for all, as compared to what might have been achieved through a cooperative approach. Meanwhile, global trends and forces exacerbate the rural situation in the American West, so that resolution of interlinked economic, environmental, and cultural problems becomes both more urgent and more difficult as time passes.

The *deeper problem* underlying this impasse, as Kemmis rightly points out, is the *inadequacy of the "formal" conception of democratic due process* that these rival actors share. This interpretation treats the Fifth and Fourteenth Amendments to the United States Constitution as requiring "notice" and "the opportunity to be heard" by the relevant government officials, but *does not require listening to each other.* Consequently, rivals talk past each other, expecting neutral third parties to make decisions about what is best, with the expectation that there can be no *common good,* but only *adversarial goods* that fall into certain patterns. However, ad-

versarial groups and individuals have learned to use lobbying, governmental procedures, and the law very effectively in "successive, mutual blocking of one another's initiatives which has . . . clouded the climate of enterprise, while at the same
time frustrating the public interest" (Kemmis 1990:53–57). In these cases, public
decision-making processes are characterized by "shrillness and indignation," "successive blocking of one another's initiatives," and "the ever more frequent with-
drawal of people from all public involvement—either because they are frustrated
with the pattern of blocked initiative or because they don't like shrillness and indignation, in themselves or in others" (p. 62). Thus, nothing is done, and hope is
lost. Less desirable outcomes are obtained than might have been achieved by a cooperative solution, and all parties are alienated from public processes. Sometimes
the obstacles to cooperative solution come from outside the particular community,
but sometimes they arise from failing to take *shared, face-to-face responsibility.*

The *root of the problem,* as Kemmis sees it, is "the total privatization of values" within our dominant American ideology. Therefore, "some conception of
shared or communal values" is necessary to its *solution* (p. 62). We tend to speak
individualistically, as if our lives and values were separate, failing to admit that
we have a "mutual stake in the shape of one another's lives" (p. 66). This *mutual
stake* cannot be adequately expressed simply by building coalitions with like-
minded others to enhance our individual political efficacy. Antagonistic coalition
building is ultimately self-defeating because, as Lester Thurow argues, a group
can never be strong enough to assure the success of their own initiatives, yet the
attempt to do so assures that their antagonists will attempt to build their own majority coalition, without the emergence of any higher common ground or public
good.[6] However, as Kemmis argues, the history and culture of the American West
contains the resources of *more deeply democratic values, practices, and virtues*
that can and must be emphasized in developing *alternative democratic processes*
that depend on *shared responsibility* for *mutually acceptable solutions that are
good for the land*—processes that can help to build "a society to match the
scenery."[7] Such a deeper conception of democratic processes implies what Kemmis calls *political re-inhabitation* of a shared place. Its ability to resolve interlinked economic, environmental, and cultural problems depends upon the success
of transformative efforts guided by his model of *economic re-location.*

By "political re-inhabitation," Kemmis means an active, behavior-guiding
recognition on the part of all the presently disputing parties that they *share a
place*—that no one is leaving, yet their actions affect each other, so they must
face the reality that their lives and futures have inevitably common aspects. They
also must recognize that they all *care about that "place,"* both the land itself and
the developed practices of a social life.

> The *polis* is, first of all, the place which a certain group of people recognize
> that they inhabit in common. Any individual or any group within that place
> may wish that others did not live there, but they recognize that removing
> them would, in one way or another, exact too high a price. Given that fact,
> politics emerges as the set of practices which enables these people to dwell

together in this place. Not the set of procedures, not the set of laws or rules or regulations, but the set of practices which enables a common inhabiting of a common place. (p. 122)

Disputing stakeholders in a shared place tend to behave differently, Kemmis argues, when they believe they are *mutually responsible for coming up with a solution to their problems,* instead of turning their unreconciled interests over to a third party for a decision.

> This kind of mediated, participatory approach to problems is happening more and more frequently in an ever wider array of situations. Wherever it does happen, people find themselves being responsible for the ultimate decision, for each other, and even for their own ideologies in ways that they may never have experienced before. *This taking responsibility is the precise opposite of the move toward the "unencumbered self." It is, quite simply, the development of citizenship.* As people learn to relate in this way to each other, they discover in their patterns of relationship a new competence, an unexpected capacity to get things done. It is not getting things done by using bureaucracies or other instrumentalities of "the government," but getting things done through the power of citizenship. (pp. 113–114, emphasis mine)

The *trust* and the *civic virtues* on which such practices of citizenship depend can only come into being through *cooperative experience over time,* and "what holds people together long enough to discover their power as citizens is their common inhabiting of a single place," especially a place that has "claimed" them (p. 117). Moreover, through shared cooperative practices that solve shared problems in a shared place, the *existential quality* of the social relationship is *transformatively deepened* over time, so that people who began to cooperate as *fellow citizens* become "*neighbors.*"

> The actual practice of finding solutions that people can live with usually reaches beyond compromise to something more like *neighborliness*—to finding within shared space the possibilities for a shared inhabitation. Such neighborliness is inconceivable without the building of trust, of some sense of justice, of reliability or honesty. This practice of being neighbors draws together, therefore, the concepts of place, of inhabitation, and of the kinds of practices from which civic virtues evolve. Most people, most of the time, do not think about these features of the art of being good neighbors. What they do know is that neighborliness is a highly prized quality of life. Where it is present, it is always near the top of people's lists of why they like a place, and where it is absent, it is deeply lamented. . . . It is in being good neighbors that people very often engage in those simple homely practices which are the last, best hope for a revival of genuine public life. (p. 118, emphasis mine)

Their *shared attachment to the place* is the critical mediating factor in motivating and sustaining the cooperative activities that allow this *relational transformation* from fellow citizens to neighbors to occur.

Extrapolating from Jane Jacobs, Kemmis argues that *regional places,* including "cities, the almost entirely fabricated element, and their largely natural hinterlands," are *our natural political entities,* whose organic character should be respected.[8]

> It may be that the boundaries which humans draw across landscapes create artificial and inefficient units both in economic and in political terms. If cities, in relation to their hinterlands, have the capacity to define working economies, then it makes sense that the same city regions which constitute economies should also be "city-states"—the manageable households within which the task of willing a common world takes place. (pp. 120–121)

If Kemmis is right, *the artificial separation* of larger natural places into *cities, suburbs,* and *rural areas,* like their practical disempowerment within modern nation–states, has been *a profound mistake* caused by an abstract, shallow conception of democracy that is dangerously unrealistic in ignoring not only our human existential needs but also the practical location–based relationships that must be taken into account if those existential needs are to be adequately and sustainably fulfilled. Kemmis offers a functional–organic argument for *recognizing regional places as integrated political units* whose operability may require fuller legal support and protection from invasive activities of other levels of government. Kemmis insightfully argues that it is important to re-empower regional governance on a cooperative, democratic participatory model because this is the level at which relational transformations can occur that both address interlinked crises and satisfy some of our basic existential needs: "Any kind of active citizenship, where different interests are directly engaged in working out their problems and possibilities among themselves, is going to work better in small than in large political entities" (p. 125).

Cooperation with multinational corporations needs to be part of revitalizing public life, Kemmis argues, because the alternative is a politics of "anybody wrecking anything." This is bad for business as well as for the public life of the community. Corporations are learning this lesson, Kemmis suggests, and also recognizing their interest in working together, guided by the civic virtues. However, because corporations' stake in a region need not be permanent, their politics will tend to become only "semi-inhabitory" at best, and thus, *the terms of corporate citizenship must be "not wholly voluntary"* within consistently applied constraints.

> Like most relationship problems, this one can probably only be solved by a mutual pattern of change and development affecting both parties. For example, a corporation which learns to practice genuine citizenship creates, by that very development, a marginally more effective body politic. (p. 135)

When citizens and corporations share responsibility for resolving problems within a shared place, all have a stake in the success of the negotiated solution, thereby giving added legitimacy to the government that allows and supports such solutions. If such collaboration is successful, Kemmis argues, corporations will tend to become advocates for this approach, partly because it is a good idea, and partly because it leads to stable business conditions while blocking "free rider" competitors from gaining the advantages of others' efforts without paying their fair share of the costs in time and in other resources (p. 136).

Kemmis focuses on the half-full rather than the half-empty glass here. In part he is right to do so, because large and multinational corporations are clearly powerful players in current struggles for the future of the American West who may be moved toward cooperative relationships by the self-interested considerations he sketches. However, given the significance of *corporations' historical and legal dependence* on *individualistic conceptions of democracy, property, land, and rational decision making,* reasonable human citizens will take a somewhat more skeptical and particularistic view of the extent and limits of the "citizen capacity" of these "nonhuman persons." This means that *greater evidence of trustworthiness* must be demonstrated on the "corporate citizen" side than on the "human citizen" side, including evidence of long-term commitment to the place and to cooperative processes. It also means that *"not all corporations are equal"* in their desirability and trustworthiness as democratic collaborative partners, and that human citizens must consider their ownership structures as well as their past patterns of behavior in deciding whether to place greater emphasis on *cooperating* with them or on *controlling* their local impacts. As democracy deepens nationally and globally through interlinked struggles that gradually transform our economic and political institutions as well as the powers, forces, and motivations to which they give rise, there will come a time when it is possible to treat economic stakeholders acting at a distance with less wariness. During our present global millennial era, to do so would be naive and foolhardy.

Nonetheless, as Kemmis rightly argues, we cannot wish ideal conditions of trustworthy neighborliness into being—*we must discover and employ our real alternatives* in transforming the real problem situation we face now. Our only real political alternative that will allow us to resolve the kind of contemporary impasse he describes is adopting *regional strategies of "political re-inhabitation"* as part of our process of deepening democracy. Such regional, collaborative decision-making strategies will allow us to find solutions to interlinked and localized economic, environmental, and cultural problems, meeting our existential needs for effective participation in shaping the public square while deepening our social relationships as neighbors. Kemmis analyzes the processes that shape regional economic futures as involving an inescapably political dimension, and rightly so. In the real world of our era, the operations of the World Bank, the International Monetary Fund (IMF), the American Federal Reserve Board, and various international trade agreements and coordinating bodies like the General Agreement on Tariffs and Trade (GATT), the North American Free Trade Agreement (NAFTA), and the European Union reveal *the political dimension* of shaping economic futures so obviously as to make this dimension of normal economic life undeniable except by the most willfully unrealistic "free-market" ideologues.

What Kemmis proposes to do differently in order to deepen democracy in ways that solve real problems is *to increase political efficacy at a regional level in shaping regional economic futures,* instead of leaving them to the vagaries of national and global forces and actors. Through *"economic re-location,"* Kemmis argues, we can *better meet the existential needs* of a region's citizen participants in cooperative political processes while *better protecting the land* and *revitalizing regional culture* at the same time. In explaining his transformative concept of "economic re-location," Kemmis once again draws upon Jane Jacobs's claim that urban–rural regions, rather than nations, are humanity's natural organic relational–locational units: "what actually makes economies grow is *import substitution*—replacing goods that were once imported with goods that are produced by the economy in question," which is done by cities and their regions (pp. 86–87, emphasis mine). Understanding this leads one to "re-place the market within a specific location," so that Adam Smith's "invisible hand" begins to become visible. This subtle theoretical shift has potentially great practical implications if it is connected to regional collaborative efforts to will into being a certain quality of shared future through political re-inhabitation.

> The partial embrace by a large number of localities of the concept of import substitution has the potential to transform very substantially the economic life of this country. . . . Almost without exception, any serious move toward import substitution by a local economic development organization goes hand in hand with an effort to identify and describe the characteristics of that locality which set it apart and give it a distinct identity. This exercise in community self-awareness is crucial to any concerned effort at import substitution. (p. 88)

In a related vein, Kemmis argues that *localized capital formation* is another key element in building a regional economy within which cooperative exercise of political power helps to assure that the land is cared for as the existential needs of the region's citizens are met (p. 96). Building *"an economy matched to its place"* would "keep locally or regionally generated capital at home, investing it in indigenous businesses, encouraging both import substitution and economic activity which respects the integrity of the local environment" (pp. 97–98, emphasis mine).

Such an increase in regional democratic economic control is both desirable and possible, but it requires progressively and pragmatically employing existing, "formally" democratic institutions in ways that *deepen democracy relationally, locationally, and transformatively* against the current of *international economic anti-trends* that are supported by the considerable influence of neocapitalist economic theorists. Operating against the ideological background of the presumptive success of American formally democratic, capitalist institutions of political economy as a world model, in combination with the international economic treaties mentioned above, and in the context of the instantaneous international movement of "virtual capital" made possible by use of the worldwide web in banking and stock transactions, the World Bank and the IMF have been playing increasingly powerful interventionary global roles in recent years. *The "invisible hand" has been unmasked,* so that the activities of particular national and corporate actors can be traced, and their operative theoretical visions can be discerned.

To play their own hand effectively in this global climate, regional cooperative citizen groups who are intent on "re-inhabiting" their political location and "re-locating" their economy must *creatively, cooperatively, and transformatively re-use* the full range of "formally" democratic institutions available to them to pressure national and international political leaders to end anti-democratic interventions like those currently practiced by the IMF, to develop more locally nuanced, collaborative alternatives like those now employed by the World Bank, and to learn some lessons about the deeper meanings of democracy in the process. When one region loses democratic economic and political semi-autonomy due to the "now-visible hands" of economistic international economic actors, all regions lose both practical control and sustainable hope in their own economic re-localization processes. Thus, though Jacobs and Kemmis are insightful as well as original in asserting the natural, organic significance of metro–regional political economies, and in calling people to meet their existential needs and to care for the land more effectively by claiming and using their potential power more effectively within metro–regional transformative coalitions, *such collaborative efforts must look beyond and link beyond their local concerns if they are to achieve their goals in real world conditions.*

The Transformative Arc: From Cross-Difference Coalition to Beloved Community

The transformative framework for rebuilding the public square that emerges from bringing together my reflections about the multifaceted unsustainability of American suburban life with West's praxis-based insights about the need for an urban-focused politics of conversion guided by a love ethic and Kemmis's insights about metro–regional "political re-inhabitation" and "economic re-location" can be given further detail by considering the lessons of three recent experiences in transformative praxis to rebuild the public square. These experiences show the overarching importance of John Dewey's deeply democratic ideal, pluralistically interpreted as Alain Locke's cosmopolitan unity amidst valued diversity, and energized as Josiah Royce's and Martin Luther King, Jr.'s vision of the Beloved Community. Taken together, these experiences sketch *a developmental trajectory* within cooperative, problem-focused processes of democratic transformation that arcs from *cross-difference coalitions* toward *beloved communities of memory and hope.*

My spouse, David Woods, and I moved to the Seattle region during the summer of 1991, when I was on sabbatical leave from my teaching position at Eckerd College, a small liberal arts college in Florida, and David, a certified urban and regional planner, was offered the opportunity to direct an experimental project in democratic citizen participation in the urban and regional planning process that would focus on planning a "city center" for suburban Lynnwood, Washington, around stations on a proposed light rail transit system for Seattle's larger metropolitan region. We fell in love with the Pacific Northwest as soon as we drove over Snoqualmie Pass and began our winding descent through mists and lush evergreen trees into the unique natural and social climate that would become our home. Perhaps it is the surrounding snow-capped mountains or the view of Puget Sound from the hills that reminds one constantly that we humans are part of a larger natural whole that should be a focus of responsibility as well as a source of healing and broader life vistas. Over the next few years, we deepened our allegiance to this place through our work, our participation in community organizations, and our rambles through the woods, developing a sustaining social network and habits of living that worked well for us. I gave up tenure at Eckerd College and began to teach at Seattle University. By the winter of 1996, we had become participants in three different kinds of local initiatives to rebuild the public square.

In the most formal, government-sponsored of these initiatives, David and I, as GreenWoods Associates, acted as professional planning consultants to Seattle's traditionally Scandinavian, Puget Sound–focused *Crown Hill/Ballard Neighborhood,* working with citizens to develop and to democratically adopt *a community vision* concerning a number of mandated elements of the city's long-range planning process. These elements included *open space, housing, transportation, economic development, human services,* and *the arts.* That citizens would participate in the urban planning process had become *a shared expectation* in this particular community over many years. This expectation was supported by shared democratic cultural tendencies, by a broadly shared working class to middle-class economic situation without distorting extremes, by shared anxieties about external economic and social forces that might undermine the quality of neighborhood life, by still-functioning civic institutions, and by experienced neighborhood leadership skills that had been developed and transmitted through involvement over the previous twenty years in a series of cooperative projects to rebuild the public square.

Recent growth management legislation at federal, state, and local levels had mandated such citizen participation in long-range urban planning, but other Seattle neighborhoods that lacked this *cultural tradition,* these *lived commonalities,* these *supporting civic institutions,* and this *grassroots leadership* had found the process of developing a shared vision very difficult, especially within the pressured time frame of the few months that the city's larger planning process allowed for this phase of neighborhood participation. However, because of the human and cultural capital Crown Hill/Ballard brought to the process, they were already well underway by the time a competitive bidding and interview process led them to choose GreenWoods Associates as their collaborative planning consultants. They chose us partly because they valued the skills and experience we could offer them, but equally importantly because they sensed our respect for their cooperative process and for the insightfulness of the transformative approach they had developed without our assistance.

This approach emphasized Saturday morning "Topical Seminars," which began with *mutual education* among diverse stakeholders to establish common ground about the history of their shared place as well as the facts about their current situation as these pertained to one of the specific topics to be covered in their

Neighborhood Vision Statement. Many of the initial speakers at these Topical Seminars were Crown Hill/Ballard residents who were professionals or long-term volunteers in the fields in question, who prepared their well-researched presentations with the aim of informing above all, though they were frank about expressing their stakes in the neighborhood's future and would not have been regarded as credible had they not done so. The *respect* with which these speakers treated all of their neighbors as well as the controversial topics under discussion was an important key to the remarkably calm energy with which participants approached the active discussion of their goals that followed. Another key was the challenge of articulating and agreeing on several tangible goals in brief small-group discussions that kept participants focused on concrete achievable particulars instead of wandering off into more vague and general discussions of abstract values, about which even those whose specific goals converged might disagree. Small group participants expressed these tangible goals in a few words on colorful sheets of construction paper. We organized these thematically on a "graffiti wall" as part of the large group summation, which also allowed for comments from participants about the emergent pattern of ideas.

A *high degree of unity* in support for these tangible collaborative goals was a characteristic outcome of these sessions. Many of the participants expressed surprise about how much agreement they found among themselves once they had *listened* to the speakers and to each other. In a Neighborhood Planning booth at Crown Hill/Ballard's traditional Norwegian Independence Day festival, we displayed summaries of the goal statements that were affirmed at these Topical Seminars and in surveys distributed at various other meetings, inviting festival participants to put colorful stickers by the goal statements they believed to be most important, and to endorse or to reject a brief overall "Vision Statement" that broadly characterized these goals. Because the level of validation expressed for these statements at the festival and through a neighborhood poll was very high, the Crown Hill/Ballard Planning Association officially adopted the Vision Statement and the topic-focused goals, reporting them to the City of Seattle as their neighborhood's conclusions from this first phase of the long-range planning process.

Predictable tensions, struggles for dominance, rival priorities, and efforts to meet various other social needs for attention and appreciation surfaced among members of the core leadership over the intense five-month period during which we worked together. However, the continuing level of commitment to the collaborative process was remarkable in involving diverse stakeholders and focusing their energies constructively in planning for their shared community's future. In addition to the steering committee's official monthly meetings, weekly one-hour breakfast meetings at a neighborhood restaurant allowed us to communicate efficiently with one another, to learn about the results of our most recent efforts, to decide on new strategies, and to divide up responsibilities. No one had time and energy to participate in everything, so it was crucial to maintain *a high level of trust* in the quality of the information, in each other's efforts, and in their mutual commitment of attention to each other's priorities. For example, those who were most interested in open space could not simply discount others' concern for housing or economic development because they would see them every week, and they knew that the possibility of achieving their own goals depended upon *cooperative support* for others' differing concerns, realizing that conflicts would eventually have to be reconciled within *mutually acceptable solutions.* Thus, although the Topical Seminars helped to bring together diverse coalitions of neighbors who shared an interest and a set of goals for one specific topical element of a comprehensive long-range plan, the leadership group became *a coalition of representatives of diverse topical coalitions* who shared *a unifying interest* in actively working out a *good common future* for the community by *reconciling their differing priorities* within an achievable overall plan for rebuilding the public square.

A crucially important part of that rebuilding process was achieved by *deepening the education, communication, trust-based collaboration, and shared vision* of citizens of the Crown Hill/Ballard neighborhood. Important as this achievement was, however, it represents only *a fragile beginning* of the larger transformation process, because it lacks adequate institutionalization and depends on the continuing active commitment and presence in the neighborhood of particular people. Thus, the Crown Hill/Ballard Planning Association is still *a cross-difference coalition* striving to persuade *residents and other stakeholders* to become *neighbors,* sharing place-related memories and committing themselves to place-related hopes within a larger urban social context in which many forces—economic, political, occupational, and cultural—make it difficult to sustain and to act upon those commitments.

A second initiative to rebuild the public square in which we were actively involved during this same period had less governmental authorization but a more stable institutional basis for the commitments of its individual members and, thus, represented *a further stage on the developmental trajectory* from cross-difference coalition to deeply democratic community of memory and hope. This was the *King County Organizing Project* (*KCOP*), a coalition of justice-focused churches, labor unions, and other "community sustaining" groups, with professional organizers to assist the volunteer core leadership group, and financial support as well as active participation as needed from member organizations. KCOP itself is a member organization of the Industrial Areas Foundation (IAF), a network of democratic change organizations that originally grew out of the efforts of Saul Alinsky and fellow community activists.[9] IAF has grown since the mid-1960s to its present national scope and deeper level of effectiveness by de-emphasizing strategies of division and alternatively emphasizing *relationship-building and cooperative pursuit of mutual interests.*[10] During our period of volunteer participation in the core leadership group, KCOP held a media-focused mass rally, at which member organizations endorsed *shared goals* focusing on job creation for poor and underemployed residents of Seattle and its larger King County as well as improved education and enhanced citizen participation in public decision making, to be pursued under the overall campaign theme of *CHANGE* (*Communities Helping to Achieve a New Generation of Equity*). The KCOP core leadership then formed committees to research various aspects of each goal and to propose specific strategies, drawing on the models of successful campaigns by other IAF organizations, such as San Antonio's "Communities Organized for Public Services" (COPS) and Baltimore's "Baltimoreans United in Leadership Development" (BUILD).[11] The goal of job creation was further divided into applicant identification and preparation, training, and placement, with research and relationship-building being conducted simultaneously by the various committees in concert with the professional organizers. As core leaders and subcommittee co-chairs, David and I participated in meetings with state and city officials as well as various agency heads who might be able to contribute information, funding, and policy support. We also met with directors of other community organizations whose past efforts had focused on providing parallel services for members of particular ethnic groups; with admissions officers of area community colleges, of vocational–technical schools, and of other educational institutions; and with human resources officers of major area employers who might be willing and able to hire appropriately trained job seekers from our member organizations. In preparation for these meetings, we read studies projecting economic development and employment prospects for the region, as well as case studies of IAF strategies employed in other regions.

An *apparent strength* of this approach was actually its *greatest weakness*: the emphasis on a relatively small, though diverse, core volunteer leadership doing all of the research and relationship-building allowed this to be done *quickly,* but *not sustainably,* because most of the core leaders had demanding jobs, families, and additional leadership responsibilities of various kinds within member organizations of the KCOP coalition. Also, this approach *failed to draw effectively upon more widely dispersed insights* and *to build deeper commitment* among other members of the KCOP member organizations. Instead, decisions would be made by the core leadership and then *"sold"* to the member organizations, who would then be asked to endorse them formally, to undertake whatever responsibilities the adopted strategy assigned to them, and to provide the quota of activists needed for a rally or other public show of strength.

The weaknesses of this less-than-deeply democratic approach became highly visible to us on one occasion when two IAF national coordinators participated in a work session during the second month of the intensely busy research and relationship-building phase of KCOP's CHANGE campaign. At that meeting, one of KCOP's professional organizers worked to "sell" us KCOP core volunteer leaders on the feasibility and desirability of joining forces with other West Coast IAF organizations for a show of strength aimed at wringing legally required public service concessions out of a major California-based bank that was seeking approval to acquire a major Seattle-based bank. The impossibility of proceeding on both the CHANGE campaign and this new interregional effort simultaneously was obvious to many of us who were already committing more time and energy to KCOP than we could sustain. Yet the intensity of effort focused on the CHANGE campaign had been achieved by evoking *a shared, contextual sense of time-related urgency* among us about its various practical facets through drawing upon *our shared, deeply motivating imperative toward substantive justice.* Thus, our energy-demanding commitment to the CHANGE campaign was undermined by the confusing and practically contradictory call to a different effort that day. A certain quality of trust between at least some of the core leaders and our highly regarded professional organizer was damaged, due to the sense that what had appeared to be shared grassroots democratic leadership had become a way to manipulate us, and that decisions were really being made by a core within or beyond "our core."

Related experiences in other contexts have convinced us of the importance of *consistently "walking the talk" of deep democracy.* Because people's existential needs are so deep and their ideal longings are so powerful, if they have managed to overcome widely shared apathy and historically well-founded suspicions in order to participate in more deeply democratic collaborative change efforts than our society usually affords them, they do not respond well to reversions to more shallowly democratic or even less-defensible operative procedures. Thus, though the KCOP and IAF organizational concept of *a coalition of communities who share certain memories and hopes* is a good one, it was flawed in its processes and in its leadership structure by failures to achieve the kind of deep democracy that would give it *stability, realism, and collective efficacy* over the long time it will take to achieve its transformative goals.

The third Seattle initiative to rebuild the public square in which we participated during this same period was the peacemaking, love-sharing, life-affirming, spirit-lifting efforts of the *Shades of Praise Gospel Choir* at St. Therese Catholic Church. A multicultural, diversity inclusive, activist faith community located in aging facilities near Seattle's poor urban core whose members' mailing addresses encompassed fifty-seven different zip codes, St. Therese Church was regarded as a "mission church" in the Roman Catholic Church's present era of declining numbers of priests and increasing needs in America's central cities. This meant that the leadership model differed from the Roman Catholic norm, because no priest was assigned as pastor. Instead, Patricia Repikoff, a brilliant woman with a Master of Divinity degree, a deep faith, a fertile imagination, a calm presence, and a charismatic preaching style served as "parochial minister," with voluntary assistance in the role of "sacramental minister" from two gifted Jesuit priests based at nearby Seattle University: Joseph McGowan, S.J., one of the handful of African American Jesuits and the friend who first invited us to "St. T's," and Philip Burroughs, S.J., a soft-spoken, California-born theologian who has since become Rector of Seattle University's Jesuit Community. This diverse trinity collaborated in spiritual leadership and rotated turns in delivering the Sunday homilies. St. Therese's practical leadership also included a diverse, outspoken Parish Council who provided organizational structure for activist undertakings focused on justice, caring, and inclusion of social outcasts.

The third element in both spiritual and practical leadership was the Shades of Praise Gospel Choir under the professional direction of Cora Jackson, a gifted African American Baptist composer, director, and performer of Gospel music, whose cultural–spiritual influence gave worship at St. T's an ecumenical nuance some members jokingly described as "Batholic." Shades of Praise was a powerful sixty-voice choir singing a four-part, Jackson–composed Catholic liturgy as well as original and traditional hymns in the call-and-response Gospel music style. The choir's membership, like St. Therese Church's, was as diverse as King's vision of the Beloved Community: black, white, Asian, Native American, and Hispanic, young and old, wealthy and poor, gay and straight, healthy and life-threateningly ill, highly educated and "still working on it," all deeply committed to each other and to the internal and external aspects of our shared transformative mission. In its *internal aspect,* within the St. Therese community and its liturgical celebrations, the mission of Shades of Praise was to "shout joyfully to the Lord a new song," singing praise to the divine Source, Sustainer, and Spirit within life on behalf of those assembled, and raising everyone's spirits in the process. In its *external aspect,* the mission of Shades of Praise was to directly express love, hope, and personal support to neighbors in the surrounding region who were going through some of life's hardest times: incarcerated juveniles at state and county lock-ups, homeless people dropping into day shelters in downtown Seattle, poor and underemployed members of church communities of different faiths, struggling organizers and heavily burdened activist participants at justice-focused KCOP rallies.

The *high level of energy and effectiveness* Shades of Praise displayed in both internal and external aspects of its ministry—its collective capacity to infuse spirit-lifting, person-transforming confidence and love into the lives of real people, binding many of them closer together into a beloved community of memory and hope—flowed forth in part from its efficacy in simultaneously meeting many of the *deep existential needs* of the choir's members. Shades of Praise provides *a multiculturally rich interpretive framework* for their life narratives, *a caring community of support* during times of poverty, illness, death, unemployment, loss of intimate partners, hard choices, and big changes, as well as *an active participatory structure for rebuilding the public square,* thereby giving substance and reality to their shared memories and hopes. Many long-term Shades of Praise members have been rehearsing and singing nearly every mass, concert, and love fest for the past twenty years. New members now join a waiting list and long to be activated, and current members almost never leave. For me, it was one of the hardest partings in my life to date to leave St. T's, Shades of Praise, Seattle University, the Crown Hill/Ballard Neighborhood, and the Pacific Northwest in order to take up my present position at Fordham University and to finish this book. Perhaps I could not have done so had not my trusted friend, Fr. Joseph McGowan, declared that "it seems like the hoof prints of an old-fashioned God are all over this thing."

This kind of *organizational stability, personal commitment, existential depth,* and *practical efficacy* in transforming the public square through a politics of conversion guided by a love ethic, working within politically re-inhabitory and economically re-locative projects, prophetically modeling the ideal that a group's members seek to achieve as they work to extend the scope of its realization, is possible only within such a *deeply democratic, diversity embracing instantiation of the Beloved Community.* To the extent that *diverse democratic coalitions* like the Crown Hill/Ballard Neighborhood Planning Association and *coalitions of justice-focused communities* individually bound together by shared memories and hopes like KCOP seek to become *more effective* in their efforts to rebuild a democratically deeper public square, they need to draw on the example of the Shades of Praise Gospel Choir within its larger prophetic context in order to discover *an ideal direction for their own developmental trajectories.*

Deepening Democracy by Rebuilding the Public Square: Toward a General Model

One question that has been implicitly addressed throughout this discussion needs a direct answer here: *Why do we need a general model of deeply democratic approaches to rebuilding the public square?* At least three praxis-based answers can be given. As to its *general* aspect, similar historical moments in humanity's ongoing struggle happen at different times in different places. Each of these similar moments gives us particular kinds of opportunity to advance to a new stage in our ongoing struggle to evolve the kinds of understandings, daily practices, and stable institutions that will meet cross-culturally shared human existential needs and promote pluralistic models of human flourishing while caring for the Earth. Therefore, we need to develop *a transformative framework and a set of transformative strategies* that are broadly insightful and useful relative to these recurring developmental moments. Of course, as Dewey pointed out, general transformative strategies are not like cookbook recipes that can simply be applied universally without attention to the particular situation. Rather, their contextualized function is to suggest how to look at a particular situation, focusing on the relevant characteristics that must be taken into account while drawing upon information and experience-based insights about other communities' struggles that may suggest some of the elements of *a specific, situationally adequate transformative solution.*

As to why such a general model must be *deeply democratic,* including all stakeholders in devising mutually satisfactory solutions to shared problems, *only shared hopes are stable.* Praxis-based experience shows that losers within adversarial struggles move or mutate, but they do not change their minds just because they are outvoted. They must be dealt with again and again, in the same location or another location, until they are at least minimally satisfied with the decision. Otherwise, as Kemmis (1990) reminds us, blocking others' actions, or some even more destructive social intervention, may be what negotiation theorists call the losers' BATNA ("best alternative to a negotiated agreement").[12]

Given the great obstacles to deeply democratic transformations—and the long period of time they take—only a transformative approach that can *sustain deeply committed, intelligently directed, situationally responsive, trust-based cooperative struggle beyond the horizon of immediate and foreseeable events* can achieve this goal. This is why the *human existential needs* and the *democratic impulse* that motivate people's initial involvement in democratic transformative struggle carry within them *an ideal directionality toward the deeply democratic community.* Our experience suggests that this developmental process must be understood as progressively embracing *cosmopolitan unity amidst valued diversity,* increasingly energized as *the Beloved Community.*

In this book, I have attempted to outline some of the main aspects of deep democracy within prophetically realized beloved communities, as well as those that are in-the-becoming. Our human existential needs and our democratic aspirations direct our yearnings toward such communities—and when we are brave enough and hopeful enough, our transformative efforts as well. I have argued that *deep democracy within beloved communities must include at least these main aspects:*

- Respect for human rights understood as common humane values
- Democratic cultural revitalization
- Lifelong education within collaborative processes of rebuilding the public square
- Political re-inhabitation
- Shared community efficacy and commitment to mutual flourishing
- Economic re-location
- A shared commitment to ecosystemic health
- Shared memories and hopes
- A web of caring within a consciously shared community life

Although it is beyond the compass of this book to fully detail a general model for rebuilding the public square in deeply democratic ways, *predictably recurring stages within collaborative democratic transformation projects include:*

- Reenergizing of semi-autonomous democratic cultural trajectories
- Critical multicultural education toward cosmopolitan unity amidst valued diversity
- Cross-difference conversations to build shared understanding
- Trust- and hope-building, coalition-based transformative cooperation
- Gradual evolution of coalitions into diverse democratic communities
- Gradual deepening of diverse democratic communities into beloved communities

The fuller development and correction of this general model is and must remain a collaborative project embracing differing times and locations, involving citizen activists, various researchers in the social and natural sciences, students, teachers, preachers, business leaders, urban and regional planners, economists, artists, and realistic, hopeful democratic visionaries of all kinds—including philosophers, whose contributions in at least four aspects of the project of rebuilding the public square are imperatively needed now.

The Role of Philosophers in Deepening Democracy: A Call to Active Engagement

Who are "the philosophers" who are hereby called to action? Some but not all of them hold Ph.D.s in philosophy and are professionally employed to teach, research, and write philosophical texts. Others hold similar credentials and positions in related fields, within which they wrestle with philosophical issues of method, social knowledge, democratic theory and practice, human welfare, environmental sustainability, education, institutional reconstruction, and cultural criticism. Still others engage these issues in theory and practice outside the academy, developing aspects of a general model and transformative strategies for rebuilding the public square, deepening democracy toward diverse and inclusive beloved communities. "Philosophy" as understood here is not a narrowly specialized academic discipline, but rather *a set of public tasks* undertaken for the transformative purpose of *human liberation and well-being* by those who share *an overlapping set of skills and techniques.* The idea that philosophy involves and must be informed by such practical consultative and transformative work is as old as Socrates, Plato, and Aristotle in the Western intellectual tradition. Many non-Western traditions also acknowledge such roles for scholars, thinkers, and wise people. What is it that these philosophers are called to do? Their contribution is needed within *a rolling cycle of elements and phases* of transformative struggle to deepen democracy. This must be a *collaborative undertaking* of many people in diverse locations and across generations, within which no one has enough time, energy, and gifts to contribute focally to all parts at once, although the best work in each area is done with an awareness of ongoing work in the other areas.

When *philosophy's ideal goal*—helping to liberate human persons and to create conditions for their mutual flourishing—is understood to require deepening democracy by rebuilding the public square, *four contributing roles for philosophers* within this ongoing collaborative transformative project become possible and even imperative. In the first of these roles, *cultural critique and intellectual reconstruction,* philosophers can bring to broader attention various symptoms of our interlinked global crises, their deeper causes, and specific areas of social life with democratic transformative potential, as John Dewey, Jürgen Habermas, and other pragmatists and critical theorists have argued they should. They can illuminate the historically unfolding implications of the democratic ideal; they can challenge intellectual obstacles to that unfolding process; and they can reconstruct various aspects of their culture's philosophical vision, interpreting experience as a source of meaning and as a guide to feeling, reflection, choice, and action.

Philosophers' contributions also are needed in *cross-disciplinary, cross-difference values research* within and between cultures, as Jane Addams, Alain Locke, and many contemporary feminists and cultural pluralists have argued. Knowledgeable philosophers are needed to collaborate in the project of identifying common humane values, valuable cultural differences to be treasured, and democratically intolerable aspects of various worldviews to be transformed. They can contribute analytical tools and synthetic insights in identifying historically power-structured tensions that must be factored into transformative strategies. They can suggest potential areas of collaboration on ends-in-view toward converging goals. They can retrieve and share accounts of how differing communities have structured their memories and hopes, and they can suggest ways to respectfully restructure these memories and hopes relative to converging cross-difference ideals and common humane values. They can participate in developing case studies of the relative efficacy of alternative democratic change strategies in culturally differing contexts.

A third area of much-needed philosophical contribution that bridges theory and practice is *construction of a general framework* for deeply democratic cross-difference transformative collaboration, including general strategies, intellectual tools, and communicative techniques. This means developing *a framework of guiding concepts* for *sustainable community planning* toward *deeply democratic goals* within *ethical side constraints* and *realistic contextual parameters,* progressively specified as *achievable ends-in-view* with *tangible benchmarks and feedback mechanisms* that can be used in assessing outcomes to confirm or show the need to change direction and strategies. It includes developing *intellectual tools* within particular, unique situations. It also includes helping to develop *an experience-based fund of effective transformative strategies* that emphasize flexibility, inclusiveness of differing epistemic locations, and progressively building shared understandings and hopes.

A fourth, much-needed philosophical role is *active consulting within deeply democratic transformative praxis.* Some philosophers have gifts and interests that will allow them to serve as resources for supporting localized collaborative stakeholder groups who are working to rebuild the public square. Acting as consultants, philosophers can contribute *situation-specific cultural critiques and intellectual reconstructions,* as well as *knowledge* gained in cross-difference research, *flexible skills* in employing a deeply democratic conceptual framework, and *fund-based information* about related efforts in other locations. Many local collaborative transformation efforts may benefit from philosophers' assistance in identifying diverse stakeholders and in finding effective ways to invite them into the collaborative process, as well as their assistance in designing a collaborative approach and in tailoring general strategies for the unique situation. Philosophical skills in *facilitation, interpretation,* and *mediation* that can bring out dispersed knowledge, new insights, and creative, mutually acceptable solutions are invaluable within cross-difference communication. Likewise, transformative coalitions may appreciate consulting support in *analyzing and synthesizing information* about realistic contextual parameters, *identifying converging and diverging goals* for transformative action, *choosing achievable ends-in-view,* and *assessing achieved outcomes* relative to agreed-upon benchmarks based on information from situation-specific feedback mechanisms. Finally, a local transformative coalition may value a philosopher's skills in the role of *"organic public intellectual"* to assist their efforts to communicate with a broader public about their findings, goals, and achievements.

As I have argued throughout this chapter, various philosopher–activists' experiences within transformative praxis have shown that it is both *possible* and *necessary* for diverse local communities to participate in rebuilding the public square in ways that deepen democracy, and that "public philosophers" can contribute in various ways to this important work. In turn, experiences in democratic praxis will help philosophers to gain *a vital new perspective* on the intellectual traditions and practices we are charged both to conserve and to transform. This is difficult work. The obstacles to doing it well are enormous. Only those who care passionately about the real and evident failures of our present institutions to meet most people's human existential needs while caring for the Earth—and who dare to hope to be part of building something better—need apply. For them, the return of such meaningful and satisfying labor will be *life-transforming.*

Notes

1. See West's *Race Matters* (1994).
2. See Sara M. Evans and Harry C. Boyte. *Free Spaces: The Sources of Democratic Change in America* (1986).
3. See West 1994:9-10 and 22-23. See also Jonathan Kozol's *Savage Inequalities: Children in America's Schools* (1991) and his *Amazing Grace: The Lives of Children and the Conscience of a Nation* (1995).
4. For one thoughtful approach to this challenge, see Sylvia Ann Hewlett and Cornel West, *The War Against Parents: What We Can Do for America's Beleaguered Moms and Dads* (1998).
5. See Daniel Kemmis, *Community and the Politics of Place* (1990).
6. See Lester Thurow, *The Zero Sum Society* (1980).
7. Kemmis 1990:69, quoting Wallace Stegner's *The Sound of Mountain Water* (1969).
8. See Jane Jacobs, *Cities and the Wealth of Nations* (1984).
9. See Saul Alinsky's *Reveille for Radicals* (1946) and *Rules for Radicals* (1971).
10. See Harry C. Boyte's case-focused philosophical study of democratic change processes, *CommonWealth* (1989).
11. See the discussion of COPS's cooperative economic initiative with the San Antonio Metro Alliance in their joint report, *Investing In People: The Story of Project Quest* (1994). For a discussion of BUILD, see Boyte, *op. cit.*
12. See Roger Fischer, William Ury, and Bruce Patton, *Getting to Yes: Negotiating Agreement without Giving In,* Second Edition (1991).

Bibliography

Addams, Jane. 1902. *Democracy and Social Ethics*. New York: Macmillan.
———. 1910. *Twenty Years at Hull House*. New York: Macmillan.
Adorno, Theodor. 1973. *Negative Dialectics*. New York: Continuum.
Aho, C. Michael. 1997. "Global Governance: Who's Minding the World Economy?" Speech at Reuters Forum at Columbia University, April 2, 1997.
Alexander, Thomas M. 1987. *John Dewey's Theory of Art, Experience and Nature: Expanding the Horizons of Feeling*. Albany: State University of New York Press.
———. 1993. "The Human Eros." In *Philosophy and the Reconstruction of Culture: Pragmatic Essays after Dewey*, ed. John J. Stuhr. Albany: State University of New York Press.
Alinsky, Saul D. 1946. *Reveille for Radicals*. New York: Random House.
———. 1971. *Rules for Radicals: A Pragmatic Primer for Realistic Radicals*. New York: Random House.
Amsden, Alice. 1997. "Free Markets—Will Reform Benefit the World's Poor?" Speech at Reuters Forum at Columbia University, February 12, 1997.
Appiah, K. Anthony, and Amy Gutmann. 1996. *Color Conscious: The Political Morality of Race*. Princeton: Princeton University Press.
Baier, Annette C. 1985. "What Do Women Want in a Moral Theory?" *Noûs* 19 (March 1985): 53–63.
Bell, Derek. 1992. *Faces at the Bottom of the Well: The Permanence of Racism*. New York: Basic Books.
Bellah, Robert N. 1975. *The Broken Covenant: American Civil Religion in Time of Trial*. New York: Seabury.
Bellah, Robert N., Richard Madsen, William M. Sullivan, Ann Swidler, and Steven M. Tipton. 1985. *Habits of the Heart: Individualism and Commitment in American Life*. Berkeley: University of California Press.
———. 1991. *The Good Society*. New York: Alfred A. Knopf.
Bearak, Barry. 1997. "Man of Vision or of Violence? Where Gang Leader Talks Peace, Police See Just Talk." *The New York Times*. November 20, 1997, B1.
Beauvoir, Simone de. 1952. *The Second Sex*. Trans. H.M. Parshley. New York: Alfred A. Knopf (original French, 1949).

Becker, Lawrence. 1977. *Property Rights.* Boston: Routledge and Kegan Paul.

Benhabib, Seyla. 1986. *Critique, Norm, and Utopia: A Study of the Foundations of Critical Theory.* New York: Columbia University Press.

————. 1987. "The Generalized and the Concrete Other: The Kohlberg–Gilligan Controversy and Feminist Theory." In *Feminism as Critique,* ed. Seyla Benhabib and Drucilla Cornell. Minneapolis: University of Minnesota Press.

————. 1989. "In the Shadow of Aristotle and Hegel: Communicative Ethics and Current Controversies in Practical Philosophy." *The Philosophical Forum* 21 (Special Double Issue on Hermeneutics in Ethics and Social Theory, ed. Michael Kelly), Fall–Winter 1989–90):1–2.

————. 1991. "On Hegel, Women and Irony." In *Feminist Interpretations and Political Theory,* ed. Mary Lyndon Shanley and Carole Pateman. University Park: The Pennsylvania State University Press.

Benhabib, Seyla, and Drucilla Cornell, eds. 1987. *Feminism as Critique.* Minneapolis: University of Minnesota Press.

Betz, Joseph. 1996. "Sandinista Nicaragua as a Deweyan Social Experiment." Presidential Address to the Society for the Advancement of American Philosophy at the Twenty-Third Annual Meeting, University of Toronto, March 1996.

Bloom, Allan. 1987. *The Closing of the American Mind.* New York: Simon and Schuster.

Bowles, Samuel, and Herbert Gintis. 1986. *Democracy and Capitalism: Property, Community, and the Contradictions of Modern Social Thought.* New York: Basic Books.

————. 1993. "A Political Case for the Democratic Enterprise." *Economics and Philosophy* 9:75–100.

Boyte, Harry C. 1984. *Community Is Possible: Repairing America's Roots.* New York: Harper & Row.

————. 1989. *CommonWealth: A Return to Citizen Politics.* New York: The Free Press.

Boyte, Harry C., Heather Booth, and Steve Max, eds. 1986. *Citizen Action and the New American Populism.* Philadelphia: Temple University Press.

Boyte, Harry C., and Frank Riessman, eds. 1986. *The New Populism: The Politics of Empowerment.* Philadelphia: Temple University Press.

Boxill, Bernard. 1976. "Self-Respect and Protest." *Philosophy and Public Affairs* 6, no. 1 (Fall 1976).

————. 1984. *Blacks and Social Justice.* Lanham: Rowman & Littlefield.

Braaten, Jane. 1991. *Habermas's Critical Theory of Society.* Albany: State University of New York Press.

Branch, Taylor. 1988. *Parting the Waters: America in the King Years, 1954–63.* New York: Simon & Schuster.

Brint, Michael, and William Weaver, eds. 1991. *Pragmatism in Law and Society.* Boulder: Westview Press.

Brown, Elsa Barkley. 1990. "African American Women's Quilting: A Framework for Conceptualizing and Teaching African American Women's History." In *Black Women in America: Social Science Perspectives,* ed. Micheline Malson et al. Chicago: University of Chicago Press.

Butler, Broadus N. 1983. "Frederick Douglass: The Black Philosopher in the United States: A Commentary." In *Philosophy Born of Struggle: Anthology of Afro-American Philosophy from 1917,* ed. Leonard Harris. Dubuque: Kendall/Hunt.

Butterfield, Fox. 1997. "Study Links Violence Rate to Cohesion in Community." *The New York Times,* August 17, 1997, A 27.

Calthorpe, Peter. 1993. *The Next American Metropolis: Ecology, Community and the American Dream.* Princeton: Princeton Architectural Press.

Campbell, James. 1992. *The Community Reconstructs: The Meaning of Pragmatic Thought.* Champaign: University of Illinois Press.

———. 1995. *Understanding John Dewey.* Chicago: Open Court.

Celik, Aliye Pekin. 1997. "Urban Development/Rural Neglect?" Speech at Reuters Forum at Columbia University, April 16, 1997.

Chichilnisky, Graciela. 1997. "The Environment and Development: Strange Bedfellows?" Speech at Reuters Forum at Columbia University, April 30, 1997.

Clark, Septima Poinsettia. 1986. *Ready from Within.* Navarro: Wild Trees Press.

Colapietro, Vincent M. 1989. *Peirce's Approach to the Self: A Semiotic Perspective on Human Subjectivity.* Albany: State University of New York Press.

Cole, Johnnetta B. 1993. *Conversations: Straight Talk with America's Sister President.* New York: Anchor Books.

Collins, Patricia Hill. 1991. *Black Feminist Thought: Knowledge, Consciousness, and the Politics of Empowerment.* New York: Routledge.

Communities Organized for Public Service and Metro Alliance. 1994. *Investing in People: The Story of Project Quest.* San Antonio: Communities Organized for Public Service.

Cone, James H. 1991. *Martin and Malcolm and America: A Dream or a Nightmare.* Maryknoll: Orbis Books.

Curry, Blanche Radford, and Judith M. Green. 1991. "Recognizing Each Other Amidst Diversity: Beyond Essentialism in Collaborative Cross-Cultural Feminist Theorizing." *Sage: A Scholarly Journal on Black Women* 8:1 (Summer 1991): 39–49.

Dahbour, Omar. 1996. "Globalization and the Contradictions of Liberal Nationalism." Paper presented at a Radical Philosophy Association Conference at Purdue University, November 1996.

Davis, Angela Y. 1969. *Lectures on Liberation.* New York: New York Committee.

———. 1981. *Women, Race and Class.* New York: Random House.

———. 1989. *Women, Culture, and Politics.* New York: Random House/Vintage Books.

Deats, Sara Munson and Lagretta Tallent Lenker. 1994. *Gender and Academe: Feminist Pedagogy and Politics.* Lanhan: Rowman & Littlefield.

de Beauvoir, Simone. 1952. *The Second Sex.* H. M. Parshley, trans. New York: Alfred A. Knopf (original French 1949).

Derrida, Jacques. 1976. *Of Grammatology.* Baltimore: Johns Hopkins University Press.

———. 1994. *Specters of Marx: The State of the Debt, the Work of Mourning, and the New International.* New York: Routledge.

Dewey, John. 1896. "The Unit of Behavior" (originally "The Reflex Arc Concept in Psychology"), *The Psychological Review* 3. Reprinted with some revisions in *Philosophy and Civilization.* New York: Minton, Balch, 1934. In *John Dewey: The Early Works, 1882–1898,* Volume 5, ed. Jo Ann Boydston. Carbondale: Southern Illinois University Press, 1972.

———. 1916. *Democracy and Education.* New York: Macmillan. In *John Dewey: The Middle Works, 1899–1924,* Volume 9, ed. Jo Ann Boydston. Carbondale: Southern Illinois University Press, 1980.

———. 1917. "The Need for a Recovery of Philosophy." In *Creative Intelligence: Essays in the Pragmatic Attitude.* New York: Henry Holt. In *John Dewey: The Middle Works, 1899–1924,* Volume 10, ed. Jo Ann Boydston. Carbondale: Southern Illinois University Press, 1980.

———. 1920. *Reconstruction in Philosophy.* New York: Henry Holt. In *John Dewey: The Middle Works, 1899–1924,* Volume 12, ed. Jo Ann Boydston. Carbondale: Southern Illinois University Press, 1982.

————. 1925. *Experience and Nature.* Chicago: Open Court. In *John Dewey: The Later Works: 1925–1953,* Volume 1, ed. Jo Ann Boydston. Carbondale: Southern Illinois University Press, 1981.

————. 1927. *The Public and Its Problems.* New York: Henry Holt. In *John Dewey: The Later Works: 1925–1953,* Volume 2, ed. Jo Ann Boydston. Carbondale: Southern Illinois University Press, 1984.

————. 1929. *The Quest for Certainty.* New York: Minton, Balch. In *John Dewey: The Later Works: 1925–1953,* Volume 4, ed. Jo Ann Boydston. Carbondale: Southern Illinois University Press, 1984.

————. 1934. *Art as Experience.* New York: Minton, Balch. In *John Dewey: The Later Works: 1925–1953,* Volume 10, ed. Jo Ann Boydston. Carbondale: Southern Illinois University Press, 1987.

————. 1935. *Liberalism and Social Action.* New York: Putnam. In *John Dewey: The Later Works, 1925–1953,* Volume 11, ed. Jo Ann Boydston. Carbondale: Southern Illinois University Press, 1987.

————. 1937. "Democracy Is Radical." *Common Sense* 6 (January 1937): 10–11. In *John Dewey: The Later Works, 1925–1953,* Volume 11, ed. Jo Ann Boydston. Carbondale: Southern Illinois University Press, 1987.

————. 1938. *Logic: The Theory of Inquiry.* New York: Henry Holt. In *John Dewey: The Later Works, 1925–1953,* Volume 12, ed. Jo Ann Boydston. Carbondale: Southern Illinois University Press, 1986.

————. 1939. *Freedom and Culture.* New York: G.P. Putnam's Sons. In *John Dewey: The Later Works, 1925–1953,* Volume 13, ed. Jo Ann Boydston. Carbondale: Southern Illinois University Press, 1988.

————. 1939. *Theory of Valuation. The International Encyclopedia of Unified Science.* Vol 2, no. 4. Chicago: The University of Chicago Press. In *John Dewey: The Later Works, 1925–1953,* Volume 13, ed. Jo Ann Boydston. Carbondale: Southern Illinois University Press, 1988.

Dewey, John, and James H. Tufts. 1932. *Ethics,* Revised Edition. New York: Henry Holt. In *John Dewey: The Later Works, 1925–1953,* Volume 7, ed. Jo Ann Boydston. Carbondale: Southern Illinois University Press, 1985.

Douglass, Frederick. 1945. *Frederick Douglass: Selections from His Writings.* Edited with an introduction by Philip Foner. New York: International Publishers.

Downs, Anthony. 1994. *New Visions for Metropolitan America.* Washington and Cambridge: The Brookings Institution and Lincoln Institute of Land Policy.

DuBois, W. E. B. 1903. *The Souls of Black Folk.* Reprinted with an introduction by Henry Louis Gates, Jr. New York: Bantam Books, 1989.

Dussel, Enrique. 1985. *Philosophy of Liberation.* Trans. Aquilina Martinez and Christine Morkovsky. Maryknoll: Orbis Books.

————. 1988. *Ethics and Community.* Trans. Robert Barr. Maryknoll: Orbis Books.

Eldridge, Michael. 1998. *Transforming Experience: John Dewey's Cultural Instrumentalism.* Nashville: Vanderbilt University Press.

Etzioni, Amitai. 1993. *The Spirit of Community: Rights, Responsibilities, and the Communitarian Agenda.* New York: Crown Publishers.

Evans, Sara M., and Harry C. Boyte. 1986. *Free Spaces: The Sources of Democratic Change in America.* New York: Harper & Row.

Firestone, David. 1997. "Giuliani Commends the Marchers, but Not All of the Message," *The New York Times,* August 30, 1997, A 26.

Fisher, Roger, William Ury, and Bruce Patton. 1991. *Getting to Yes: Negotiating Agreement without Giving In,* Second Edition. New York: Penguin Books.

Foner, Philip, ed. 1945. *Frederick Douglass: Selections from His Writings.* New York: International Publishers.

Forester, John, ed. 1985. *Critical Theory and Public Life.* Cambridge: MIT Press.

———. 1996. "Beyond Dialogue to Transformative Learning: How Deliberative Rituals Encourage Political Judgment in Community Planning Processes." In *Political Dialogue: Theories and Practices,* ed. Stephen L. Esquith. *Poznan Studies in the Philosophy of the Sciences and the Humanities,* Vol. 46.

———. 1998. "Rationality, Dialogue, and Learning: What Community and Environmental Mediators Can Teach Us about the Practice of Civil Society." In *Cities for Citizens,* ed. Michael Douglas and John Friedmann. New York: Wiley.

Fraser, Nancy. 1989. *Unruly Practices.* Minneapolis: University of Minnesota Press.

Freire, Paolo. 1970. *Pedagogy of the Oppressed.* Myra Bergman Ramos, trans. New York: Continuum.

Friedman, Milton. 1962. *Capitalism and Freedom.* Chicago: University of Chicago Press.

———. 1970. "The Social Responsibility of Business Is to Increase Its Profits." Originally published in *The New York Times Magazine,* 13 September 1970, and widely anthologized, including in *Business Ethics: Readings and Cases in Corporate Morality.* Second Edition, ed. W. Michael Hoffman and Jennifer Mills Moore. New York: McGraw-Hill, 1990.

Fukuyama, Francis. 1992. *The End of History and the Last Man.* New York: The Free Press.

Fuller, Margaret. 1843. "The Great Lawsuit." *The Dial,* July 4, 1843, expanded into *Woman in the Nineteenth Century* (1845), excerpted in *The Transcendentalists,* ed. Perry Miller. Cambridge: Harvard University Press, 1950, and in *The Feminist Papers from Adams to de Beauvoir,* ed. Alice S. Rossi. Boston: Northeastern University Press, 1973.

Gates, Henry Louis, Jr., and Cornel West. 1996. *The Future of the Race.* New York: Alfred A. Knopf.

Gevisser, Mark. 1997. "The Witnesses." *The New York Times Magazine,* June 22, 1997, 32–38.

Gilligan, Carol. 1982. *In a Different Voice: Psychological Theory and Women's Development.* Cambridge: Harvard University Press.

Gilman, Charlotte Perkins. 1898. *Women and Economics: A Study of the Economic Relation between Men and Women as a Factor in Social Evolution.* Boston: Small, Maynard.

Gordon, Jill. 1995. "By Any Means Necessary: John Locke and Malcolm X on the Right to Revolution." *Journal of Social Philosophy* 26:53–85 (Spring 1995).

Gould, Carol C. 1988. *Rethinking Democracy: Freedom and Social Cooperation in Politics, Economy, and Society.* Cambridge: Cambridge University Press.

Green, Judith M. 1992. "King's Historical Location of Political Concepts." *American Philosophical Association Newsletter on Philosophy and the Black Experience* 91–92 (Fall 1992), 12–14.

———. 1994. "King's Pragmatic Philosophy of Political Transformation." *Journal of Social Philosophy* 25:1 (Spring 1994): 160–169.

———. 1995. "Retrieving the Human Place in Nature." *Environmental Ethics* 17:1 (Winter 1995): 381–396.

———. 1995. "The Diverse Community or the Unoppressive City: Which Ideal for a Transformative Politics of Difference." *Journal of Social Philosophy* 26:1 (Spring 1995): 86–102.

———. 1998. "Educational Multiculturalism, Critical Pluralism, and Deep Democracy." In *Theorizing Multiculturalism: A Guide to the Current Debate,* ed. Cynthia Willett. New York: Blackwell Publishers.

————. 1999. "Alain Locke's Multicultural Philosophy of Value: A Transformative Guide for the Twenty-First Century." In *The Critical Pragmatism of Alain Locke: A Reader on Value Theory, Aesthetics, Community, Culture, Race, and Education,* ed. Leonard Harris. Lanham: Rowman & Littlefield.

————. 1999. "Deepening Democratic Participation through Deweyan Pragmatism." In *Beyond the Tower: Philosophy and Service Learning,* ed. David Lisman. Washington: American Association of Higher Education.

Green, Judith M., and Blanche Radford Curry. 1996. "Notorious Philosopher: The Transformative Life and Work of Angela Davis." In *Hypatia's Daughters: 1500 Years of Women Philosophers,* ed. Linda Lopez McAlister. Bloomington: Indiana University Press.

Gurwitt, Rob. 1993. "A User's Guide to Communitarianism (Communitarianism: You Can Try It at Home)." *Governing: The Magazine of States and Localities* 6:11 (August 1993).

Gutmann, Amy, ed. 1994. *Multiculturalism.* Princeton: Princeton University Press.

Habermas, Jürgen. 1970. *Toward a Rational Society.* Trans. Jeremy Shapiro. Boston: Beacon Press.

————. 1975. *Legitimation Crisis.* Trans. Thomas McCarthy. Boston: Beacon Press (first published in German, 1973).

————. 1984. *The Theory of Communicative Action, Volume One: Reason and the Rationalization of Society.* Trans. Thomas McCarthy. Boston: Beacon Press (first published in German, 1981).

————. 1987. *The Theory of Communicative Action, Volume Two: Lifeworld and System: A Critique of Functionalist Reason.* Thomas McCarthy, trans. Boston: Beacon Press (first published in German, 1981).

————. 1989. "Justice and Solidarity: On the Discussion Concerning 'Stage 6'." In *The Philosophical Forum* 21:1–2 (Special Double Issue on Hermeneutics in Ethics and Social Theory, ed. Michael Kelly, Fall–Winter 1989–90): 32–52.

————. 1990. *Moral Consciousness and Communicative Action.* Trans. Christian Lenhardt and Shierry Weber Nicholsen. Cambridge: MIT Press.

————. 1992. *Postmetaphysical Thinking: Philosophical Essays.* Trans. William Mark Hohengarten. Cambridge: The MIT Press (originally published in German in 1988, except for "Peirce and Communication").

————. 1993. *Justification and Application: Remarks on Discourse Ethics.* Trans. Ciaran Cronin. Cambridge: MIT Press.

————. 1994. "Struggles for Recognition in the Democratic Constitutional State." In *Multiculturalism,* ed. Amy Gutmann. Princeton: Princeton University Press.

————. 1995. "Reconciliation through the Public Use of Reason: Remarks on John Rawls's Political Liberalism." *The Journal of Philosophy* 92:3 (March 1995): 109–131.

Hallin, Daniel. 1985. "The American News Media: A Critical Theory Perspective." In *Critical Theory and Public Life,* ed. John Forester. Cambridge: MIT Press.

Harding, Sandra. 1993. "Rethinking Standpoint Epistemology: What Is 'Strong Objectivity'?" In *Feminist Epistemologies,* ed. Linda Alcoff and Elizabeth Potter. New York: Routledge.

Harris, Leonard. 1983. *Philosophy Born of Struggle: Anthology of Afro-American Philosophy from 1917.* Dubuque: Kendall/Hunt.

————. 1989. *The Philosophy of Alain Locke: Harlem Renaissance and Beyond* (with introduction, commentaries, and an interpretive essay). Philadelphia: Temple University Press.

————. 1999. *The Critical Pragmatism of Alain Locke: A Reader on Value Theory, Aesthetics, Community, Culture, Race, and Education.* Lanham: Rowman & Littlefield.

Hartsock, Nancy C. M. 1983. "The Feminist Standpoint: Developing the Ground for a Specifically Feminist Historical Materialism." In *Discovering Reality: Feminist Perspectives on Epistemology, Metaphysics, Methodology, and Philosophy of Science,* ed. Sandra Harding and Merrill B. Hintikka. Boston: D. Reidel.

Heilbroner, Robert. 1989. "Reflections on the Triumph of Capitalism." Originally published in *The New Yorker* 64 (January 23, 1989): 98–109, and collected in *Moral Issues in Business,* 5th Edition, ed. William H. Shaw and Vincent Barry. Belmont: Wadsworth, 1992.

Henderson, Hazel. 1991. *Paradigms in Progress: Life Beyond Economics.* Indianapolis: Knowledge Systems.

Hewlett, Sylvia Ann, and Cornel West. 1998. *The War Against Parents: What We Can Do For America's Beleaguered Moms and Dads.* Boston: Houghton Mifflin Company.

Hickman, Larry A. 1990. *John Dewey's Pragmatic Technology.* Bloomington: Indiana University Press.

————, ed. 1998. *Reading Dewey: Interpretations for a Postmodern Generation.* Bloomington: Indiana University Press.

Honore, A. N. 1961. "Ownership." In *Oxford Essays in Jurisprudence,* ed. A.G. Guest. Oxford: Clarendon Press.

hooks, bell (Gloria Watkins). 1984. "Sisterhood: Political Solidarity between Women." In *Feminist Theory: From Margin to Center.* Boston: South End Press.

hooks, bell, and Cornel West. 1990. "Black Women and Men: Partnership in the 1990s." In *Yearning: Race, Gender, and Cultural Politics.* Boston: South End Press.

Hoopes, James, ed. 1991. *Peirce on Signs: Writings on Semiotic by Charles Sanders Peirce.* Chapel Hill: University of North Carolina Press.

Houser, Nathan, and Christian Kloesel, ed. 1992 and 1998. *The Essential Peirce: Selected Philosophical Writings,* Two Volumes. Bloomington: Indiana University Press.

Jacobs, Jane. 1961. *The Death and Life of Great American Cities.* New York: Random House, Inc.

Jaggar, Alison M. 1983. *Feminist Politics and Human Nature.* Totowa: Rowman & Allanheld. Reprinted by Rowman & Littlefield, 1988.

James, William. 1879 and 1882. "The Sentiment of Rationality." *Mind* (July 1879) and *Princeton Review* (July 1882), reprinted as a unified essay in *The Will to Believe and Other Essays in Popular Philosophy.* New York: Longmans, Green & Co., 1897.

————. 1884. "The Dilemma of Determinism," *Unitarian Review* (September 1884), reprinted in *The Will to Believe and Other Essays in Popular Philosophy.* New York: Longmans, Green & Co., 1897.

————. 1890. *The Principles of Psychology,* 2 vols. New York: Henry Holt & Co.

————. 1907. "Pragmatism's Conception of Truth." In *Pragmatism: A New Name for Some Old Ways of Thinking.* New York: Longman's, Green and Co.

————. 1968. *The Writings of William James,* ed. John J. McDermott. New York: Modern Library.

Kemmis, Daniel. 1990. *Community and the Politics of Place.* Norman: University of Oklahoma Press.

————. 1995. *The Good City and the Good Life: Renewing the Sense of Community.* Boston: Houghton Mifflin Company.

Kennedy, Robert F., Jr. 1997. "The Environment and Development: Strange Bedfellows?" Speech at Reuters Forum at Columbia University, April 30, 1997.

Kifner, John. 1997. "Giuliani Ignored Anti-Brutality Advice: Mayor's Own Commissioners Urged Ways to Answer Complaints." *The New York Times,* August 25, 1997, B3.

————. 1997. "Thousands Call on City Hall to Confront Police Brutality." *The New York Times,* August 30, 1997, A1

King, Martin Luther, Jr. 1963. "Letter from Birmingham Jail." In *A Testament of Hope: The Essential Writings and Speeches of Martin Luther King, Jr.,* ed. James M. Washington. San Francisco: HarperCollins, 1986.

————. 1967. *Where Do We Go from Here: Chaos or Community?* New York: Harper & Row.

Kocieniewski, David. 1997. "Facing Storm of Rage, Officers Are Impassive: Countless Encounters with Peaceful Ends." *The New York Times,* August 30, 1997, A26.

Kozol, Jonathan. 1991. *Savage Inequalities: Children in America's Schools.* New York: Crown Publishers.

————. 1995. *Amazing Grace: The Lives of Children and the Conscience of a Nation.* New York: Crown Publishers.

Kristeva, Julia. 1977. *Polylogue.* Paris: Editions du Seuil.

Kuhn, Thomas S. 1962. *The Structure of Scientific Revolutions. The International Encyclopedia of Unified Science,* 2, no. 2. Chicago: University of Chicago Press.

Lachs, John. 1993. "Aristotle and Dewey on the Rat Race." In *Philosophy and the Reconstruction of Culture: Pragmatic Essays after Dewey,* ed. John J. Stuhr. Albany: State University of New York Press.

Lasch, Christopher, ed. 1965. *The Social Thought of Jane Addams,* with Introduction and Commentaries by the Editor. New York: Bobbs-Merrill.

Lee, Kyu Sik. 1997. "Urban Development/Rural Neglect?" Speech at Reuters Forum at Columbia University, April 16, 1997.

Lewis, David Levering. 1970. *King: A Biography.* Urbana: University of Illinois Press.

Lipsey, R.G., and Kelvin Lancaster. 1956. "The General Theory of Second Best." *Review of Economic Studies* 24:63, 11–32.

Lisman, David, ed. 1999. *Beyond the Tower: Philosophy and Service Learning.* Washington: American Association of Higher Education.

Locke, Alain LeRoy. 1987. *The Philosophy of Alain Locke: Harlem Renaissance and Beyond.* ed. Leonard Harris. Philadelphia: Temple University Press.

————. 1992. *Race Contacts and Interracial Relations* (1915–16 Lecture Series at Howard University). Edited with an introduction by Jeffrey C. Stewart. Washington: Howard University Press.

————, ed. 1925. *The New Negro.* Reprinted with an introduction by Arnold Rampersad. New York: Atheneum, 1992.

Locke, Alain LeRoy, and Bernhard J. Stern, ed. 1942. *When Peoples Meet: A Study of Race and Culture Contacts.* New York: Committee on Workshops, Progressive Education Association.

Lodge, George Cabot. 1995. *Managing Globalization in the Age of Interdependence.* San Diego: Pfeiffer & Company.

————. 1997. "Global Governance: Who's Minding the World Economy?" Speech at Reuters Forum at Columbia University, April 2, 1997.

Lugones, Maria C., and Elizabeth V. Spelman. 1983. "Have We Got a Theory for You! Feminist Theory, Cultural Imperialism and the Demand for 'the Woman's Voice'." *Women's Studies International Forum* 6:6, 573–581.

MacIntyre, Alasdair. 1984. *After Virtue*. 2nd Ed. Notre Dame: Notre Dame University Press.

Macpherson, C. B. 1973. *Democratic Theory: Essays in Retrieval*. Oxford: Clarendon Press.

Manning, Rita. 1992. "Just Caring." In *Explorations in Feminist Ethics: Theory and Practice*, ed. Eve Browning Cole and Susan Coultrap-McQuin. Bloomington: Indiana University Press.

Marcuse, Herbert. 1964. *One-Dimensional Man*. Boston: Beacon Press.

———. 1969. *An Essay on Liberation*. Boston: Beacon Press.

Marsalis, Wynton. 1994. "Blood on the Fields: A Jazz Oratorio." Performed by the Lincoln Center Jazz Orchestra. Wynton Marsalis, Composer and Conductor.

Marsh, James L. 1994. "Specters of Dewey, Derrida, Marx, and the New World Order." Paper presented at a session on "Postmodernism and Democracy" organized by the Society for the Advancement of American Philosophy at the Annual Meetings of the Society for Phenomenology and Existential Philosophy, sponsored by Seattle University, September 29, 1994.

———. 1995. *Critique, Action, and Liberation*. Albany: State University of New York Press.

———. 1996. "What's Critical About Critical Theory?" Paper presented at a conference of the Radical Philosophy Association at Purdue University, November 1996. Forthcoming in a volume of *The Library of Living Philosophers* on the work of Jürgen Habermas, ed. Lewis Edwin Hahn. LaSalle: Open Court.

———. 1999. *Process, Praxis, and Transcendence*. Albany: State University of New York Press.

Marx, Karl. 1845. "Theses on Feuerbach." In *Karl Marx: Selected Writings*, ed. David McLellan. Oxford: Oxford University Press, 1977.

Mason, Ernest. 1988. "Deconstruction in the Philosophy of Alain Locke." In *Transactions of the Charles S. Peirce Society* 24 (Winter): 85–106.

Matustik, Martin. 1994. "Specters of Deconstruction." Paper presented at a special session on Jacques Derrida's *Spectres de Marx* at the 1994 Annual Meetings of the Society for Phenomenology and Existential Philosophy, sponsored by Seattle University, October 1, 1994.

———. 1998. *Specters of Liberation: Great Refusals in the New World Order*. Albany: State University of New York Press.

McCarthy, Thomas. 1985. "Reflections on Rationalization." In *Habermas and Modernity*, ed. Richard Bernstein. Cambridge: MIT Press.

McDermott, John J. 1976. *The Culture of Experience: Philosophical Essays in the American Grain*. New York: New York University Press.

———. 1986. *Streams of Experience: Reflections on the History and Philosophy of American Culture*. Amherst: University of Massachusetts Press.

———. 1993. "Why Bother: Is Life Worth Living? Experience as Pedagogical." In *Philosophy and the Reconstruction of Culture: Pragmatic Essays after Dewey*, ed. John J. Stuhr. Albany: State University of New York Press.

———, ed. 1969. *The Basic Writings of Josiah Royce*. Chicago: The University of Chicago Press.

McDermott, John J., ed. 1997. *The Writings of William James: a Comprehensive Edition*. Chicago: The University of Chicago Press.

McGary, Howard. 1997. "Racism, Social Justice, and Interracial Coalitions." *The Journal of Ethics* 1:3, 249–64.

———. 1998. *Race and Social Justice*. New York: Blackwell Publishers.

McPherson, Dennis H. and J. Douglass Rabb. 1993. *Indian from the Inside: A Study in Ethno-Metaphysics*. Thunder Bay: Lakehead University Centre for Northern Studies.

Morrison, Toni. 1987. *Beloved*. New York: Alfred A. Knopf.

―――. 1992. *Playing in the Dark: Whiteness and the Literary Imagination*. New York: Vintage Books.

Morrison, Toni, ed. 1992. *Race-ing Justice, En-gendering Power: Essays on Anita Hill, Clarence Thomas, and the Construction of Social Reality*. New York: Pantheon Books.

Moses, Greg. 1997. *Revolution of Conscience: Martin Luther King, Jr., and the Philosophy of Nonviolence*. New York: The Guilford Press.

Mead, George Herbert. 1910. "Social Consciousness and the Consciousness of Meaning." *The Psychological Bulletin*. 7:397–405. Reprinted in *Pragmatism: The Classic Writings*, ed. H. S. Thayer. Indianapolis: Hackett, 1982.

―――. 1913. "The Social Self." *The Journal of Philosophy, Psychology, and Scientific Method* 10:374–380. Reprinted in *Pragmatism: The Classic Writings*, ed. H. S. Thayer. Indianapolis: Hackett, 1982.

―――. 1936. *Mind, Self, and Society: From the Standpoint of a Social Behaviorist*, ed. Charles W. Morris. Chicago: The University of Chicago Press.

Mill, John Stuart, and Harriet Taylor Mill. 1869. *The Subjection of Women*. Reprinted in *Essays on Sex Equality*, ed. Alice S. Rossi. Chicago: The University of Chicago Press, 1970.

Miller, Richard. 1997. "Free Markets—Will Reform Benefit the World's Poor?" Speech at Reuters Forum at Columbia University, February 12, 1997.

Mills, Charles W. 1997. *The Racial Contract*. Ithaca: Cornell University Press.

Miringoff, Marc L. 1987–1998. *The Index of Social Health*. New York: Fordham University Institute for Innovation in Social Policy.

Moussa, Mario. 1991. "Misunderstanding the Democratic 'We': Richard Rorty's Liberalism and the Radical Urge for a Philosophical Foundation." *Philosophy & Social Criticism: An International, Interdisciplinary Quarterly Journal* 17:4.

Moynihan, Daniel Patrick. 1965. *The Negro Family: The Case for National Action*. Washington: U. S. Department of Labor. Reprinted in Lee Rainwater and William L. Yance, *The Moynihan Report and the Politics of Controversy*. Cambridge: MIT Press, 1967.

Nelessen, Anton C. 1994. *Visions for a New American Dream: Process, Principles and an Ordinance to Plan and Design Small Communities*. Chicago: American Planning Association Press.

Nelson, Julie A. 1996. *Feminism, Objectivity and Economics*. New York: Routledge.

―――. 1996. "The Masculine Mindset of Economic Analysis." *The Chronicle of Higher Education*, June 28, 1996, B3.

Nozick, Robert. 1974. *Anarchy, State, and Utopia*. New York: Basic Books.

Nyerere, Julius. 1968. *Uhuru na Ujamaa: Freedom and Socialism*. New York: Oxford University Press.

Olson, Mancur. 1997. "Free Markets—Will Reform Benefit the World's Poor?" Speech at Reuters Forum at Columbia University, February 12, 1997.

Outlaw, Lucius T., Jr. 1996. *On Race and Philosophy*. New York: Routledge.

Pareles, Jon. 1997. "Out of the Mouths of Black Poets." *The New York Times*, February 11, 1997, C 11.

Patton, Carl V., and David S. Sawicki. 1986. *Basic Methods of Policy Analysis and Planning*. Englewood Cliffs: Prentice-Hall.

Peirce, Charles Sanders. 1991. *Peirce on Signs: Writings on Semiotic by Charles Sanders Peirce*, ed. James Hoopes. Chapel Hill: University of North Carolina Press.

―――. 1992 and 1998. *The Essential Peirce: Selected Philosophical Writings*, Two Volumes, ed. Nathan Houser and Christian Kloesel. Bloomington: Indiana University Press.

Randall, John Herman, Jr. 1939. "Dewey's Interpretation of the History of Philosophy." In *The Philosophy of John Dewey.* Vol. 1 in *The Library of Living Philosophers,* ed. Paul Arthur Schilpp and Lewis Edwin Hahn. La Salle: Open Court.

Rawls, John. 1971. *A Theory of Justice.* Cambridge: Harvard University Press.

————. 1974. "Independence of Moral Theory," *Proceedings of the American Philosophical Association* 49.

————. 1980. "Kantian Constructivism in Moral Theory," *Journal of Philosophy* 77 (September 1980).

————. 1993 and 1996. *Political Liberalism.* New York: Columbia University Press.

————. 1995. "Reply to Habermas." *The Journal of Philosophy* 92:3 (March 1995): 132–180.

Reagon, Bernice Johnson. 1983. "Coalition Politics: Turning the Century." In *Home Girls: A Black Feminist Anthology,* ed. Barbara Smith. New York: Kitchen Table Press. Reprinted in *Race, Class, and Gender: An Anthology,* ed. Margaret L. Andersen and Patricia Hill Collins. Belmont: Wadsworth Publishing Company, 1992.

Rockefeller, Steven C. 1991. *John Dewey: Religious Faith and Democratic Humanism.* New York: Columbia University Press.

Rorty, Richard. 1985. "Solidarity or Objectivity?" In *Post-Analytic Philosophy,* ed. John Rajchman and Cornel West. New York: Columbia University Press.

Rose, Tricia. 1994. *Black Noise: Rap Music and Black Culture in Contemporary America.* Hanover: University Press of New England.

Rosengarten, Theodore. 1997. "Songs of Slavery Lifted by a Chorus of Horns." *The New York Times,* February 23, 1997, H1.

Rosenthal, Sandra B. 1986. *Speculative Pragmatism.* LaSalle: Open Court.

————. 1993. "The Individual, the Community, and the Reconstruction of Values." In *Philosophy and the Reconstruction of Culture: Pragmatic Essays after Dewey,* ed. John J. Stuhr. Albany: State University of New York Press.

Rousseau, Jean Jacques. 1762. *The Social Contract.* Reprint, New York: Hafner, 1947.

Royce, Josiah. 1908. *The Philosophy of Loyalty.* New York: Macmillan. Republished with an introduction by John J. McDermott. Nashville: Vanderbilt University Press, 1995.

————. 1908. *Race Questions, Provincialism, and Other American Problems.* New York: Macmillan. Reprint, Freeport: Books of Libraries Press, 1967.

————. 1916. *The Hope of the Great Community.* New York: Macmillan.

————. 1918. *The Problem of Christianity.* New York: Macmillan. Republished with an introduction by John E. Smith. Chicago: University of Chicago Press, 1968.

Sachs, Jeffrey. 1993. *Poland's Jump to the Market Economy.* Cambridge: MIT Press.

Sandel, Michael. 1982. *Liberalism and the Limits of Justice.* Cambridge: Cambridge University Press.

Sanger, David E. 1998. "Policy Means Nothing if the Shelves Are Bare." *The New York Times,* September 27, 1998, Section 3, 4.

————. 1998. "Dissension Erupts at Talks on World Financial Crisis: I.M.F.'s Austerity Policies Draw Criticism." *The New York Times,* October 7, 1998, A6.

Schaar, John. 1967. "Equality of Opportunity, and Beyond." In *Nomos IX: Equality,* ed. J. Roland Pennock and John W. Chapman. New York: Atherton Press.

Serageldin, Ismail. 1997. "The Environment and Development: Strange Bedfellows?" Speech at Reuters Forum at Columbia University, April 30, 1997.

Seidman, Steven, ed. 1989. *Jürgen Habermas on Society and Politics: A Reader.* Boston: Beacon Press.

Seigfried, Charlene Haddock. 1991. *William James's Radical Reconstruction of Philosophy.* Albany: State University of New York Press.

————. 1991. "Where Are All the Pragmatist Feminists?" *Hypatia: A Journal of Feminist Philosophy* 6:2 (Summer): 1–20.

————. 1991. "The Missing Perspective: Feminist Pragmatism." *Transactions of the Charles S. Peirce Society* 27:4 (Fall): 405–416.

————. 1992. "Like Bridges without Piers: Beyond the Foundationalist Metaphor." In *Anti-Foundationalism Old and New,* ed. Tom Rockmore and Beth J. Singer. Philadelphia: Temple University Press.

————. 1993. "Validating Women's Experiences Pragmatically." In *Philosophy and the Reconstruction of Culture: Pragmatic Essays after Dewey,* ed. John J. Stuhr. Albany: State University of New York Press.

————. 1996. *Pragmatism and Feminism: Reweaving the Social Fabric.* Chicago: University of Chicago Press.

Seigfried, Charlene Haddock, ed. 1993. Special Issue on Feminism and Pragmatism. *Hypatia: A Journal of Feminist Philosophy,* 8:2 (Spring 1993).

Shabazz, Malcolm (X), with Alex Haley. 1964. *The Autobiography of Malcolm X.* New York: Ballantine Books.

Shabazz, Malcolm (X). 1970. *By Any Means Necessary,* ed. George Breitman. New York: Pathfinder Press.

Sherover, Charles. 1994. "Postmodernism and Democracy." Paper presented at a session on "Postmodernism and Democracy" sponsored by the Society for the Advancement of American Philosophy at the 1994 Annual Meetings of the Society for Phenomenology and Existential Philosophy, sponsored by Seattle University, September 29, 1994.

Solemano, Andres. 1997. "Free Markets—Will Reform Benefit the World's Poor?" Speech at Reuters Forum at Columbia University, February 12, 1997.

Solomon, Paul. 1994. "Bootstrap Economics." *The MacNeil–Lehrer Newshour,* February 17, 1994. Washington: PBS Video.

Sleeper, R.W. 1993. "The Pragmatics of Deconstruction and the End of Metaphysics." In *Philosophy and the Reconstruction of Culture: Pragmatic Essays after Dewey,* ed. John J. Stuhr. Albany: State University of New York Press.

Stanton, Elizabeth Cady, et al. 1848. "Declaration of Sentiments." Adopted at the 1848 Woman's Rights Convention at Seneca Falls, New York. In *History of Woman Suffrage,* ed. Elizabeth Cady Stanton, Susan B. Anthony, and Matilda J. Gage. Rochester: Charles Mann, 1881. Reprinted in *The Feminist Papers from Adams to de Beauvoir,* ed. Alice S. Rossi. Boston: Northeastern University Press, 1973.

Stegner, Wallace. 1969. *The Sound of Mountain Water.* New York: Doubleday & Company.

Stewart, Jeffrey C., ed. 1992. *Race Contacts and Interracial Relations* (Alain LeRoy Locke's 1915–16 Lecture Series at Howard University). Washington: Howard University Press.

Stikkers, Kenneth L. 1999. "Instrumental Relativism and Cultivated Pluralism." In *The Critical Pragmatism of Alain Locke: A Reader on Value Theory, Aesthetics Community, Culture, Race, and Education,* ed. Leonard Harris. Lanham: Rowman & Littlefield.

Stuhr, John J., ed. 1987. *Classical American Philosophy: Essential Readings and Interpretive Essays.* New York: Oxford University Press.

————. 1993. "Democracy as a Way of Life." In *Philosophy and the Reconstruction of Culture: Pragmatic Essays after Dewey,* ed. John J. Stuhr. Albany: State University of New York Press.

Taylor, Charles. 1994. "The Politics of Recognition." In *Multiculturalism: Examining the Politics of Recognition,* ed. Amy Gutmann. Princeton: Princeton University Press.

Thompson, Phillip. 1997. "Urban Development/Rural Neglect?" Speech at Reuters Forum at Columbia University, April 16, 1997.

Thurow, Lester. 1980. *The Zero-Sum Society: Distribution and the Possibilities for Economic Change.* New York: Basic Books.

Tocqueville, Alexis de, Alexis de. 1835 and 1840. *Democracy in America.* Republished, trans. George Lawrence. J. P. Mayer. New York: Doubleday/Anchor Books, 1969.

United Nations. 1996. *The Habitat Agenda: Goals and Principles, Commitments and Global Plan of Action.* Adopted at the United Nations Conference on Human Settlements (Habitat II), June 3–14, 1996.

Walker, Alice. 1982. *The Color Purple.* New York: Harcourt Brace Jovanovich.

———. 1983. *In Search of Our Mothers' Gardens.* New York: Harcourt Brace Jovanovich.

———. 1989. *The Temple of My Familiar.* New York: Simon & Schuster.

Walzer, Michael. 1983. *Spheres of Justice.* New York: Basic Books.

Washington, Booker T. 1895. "Atlanta Exposition Address." In *I Am Because We Are: Readings in Black Philosophy,* ed. Fred Lee Hord (Mzee Lasana Okpara) and Jonathan Scott Lee. Amherst: University of Massachusetts Press, 1995.

Washington, Johnny. 1983. "Alain L. Locke's 'Values and Imperatives': An Interpretation." In *Philosophy Born of Struggle: Anthology of Afro-American Philosophy from 1917,* ed. Leonard Harris. Dubuque: Kendall/Hunt.

———. 1986. *Alain Locke and Philosophy: A Quest for Cultural Pluralism.* New York: Greenwood Press.

———. 1994. *A Journey into the Philosophy of Alain Locke.* New York: Greenwood Press.

Wells, Ida B. 1970. *Crusade for Justice: The Auto-Biography of Ida B. Wells,* ed. Alfreda M. Duster. Chicago: University of Chicago Press.

West, Cornel. 1986. "Populism: A Black Socialist Critique." In *The New Populism: The Politics of Empowerment,* ed. Harry C. Boyte and Frank Riessman. Philadelphia: Temple University Press.

———. 1989. *The American Evasion of Philosophy: A Genealogy of Pragmatism.* Madison: University of Wisconsin Press.

———. 1992. "Learning to Talk of Race." In *The New York Times Magazine,* August 2, 1992. Reprinted in *I Am Because We Are: Readings in Black Philosophy,* ed. Fred Lee Hord (Mzee Lasana Okpara) and Jonathan Scott Lee. Amherst: University of Massachusetts Press, 1995.

———. 1993. *Prophetic Thought in Postmodern Times.* Monroe: Common Courage Press.

———. 1994. *Race Matters.* New York: Vintage Books (originally published Boston: Beacon Press, 1993).

Westbrook, Robert B. 1991. *John Dewey and American Democracy.* Ithaca: Cornell University Press.

Wheeler, David L. 1996. "Evolutionary Economics: Scholars Suggest that Much of World Trade May Be Controlled by Biologically Based Behaviors." *The Chronicle of Higher Education,* July 5, 1996, A8.

Wilgoren, Jodi. 1999. "Diallo Rally Focuses on Call for Strong Oversight of Police: Thousands March Across the Brooklyn Bridge," *New York Times,* April 16, 1999, B1.

Willett, Cynthia, ed. 1998. *Theorizing Multiculturalism: A Guide to the Current Debate.* New York: Blackwell Publishers.

Wills, Garry. 1978. *Inventing America: Jefferson's Declaration of Independence.* New York: Random House.

Wittgenstein, Ludwig. 1958. *Philosophical Investigations,* 3rd Ed. Trans. G.E.M. Anscombe. New York: Macmillan.

———. 1969. *On Certainty.* Trans. Denis Paul and G.E.M. Anscombe, Ed. G.E.M. Anscombe and G.H. von Wright. New York: Harper & Row.

Woods, David W. 1993. "Lynnwood Legacy: A Collaborative Planning Model for the 1990s." *Urban Design and Planning* (Special Issue: Social Equity in Urban Planning? June 1993).

————. 1994. "Collaborative Planning for the Lynnwood Legacy: A Successful Alternative to 'Traditional' Planning." Compendium of Papers for the 15th Annual International Pedestrian Conference, sponsored by the City of Boulder, Colorado (September 1994).

Wolf, Susan. 1994. "Comment." *Multiculturalism,* ed. Amy Gutmann. Princeton: Princeton University Press.

Woolf, Virginia. 1929. *A Room of One's Own.* London: Hogarth Press.

Wollstonecraft, Mary. 1792. *A Vindication of the Rights of Woman.* Reprinted in a critical edition, ed. Carol H. Poston. New York: W.W. Norton & Company, 1975.

Young, Iris Marion. 1990. "The Ideal of Community and the Politics of Difference." In *Feminism/Postmodernism,* ed. Linda J. Nicholson. New York: Routledge.

Yunus, Mohammed. 1997. "Global Financial Integration: Closing the Wealth Gap." Speech at Reuters Forum at Columbia University, January 29, 1997.

Zack, Naomi. 1993. *Race and Mixed Race.* Philadelphia: Temple University Press.

Index

About the Author

Judith M. Green teaches philosophy at Fordham University in New York City, including courses in democratic theory, American pragmatism, ethics, African American philosophy, and Native American philosophy. She earned her doctorate in philosophy, with supporting work in aesthetics and political economy, at the University of Minnesota. Her previously published essays have focused on social philosophy, political economy, educational multiculturalism, environmental ethics, African American philosophy, and feminist theory. Green is a principal of Green Woods Associates, a consulting firm specializing in community-building through fostering collaborative citizen participation in planning processes that promote social equity and environmental sustainability.